The Pirate's Fiancée

The Pirate's Fiancée
Feminism, reading, postmodernism

MEAGHAN MORRIS

VERSO

London · New York

This edition published by Verso 1988
Second impression 1990
© 1988 Meaghan Morris
All rights reserved

Verso
UK: 6 Meard Street, London W1V 3HR
USA: 29 West 35th Street, New York, NY 10001-2291

Verso is the imprint of New Left Books

British Library Cataloguing in Publication Data

Morris, Meaghan
        The pirate's fiancée : feminism, reading,
        postmodernism.—(Questions for feminism).
        1. Popular culture. Influence of women
        I. Title   II. Series
        306´.1

ISBN 0-86091-212-4
ISBN 0-86091-926-9 (pbk.)
        .

US Library of Congress Cataloging in Publication Data

Morris, Meaghan.
        The pirate's fiancée.
        (Questions for Feminism)
        Bibliography: p.
        1. Feminism.   2. Feminist criticism.   I. Title.
        II. Series
HQ1154.M685   1988   305.4´2   88-17209

ISBN 0-86091-212-4
ISBN 0-86091-926-9 (pbk.)
        ,

Typeset by Leaper & Gard, Bristol, England
Printed in Great Britain by Bookcraft (Bath) Ltd, Midsomer Norton, Avon.

For Joyce Morris

QUESTIONS FOR FEMINISM

Edited by Michèle Barrett, Annette Kuhn, Anne Phillips and Ann Rosalind Jones, this socialist feminist series aims to address, in a lively way and on an international basis, the wide range of political and theoretical questions facing contemporary feminism.

Other Titles in the Series

UNEQUAL WORK by Veronica Beechey

THE WEARY SONS OF FREUD by Cathérine Clément

THE POLITICS OF DIVERSITY: FEMINISM, MARXISM AND NATIONALISM edited by Roberta Hamilton and Michèle Barrett

FEMALE SEXUALIZATION: A COLLECTIVE WORK OF MEMORY by Frigga Haug and others

SEA CHANGES: CULTURE AND FEMINISM by Cora Kaplan

CONSUMING FICTION by Terry Lovell

ABORTION AND WOMAN'S CHOICE: THE STATE, SEXUALITY AND REPRODUCTIVE FREEDOM by Rosalind Pollack Petchesky

READING THE ROMANCE: WOMEN, PATRIARCHY AND POPULAR LITERATURE by Janice A. Radway

FEMALE SPECTATORS: LOOKING AT FILM AND TELEVISION edited by E. Deidre Pribram

GRAFTS: FEMINIST CULTURAL CRITICISM edited by Susan Sheridan

Contents

Acknowledgements

Any collection such as this is indebted to the advice, criticism and encouragement of many people in different times and places.

My thanks must first go to Paul Foss, who has been both friend and colleague from the first to the last essay in the book. My thanks also to Annette Kuhn and Anna del Nevo of Verso for their help with the manuscript and for entertaining my specific requests regarding the book's style and design; and to Juan Davila, Richard Dunn and Lynn Silverman for their kind permission to reproduce their work.

For discussions that over many years have informed and directed my work, I thank Virginia Coventry, Peter Cryle, Anne Freadman, John Frow, Ross Gibson, Colin Gordon, Helen Grace, Elizabeth Grosz, Colin Hood, Lynne Hutton-Williams, Elizabeth Jacka, Laleen Jayamanne, Tina Kaufman, Sylvia Lawson, Adrian Martin, Tom O'Regan, Paul Patton, Jean-Michel Raynaud, Julie Rose, Sam Rohdie, Lesley Stern, Hugh Tomlinson and Paul Willemen. My gratitude and affection to Kate Jennings, who helped me to start writing, and to Ross Chambers, who introduced me to most of the writing that I wanted to read.

My love to Joyce and Keith Morris, without whose support and endurance very few of these essays could have been begun, and to André Frankovits — without whom none of them would have been finished.

'The Pirate's Fiancée' originally appeared in Meaghan Morris and Paul Patton, eds, *Michel Foucault: Power, Truth, Strategy*, Sydney 1979, and is published by permission of Feral Publications.

'On the "On" of *On Photography*' appeared in *Photo-Discourse*, edited and published by Sydney College of the Arts, 1981.

'Operative Reasoning: Reading Michèle le Doeuff' appeared originally in *I&C*, no. 9, 1981/82, and is published by permission of Colin Gordon.

'A-mazing Grace: Notes on Mary Daly's Poetics' appeared originally in *Intervention*, no. 16, 1982.

'Indigestion: A Rhetoric of Reviewing' appeared originally in *Filmnews*, vol. 12, no. 6, June 1982, and is published by permission of Tina Kaufman.

'Two Types of Photography Criticism Located in Relation to Lynn Silverman's Series' appeared originally in *Art & Text*, no. 6, 1982, and is published by permission of Paul Foss.

'Room 101 Or A Few Worst Things In The World' appeared originally in André Frankovits, ed., *Seduced and Abandoned: The Baudrillard Scene*, Sydney 1984, and is published by permission of Stonemoss Services.

'Postmodernity and Lyotard's Sublime' appeared originally in *Art & Text*, no. 16, 1984, and is published by permission of Paul Foss.

'Politics Now (Anxieties of a Petty-bourgeois Intellectual)' appeared originally in *Intervention*, no. 20, 1986.

'Apologia: *Beyond Deconstruction*/"Beyond What?"' appeared originally in *Scripsi*, vol. 4, no. 4, 1987, and is published by permission of Peter Craven and Michael Heyward.

'Intrigue' appeared originally in *Sighting References*, exhibition catalogue, curated by Gary Sangster, Artspace, Sydney 1987, and is published by permission of Artspace.

Earlier versions of 'Tooth and Claw: Tales of Survival and *Crocodile Dundee*' appeared originally in *Art & Text*, no. 25, 1987, and in Andrew Ross, ed., *Universal Abandon? The Politics of Postmodernism*, Minneapolis 1988. It is published here by permission of Paul Foss.

Introduction: feminism, reading, postmodernism

Some time in the early 1970s, a Women's Film Festival in Sydney tried to screen Nelly Kaplan's film *La Fiancée du pirate* (*A Very Curious Girl*, 1969). It was not a great success. One reel turned out to be unsubtitled and, if I remember rightly, the reels were screened out of order. At the time, this seemed like an omen against the use in feminist cinema of large narrative structures – then in question, in theory, as being somehow intrinsically 'male'. As images of a women's truth, eloquent in any order, the festival documentaries and expressive experimental shorts proved more resistant to accidents of context than Kaplan's tightly organized fiction.

Nevertheless, Kaplan's film made a profound impression on many women in the audience, and I have never forgotten it. I have also never been able to see it again – so it has acquired in my memory the abstraction of a multi-purpose myth. It was certainly a fable. Kaplan's 'fiancée' lived on the edge of a village with her goods and chattels, her goat, and her bit of high-tech – a tape recorder. She makes money from men, and from cleaning. In town, the villagers spurn her and fear her because of her reputation and her sharp, insolent tongue. But in her house, the village men confide in her, depend on her, trust her (while allowing increasingly vicious attacks on her establishment). But she has saved their money, and with her recorder she has saved their words. One day she leaves: and as she sets off on the road, she leaves behind a village listening in horror not to the voice of the curious girl, but to its own most intimate secrets and confessions – playing loudly, in public, for all to hear.

As an allegory of vengeance and liberation, *La Fiancée du pirate* could be read as an improvement on another text popular in the enthusiastically uncompromising *ambience* of the early women's movement – the Brecht–Weill song from *The Threepenny Opera*, 'Pirate Jenny'. As a cleaning-woman's dream of being recognized as a pirate

1

queen, possessing a secret knowledge that will give her the power to humiliate and destroy everyone who has ever humiliated her, 'Pirate Jenny' was often savoured straight as a bloodthirsty declaration of feminist utopian desires. But it maintains an ambivalent edge. 'Pirate Jenny' is Polly's song, an embedded fiction of a fantasy, and she sings it at her wedding to MacHeath. Polly presents 'Pirate Jenny' as an 'imitation' of another woman posed as distant from herself. Jenny lives in a squalor that Polly pretends to transcend; Polly has actually married her bandit, while Jenny's is always about to arrive. But Polly's dream of action, just like Jenny's, is limited to waiting and watching till her ship comes in – commanded by a masculine saviour. Even her act of mimesis as Jenny is severely restricted. At the end of the song, Mac publicly praises Polly's 'art' to the other men – but then tells her in an undertone, 'I don't like you play-acting; let's not have any more of it'.[1]

Kaplan's narrative did away with the pirate, as well as with the heroine's oppressors. It also substituted, for Jenny's grim vision of having everyone massacred, a much more subtle form of poetic – and pragmatic – justice. The village society is undone by the broadcast of its own presuppositions, and the village economy is wrecked by an intensification of its own exploitative logic.

Kaplan's fiancée doesn't dream of waiting for her hero to arrive on stage in a moment of revolutionary rupture. She makes do herself by acting critically upon her everyday conditions of existence – to transform her position within them. She is not reduced to silence after her own 'play-acting'. Instead of performing another woman, she plays herself; then shifts from performer to director when she 'stages', by borrowing and quoting in an altered context, the voices of her former masters. It is their everyday conduct that is now framed as 'play-acting' – and after the performance there can't be any more of it in quite the same old way.

It was only some years after seeing *La Fiancée du pirate* that it became possible for me to think about Kaplan's achievement in quite those terms. At the time, the discussion was mainly about 'images of women', 'distribution of gender roles', and 'reflection of class position'. Those terms worked very well for debating the logic of the fiction, but by eliding (at least as we used them) the question of the practice of narration, they encouraged a hasty jump to debating (not for the first time in the history of modern aesthetics) whether such 'fiction' was generally *desirable*. However, work by feminist writers engaging with these issues, and with the history of aesthetics, soon provided a framework in which Kaplan's film could be read not only as a fable of political action, but as a political act of transforming fables (a song from *The Threepenny Opera*, but also a store of legends about witches, wicked

women and outcast girls). For example, this passage from Anne
Freadman's analysis of George Sand's *Indiana* in 'Sandpaper':

> My major methodological presupposition will be that any text is a rewriting of
> the field or fields of its own emergence, that to write, to read, or to speak is
> first of all to turn other texts into discursive material, displacing the enuncia-
> tive position from which those materials have been propounded. I mean that
> 'use' can always do something a little different from merely repeating 'usage'.
> In an attempt to do something towards specifying 'women's writing', I shall
> suppose that it is in the business of transforming discursive material that, in its
> untransformed state, leaves a woman no place from which to speak, or
> nothing to say.[2]

Freadman goes on to suggest that 'the production of a speaking-
position, with respect to discursive material that is both given and
foreign' can be studied by a 'feminist formalism'. Her own paper, in
turn, can be read in this way. For example, by analysing the novel
Indiana as a set of rhetorical and generic strategies rewriting the
material of two discourses – the story of Don Juan, and the myth of the
Muse – Freadman is able to produce a position from which the 'George
Sand' of the history books ('prolix and repetitive when she is not just
telling a good story, and when she is, a downright embarrassment to the
modernist critic')[3] can be rewritten for a feminist literary *history*.

So she too transforms two discourses: one an essentialist theory of
'women's writing', the other a polemic against 'formalism'. The former,
insisting on biological authorship as a source of meanings, threatens to
leave a feminist *formalist* with nothing to say. If we reject 'femininity' as
an *a priori* of feminist criticism, then 'how (it may well be asked) could
feminist criticism select a corpus of women's writing?'[4] Freadman's
response is to say that the woman writer *is* a given – but a given in (and
by) discourse. 'I can read that discourse, and rewrite it'. This move in
turn allows Freadman to transform an opposition between 'history' and
'form' that might leave a *feminist* formalist no place from which to
speak. Since her rewriting of 'George Sand' as a discursive object
involves a history of transformations produced in 'social conditions of
some specificity', then Freadman's formalism could not be opposed to a
political practice of reading and writing. On the contrary it would be one
of the enabling conditions for such a practice. It is a way of writing a
political history, as well as a theory, or how changes may take place in
particular circumstances.

'Formalism' is still (like 'fiancée') a discomfiting term,[5] never easily
disentangled from memories of the history of its uses. Many theorists
now prefer to avoid it, rather than rewrite it, confining it to the museum

of dead terms sometimes revisited by those renewing their own speaking-position as always already 'beyond'. In beginning this introduction by rereading a film and an essay that have been important to my work over several years, it would perhaps be easier now to situate both of them in the field of postmodernism, and in recent debates about appropriation, strategies of quotation, revision, mimicry, and, for that matter, of image and discourse *piracy* (or, more recently, 'poaching').

Indeed, in reading over again those texts that not only made me want to write about them, but changed the ways that I wanted to read, it occurred to me that much the same move of relocation 'in' postmodernism could easily be imposed on the project of Michèle Le Doeuff's *L'Imaginaire philosophique.* Le Doeuff's essays develop a number of themes about femininity, pleasure and power, the politics of 'style', the limitations of *philosophical* Reason, the work of figuration in discourse, the function of Other-ness in meta-discourse, and the complexity of historical relations between a philosophical imaginary and popular culture[6] – themes that have become key reference-points for 'postmodernism' insofar as that term defines a place for making generalizations about the stakes of otherwise disparate debates. *L'Imaginaire philosophique* also develops a theory of quotation (and a practice of reading differences between particular acts of quoting) that moves away from the mourning and melancholia associated with quotation by Susan Sontag (for the context of photography), and Jean Baudrillard (in his myth of the simulacrum).[7] Her intricate analyses of how the act of referring to a previous 'image' can *work* in philosophy to formulate, solve or banish problems can then provide the more useful methodological precedent for thinking about much insistently lively contemporary art and commercial cinema. And her own practice of essay writing can be read as a transformation of the specific discourses she addresses in criticism – a subtle transformation, but one no less substantial than those performances of a 'feminine' writing in whose play she declines to participate.

But if it would be easy to re-present Le Doeuff's work in this way to produce a postmodern image, it is not so easy to say what would be gained by ignoring the specificity of its moves between the history of philosophy on the one hand, and the discourses of feminism on the other. It is her critical analysis of the function of images in both of them, and between them, that makes the politics of her writing make sense.

In the same way, it is significant for me that the precision of Anne Freadman's project is matched by few of the non-'formalist' theories of a strategic rewriting of cultural materials (from pop analyses of bricolage and recoding to Jean-François Lyotard's revision of the theory of language games) that have been so influential in recent years. One problem now emerging as a result is that as the *terms* of such analyses become commodified to the point of becoming dated ('strategy', 'bricolage' and 'recoding' have the aura of the remainder sale about them now, too old to surprise, too new to seduce ...), they offer little resistance to the wearing effects of overuse. When any and every text can be read indifferently as another instance of 'strategic rewriting', another illustration of an established general principle, something more (and something more specific) is needed to argue how and why a particular event of rewriting might matter.

In this context, it is worth revisiting Barthes' comment in *Mythologies* 'that a little formalism turns one away from History, but that a lot brings one back to it'.[8] The history I want to return to here is one in which the question of rewriting 'discourses' emerges from a political critique of the social positioning of women. Just as a transformation of the meaning of a woman's 'play-acting' occurs in Kaplan's fiction as a solution to a local experience of sexual and class oppression (*and* as an alternative to the melancholy romance of Pirate Jenny's dream), so too, I think, does Freadman's feminist formalism depend on the political projects of the women's movement for its insistence that we say what *kinds* of discursive changes will matter, why, and for whom. In this way, the notion of a 'textual strategy' cannot become a sort of free-floating aesthetic ideal, interchangeable with any other general concept of action or a vague thematics of 'doing something'. On the contrary: 'strategy' here is a value that not only refers to and derives from the political discourses of feminism, but remains open to revision *by* them.

So rather than resituate *La Fiancée du pirate* and 'Sandpaper' in relation to postmodernism, I prefer initially to make a framework of introduction by relating them to each other like this: both can be read as 'formalist' practices in Freadman's sense; both are in the business of transforming discursive material that otherwise 'leaves a woman no place from which to speak, or nothing to say'. Both therefore actively assume that the movement of women to a position of power in discourse is a political necessity, and a *practical* problem.

It doesn't follow that I think their methods and interests are the same. It doesn't follow that, in making connections between a narrative film about a village outcast and an academic essay about reading women's writing, I would then rush on to an analogy between prostitutes, witches and academic feminist critics, or conflate a film or an essay with the social conditions that they may refer to or discuss. And it doesn't follow for one moment that I consider the activity of 'transforming discursive material' as sufficient to, or coextensive with, the tasks of feminist political struggle now or in the future.

But it does follow that I think such activity is part of that struggle and, more strongly, that it can be one of the enabling conditions for realizing, securing and renewing its wider political projects.

These qualifications are necessary, I think, because at a time of inflationary rhetoric about the importance of 'cultural' studies and criticism, it becomes all too easy in reaction to go back to 'basics' and declare that work on women's writing, after all, has nothing to say – and no place in politics.

Most of the essays in this volume were written as an effort to produce a speaking-position in a particular political, critical and publishing context. Some, like the essays on Mary Daly, Jean Baudrillard and *Crocodile Dundee*, dealt with discourses tending to deny *all* critics (even feminist ones for Daly, feminists in particular for Baudrillard and Paul Hogan) a place from which to speak, or the possibility of having something to say. In each case, I have tried not simply to find a way to 'answer back', but to read the texts in question sympathetically in order to understand them *as* criticisms of those answers that my feminism might automatically provide, and so to use them to question my own assumptions and practices in the process of reading theirs.

Some essays were written directly in response to work which is explicitly concerned with the positioning of women, and with thinking about subjectivity, modes of address, and reference, in particular historical contexts. Since these preoccupations are often now considered to be the signs of an academic 'feminist theory', I want to stress here the artworks of Lynn Silverman and Richard Dunn. Both artists ask us to consider our relationship to the images each provides of subjectivity not as a source of meanings, or as an object of quests, but as an elusive *reference-point*. Silverman's boots, recurring from image to image across the bottom of the bottom line, introduce the trace of a history in the mythic space of the so-called 'timeless land' of the (white) Australian interior.[9] Dunn's formal portraits construct a set of stylized positions – of which the most intriguing, for me, remains the image of the young woman (a fiancée, perhaps) from the far right of the series, gazing through fire at a story of her own positioning in that place. Each artist asks us to analyse the process of representation both arriving at and departing from that elusive reference-point – and allows us then to transform it by imagining a story in turn.

Finally, other essays pursued a feminist analysis of contemporary writing which, from Howard Felperin to Roland Barthes, Susan Sontag and Jean-François Lyotard, attempts to debate presumed general dilemmas about critical 'speaking' today. Sometimes the feminism of the essays is an explicit and polemical position. Sometimes it operates implicitly, as a set of theoretical and political assumptions about the questions that criticism might ask. In some of the more recent essays a 'feminist speaking-position' is framed as today defining a recognizable *genre* in criticism, which may in turn begin to impose new difficulties for the further work of (feminist) women.

In none of these essays, however, is the production of a speaking-position understood as a matter of inventing a 'personal voice' for '*me*'. None of them is presented as an instance of a subjective or 'reader' response. On the contrary, I think that producing a 'position' is a problem of rhetoric, of developing enunciative strategies (or ways of 'play-acting', in MacHeath's sense) precisely in relation to the cultural and social conventions that make speaking difficult or impossible for *women*.

To stress a relation to those conventions is to say that I think it is important to think of the 'production of a speaking-position' *as* a matter of strategies of reference,[10] rather than simply of 'the subject' or even 'subjectivity'. Several essays in this volume explore that argument further. One of the reasons that I think it worth pursuing is that in the uncertainty and confusion that attends speculation about the relations between semiotics, marxism, feminism and politics, the one polemical position that for me has proved itself quite useless is that which insists on retaining 'in the last instance' an empiricist conception of '*the* referent' as 'the thing', as privileged synecdoche of 'the real (material) world'.[11] It may be useless for its own political purposes: few other theories of reference are quite so rhetorically vulnerable to the mega-empiricism of a Jean Baudrillard discovering, on a trip to Disneyland or on a quick run through some meta-*vérité* TV or high-tech Japanese videos, that 'the referent', and therefore 'reality', is dead.

The only other comment I wish to make to situate the essays that follow is that most of them were written for fun, or as a 'leisure' occupation. Fun, of course, can incorporate any number of reasons for writing something – enthusiasm, amusement, admiration, a sense of a challenge to learn, but also concern, irritation, anxiety or bemusement, a desire to confront something bothersome.

From 1978 to 1985, I worked primarily as a film reviewer for newspapers (the *Sydney Morning Herald*, and then *The Australian Financial Review*). While I also often taught part-time in several art and media colleges, the arduous physical and intellectual conditions of a job in which I might see up to a dozen films a week, and have to find 'something to say' about most of them, meant that while I have always understood mass-media work as an ideological practice involving acts of theorization, the activity of thinking and writing about *theories* that might inform my practice had to be cherished as a hobby.

This experience has influenced my work in a number of ways. I became as interested in addressing the theoretical debates that circulate in and as popular culture as I am in academically situated theoretical work *about* popular culture. In the process, maintaining the distinction I've just reiterated between the 'popular' and the 'academic' became increasingly awkward for any purposes of generalization. I make it again here only in order to say that I think some theories in wide circulation (like the 'gut reaction' theory of criticism discussed below in 'Indigestion' or the big-cinema theory of mass pleasure discussed in 'Tooth and Claw') are still insufficiently addressed by academic work. The basic premises of each are so much in conflict that the former is simply dismissed as 'wrong', or ignored as *non*-theoretical. Yet serious engagement with popular culture must eventually accept to take issue with it and in it, as well as about it, and I think this means writing seriously about popular theories as well as (or even rather than) writing 'popular' spin-offs from academic theories.

However, many of the essays in this volume were initially written *for*, if not 'from', an academic context. Others were not; but in neither case did the kind of critical response that helps any writer to shift her position (or change her mind) necessarily come from the imaginary addressee I may have inscribed as I wrote them. Perhaps the most demanding and useful criticism an intellectual can receive comes from the kind of 'mixed' public to be encountered at events organized on thematic or political, rather than purely professional, principles. So the experience of moving between a number of different social sites of debate and discussion about cultural politics has also left me very cautious about some aspects of recent attempts to come to terms with the limitations and specificities of 'academic' practice.

On the one hand, Foucault's notion of the 'specific intellectual', for example, has been particularly useful both in allowing institutional struggles to occupy a field of 'everyday life' rather than being relegated to an 'ivory tower' divorced from a 'real world', and in making it possible to criticize the moment in which a theory 'mistakes the liberal academy as the collective subject of a universally useful knowledge'.[12] Feminism has both profited from, and helped to produce, this kind of reconceptualization of academic politics. On the other hand, something slightly different seems to be happening when it becomes possible to claim, as Paul Smith does in an essay in *Men in Feminism*, that poststructuralist feminist theory 'however "feminist" it may be, and howsoever "feminist" is construed – *does not exist outside the academy*' (my emphasis).[13] Smith stresses in a note that he is referring only to what is known 'in the academic vernacular as feminist theory (the structuralist/ poststructuralist variety)'.

But I wonder – whose academic vernacular? Many feminist theorists involved in an academic practice (Mary Daly comes immediately to mind, but one might find any number in various disciplines) would be astonished and annoyed to find their work either categorized as post-structuralist or consigned to nonexistence. Furthermore, this 'vernacular' equation between a reified 'poststructuralism' and an equally reified 'theory' is not confined to the academy. As one of the means by which any part of a field of activity promotes itself as co-extensive with the whole, the term 'theory' can be used in precisely that shorthand way (at least in my cultural context) by administrators and curators and bureaucrats in the visual and performing arts, by journalists, by film-makers ...

One must be passionately careful here, precisely because to state that a given activity has 'no existence' outside one's own immediate sphere of operations is to accept and reinforce as absolute, rather than to challenge and transform, prevailing *local* conventions about the available places from which people (and in this case, feminists) can be allowed to be saying something. If we extend the realm of the 'academy' to include a whole range of activities shuttling between pedagogical institutions and the culture industries, then we are no longer talking about the specificities and limitations of the former, but rather using a vaguely expansive metonym of 'the institution' to blur away a number of questions about *class* and cultural practice in specific sites today. We are, once again, universalizing the 'academy' (and in the name of only one of its elements).

A response to this objection is that an incessant 'shuttling' (of personnel as well as of activities) into other social sites is precisely what characterizes a primary function of the academy in post-industrial societies. Modern academies no doubt have always done this: but as they come to act not only as training grounds for a future élite diaspora, but *also* as pre-unemployment waiting rooms or as anti-unemployment therapy and 'personal improvement' centres, their ideological role in *moving discourses around* becomes increasingly complex (in a way which varies considerably, too, from country to country). But it is precisely when we begin to come to terms with this development that it becomes impossible to claim that a given theoretical activity 'does not exist outside' the academy. This can only be true in an academy imagined as without students who do not proceed to become professors, or with students who remain untouched by their own working experiences.

Furthermore, this academy functions in a world without bookshops, without 'amateur' readers and writers of theoretical work, without theorizing artists, without those ambiguous 'art-world' figures (critics, and especially curators) who can frame artists' work as 'theoretical' whether they wish it so or not, without TV chat-shows and intellectual talking-heads, without interviews, without media jokes about semiotics and poststructuralism, without private reading groups, without public forums, without young film-school graduates making both small film-essays and big blockbusters, without other than academic audiences for any of these, or anyone anywhere to go on to make something different from them: it is a world without any 'dissemination' of ideas, and finally without the rampant commodification of thought and feeling that makes it possible to speak of 'Theory' – in a vernacular sense – as a practice, as a problem, as a *genre*, and as a 'zone' of possible contestation.

I take issue with Paul Smith's comment in such detail because it seems to be one of the more careful formulations of a myth of institutional and discursive *closure* which may emerge from the important academic attempt to 'know your limitations', in Clint Eastwood's phrase, but which sometimes ends (as I have seen it do in feminist discussion groups) with a self-lacerating and ultimately self-defeating lament by 'theorists' that we (or 'they') aren't doing something else – something, perhaps, with more *power* to change prevailing conditions of existence.

It's a reasonable anxiety. Without worrying about the disconnections and the failures of intellectual work, we cannot transform it politically. Yet one of the most important consequences of the notion of the 'specific intellectual' is not to translate 'specificity' as 'confinement', but rather to begin to accept firstly that work produced in an academic context (even the writings of Foucault, even poststructuralist feminist theory) can be used and rewritten in unpredictable ways (and various media) elsewhere: and secondly that this movement can run the other way: academic theorization can and should transform its practices by learning from the experiences, the concepts, and the methodologies developed by people in broader social and political movements.

The relationship between feminist theory and the various women's movements has operated historically in this two-way sense, and I would add that non-academically constituted feminist groups provided an excellent training ground in not deducing people's reading habits or their intellectual interests from their social occupations. It is perhaps true today that the emergence of modes of feminist theorizing inflected by 'poststructuralism' corresponds both to an intensified discussion *of* feminism in the academies, and to the development of a more complex and indirect relationship between that discussion, a range of broad political struggles involving women, and a rapidly changing, sometimes weakened, sense of 'feminism' as a social force. But at that point it becomes crucial not only to ask, as Michèle Le Doeuff does of the work of Simone de Beauvoir (or as I would still wish to ask of the work of

Mary Daly), what is it that has allowed this practice of theory to 'dynamize' so many diverse women's movements?; but also to ask how social movements *now* can generate changes in (even poststructuralist) feminist theory, and in our practice of feminist politics.

A declaration that a certain kind of feminist theory does not exist outside a specific institutional space may function as a way of denying certain women a place from which to speak, but it does so haphazardly, by the kind of accident that befalls any generalization. I should like to conclude by considering a much more coherently motivated denial (in a structural, not an individual, sense of 'motivation') that occurs when it is stated that women have had nothing to say about a particular topic.

In a number of recent discussions of postmodernism, a sense of intrigue develops around a presumed absence – or withholding – of women's speech in relation to what has certainly become one of the boom discourses of the 1980s. Feminists in particular, in this intrigue, have had little or nothing to say about postmodernism. This very curious *doxa* emerges from texts by male critics referring primarily to each other commenting on the rarity of women's speech.

In 1983, in a text commenting on his own 'remarkable oversight' in ignoring the question of sexual difference in his previous critical practice, Craig Owens noted 'the fact that few women have engaged in the modernism/postmodernism debate'.[14] In an essay first published the following year, Andreas Huyssen – warmly agreeing with Owens that feminist work in art, literature and criticism has been 'a measure of the vitality and energy' of postmodern culture – nonetheless found it 'somewhat baffling that feminist criticism has so far largely stayed away from the postmodernism debate which is considered not to be pertinent to feminist concerns'.[15]

Both of these critics stressed the complexity and importance of a feminist contribution to what *they*, in turn, wished to describe as a 'postmodern' culture. Owens in particular was careful to disclaim any desire to efface the specificity of feminist critique, and to insist that his own project was to consider the implications of an *intersection* of feminism and postmodernism.

More recently, however, Jonathan Arac stated baldly in his Introduction to *Postmodernism and Politics*:

> ... *almost no women have figured in the debate*, even though many analysts include current feminism among the features of postmodernity. Nancy Fraser's important feminist critique of Habermas ('What's Critical') stands nearly alone (see also Kristeva), although Craig Owens and Andrew Ross have effectively situated feminist work by women in relation to postmodernism.[16]

In the bibliography which concludes Arac's Introduction, very few women do figure beside Fraser and Kristeva: five, to be precise, out of more than seventy individual and collaborative authorial entries. One of the five is Virginia Woolf. Another is Hannah Arendt.[17] Any bibliography, it is true, must be exclusive. This one is, when it comes to gender, *very* exclusive.

The interesting question, I think, is not whether feminists have or have not written about postmodernism, or whether they should have (for despite the 'baffled' expectation, the hope, perhaps, of eventual *fiançailles*, there is no suggestion here that feminism in any sense *needs* postmodernism as complement or supplement).[18] My question is rather under what conditions women's work *can* 'figure' currently in such a debate. There is general agreement between the male critics I've cited that 'feminist work *by women*' can figure when appropriately framed ('effectively situated') by what has mainly been, apparently, a man's discourse. But by what criteria does feminist work by women come to figure, or *not* to figure when it comes raw-edged, without a frame?

Common sense suggests that perhaps all that is meant by these remarks is that few women so far have written articles explicitly entitled 'Feminism and Postmodernism'; or that few have written analyses focussed on the standard (male) referents of present debate – Habermas, Lyotard, Rorty, Jameson, Huyssen, Foster, Owens, and so on. If we accept that this is true (or that many of the texts that fulfil these conditions are quite recent) then perhaps feminists have merely been busy doing other things. It would be hard to deny that in spite of its heavy (if lightly acknowledged) borrowings from feminist theory, its frequent celebrations of 'difference' and 'specificity', and its critiques of 'Enlightenment' paternalism, postmodernism as a publishing phenomenon has pulled off the peculiar feat of re-constituting an overwhelmingly male pantheon of proper names to function as ritual objects of academic exegesis and commentary. It would be easy to shrug away a presumed feminist noninvolvement with postmodernism as a wise avoidance by women of a singularly ponderous, phallo-centred conversation – and to point out with Michèle Le Doeuff that the position of faithful reader to the great male philosopher is one that women have good reason to approach with caution. Many feminist criticisms of theories of postmodernism have occurred, in fact, in passing, in the context of saying something else as well.

Yet the matter is not quite so simple. *If* it is true that few women have explicitly inscribed their work in relation to postmodernism (and I am sceptical of such claims, since they tend to present the limits and biasses of our local reading habits as a satisfactory survey of the state of the world), it should also be true that only male writers who *do* so inscribe their work then come to 'figure' in the debate.

Yet in Arac's bibliography, we find numerous figures whose contribution could only strictly be described as formative, enabling and/or indirect: Adorno and Horkheimer, Derrida, Heidegger, Lacan, Foucault (not to mention Althusser, Perry Anderson, Lukács and Raymond Williams). Their work can only be part of a debate about postmodernism when 'effectively situated' in relation to it by subsequent commentary and citation. But a formative or indirect role in postmodernism has been willingly accorded, by men cited by Arac, to feminism. Why then, alongside the names of those men, do we not find references to (for example) the closely and critically associated work of Catherine Clément, Hélène Cixous, Luce Irigaray, Shoshana Felman, Jane Gallop, Sarah Kofman, Alice Jardine, Michèle Le Doueff, Gayatri Chakravorty Spivak, or Jacqueline Rose?

One could continue this line of questioning. For example, it might be argued that the 'enabling' male figures have at least explicitly theorized 'modernity', and so provide the bases for thinking postmodernity. But then not only would my brief list of women recur with even greater insistence, but it would need immediate expansion: Janet Bergstrom, Mary Anne Doane, Elizabeth Grosz, Barbara Johnson, Donna Haraway, Teresa de Lauretis, Angela McRobbie, Patricia Mellencamp, Tania Modleski, Nancy K. Miller, Naomi Schor, Kaja Silverman, Judith Williamson ... (many of whom have had, in fact, quite a bit to say about postmodernism). Furthermore, if the 'politics' in the conjunction of *Postmodernism and Politics* authorizes the figuring under that rubric of the work of a Perry Anderson – then surely we might also expect to find listed works by Nancy Hartsock, Carole Pateman, Juliet Mitchell or Chantal Mouffe?

At this point, however, it becomes difficult to keep restricting my own enquiries to the names of (mostly white and Western) women. In the first and last sentence of his introductory text, Arac invokes 'the world' as the context of criticism. So why would a bibliography of 'postmodernism and *politics*' today still privilege only the great names of Western Marxism and their American academic heirs – at the expense of new theorizations of politics and culture by writers differently placed in histories of racism and colonialism? Rasheed Araeen, Homi K. Bhabha, Eduardo Galeano, Henry Louis Gates Jr, Geeta Kapur, Trinh T. Minh-ha, Nelly Richard.... After all, if postmodernism really has defined a useful sphere for political debate, it is because of the awareness it can foster that its 'world' is finally not so small, so clearly 'mapped'.

It is, as a Derridean might observe, all a matter of border lines and frames. Any bibliography 'frames', as it defines, its field of representation.

But the paradox of the frame does not prevent us from asking, in relation to any instance of framing, where and why a line is drawn. As John Frow has argued in *Marxism and Literary History*, the paradox of the frame is most useful precisely for framing a political project of working on 'the limits of reading'.

In reading the limits of Arac's bibliography, it becomes particularly difficult to determine the difference between an act of re-presenting a presupposed historical not-figuring of women in postmodernism debates, and an act of re-*producing* the not-figuring, not counting, of women's work, by 'simple' omission (writing it out of history, by writing its absence into history).

I have a similar difficulty with the more sensitive comments of Owens and Huyssen. Why do women artists and feminist theorists count *as* postmodernist (and as objects of commentary) for Owens, but not as 'engaging' in a debate? Doesn't this distinction return us precisely to that division between a (feminized) object-language and a (masculine) meta-language that feminist theory has taught us to question for its political function, rather than for its epistemological validity? How can Huyssen simply cite and confirm what Owens says, while conceding that crucial aspects of postmodernism now would be 'unthinkable'[19] without the impact of feminist thought?

After all, it is Huyssen himself who has stressed in his feminist reading of 'Mass Culture as Woman: Modernism's Other' that male authors' preoccupation with imaginary femininity 'can easily go hand in hand with the exclusion of real women from the literary enterprise'.[20] Following Huyssen, then, a 'male' postmodernism could be seen as renewing one of the inaugural gestures (in Lyotard's sense) of modernism: inscribing its 'bafflement' by an imaginary, 'absent', silent femininity, while erasing and silencing the work of real women in the history and practice of the theoretical enterprise.

Given the persistence of the figure of woman as mass culture (the irony of modernism), it is no accident that a debate about a presumed silence and absence of women has already taken place in relation to the work on popular culture that is in turn a component of postmodernism.[21] But the bafflement about women that besets both is also perhaps the latest version of the 'why have there been no great women artists (mathematicians, scientists ...)?' conundrum – a badly posed question that assumes a negative response to a previous question, which remains, by default, unasked and unexamined.

How can this happen again? Again, there are some obvious responses that feminists might make. We could say that 'feminist theory' has come to function in academic publishing as a limiting category to a certain extent. It's now too easy to assume that if a text is labelled 'feminist' theory, then it can't properly 'count' or 'figure' as anything else ('woman's sphere', again). We could adopt a complacent paranoia, and assume that the male pantheon of postmodernism is merely a twilight of the gods – the last ruse of the patriarchal University trying for power to fix the meaning, and contain the damage, of its own decline. Or we could claim, probably with some justice if much brutality, that in spite of many rhetorical flourishes from men about their recognition and acceptance of feminism's 'contribution' to cultural and political theory, not very many men have really read extensively, or kept on reading, very many women's books and essays – particularly those published off the fast-track of prestige journals, or in strictly feminist contexts. The bottom line of any working bibliography is not, after all, a frame, but a practical prerequisite: you have to know it to use it.

The problem that interests me, however, is rather the difficulty that a feminist critic now faces in *saying* something about this – in trying to point out, let alone come to terms with, what seems to be a continued, repeated, basic *exclusion* of women's work from a highly invested field of intellectual and political endeavour. What woman writer wants to say, in 1987, that men still aren't reading feminist work?; that women are being 'left out again'?; thus running the risk of being suspected of talking about herself ('if she writes about women's experiences, especially the unpleasant ones, declare her hysterical or "confessional"').[22]

In addressing the myth of a postmodernism still waiting for its women we can find an example of a genre, as well as a discourse, which in its untransformed state leaves a woman no place from which to speak, or nothing to say. For by resorting to the device of listing 'excluded' women, women excluded for no obvious reason except that given by the discourse – their gender – I have positioned myself in a speech-genre all too familiar in everyday life, as well as in pantomime, cartoons, and sitcoms: the woman's complaint, or *nagging*. One of the defining generic rules of 'nagging' is unsuccessful repetition of the same statements. It is unsuccessful, because it blocks change: nagging is a mode of repetition which fails to produce the desired effects of difference that might allow the complaint to end. In this it is quite close to what Anne Freadman, in her analysis of *Indiana*, calls the lament: a 'powerless text'. (A conventional comic scenario goes: she nags, he stops listening, nothing changes, she nags.) Yet there is always a change of sorts implied by repetition: in this case, her 'place' in speech becomes, if not strictly nonexistent, then insufferable – leaving frenzy or silence as the only places left to go. It is an awesome genre, and I am not sure, I confess, how to transform it.

A traditional method has always been for the nagger somehow to lose interest, and so learn to change her subject (and her addressee). One possibility in this context is to follow up Dana Polan's suggestion that postmodernism is a 'machine for producing discourse'.[23] Polan argues that as the input to this machine begins to determine what it is possible to say in its name, so it becomes increasingly difficult to generate as output anything non-repetitive. Participants in a postmodernism debate are 'constrained' to refer back to previous input, and to take sides in familiar battles on a marked-out, well-trodden, terrain ('Habermas v. Lyotard', for example). The solution to feminist complaint might then be a simple one – switch position from nagger to nagged, then switch off.

But assuming a calculated deafness to discussion about postmodernism is not much of a solution for feminist women. To choose to *accept* a given constraint is not to challenge, overcome or transform anything. Besides, one of the fascinating paradoxes of the postmodernism machine is precisely how difficult it can be to switch it off (or switch off to it). Many of its best operators (Lyotard and Baudrillard, for example) have tried, and failed. As a discourse which runs on a 'paradoxical concern with its own lateness', as Andrew Ross points out (in one of the few essays relating feminism to postmodernism without attributing silence to women),[24] postmodernism has so far proved compatible with, rather than vulnerable to, vast quantities of input about its obsolescence or imminent breakdown.

A different response worth making would be, it seems to me, to make a generically feminist gesture of reclaiming women's work, and women's names, as a context *in* which debates about postmodernism might further be considered, developed, transformed (or abandoned).

The bibliography of women's writing at the end of this introduction is put forward in that spirit. It does not propose to present – or to 'effectively situate' – feminist theory *as* 'postmodernist', and it certainly does not propose to salvage feminism *for* postmodernism. It does presuppose that since feminism has acted as one of the enabling conditions of discourse *about* postmodernism, it is therefore appropriate to use feminist work to frame discussions of postmodernism, and not the other way around. To make this gesture of changing frames is to propose at least one alternative to nagging – and to wasting time waiting and watching for imaginary acts of piracy.

Bibliography

For the reasons discussed in the Introduction, I have included in this bibliography only works signed or cosigned as written by women. Since it combines entries about feminism, theories of reading, and post-modernism, it is for practical reasons mostly limited to works I have drawn on in some way for the essays in this book. Essays published in anthologies are not listed separately under their authors' names.

Abel, Elizabeth, ed., *Writing and Sexual Difference*, Brighton 1982.

Allen, Judith and Grosz, Elizabeth, eds, *Feminism and the Body*, *Australian Feminist Studies*, no. 5, 1987.

Allen, Judith and Patton, Paul, eds, *Beyond Marxism? Interventions After Marx*, Sydney 1983.

Atkinson, Ti-Grace, *Amazon Odyssey*, New York 1974.

Bell, Diane, *Daughters of the Dreaming*, Melbourne 1983.

Bergstrom, Janet, 'Enunciation and Sexual Difference (Part 1)', *Camera Obscura*, nos. 3–4, 1979.

Bergstrom, Janet, 'Violence and Enunciation', *Camera Obscura*, nos. 8/9/10, 1982.

Bergstrom, Janet, 'Androids and Androgyny', *Camera Obscura*, no. 15, 1986.

Bernstein, Cheryl, 'Performance as News: Notes on an Intermedia Guerilla Art Group', in Michel Benamou and Charles Caramello, eds, *Performance in Postmodern Culture*, Milwaukee 1977.

Braidotti, Rosi, *Féminisme et philosophie: La philosophie contemporaine comme critique du pouvoir par rapport à la pensée féministe*, Université de Paris-1, 1981.

Brooke-Rose, Christine, *A Rhetoric of the Unreal*, Cambridge 1981.

Brown, Denise Scott, Izenour, Steven and Venturi, Robert, *Learning from Las Vegas: The Forgotten Symbolism of Architectural Form*, Cambridge, Mass. and London 1977.

Bruno, Giuliana, 'Postmodernism and *Blade Runner*', *October*, no. 41, 1987.

Bruss, Elizabeth W., *Beautiful Theories: The Spectacle of Discourse in Contemporary Criticism*, Baltimore and London, 1982.

Burchill, Louise, 'Either/Or: Peripeteia of an Alternative in Jean Baudrillard's *De la séduction*' in André Frankovits, ed., *Seduced and Abandoned: The Baudrillard Scene*, Sydney 1984.

Cameron, Deborah, *Feminism and Linguistic Theory*, London 1985.
Chow, Rey, 'Rereading Mandarin Ducks and Butterflies: A Response to the "Postmodern" Condition', *Cultural Critique*, no. 5, 1986–7.
Cixous, Hélène *et al.*, *La Venue à l'écriture*, Paris 1977.
Clément, Catherine, and Cixous, Hélène, *La Jeune Née*, Paris 1975.
Clément, Catherine, *Miroirs du sujet*, Paris 1975..
Clément, Catherine, *Les Fils de Freud sont fatigués*, Paris 1978; *The Weary Sons of Freud*, London 1987.
Clément, Catherine, *Vies et légendes de Jacques Lacan*, Paris 1981; *The Lives and Legends of Jacques Lacan*, New York 1983.
Collins, Felicity, 'A (Sad) Song of the Body', *Screen*, vol. 28, no. 1, 1987.
Cornillon, Susan Koppelman, *Images of Women in Fiction: Feminist Perspectives*, Ohio 1972.
Coventry, Virginia, *The Critical Distance: Work With Photography/Politics/Writing*, Sydney 1986.
Coward, Rosalind, *Female Desire*, London 1984.
Coward, Rosalind and Ellis, John, *Language and Materialism: Developments in Semiology and the Theory of the Subject*, London 1977.
Creed, Barbara, 'From Here to Modernity – Feminism and Postmodernism', *Screen*, vol. 28, no. 2, 1987.
Daly, Mary, *Beyond God the Father; Towards a Philosophy of Women's Liberation*, Boston 1973.
Daly, Mary, *Gyn/Ecology: The Metaethics of Radical Feminism*, Boston 1978.
Davidson, Robyn, *Tracks*, London 1980.
Delphy, Christine, *The Main Enemy: A Materialist Analysis of Women's Oppression*, London 1977.
Doane, Mary Ann, 'Woman's Stake: Filming the Female Body,' *October*, no. 17, 1981.
Doane, Mary Ann, 'Film and the Masquerade: Theorizing the Female Spectator', *Screen*, vol. 23, no. 24, 1982.
Doane, Mary Ann, 'When the Direction of the Force Acting on the Body is Changed: The Moving Image', *Wide Angle*, vol. 7, nos. 1–2, 1985.
Doane, Mary Ann, *The Desire to Desire: The Woman's Film of the 1940s*, Indiana 1987.
Dubreuil-Blondin, Nicole, 'Feminism and Modernism: Paradoxes' in Benjamin Buchloh, *et al.*, eds, *Modernism and Modernity*, Nova Scotia 1983.
Duras, Marguerite and Gauthier, Xavière, *Les Parleuses*, Paris 1974.
Ecker, Gisela, ed., *Feminist Aesthetics*, London 1985.
Eisenstein, Hester and Jardine, Alice, eds, *The Future of Difference*, Boston 1980.
Ellmann, Mary, *Thinking About Women*, London 1969.
Ewen, Elizabeth and Ewen, Stuart, *Channels of Desire: Mass Images and the Shaping of American Consciousness*, New York 1972.
Felman, Shoshana, *La Folie et la chose littéraire*, Paris 1978; *Writing and Madness*, Ithaca 1986.
Felman, Shoshana, ed., *Literature and Psychoanalysis, the Question of Reading: Otherwise, Yale French Studies*, nos. 55–6, 1977.
Felman, Shoshana, *Le Scandale du corps parlant: Don Juan avec Austin ou la séduction en deux langues*, Paris 1980.
Ferguson, Frances, 'The Nuclear Sublime', *Diacritics*, vol. 14, no. 2, 1984.
Fraser, Nancy, 'The French Derrideans: Politicizing Deconstruction or Decon-

structing Politics', *New German Critique*, no. 33, 1984.

Fraser, Nancy, 'What's Critical About Critical Theory? The Case of Habermas and Gender', *New German Critique*, no. 35, 1985.

Freadman, Anne, 'On Being Here and Still Doing It', in P. Botsman, C. Burns and P. Hutchings, eds, *The Foreign Bodies Papers*, Sydney 1981.

Freadman, Anne, 'Sandpaper', *Southern Review*, vol. 16, no. 1, 1983.

Freadman, Anne, 'Riffaterra Cognita: A Late Contribution to the "Formalism" Debate', *SubStance*, no. 42, 1984.

Freadman, Anne, 'Reading the Visual', *Framework*, nos. 30–31, 1986.

Gaines, Jane, 'White Privilege and Looking Relations: Race and Gender in Feminist Film Theory', *Cultural Critique*, no. 4, 1986.

Gallop, Jane, *Intersections: A Reading of Sade with Bataille, Blanchot, and Klossowski*, Nebraska 1981.

Gallop, Jane, *Feminism and Psychoanalysis: the Daughter's Seduction*, London 1982.

Gallop, Jane, *Reading Lacan*, Ithaca and London 1985.

Gaudin, Colette, *et al.*, *Feminist Readings: French Texts/American Contexts*, *Yale French Studies*, no. 62, 1981.

Gould, Carol, C. and Wartofsky, Marx W., eds, *Women and Philosophy: Toward a Theory of Liberation*, New York 1976.

Gross, Elizabeth, 'Derrida, Irigaray and Deconstruction', *Leftwright, Intervention*, no. 20, 1986.

Gross, Elizabeth, 'Irigaray and the Divine', Local Consumption Occasional Paper 9, Sydney 1986.

Grosz, Elizabeth, 'Every Picture Tells a Story: Art and Theory Re-examined', in Gary Sangster, ed., *Sighting References*, Sydney 1987.

Grosz, Elizabeth, 'The "People of the Book": Representation and Alterity in Emmanuel Levinas', *Art & Text*, no. 26, 1987.

Grosz, Elizabeth, *et al.*, eds, *Futur*fall: Excursions into Post-Modernity*, Sydney 1986.

Gunew, Sneja, 'Feminist Criticism: Positions and Questions', *Southern Review*, vol. 16, no. 1, 1983.

Gunew, Sneja, and Reid, Ian, *Not the Whole Story*, Sydney 1984.

Gusevich, Miriam, 'Purity and Transgression: Reflections on the Architectural Avantgarde's Rejection of Kitsch', Working Paper, Center for Twentieth Century Studies, University of Wisconsin-Milwaukee, 1986.

Haraway, Donna, 'A Manifesto for Cyborgs: Science, Technology and Socialist Feminism in the 1980s', *Socialist Review*, no. 80, 1985.

Hartsock, Nancy C.M., *Money, Sex, and Power: Toward a Feminist Historical Materialism*, Boston 1985.

Hermann, Claudine, *Les Voleuses de langue*, Paris 1976.

Hill, Ernestine, *The Great Australian Loneliness*, Melbourne 1940.

Hutcheon, Linda, *Narcissistic Narrative: the Metafictional Paradox*, Ontario 1980.

Hutcheon, Linda, 'A Poetics of Postmodernism', *Diacritics*, vol. 13, no. 4, 1983.

Hutcheon, Linda, *A Theory of Parody: The Teachings of Twentieth Century Art Forms*, New York and London 1985.

Hutcheon, Linda, 'Beginning to Theorize Postmodernism', *Textual Practice*, vol. 1, no. 1, 1987.

Irigaray, Luce, *Speculum de l'autre femme*, Paris 1974; *Speculum of the Other Woman*, Ithaca 1985.

Irigaray, Luce, *Ce sexe qui n'en est pas un*, Paris 1977; *This Sex Which is Not One*, Ithaca 1985.

Jacobus, Mary, ed., *Women Wri*ᵗⁱᵗᵍ *and Writing About Women*, London 1979.

Jardine, Alice, *Gynesis: C*ᵒ*.ifigurations of Woman and Modernity*, Ithaca and London 1985.

Jardine, Alice, and Smith, Paul, *Men in Feminism*, New York and London 1987.

Jayamanne, Laleen and Rodrigo, Anna, 'To Render the Body Ecstatic', *Fade to Black*, Sydney College of the Arts Occasional Publication, 1985.

Jayamanne, Laleen, Kapur, Geeta and Rainer, Yvonne, 'Discussing Modernity, "Third World", and *The Man Who Envied Women*', *Art & Text*, nos. 23/4, 1987.

Jennings, Kate, *Come To Me My Melancholy Baby*, Melbourne 1975.

Johnson, Barbara, *The Critical Difference: Essays in the Contemporary Rhetoric of Reading*, Baltimore and London 1980.

Johnson, Barbara, 'Thresholds of Difference: Structures of Address in Zora Neale Hurston', in Henry Louis L. Gates, ed., *'Race', Writing, and Difference, Critical Inquiry*, vol. 12, no. 1, 1985.

Johnston, Jill, *Gullibles Travels*, New York and London 1974.

Jones Lyndal, 'Prediction Piece #9', *Art & Text*, no. 9, 1983.

Kaplan, Cora, *Sea Changes: Culture and Feminism*, London 1986.

Kelly, Mary, 'Re-viewing Modernist Criticism', *Screen*, vol. 22, no. 3, 1981.

Kofman, Sarah, *Nietzsche et la métaphore*, Paris 1972.

Kofman, Sarah, *Comment s'en sortir?*, Paris 1983.

Kofman, Sarah, *Un métier impossible*, Paris 1983.

Kofman, Sarah, *L'Enigme de la femme*, Paris 1980; *The Enigma of Woman*, Ithaca 1985.

Kramarae, Cheris and Treichler, Paula A., *A Feminist Dictionary*, Boston, London and Henley 1985.

Krauss, Rosalind E., *The Originality of the Avant-Garde and Other Modernist Myths*, Cambridge, Mass. and London 1985.

Kristeva, Julia, *Desire in Language: A Semiotic Approach to Literature and Art*, Oxford 1980.

Kristeva, Julia, *The Kristeva Reader*, ed., Toril Moi, Oxford 1986.

de Lauretis, Teresa, *Alice Doesn't: Feminism, Semiotics, Cinema*, Indiana 1984.

de Lauretis, Teresa, ed., *Feminist Studies/Critical Studies*, Indiana, 1986.

de Lauretis, Teresa, *Technologies of Gender: Essays on Theory, Film and Fiction*, Indiana 1987.

Lawson, Sylvia, *The Archibald Paradox: A Strange Case of Authorship*, London and Sydney 1983.

Le Doeuff, Michèle, 'Women and Philosophy', *Radical Philosophy*, no. 17, 1977.

Le Doeuff, Michèle, 'Operative Philosophy: Simone de Beauvoir and Existentialism', *Governing the Present, I&C*, no. 6, 1979.

Le Doeuff, Michèle, *L'Imaginaire philosophique*, Paris 1980.

Le Doeuff, Michèle, 'Pierre Roussel's Chiasmas', *Life, Labour and Insecurity, I&C*, no. 9, 1981/2.

Lewitt, Vivienne Shark, 'Why Egyptian Mods Didn't Bother to Bleach Their Hair or More Notes about Parkas and Combs', *Art & Text*, no. 3, 1981.

Lewitt, Vivienne Shark, 'The End of Civilisation Part 2: Love Among The Ruins', *Art & Text*, no. 10, 1983.

Lippard, Lucy, *Changing: Essays in Art Criticism*, New York 1971.

Lloyd, Genevieve, *The Man of Reason: 'Male' and 'Female' in Western Philosophy*, London 1984.

Long, Elizabeth, 'Reading Groups and The Postmodern Crisis of Cultural Authority', *Cultural Studies*, vol. 1, no. 3, 1987.

McRobbie, Angela, 'Settling Accounts with Subcultures', *Screen Education*, no. 34, 1980.

McRobbie, Angela, 'The politics of Feminist Research: Between Talk, Text and Action', *Feminist Review*, no. 12, 1982.

McRobbie, Angela, 'Strategies of Vigilance, an Interview with Gayatri Chakravorty Spivak', *Block*, no. 10, 1985.

McRobbie, Angela, 'Postmodernism and Popular Culture', *Postmodernism*, ICA Documents 4, London 1986.

McRobbie, Angela and Nava, Mica, eds, *Gender and Generation*, London 1984.

Marini, Marcelle, *Territoires du féminin avec Marguerite Duras*, Paris 1977.

Marks, Elaine and de Courtivron, eds, *New French Feminisms*, Amherst 1980.

Mellencamp, Patricia, 'Film History and Sexual Economics', *Enclitic*, vol. 7, no. 2 1983.

Mellencamp, Patricia, 'Postmodern TV: Wegman and Smith', *Afterimage*, vol. 13, no. 5, 1985.

Mellencamp, Patricia, 'Situation and Simulation', *Screen*, vol. 26, no. 2, 1985.

Mellencamp, Patricia, 'Uncanny Feminism: The Exquisite Corpses of Cecilia ˙ Condit', *Framework*, nos. 32/3, 1986.

Mellencamp, Patricia, 'Images of Language and Indiscreet Dialogue – "The Man Who Envied Women"', *Screen*, vol. 28, no. 2, 1987.

Mellencamp, Patricia, 'Last Seen in the Streets of Modernism', Hawaiian Film Festival, publication forthcoming.

Miller, Nancy K., ed., *The Poetics of Gender*, New York 1986.

Millett, Kate, *Sexual Politics*, London 1970.

Minh-ha, Trinh T., 'The Plural Void: Barthes and Asia', *SubStance*, no. 36, 1982.

Minh-ha, Trinh T. ed., *The Inappropriate/d Other*, *Discourse*, no. 8, 1986/7.

Mitchell, Juliet, *Woman's Estate*, London 1971.

Mitchell, Juliet, *Psychoanalysis and Feminism*, London 1974.

Mitchell, Juliet, and Oakley, Anne, eds, *The Rights and Wrongs of Women*, Harmondsworth 1976.

Modleski, Tania, *Loving with a Vengeance: Mass-Produced Fantasies for Women*, New York and London 1982.

Modleski, Tania, 'Femininity as Mas(s)querade: A Feminist Approach to Mass Culture' in Colin MacCabe, ed., *High Theory/Low Culture*, Manchester 1986.

Modleski, Tania, ed., *Studies in Entertainment: Critical Approaches to Mass Culture*, Indiana 1986.

Moi, Toril, *Sexual/Textual Politics: Feminist Literary Theory*, London and New York 1985.

Montrelay, Michèle, *L'Ombre et le nom, sur la fémininité*, Paris 1977.

Moore, Catriona and Muecke, Stephen, 'Racism and the Representation of Aborigines in Film', *Australian Cultural Studies*, vol. 2, no. 1, 1984.

Morgan, Robin, ed., *Sisterhood is Powerful*, New York 1970.

Morgan, Robin, *Monster*, private printing, 1972.

Mouffe, Chantal, 'Radical Democracy: Modern or Postmodern' in Andrew Ross, ed., *Universal Abandon? The Politics of Postmodernism*, publication forthcoming, Minnesota 1988.

Mouffe, Chantal and Laclau, Ernesto, *Hegemony and Socialist Strategy: Towards a Radical Democratic Politics*, London 1985.

Mulvey, Laura, 'Visual Pleasure and Narrative Cinema', *Screen*, vol. 16, no. 3, 1975.

Pateman, Carole, *The Problem of Political Obligation*, Cambridge 1985.

Pateman, Carole and Gross, Elizabeth, eds, *Feminist Challenges: Social and Political Theory*, Sydney, London and Boston 1986.

Penley, Constance, 'The Avant-Garde and Its Imaginary', *Camera Obscura*, no. 2, 1977.

Penley, Constance, 'Time Travel, Primal Scene, and the Critical Dystopia', *Camera Obscura*, no. 15, 1986.

Petro, Patrice, 'Mass Culture and the Feminine: The "Place" of Television in Film Studies', *Cinema Journal*, vol. 25, no. 3, 1986.

Petro, Patrice, 'Modernity and Mass Culture in Weimar: Contours of a Discourse on Sexuality in Early Theories of Perception and Representation', *New German Critique*, no. 40, 1987.

Petro, Patrice, *Joyless Streets: Women and Melodramatic Representation in Weimar Germany*, publication forthcoming, Princeton 1988.

Pratt, Mary Louise, 'Interpretive Strategies/Strategic Interpretations: On Anglo-American Reader-Response Criticism', in Jonathan Arac, ed., *Postmodernism and Politics*, Manchester 1986.

Probyn, Elizabeth, 'Bodies and Anti-Bodies: Feminism and the Postmodern', *Cultural Studies*, vol. 1, no. 3, 1987.

Rich, Adrienne, *Of Woman Born: Motherhood as Experience and Institution*, London 1977.

Rich, Adrienne, *On Lies, Secrets and Silence, Selected Prose 1966–1978*, London 1980.

Richard, Nelly, 'Body Without Soul: On the Mechanism of Quotation in the Pictorial Materialism of Juan Davila', *Art & Text*, nos. 12–13, 1984.

Richard, Nelly, 'Notes Towards A (Critical) Re-evaluation of the Critique of the Avant-Garde', *Art & Text*, no. 16, 1984.

Richard, Nelly, 'Love in Quotes: On the Painting of Juan Davila', in Paul Taylor, ed., *Hysterical Tears: Juan Davila*, Melbourne 1985.

Richard, Nelly, 'Margins and Institutions: Art in Chile Since 1973'. *Art & Text*, no. 21, 1986.

Rose, Jacqueline, *Sexuality in the Field of Vision*, London 1986.

van Rossum-Guyon, Françoise, ed., *Ecriture, fémininité, féminisme, Revue des sciences humaines*, no. 168, 1977—4.

Rowbotham, Sheila, *Hidden from History*, London 1974.

Russ, Joanna, *How to Suppress Women's Writing*, Austin 1983.

Schor, Naomi, *Breaking the Chain: Women, Theory and French Realist Fiction*, Columbia 1985.

Schor, Naomi, *Reading in Detail: Aesthetics and the Feminine*, New York and London 1987.

Schor, Naomi and Majewski, Henry F., eds, *Flaubert and Postmodernism*, Nebraska 1984.

Showalter, Elaine, *A Literature of Their Own; British Women Novelists from Bronte to Lessing*, Princeton 1977.

Showalter, Elaine, ed., *The New Feminist Criticism: Essays on Women, Literature, Theory*, New York 1985.

Silverman, Kaja, *The Subject of Semiotics*, New York and Oxford, 1983.
Smock, Anne, 'Learn to Read, She Said', *October*, no. 41, 1987.
Solanas, Valerie, *The Scum Manifesto*, London 1983.
Sontag, Susan, *Against Interpretation*, New York 1966.
Sontag, Susan, *On Photography*, London 1977.
Sontag, Susan, *I, etcetera*, London 1979.
Sontag, Susan, *Under the Sign of Saturn*, New York 1981.
Spivak, Gayatri Chakravorty, 'Displacement and the Discourse of Woman', in Mark Krupnick, ed., *Displacement: Derrida and After*, Indiana 1983.
Spivak, Gayatri Chakravorty, *In Other Worlds: Essays in Cultural Politics*, New York and London 1987.
Stanton, Domna C., ed., *The Female Autograph*, New York, 1984.
Stein, Gertrude, *How Writing is Written*, Los Angeles 1974.
Stein, Gertrude, *How to Write*, Toronto and London 1975.
Stern, Lesley, 'The Body as Evidence', *Screen*, vol. 23, no. 5, 1982.
Suleiman, Susan Rubin, *Authoritarian Fictions: The Ideological Novel As a Literary Genre*, New York 1983.
Suleiman, Susan Rubin, ed., *The Female Body in Western Culture*, Cambridge, Mass. and London 1986.
Whiteside, Anna and Issacharoff, Michael, eds, *On Referring in Literature*, Indiana 1987.
Williamson, Judith, *Consuming Passions: The Dynamics of Popular Culture*, London and New York 1986.
Wilson, Elizabeth, *Adorned in Dreams: Fashion and Modernity*, London 1985.
Wolff, Janet, 'The Invisible Flaneuse: Women and the Literature of Modernity', *The Fate of Modernity, Theory Culture & Society*, vol. 2, no. 3, 1985.

PART I

1

A-mazing Grace: Notes on Mary Daly's Poetics

1. Definitions

A-mazing process:

Within a culture possessed by the myth of feminine evil, the naming, describing, and theorizing about good and evil has constituted a maze/haze of deception. The journey of women becoming is breaking into free space, which is an a-mazing process.[1]

Mary Daly, *Gyn/Ecology*

Grace:

1. *-n.... elegance or beauty of form, manner, motion or act.... (cap.)* **Class. Myth**. *one of three sister goddesses, commonly given as Aglaia (brilliance), Euphrosyne (joy) and Thalia (bloom), presiding over all beauty and charm in nature and humanity.*
2. **Theol**. *a. the free, unmerited favour and love of God. b. the influence or spirit of God operating in man (sic) to regenerate or strengthen. c. a virtue or excellence of divine origin:* **the christian graces ... state of grace. Theol**. *a. a condition of being in God's favour. b. condition of being one of the elect.*

A reordered selection from *The Macquarie Dictionary*.

Poetics:

general theory of textual forms, from Greek **poiesis** *– 'making'. Also, a genre in which that theory is written. Used here in opposition to:* **Rhetoric**, *theory of the art of language as persuasion.*

Poetry:

I speak as a member of the third world women's group and also as a former Catholic. Your talk is at best bad poetry and at worst anti-feminist. I say bad poetry not because I have a notion of good poetry based on certain aesthetic criteria but because your language is derived from western philosophy and from the following discourses in particular: Catholicism, 19th century Romanticism, Existentialism – all of which are incompatible with feminism.[2]

Laleen Jayamanne, statement at Mary Daly event, Sydney, 24 August 1981

27

2. Reasons

Gyn/Ecology is probaby the most important and influential single work
to come out of the American women's movement since Kate Millett's
Sexual Politics. It is important to feminists, because it represents a major
attempt to produce a general philosophy of radical feminism: a philosophy which combines a critique of history, a treatise on religion, a
theory of language and a guide to how to live. It is influential because it
has been read by an enormous number of women, because it elicits
positive responses from feminists who might not otherwise agree on
anything else, and because it has helped to shape at least some of the
broad debates in the women's movement for quite some time.

A work of *Gyn/Ecology's* scope and passionate intensity can hardly
fail to generate controversy. Mary Daly has been criticized for promoting a racist rhetoric, for abrogating the right of third world women to
determine the analysis of their own culture and their own oppression,
and for minimizing the material conditions of women's lives.[3] I agree
with those criticisms; but my concern in this article is a much more
limited one. I want to discuss some aspects of Mary Daly's poetics (her
theory and practice as a writer); take up the connection made by Laleen
Jayamanne between the politics of Daly's writing, and her relationship
to romanticism; and then make a couple of comparisons between *Gyn/
Ecology* and the work of Luce Irigaray, another feminist for whom work
in and with language is of prime political importance.

In the context of *Intervention*, I'm assuming that there is no need to
argue for a critical and theoretical engagement with the work of Mary
Daly.[4] That is, I'm not assuming an imaginary audience of uncritical
Daly-ites, nor of rabidly hostile readers of her work. But I probably *am*
assuming an imaginary group of sociologists, economists, historians who,
having been trained in the 'hard reality' discourses of our knowledge
institutions, are bowled over backwards by a bit of alliteration when it
bobs up in their area. For my assumption is that Mary Daly's use of
language and the Literature Effect (punning, alliteration, word-play,
allegory and the Great Metaphor of the Voyage) cannot be easily
divorced from the politics of *Gyn/Ecology*: that the coherence of Daly's
position is such that the pleasure of the text is bound up in the pleasure
of participating in the political scenario of the Feminist Western, where
good (*some* women) battles evil (males + 'fembots'), and where Athena
wears the black hat while Artemis wears the white. Both the use of
language and the politics depend on a strategy of 'righteous' identification between the reader and the terms of the text.

In an excellent and appreciative review of *Gyn/Ecology* in *Gay
Information 5*, Jill Matthews wrote about the possible negative political

consequences which could follow 'if *Gyn/Ecology* is read as a book of strategy *rather than* poetry' (my emphasis).[5] I think that in this case, the poetry IS strategic. In this sense, my disagreement is probably less with Mary Daly than with those feminist discourses which – unlike Daly's – continue to rely on an implied divorce between language and action, and to draw on the petit-bourgeois vision of Literature as the realm of innocent, or purely spiritual, pleasures.

These are notes, because I'm not making a 'case' against Mary Daly and because I want to make a long digression. But there is one argument throughout: that *Gyn/Ecology* is a politics of subverting isolated signs, not one of transforming discourse. I think that this is a serious problem because I think it is one of the reasons that we find, at the end of Daly's voyage through the maze/haze of patriarchy's deceptions, yet another image of the evil of Other women.

3. Grace (1)

The charm (that is, the power) of Mary Daly's writing is strong and intense. It seems to produce an exhilarating rush which sweeps the sympathetic reader along from page to page, then arrests her with a word or a phrase. Daly has a tremendous control of verbal rhythm, to the point that she can – with a well-placed pun, or a densely packed neologism after an easy passage of delightful abuse – isolate and indicate the spots where you are to *think*. As a 'way of wrenching back some word-power' (p. 9), *Gyn/Ecology* is stunningly succesful. Yet the rush of the rhetoric tends to make the language itself seem unquestionable. As a feminist friend said recently, 'Oh, I didn't try to analyse the language, I just let it sort of flow over me'.

Well, to analyse it a little bit: one focus of Daly's interest in *Gyn/Ecology* is the possibilities offered by changing *particular words* (those items in the dictionary, i.e. the available code – or *langue* – of patriarchal English). She de-constructs and de-forms them in their inert state as signs whose only context *is* the dictionary, and then puts them to work in discourse. Sometimes she trots out her Merriam-Webster to revive old meanings (*glamour, spell, haggard*) and sometimes points to meanings which should be in the dictionary but aren't (*re-search* as the rite of repetition in academic training). Sometimes she produces new definitions herself by pointing to puns already implicit in single words (*stagnation: stag-nation*), and sometimes she creates new signs (*gynaesthesia, biophilic*). Like Dale Spender in *Man Made Language*, she insists that signs (that is, not just word-units, but also prefixes, and compounds like *Sado-Ritual Syndrome*) work to produce our knowledge

of reality; that they are powerful weapons, and that the limitations
of a language in which 'necrophilia' appears but 'biophilia' does not are,
in a real sense, the limitations of a world.[6]

Her strategy is to warp the words of the patriarchal dictionary, to
bend the code back against itself until it snaps to our shrieks of derision.
In this respect (and this respect only), Daly's use of the vocabulary of
christianity, for example, is not a simple takeover or a repetition, but a
deliberate deformation. Like the so-called Black Mass, *Gyn/Ecology* is
the christian code said backwards – and of course for Daly, it is the
original truth of our female integrity which we re-member during the
process of going back. She calls this process 'reversing the reversals'.

The tactics she uses are few in number, but sufficiently striking to
acquire the force of an Authorial style. It's a style which both solicits
and forbids imitation, since to write like Mary Daly is to copy her
signature – to sign one's allegiance in an act of subordination which no
loyal Daly-ite could possibly assume. But the methods she proposes are
as suggestive as her concepts – for example, her play with the histories of
words. It's probably poetic justice that when I looked up the word *grace*
to make sure that it was indeed the religious term I wanted, what jumped
up alongside the sought-for word *elect* was precisely an example of the
kind of reversal that Mary Daly contests: not only the christian conversion of the Graces into a gift of the male God, but the demeaning
refeminization of the concept as 'the accomplishments and refinements
expected of a young person, esp. a young woman, who belongs to or
wishes to enter the upper levels of society'.[7]

It's rather like a game of buried treasure, an illuminating search
through the store-house of signs made pleasurable as well as instructive
by the evident joy that Mary Daly takes in working with words. Whatever one thinks of the style, the sheer excessiveness of the signs of
literary-ness in phrases like 'absolutely Anti-androcrat, A-mazingly
Anti-male, Furiously and Finally Female' provides a powerful antidote
to the deadening effect of left puritanism in language.

But reworking 'words' as dictionary items (subverting the code) is not
the same thing as paying attention to the ways that words work together
in discourse, or *language in use*.

At the simplest level, it's curious that Mary Daly shows little interest
in playing with the possibilities of syntax. She does draw on the work of
feminist linguists like Julia Stanley for notions such as the Passive Voice,
'agent deletion', and the erasure of responsibility in professional language which gives rise to formations like *untreated menopause*. In an
extended listing of examples, Daly uses these notions as powerful critical
tools in a politicized version of Close Reading. She also refers to the
work on pronouns carried out by the linguists, and by the writer

Monique Wittig. But if for Daly, as well as for Wittig, 'women are silenced/split by the babble of grammatical usage',[8] Daly nevertheless treats the usages she mentions as isolated *'features'* of a thing called language (and not part of a process of discourse). The 'usages' are further items in the repertoire of the universal code of patriarchy. The consequence of this is that 'meanings' are regarded as being inherent in the sign – frozen in there waiting to be unpicked and unpacked, and the 'false' replaced by the 'true'.

I want to come back to this problem later, to talk about why it matters. But an example can be found in Daly's rewriting of Wittig on the pronoun 'I'. Wittig says, 'the "I" (*Je*) who writes is alien to her own writing at every word because this "I" (*Je*) uses a language alien to her; this "I" (*Je*) experiences what is alien to her since this "I" (*Je*) cannot be *"un"* ecrivain ... *J/e* poses the ideological and historic question of feminine subjects.'[9] Wittig is talking about the *relationship between* the *Je* and the *un*, between the 'I' of a woman writer and the rest of the discourse process; and in posing her split *J/e*, she connects the question of this relationship to the question of the constitution of femininity in ideology and history. Daly collapses these connections into person- alized drama starring the *'spooks* of grammar'. She says, 'The false/evil "I" (the ghostliest pronoun) must be burned into impotence by the Evil Eyes of watchful Witches' (p. 327). Daly now is no longer talking about the 'I' *in* discourse, or about relationships with verbs, adverbs and articles (although when she analyses the 'elasticity' of *we* and *us* in particular texts, or in sentences like 'We failed in Vietnam', she is obliged to do just that). Instead, with the Tolkienesque touch for character which makes much of *Gyn/Ecology* read like a feminist *Lord of the Rings*, she inhabits the 'I' with evil spirits. She gives it an intrinsic being, an identity of its own – the 'I' as a particular word becomes inherently false and evil.

My point here is not that Daly 'distorts' Wittig, and it is certainly not that her representation of syntax as a set of items is incorrect in the terms of some other theory. What I am stressing is the difference between Wittig's work and Daly's, as part of my argument that Daly pursues a politics of subverting isolated signs, not discourses. The 'word' is what carries, conveys and contains 'meaning'. The emblem of this is Daly's curious rewriting of a quotation from Gertrude Stein at the beginning of *Gyn/Ecology* (facing p. viii), where Stein's flow of syntactical humour is blocked off and transformed into slabs of statement. Thus:

Patriarchal Poetry is the same as Patriotic poetry is the same as patriarchal poetry is the same as Patriotic poetry is the same as patriarchal poetry is the same.

becomes:

> Patriarchal Scholarship is the same as Patriotic scholarship is the same
> as patriarchal scholarship is the same as patriarchal poetry.

Where Stein has three elements (Patriarchal Poetry, Patriotic poetry,
patriarchal poetry) which recur in an assymetrical pattern (1/2/3/2/3),
Mary Daly gives us the march of a right-on 1/2/3/4 (Patriarchal
Scholarship, Patriotic scholarship, patriarchal scholarship, patriarchal
poetry). But above all, Stein in ending with '*is the same*' is making a joke
about the mechanisms for stating equivalence and identity (i.e., a joke
about poetry and syntax). Daly snaps the full stop back to its 'proper'
place, and so simply produces an equation – she states only that these
things ARE the same. She cuts out Stein's concern with the process of
discourse, and what's left is an assertion of the identity of four signs.
(The same thing happens on the level of the comment on capitalisation:
Stein's flux – PP/Pp/pp/Pp/pp – becomes a step-by-step reduction –
PS/Ps/ps/pp).

At the end of one of the most graceful and inspiring passages in the
book, Mary Daly calls for the transformation of 'static "bodies of
knowledge"': 'It is women's own Gyn/Ecology that can break the
brokenness of the "fields", deriding their borders and boundaries,
changing the nouns of knowledge into verbs of know-ing' (p. 11). What
I'd like to say next is that Mary Daly's concern is with the noun of
speech, rather than the verb of speak-ing (in other words, with the
semantics of the said, rather than the enunciative strategies of saying) –
and that this limitation has a political function in her work which *is the
same* as what Jayamanne calls 'bad poetry'. But first, a digression on
discourse.

4. Digression on Discourse

There is something ludicrous about writing a technical paper on Mary
Daly's poetics for *Intervention*. It isn't entirely mad (as it would be to
send the above piece of unabashed Athena-ite pedantry to a radical
feminist journal of Female Creativity) or entirely inappropriate (as it
would be to submit it to a newspaper, or read it aloud at a forum). But
neither is it entirely reasonable and meaningful, as it would be to write it
for a feminist journal of semiotics. (Unlike Mary Daly, I do not believe
that 'meanings' are in 'words', but that meaning is produced in specific
contexts of discourse). It does make some sense, because *Intervention* is
a theoretical as well as a political journal, and because part of its current

publishing project is to open up traditional left discourse on politics and economics to different questions and formulations.

But if it still seems ludicrous, it's partly because of a stereotyped notion I have of the questions imposed by the *Intervention* context: questions of defining the issue politically, of making the politics clear or *visible* in terms which make sense in *Intervention*, and of trying (and no doubt failing) to maintain some consistency in the terms of my analysis while avoiding 'too much' use of a language which is frequently called intimidating, mystifying and élitist.

To mention this is not to brighten up my article by fabricating a polemical relationship with its context. It is partly to illustrate what it means NOT to believe that meanings inhere in words: to assume that a context – in particular, at least an image of an audience – plays a part in what is said and how it's said. Mary Daly's approach can imply the opposite: because you have 'true meanings' to articulate, you are likely to say the same thing in the same way in the same language in any circumstances to anyone to whom you accept to speak politically. It is then up to the audience to situate itself/themselves accordingly. To do otherwise would be to speak 'falsely' – to use 'mere rhetoric' in the pejorative sense which is part of the common sense of post-romantic culture. (I say Daly's *approach* implies this, because people's practices are not identical with or deducible from their theories; and many people who would insist that words simply mean what they mean, would also never dream of reading a densely written article aloud and expect it to make sense. In practice, this 'approach' is probably quite rare; the Sparticists provide one example). This is one way in which Mary Daly offers feminism a Poetics, and not a Rhetoric – a 'form', and not a politics, of speech.

But to describe my image of *Intervention* is also a way of defining my basic concern in this article: that while traditional left suspicion of – or caution about – what is sometimes called 'the language stuff' may well be quite reasonable, it has allowed a waffly, homogenized notion of language as a 'method' to emerge – which makes the political differences which do exist between feminists working on language become practically invisible, and so outside discussion. (Whether this work *can* ever count as 'visible politics' is another problem again.)

One obstacle in the theoretical debates about Language on the left has long been, I think, the Daly-esque idea that some words '*are*' intrinsically intimidating; that there is an inherent and insurmountable obscurity at work in the conceptual vocabularies of theories of discourse, which is absent from the limpid languages of the social sciences. Raymond Williams once analysed a similar belief, held by British intellectuals of the Leavisite persuasion in literary criticism, when they contested Marxist approaches to literature and society by assimilating them to the dangers of the use of language to 'disguise' the realities of industrial society:

> Very aware of this danger, which does not have to be called but can be called dehumanising and mystifying, English thinkers could easily, too easily, fall back on their older habits, professing not to understand abstractions like a power structure though they could traditionally understand a microcosm, or not to understand reification though they could understand the objective correlative, and not to know mediation though they knew catharsis. Certain received habits of mind, a very particular and operative selection of traditional and predemocratic concepts and adjustments, acquired, by what one has to call alchemy, the status of concrete, or of minute particulars.[10]

While there is certainly a different history involved, a similar alchemy transforms *énonciation*[11] into an intimidating term while *labour market segmentation* is not, *text* into an élitist term while *ideology* is not, and *discourse* into a mystifying term – while *mystification* is not. Part of the alchemy – which also renders wispy and unreal the objects analysed in semiotics, while objects in economics are concrete in their reality – is probably the systematic evacuation of language about language (i.e. the minimal tools for talking about language at all) from and by our schooling systems. If the politics of language debates seem invisible, it is *in part* because verbal language is the most intensely naturalized – i.e. transparent – mode of social control at work in our culture. It's sometimes said that *labour market segmentation* is easy to explain because it affects people's lives: but *énonciation* is a concept dealing with something that everybody does every time that they open their mouths (to good or evil effect).

But this is a debate so old that it's practically cosy. I'm more concerned about the problems of manoeuvring within it, which are rather of the order of Catch 22. Given the relatively restricted dissemination of linguistic and semiotic concepts, and the myths which surround their use, to employ them can be tantamount to making oneself incomprehensible. On the other hand, not to employ them, and to sweat over sneaky uses of 'simple language', can simply provide further evidence that the theories are not necessary in the first place. To refuse to recognise the problem of accessibility is to be 'élitist', while to discuss it is to be 'inward' and 'self-reflective'. The *effect* of this is to maintain the aura of confusion and uncertainty surrounding much feminist work on discourse as it circulates in the broad women's movement, because it rarely circulates publicly in a developed state.

Finally, on a less polemical note, there is the problem of definitions. It is sometimes said in the women's movement that it would be a help if writers in semiotics (or indeed, academic feminists writing in the terms of any discipline) provided a glossary of terms. In fact, this doesn't always help at all; since a set of definitions – and the dictionary here is the best example – is a self-referring system. Words in dictionaries do not 'refer' to anything except all the other words in the dictionary; and to understand the definition of one item, it is necessary to understand the code of which the item is a part. That is why it is impossible to learn a foreign language using nothing but the dictionary of that language; that is why, if one accepts Mary Daly's concept of patriarchy, as the dominant code of culture, then Mary Daly's use of the dictionary as a means of unravelling both code and culture makes a-mazing sense; and that is also why the attempt to be both accessible and consistent in a technical discourse often fails in spite of the best intentions.

However, a definition working in a context (discourse) is something different from a glossary ('words' and their 'meanings'); and in the intention, at least, of clarity, I'd like to define the terms *discourse* and *énonciation* as I am using them *in this article*. Discourse in particular is a tricky term. On the one hand, there is the basic definition of discourse as 'things said or written'. On the other hand, there are the eleven distinct uses of the term noted by A.J. Greimas and J. Courtés in their dictionary *Sémiotique: dictionnaire raisonné de la théorie du langage* (referring to over forty other terms listed by that same dictionary, and without including the specific uses of *discourse* in the work of philosophers like Foucault and Derrida).[12] Eleven entries is probably not bad going if you consider what a dictionary of marxisms would have to do with *ideology*, but it does indicate the way that, historically, the term *discourse* has been used to take up the slack in inadequate theories of language – which may perhaps be the reason that Ducrot and Todorov's *Encyclopedic Dictionary of the Sciences of Language* does not register *discourse* as a separate item at all. But one general definition I've heard would cover all the entries in Greimas and Courtés, and would probably extend to Foucault and Derrida as well: *discourse* may be defined as '*constraints* on semiosis', semiosis being defined as the production of meaning by signs *in continuous action*.[13] Finally, alongside 'things said or written' and the technical uses, there is the vague but functional use of the term in expressions like 'romantic discourse', 'traditional left discourse', 'feminist discourse', to designate an assumed – or momentarily posited – unity.

In arguing that Mary Daly works to transform signs, but not discourse, I'm using one of the Greimas/Courtés Eleven – *discourse* as defined by Emile Benveniste is 'the product of a speaking position'. A summary of Benveniste's argument – given in Anne Freadman's paper 'On Being Here and Still Doing It', – is reproduced below.[14] But I want to stress here that what makes discourse possible is the mechanism of the *énonciation*: the way that in its function as 'the nexus of linguistic space-time coordinates – the tense structures, the indicative pronouns ('this' and 'that'), adverbs of time and place, articles – the pronoun 'I' defines what is 'you' and what is 'he/she/it', what is 'here' and what is 'there', what is 'now' and what is 'then'. This is why discourse – by definition – does and must refer, in a way that dictionaries, equally by definition, cannot.

Finally, an example of the possible use of these concepts in relation to two texts too remote to be controversial. In the novels of the eighteenth century in France, it was a common narrative device to reunite the hero and the heroine by placing the latter in an overturned chariot when the former just happened to be riding by. Two women writers in the 1730s dealt with the embarrassment of producing this cliché in these two different ways:

> One expects, of course, that it was Adelaide and her mother in the chariot: and in effect, it was them.
>
> Mme de Tencin, *Mémoires du Comte de Comminge*

> I cannot resist arresting the reader's attention here; what I am about to relate has something so singular about it, that it is good to stop for breath. I simply beg the reader to reflect upon the effects of chance. However little he may have lived, he will perhaps find even more surprising examples in his own career; extraordinary things happen every day ... Hmmm! Who would not have been amazed by such an encounter? Madame de Nerville ... Yes, it was she whom an unforeseen good fortune had led us to succour.[15]
>
> Mme Méheust, *Les Mémoires du Chevalier de ...*

Without listing all the differences in the marks of *énonciation* in these texts, it's enough to note that the first one binds the narrator and the reader in the urbanity of the '*One* expects', with a gesture of the order of a wink; that the distinction between the present tense of the reading "One *expects*') and the past tense of the story "It *was* Adelaide') assumes a clear separation between the reading and the read-about; and that the closure with a further wink 'in effect' has the function of pointing to the chariot device AS device. It is an approach which might today be called 'formalist'; but which affirms a *common cultural code* about what one expects to find in novels, and the pleasure of finding what one expects. (It may be worth noting that Mme de Tencin moved in court and aristocratic circles.)

The second text separates narrator and reader by addressing the latter (the 'he' is an oblique 'you'). Instead of affirming a literary *device* as a *literary* device, the text justifies its chariot by an appeal to experience and reality; the move from the present tense of the narrating ('I *cannot* resist') to the subjunctive and future ('However little he *may have lived,* he *will*') to a generalized '*Who would not*' and straight into the past of the story ('*it was* she') blurs completely and deliberately the distinction between life, the story, and the act of reading a novel. It invokes the life/art relation that was to play such a vital part in both romanticism and realism – conflicting cultural and political movements, which nevertheless shared a set of assumptions about Art and Life, Reality and Imagination, which have no place in the culture defined by Mme de Tencin. (Mme Méheust was a *bourgeoise*, with recognizable feminist leanings).

Both of these books are fictional memoirs; that is, both are examples of what is usually and misleadingly called 'first-person narration'. Both are 'women's discourse', in the sense of things written by women. Both could be called 'literary' or 'novelistic' discourse, in the sense that it is possible (if not necessarily desirable) to posit both the literary and the novel as unified objects or fields of enquiry. But in the sense derived from Benveniste, they would constitute two *different* modes of *énonciation*, two different types of discourse.

It is in this sense that I'd now like to discuss the discourse of Mary Daly, and its relationship to the romantic aesthetic.

5. Grace (2)

Mary Daly is a political élitist. I don't mean that in the abusive sense used by feminists to denounce the imagined motives behind work which they dislike or do not understand. I mean that she's an élitist because she says she is.

It's not just that her work is not addressed to 'all women', or to fictional constructs like The Ordinary Woman. Neither is this article, neither is *Intervention*, and neither is any work which assumes that there can be class, cultural and political differences between women. It's rather that Mary Daly distinguishes between women who are too 'damaged'[16] to free themselves spiritually from patriarchy, and those who are not; that she actively constructs an imaginary order – or Convocation – of the companions of *Gyn/Ecology* on the basis of their Be-ing, their spiritual qualities and capacities; and that she projects this notion on to the history of women to the point that the targets of the witchburnings become 'primarily a spiritual/moral/know-ing élite cross-section of the female population of Europe' (p. 194). The restriction 'élite cross-section' is in no way required by a traditional radical feminist interpretation of the witchburnings as a chapter in the history of war waged by men against women.

In her *Gay Information* review, Jill Matthews describes the way that this élitism works in the structure of argument in *Gyn/Ecology*.

> It is beautifully crafted, an incredibly complex book, creating a self-enclosed and self-justified system of thought which disarms criticism by prejudging her critics and denying their legitimacy. To disagree with her is to put oneself outside the circle of the elect for whom the book is written. The critic is, by definition, one of the enemy.[17]

It also works in the discourse, and the function accorded to poetry as a means of dividing the false from the true.

At the end of the first note on Grace, I said that Mary Daly's main concern is with the 'noun' of speech rather than the 'verb' of speak-ing – with semantics rather than with the *énonciation*. That is an interpretation of her practice as a reader of the patriarchal dictionary, and her tactics as a producer of new 'words'. But to say that she pursues a politics of subverting isolated signs is not to say that she doesn't produce discourse (since in my terms, it would make no sense to say so) – nor that she doesn't provide us with a model of her own mode of *énonciation*.

I want to produce two examples of what that model is, and how it works. One is an allegory I'm inventing myself, by narrating some aspects of a lecture given by Mary Daly: the other is an interpretation of the passage 'The Dissembly of Exorcism' (from *Gyn/Ecology*) read *as* an allegory of a type of discourse. Both examples imply, I think, that discourse is a social ritual for sorting the sheep from the goats, for dividing the elect-in-a-state-of-grace from those beyond the pale: and that the principle for making this division is a test of whether or not it is possible for the 'you' to commune in a 'we' with the 'I' of Gyn/Ecological discourse.

In August 1981, Mary Daly gave a lecture in Sydney to a large assembly of feminists from many different tendencies of the women's movement. Although it was a Women Only event, much of the controversy was subsequently discussed in public media. Mary Daly read aloud from a written text of some sort, but relieved the difficulty of this for the listeners by digressing and chatting as she went along. The second part of the lecture was purely informative, since it was an outline of new work later to be made public in her book, *Pure Lust*.[18] The first part, however, had a more complex function, since it was a long summary of sections of *Gyn/Ecology*.

Presumably this had an informative function for women who had not read the book. For those who had, the repetition could only function as a reminder or – in an ancient tradition of both academic and priestly discourse – as a ritual and pleasurable reaffirmation of what has already been said before: an *act* of repetition of shared statements which – like the Communion Service – ritually reunites both speaker and hearers in an affirmation of their common identity. (Here, I'm not attempting to diagnose Mary Daly's *motives* for speaking in this way – which for all I know may have been of the order of having to throw something together at short notice, or anxiety at being put up on display in front of an unknown audience in an alien land. I'm simply pointing to the function of the strategy she adopted, and the speaking traditions from which it comes.)

The *we*-ness of the address was ruptured, however, by a woman who called out 'Mary, you're not speaking to *me* ...'. As the speaker, Mary Daly replied that the woman who interjected had a choice: she could stay (i.e. accept the speech) or she could go (i.e. reject it altogether). This reply (and again, I'm not claiming to know Daly's motives for making it, or to judge her feeling at the time) amounted to a refusal to change rhetorics, or to change the mode of *énonciation* to deal with this new 'I' that had emerged by posing Mary Daly as the 'you'; that posed *itself* as defining the 'here/now' in opposition to the 'not-here/not-now' defined as Mary Daly's discourse. Daly's refusal to change in response – her refusal to address the new 'I' on its own terms, or to modify the *we*-ness of her address in any way – was immediately identified as a school-room tactic by women in the audience. This tactic was later reinforced by Daly's refusal to discuss the relationship between social class, education, and language use; and by her positioning of most subsequent questions and criticisms as attacks (whether or not they were made by women who agreed with the initial interjection). She unified all statements made with any degree of distance from her own speech as the product of a hostile '*you*' (thereby conflating the positions of some lesbian separatists with those of communist women, and so on).

A number of interpretations were made of this event: for example, that it was a case of feminist star-bashing, of Australian intellectual-thumping, or of cross-cultural misunderstanding. I think that these are probably all quite true. But my point here is that Daly's mode of address in her lecture, and her refusal to change that mode enough to enter into an exchange with women speaking from positions different from her own, is ALSO perfectly consistent with the idea at work in *Gyn/Ecology* that discourse is a way of distinguishing those who are For you from those who are Against. Those who are For you can share your speech, those who are Against cannot.

'The Dissembly of Exorcism' is an extremely vivid and funny drama about precisely this distinction, written rather in the manner of a biblical parable. I don't have space to summarize it, so I'll just refer to pages

418–22 of *Gyn/Ecology*. It is about the breaking of the spell of 'the crude Deceptions of the Demons who persist in trying to *blend their voices* into *our Hearings*' (my emphases). Each group of demons (who re-present the Sins of the Fathers) makes a speech to the convocation of Gyn/Ecologists: and each speech is an example of deceptive language. Some attempt to persuade the Convocation with their sweet talk, while others go so far as to attempt to assume the Gyn/Ecological position (those who say 'I like dykes' or 'I am a lesbian-feminist male-to-female transsexual. Take me in'). At the end, they all unravel to the roaring of the Revolted Hags.

Without insisting too much, I'd argue that this is not only about the impossibility of *dialogue* (between males and females, evil and good) but also about the idea that discourse tells you who people 'are', and if you know who they are then you can't be deceived by their discourse – including their attempts to share, to join, to make contact or connect with your speech. 'The Dissembly of Exorcism' describes a ritual performance of this idea, since this time (i.e. at this place in the process of reading *Gyn/Ecology*) the convocation of Gyn/Ecologists/good readers of *Gyn/Ecology* know who the demons ARE before they even begin to speak. 'We are ready for them now': and so the point of the whole performance is to demonstrate a process of deceptive discourse deceiving itself (the invoked demons must have 'ample opportunity to expose themselves'); and to affirm the importance of *Gyn/Ecology* in giving women the power to turn back the linguistic lures of their enemies. It is a drama of discourse as an Anti-communication: a celebration of the State of Complete Closure constituted by the *Gyn/Ecological* speaking-position.

Mary Daly's affirmation of the communion of the élite, her concept of election as a state of 'spiritual/moral/knowing' potential, and her preemptive disqualification of critics as hostile, unknowing *beings* (damaged or deadly by nature),[19] produces a posture in strong affinity with romantic theories of the redemptive function of Art, and the special nature of Be-ings called Artists. Since Mary Daly works explicitly by reversing the reversals of patriarchal culture, it is no criticism of her work to discern within it the traces of various traditions which she has wittingly twisted, rewritten or transformed. But of all such traces, it is the function of a largely untransformed romantic discourse on meaning which concerns me most: a romantic speaking-position, and a romantic position on speaking.

It's easy enough to produce abusive generalizations about romanticism, stirring a couple of centuries' worth of diverse activities into a single, bland Bad Thing. Romanticism, for example, does not necessarily entail political or even artistic élitism: many of the early romantics were, in the terms of their times, democrats, Enthusiasts, and revolutionaries, concerned to free language from the particular class constraints of classical culture. But it's possible to point to a couple of common features. One is the way that romanticism constructs a special affinity between Woman and the forces of nature; an image, or a 'pleasant reverie of a womanhood enclosed in itself',[20] which is sharply distinguished from the earlier eighteenth-century concept of women as the forces of social and political cohesion. Another is the preeminence accorded to the Imagination: 'when we turn our back on the world and invent, only then is truth'.[21] Both of these features are strongly present in *Gyn/Ecology*, with its metaphorics of wind and water, its concept of the woman-centred Self, and its assertion that patriarchy may be left behind by the process of spiritual metamorphosis.

But above all, romanticism implies a doctrine of Self-expression – in which the qualities of the 'self' in a sense, can be held to determine qualities of language. Reading (or in Daly's terms, Hearing) can then become a process of reaching through language to seize the quality of the self which is therein expressed. If romanticism does not necessarily entail an élitism, it is in part because the romantic stress on inspiration and creativity could be generalized as a 'belief in the irreducible specialness of each individual'[22] – although in the kind of romanticism which is still alive and well and living in the Art Schools, as well as that spoken by Mary Daly, the irreducible specialness has become the defining characteristic of a particular group (Creative People in one case, Gyn/Ecologists in the other). At the same time, as Peter Wollen points out, this belief directly threatened the function of art as communication – a threat which was dealt with by such notions as 'identification' and 'empathy'.[23]

Communing through the text is precisely the option Mary Daly offered to women in an interview when – in response to a question about her criticisms of reformist women – she concluded 'I have to say – you know – let she who has ears to hear ...'.[24] Communication is a matter of equipment: biological (you must be a woman) and then spiritual (you must be a less-damaged woman, with Woman-Identified ears). These qualifications are necessary for both speakers and hearers *before* Gyn/Ecological discourse can take place; and before the 'vast, incredible differences' which Mary Daly (in that same interview) quite willingly allows for 'within our understanding of Radical Feminism', can take their place in discussion.

It is in the matter of biological and spiritual equipment that Be-ing, for Mary Daly, determines the possibilities of discourse. This is why it is possible to *see through* deceptive discourse to reveal who the speakers really 'are' – and thus, to name them truly with a word which fits their

being. This is why discourse can be a recognition ritual for finding out
who people are (or rather, who *women* are – since a male is a male is a
male): and for separating 'we' women from Other women. And I think
this is probably why discourse itself (rather than words and their
meanings) cannot be a site of experiment to Gyn/Ecological practice:
the mode of *énonciation* must be relatively fixed, since it is the means by
which 'the *multiply mobile*: the movers, the weavers, the Spinners'
(p. xiv) may find themselves identified, and identify each other. This is
another sense in which *Gyn/Ecology* could be said to offer feminism a
Poetics: it is a theory of the textual forms held to 'fit' a certain sort of
spirit.

In this context, Mary Daly's affirmation of Big Words for 'big, strong
women'[25] acquires its full force. Strength calls to strength, language
echoes spirit: and thus it can only be a confession of weakness for a
woman to assert class, cultural or educational difference in response to
Mary Daly's speech. The density of the poetry is then comparable in
function to a spiritual exercise which prepares women for seeing through
the progressively transparent discourse of others, for naming the false
and the true. 'Words' are like the magic formulae of the alchemist: they
transform the user, not the material world. And just as spiritual strength
is inherent in all women (but more so in some than others), so there is a
strength-potential in isolated signs which is sufficient to overcome the
histories of their use. The word *race*, for example, can be cheerfully put
to 'new' political purposes by reviving the dictionary 'meanings' of
rushing onwards, or of two tides meeting in a choppy sea[26] – while the
function of *race* in certain particular discourses, the history of those discourses, and the histories which those discourses have made and still
make possible, remains, in Mary Daly's poetics, entirely beside the
point.

There remains the question of the visible politics of such language
'games'. For just as to talk of élites and election can be an unkind way of
describing a simple restriction, so to call Mary Daly's discourse romantic
can be a mere assertion of guilt by association. My argument is rather
that the bad poetry of *Gyn/Ecology* consists in the strategic function
played by the romanticism, by the identification-games played through
the closure of the discourse in contrast to the opening up of the sign.
That function is to maintain a *necessary* image of Other women as
wanting, lacking, incomplete, blinded, damaged or downright malevolent.
This is the excluded She of Gyn/Ecological discourse; and as Mary Daly
points out, 'Her name is legion' (p. 335). However some of Her names
are fembot (female robot), Athena, token woman, and the Painted Bird.

These creatures are – like the false Athena born from the head of
Zeus – repeatedly reproduced by the rulers; and their function is far

from innocent. For example, 'token women are trained to kill off feminists in patriarchal professions' (p. 8). In the section 'Painted Birds: the State of Total Tokenism' (pp. 333–6), these women are compared to prostitutes turning tricks, disease carriers, poisoners and torturers. This section is another case of 'reversing the reversals' at the level of a single (complex) sign. The image of the Painted Bird is taken from Thomas Szasz's interpretation of a novel by Jerzy Kosinski: 'The Painted Bird is the perfect symbol of the Other, the Stranger, the Scapegoat.' Daly says that this could be applied to the situation of women under patriarchy; but the image would then be inadequate and a reversal. To *reverse* the reversal, it is necessary to understand that it is the woman who *sheds* her paint who is treated as a Freak (i.e. the Other) under patriarchy. Under patriarchy, Painted Birds are the norm.

What remains discreetly *un*-reversed by this process is the structural necessity FOR a symbol of the Other (who now becomes a woman as well). In Daly's double reinterpretation of the image, the mode of discourse invoked by Szasz remains unchanged.

The feminist philosopher Michèle Le Doeuff has argued that certain philosophical discourses produce their own identity by projecting an image of an Other who lacks that same identity (thus *creating* that Other in the process); and that the history of the misogyny of philosophy is in part the history of such projections on to women. She argues that classical rationalist discourse, for example, depends upon an image of Womanly Unreason; and that the famous 'holes and slime' imagery in Sartre's metaphysics provides the counterfigure which is indispensable to the existentialist system. For Le Doeuff, it is precisely because Simone de Beauvoir was able to transpose the existentialist problematic from the status of system to that of a point of view 'trained on *a* determinate and partial field of experience', that she was able to eliminate the need for a counterfigure – and thus transform a particularly unpromising philosophical framework in order 'to reach conclusions about which the least one can say is that they have dynamized women's movements in Europe and America over the last thirty years'.[27]

My objection to the image of the Painted Bird in *Gyn/Ecology* is that its function is comparable to that of Sartre's holes and slime: it's not that it isn't very nice to talk about other women that way, or that Daly's language here ranges from tart to vitriolic, but that the projection of an image of evil in other women is indispensable to the Gyn/Ecological speaking position. 'Evil in other women' may be unfair, since it is a matter of what patriarchy has done to such women. But in that case, Daly deprives them again of identity: they are women no-longer Women, male creations, non-Identified women; the ones *produced by* Daly's question in her Preface, 'just *who* are "the women"?' (p. xv).

This division made amongst women seems to me to be a particularly deadly one: BOTH because it returns us to the perfectly classical mode of philosophical discourse analysed by Michèle Le Doeuff (or to the speaking position of patriarchal theory, with its phantasmagorical Processions of Others) AND because of the politics it can imply.

The first problem is that Mary Daly produces her images of fembots and Painted Birds inside a completely coherent mythical – and philosophical – system. She isn't just writing a spirited attack on the politics of feminist bureaucrats, or waging an angry polemic against reformist practices, or criticizing the function of women's studies courses in the local university. To do so might require a different mode of discourse; for to adopt a position against an opponent is not to produce a full-blown symbolic Other. Instead, the Painted Birds and the fembots take their place in a complex narrative and symbolic system for interpreting the whole of patriarchal history – and for interpreting patriarchy as the religion of the whole planet – in terms of false and true, evil and good, males (+ fembots) and females (− fembots).

With great good will and determination to be blind and deaf to the rhythms of the writing, this might be read as parodic of the global pretentions of patriarchal theory. But the Painted Birds then pose a second problem – this time at the level of myth. *Gyn/Ecology* – *as writing* – does not proceed from the observation that tokenism poses a threat or a problem to feminists, and then work through to explanations, polemics, countertactics, proposals or persuasions. Instead, the Painted Birds are produced as symbols illustrating a much wider general phenomenon which the whole Journey of *Gyn/Ecology* exists to explain – and which consequently places these 'creatures' in a paradigm (or a complicity set-up) with witch-burners, foot-binders and Nazi medicos. The myth structure explains the phenomenon of tokenism: the phenomenon of tokenism does not generate the myth. In this sense, *Gyn/Ecology* could hardly be described as a parody of a global theory, but rather a perfect replica.

The third problem is the way that the difference between Painted Birds and Gyn/Ecologists is represented in the text. Apart from the contempt in the language (Painted Birds are 'mutants' (p. 334), they 'turn their tricks in all the prescribed positions' (p. 335) as well as 'double-crossing (their) sisters, polluting them with poisonous paint' (p. 336)), this difference is consistently founded by Mary Daly in a machismo of the spirit possessed by Gyn/Ecologists. They are 'those women *strong enough* to resist the paint infection' (p. 336 my emphasis). In spite of occasional gestures in *Gyn/Ecology* towards an ultimate desirable state in which all women would be returned to their original integrity of Be-ing, the insistent theme in the book is the moral and spiritual superiority of the strong as opposed to the contemptible, menacing wiles of the weak. The basic schema of the book is intractable: the universe may be understood on the basis of 1) primary, determining biological difference between males and females, then 2) secondary but equally determining spiritual difference beween women. And it is on this schema that the poetics of *Gyn/Ecology* rests, with its 'fit' beween spirit and sign.[28]

For the Painted Birds and the fembots are, in fact, the floating signifiers of difference. It is their tittering (p. 17) which allows the roaring of the Hags to be heard. It is their lack of strength, their greater numbers and their 'common condition' (p. 334) which allows the strong, s/elect State of Gyn/Ecology to consolidate its identity and emerge in its difference – not just from men, not just from most women, but also *from other forms of feminism.* For this reason, the images of the fembot and the Painted Bird are absolutely necessary to the Gyn/Ecological system: for without them, the complex identification strategies of Gyn/Ecological discourse and its poetics of perfect coherence – would, strictly speaking, make no sense.

6. Difference

For women to undertake tactical strikes, to keep themselves apart from men long enough to learn to defend their desire, especially through speech, to discover the love of other women while sheltered from men's imperious choices that put them in the position of rival commodities, to forge for themselves a social status that compels recognition, to earn their living in order to escape from the condition of prostitute ... these are certainly indispensible stages in the escape from their proletarization on the exchange market. But if their aim were simply to reverse the order of things, even supposing this to be possible, history would repeat itself in the long run, would revert to sameness; to phallocratism. It would leave room neither for women's sexuality, nor for women's imaginary, nor for women's language to take (their) place.[29]

To make a point for point comparison between the work of Luce Irigaray and that of Mary Daly would be an exhausting, and pointless process. My purpose anyway is not to represent them as diametrical opposites, but to indicate some ways in which feminist work on language can imply quite different political tendencies within – and across – the women's movement.

Irigaray and Daly could be compared, for example, in terms of an equal commitment for the dismantling of the assumptions of patriarchal thought: Irigaray's study of Freud in *Speculum – de l'autre femme* is

quite close in many respects – including the method of detailed analysis
of passages from texts – to the long assault on scholarship in The Second
Passage of *Gyn/Ecology*. Both work with very long spans of time; Daly
with the whole history of patriarchy treated as one regime, Irigaray with
the history of the Western *logos* since Plato. And both recommend – in
distinction from one radical feminist position on Never Reading Men's
Books – a thorough and meticulous study of the canons of masculine
culture.

But the differences between them are, nevertheless, sharp and
fundamental. Mary Daly advocates a particular *type* of radical feminist
separatism, based not only on dissociation from men, but on dis-
association from women who are not of the 'race' of women. Luce
Irigaray supports the necessity for women to adopt a separatist practice,
in places and times of their own choosing, in order to 'escape their
proletarization on the trade market'. If radical feminism is defined as
a *politics* which works on whatever all women have in common, in full
recognition of the differences between them, then Luce Irigaray could
probably be described as a radical feminist.[30] But if radical feminism is
defined as a *theory* of the determining role played by sex over class,
economic and cultural factors in the oppression of women, then Luce
Irigaray is not   radical feminist. As her essay 'Commodities Among
Themselves' makes quite clear,[31] for her these questions are indissoci-
able. Finally, these feminisms differ in the role they accord to discourse.
For Mary Daly, the 'living Speech' of the Crones is intrinsically transgressive, and liberatory: 'The point is not to save society or to focus on
escape ... but to release the Spring of be-ing. To the inhabitants of
Babel, this Spring of living speech will be unintelligible ... So much the
better for the Crone's Chorus. Left undisturbed we are free to find our
own concordance, to hear our own harmony, the harmony of the
spheres' (p. 22). For Luce Irigaray, the importance of discourse IS its
imbrication in the social; and as Rosi Braidotti puts it, 'Irigaray is thus in
solidarity with the current of feminist thought according to which the
oppression of women is simultaneously real, and symbolic – that is, that
it rests as much on material structures of repression as it does on
philosophical pre-suppositions'.[32]

One of the reasons for this difference is precisely the value which
each accords to the term 'phallocracy'. For Mary Daly, phallocracy is
the State of rule by males – i.e. not-women with penises. For Luce
Irigaray, phallocracy is something like the political economy of phallo-
centrism: the idea, as Michèle Le Doeuff puts it, 'that there is only one
sex, the male one – the other half of heaven being eunuch'.[33] According
to the logic of the One sex, the feminine sex is represented as an
absence, a lack, a blank, a minus, or a zero. Irigaray's project in *Speculum*,

and in the essays of *Ce sexe qui n'en est pas un,* is to dismantle that logic, and to subvert those representations – to contest the culture of the Same and the One, and to affirm the *non-symmetrical difference* of the feminine sex. This is why, for her, a reversal of the existing order (even 'merely' in discourse) would be a return to phallocratism: for an imaginary order based only on the feminine sex (in which persons with penises would be simply not-women) can only return women to the economy of the Same and the One which denied their difference in the first place. An example of such a reversal would be the famous formula in *The Scum Manifesto* that the 'Y' chromosome is only a deficient 'X' chromosome; and in terms of defining masculinity as a lack of positive qualities, I think that the reversed reversals of *Gyn/Ecology* produce much the same result in the end.

Several things follow from this. Firstly, in her attack on the logic of the One, Luce Irigaray adopts an image of the multiplicity of the feminine (notably in *This Sex Which is not One*). This image is developed to represent something in common to *all* women: and it is opposed in its common-ness (symbolically founded in women's bodies) to Mary Daly's concept of 'the *multiply mobile*: the movers, the weavers, the Spinners' (p. xiv), which names a particular group of women distinguished from the others by their real, spiritual, capacities. So for Luce Irigaray, a common feminist politics consists *in* a multiplicity of different positions, struggles, and theoretical projects: while for Mary Daly, difference is only possible after a common and restricted Gyn/Ecological identity (the Convocation of the Ones) has been established.

This entails another difference in their work. *Gyn/Ecology* really is based on a biological determinism; the difference between males and females is clear, absolute, and initially anatomical. But this is just the preliminary assumption of *Gyn/Ecology* which is not concerned in any immediate way with sexual difference, or with women's bodies and sexualities (beyond the massive documentation of the damage done to them in patriarchy); but with elaborating a politics of the spiritual. Luce Irigaray does not argue that biology is destiny, but rather examines the effects that various representations of Woman, the feminine, and female bodies have had on and in the destinies of women. Since she argues that female difference has been suppressed – in the discourses of philosophy, psychoanalysis and the social sciences – she is particularly concerned with working on ways to make it possible for women to *speak* their bodies and sexualities. She *therefore* founds her own discourse of difference in a rhetoric of the female body.

So far, I've made some general remarks on the political and philosophical differences between Daly and Irigaray (without venturing into the major gulf which separates them, namely their respective interpretations of psychoanalysis, and the history of Western philosophy). What I want to do now is to make some schematic (and therefore simplistic) distinctions between their language practices.

If Mary Daly explicitly pursues a politics of subverting the signs of the patriarchal code, Luce Irigaray is rather concerned with dismantling discourses. Like Daly, she mimics the procedures of her opponents, in order to pull them apart. But unlike Daly, she is concerned with the discursive (as well as the semantic) modes of phallocratic knowledge; and the focus of her own writing is on the conditions of possibility for women's *speak-ing* (their bodies, their desires, their oppressions, their differences) and not on producing a model of realized female *speech.*

Secondly, there is a difference at the level of the discourse(s) used by each. There is no equivalent anywhere in *Speculum* or in *Ce sexe qui n'en est pas un* of Daly's coherent myth of the Voyage, her structure of opposites and Others, and her stress on the transcendant, s/elective function of the 'we'; and nor could there be, since Irigaray's conception of both femininity and feminism requires not only a critical denunciation of such mechanisms as part of a strategy of the Same, but also a multiplication of the modes – and the means – of *énonciation* to be diverted to, and invented for, the speak-ing of women. Both *Speculum* and *Ce sexe qui n'en est pas un* are composed of the juxtaposition of different discourses, different modes of address, and experiments in different genres (polemic, abusive generalisation, meticulous analysis, authoritative criticism, lyric poetry, speculative theory ...): while *Gyn/Ecology* is rather an opus displaying the range of variations opened up by a single exemplary speaker.

Thirdly, if *Gyn/Ecology* can be loosely described as a Poetics – a theory of textual forms – then I think that *Speculum* and *Ce sexe qui n'en est pas un* could (with the same degree of looseness) be described as providing some suggestions for a Rhetoric. I'm using this distinction as a heuristic device (i.e. to see what happens if it's made). Obviously both Daly's and Irigaray's writings could be described as 'poetic' in the colloquial sense; and both *Gyn/Ecology* and *Speculum* are rhetorical in that they both, inevitably, employ persuasive devices as all texts do. And along with its practice of discovering True Names, *Gyn/Ecology* is also quite comfortable about recommending rhetorical practices to the possessors of True Names: 'We know that there is not one tactic for each specific situation. At one time and place "outspokenness" may be more useful; at another time and place, camouflage. At all times, we are speaking our Selves, hearing and following the call of our undomesticated, wild be-ing' (p. 343).

In calling *Gyn/Ecology* a poetics, I was referring to its theory of the fitting-ness of sign and spirit, meanings and Big Strong Women. In this sense, it is a theory of linguistic appropriateness; and it is up to '*you*' to situate your-Self accordingly in the order of language and be-ing. In calling Irigaray's work a rhetoric, I mean that hers is primarily a politics of *address*: adroitness, subtlety, but above all a double labour of both direct and indirect engagement with the master-thinkers of phallocracy on the one hand, and with the political and symbolic struggles of women on the other. The 'I' of Irigaray's discourse is always involved with a she-who-might-be-possible; and in each case, in each text, a desired effect on a variable 'you' is openly assumed in the process of writing. For Iriga-ray, there can be no appropriate language for, or of, women – not only because Woman, for her, is *not yet*, but because the project of determin-ing the being of women (and thus, the words which would fit them) is precisely the project of phallocracy.

This Sex Which Is Not One is sometimes described as an attempt to make women's language fit the 'form' of the female sex.[34] Yet its image of a woman's two open lips is not presented as a form discovered in nature which is appropriate to an existing female language, but rather as a *metaphor-addressed-to*. On the one hand, it is addressed to the dis-course of psychoanalysis; as Rosi Braidotti points out, it is an 'image chosen for its value of metaphorical subversion, in response to the Lacanian image of the black hole'.[35] On the other hand, it is addressed to women engaged in inventing an imaginary:

> And to try to rediscover a possible imaginary for women through the re-touching movement of two lips does not signify a regressive return to the ana-tomical, nor to a concept of 'nature', and nor to a recall of genital norm.... Rather, it is a matter of re-opening the autological and tautological circle of representative systems – and of their discourses – so that women may speak of their sex.[36]

The 'may', here, is an operative word. One last distinction I want to make between Daly and Irigaray is one between the present tense and the conditional. For Daly, women's speech IS – at least, after it has been established 'who are the women'. Fembots titter, Hags roar: and *Gyn/ Ecology* itself is an example of female speech (although without presenting itself as representative, or claiming to fix the speech of those who qualify as females). For Irigaray, women's speaking MAY BE: it has no triumphant, concrete existence, and everything is yet to be fought for (and won – for Irigaray's proposal is not for an infinite deferment, but for a long and difficult struggle). There are a number of philosophi-cal arguments in her work for the importance of this position, but one simple and equally important political argument is this: that women's struggles against their confinement by the 'circles' of representative

systems cannot be waged in isolation from their political struggles
against material oppression. To assert that a women's language miracu-
lously IS, and may be spoken by I – here – now, is to return from an
imaginary closure, which is all the more dangerous because it closes
itself *from* the multiple, diverse and diffused movements of women.

This necessary open-ness is another reason for describing Irigaray's
work as a rhetoric. It proposes to provide a set of possible methods for
contesting and inventing discourse – but no more than that. The rest is
up to women, and there are no spiritual restrictions placed on that
category. I think this is why (although it is possible to imitate an
Irigarayan text, just as it is possible to write in a Dalyesque style) one
can plausibly speak of a 'Dalyite line' in feminist politics – while there is
no such thing as an Irigarayan '*line*'. Daly's poetics of coherence can
imply an identifiable politics, because it is part of a general theory of
Patriarchy – including fembots, Painted Birds, and weak-spirited Third
World women who can't cope with new meanings of *race*, and may wish
to analyse their own cultures themselves. Irigaray's rhetoric is not
founded in a general theory, and does not found a general theory – and
its images of 'multiplication' and 'openness' depend on affirming a
political need for all women to begin speak-ing their difference – and
their differences – together.

Mary Daly is fond of paraphrasing Virginia Woolf: 'as a woman I have
no country, as a woman I want no country. As a woman my country is
the whole world, the whole cosmos.'[37] Luce Irigaray's work implies
rather that a 'global feminism' (in Mary Daly's phrase) is best achieved
by women assisting women to deal with their own countries; and if Luce
Irigaray's work with language seems to me to be more useful than Mary
Daly's it is because it implies – along with the rigorous debate and
exchange which *Gyn/Ecology* precludes – a feminist politics like this:

> For my part, I refuse to let myself be locked into a single 'group' within the
> women's liberation movement. Especially if such a group becomes ensnared
> in the exercise of power, if it purports to determine the 'truth' of the feminine,
> to legislate as to what it means to 'be a woman', and to condemn women who
> might have immediate objectives that differ from theirs. I think the most
> important thing to do is to expose the exploitation common to all women and
> to find the struggles that are appropriate for each woman, right where she is,
> depending upon her nationality, her job, her social class, her sexual experi-
> ence, that is, upon the form of oppression that is for her the most immediately
> unbearable.[38]

2

The Pirate's Fiancée

Lacking faith in their ability to change anything,
resigned to the status quo, they have *to see beauty in*
turds because, so far as they can see, turds are all
they'll ever have.[1]

I would like to make a few slanted suggestions about the possible value
of Foucault's work to those feminists who might be reading it. This isn't
a theoretical text; though that is not because I wish to avoid being
caught at commentary, or to tick down my allegiance automatically to a
politics (which I do support) of the provisional and the definitely
uncertain. Still less does it claim to have anything to do with a gene-
alogical analysis; far from being patiently documentary, it's rather a
matter of some impatient speculations on some affairs currently absorbing (in theory) a small section of the women's movement.

Discipline and Punish and *The History of Sexuality 1* arrive in troubled
times: their propositions have a kind of rampant inappropriateness
around them. Foucault's recent work is not enamoured of psychoanalysis, being much more concerned with the possibility of its emergence. It displaces some of the traditional concerns of marxism, and has
scant respect for semiotics:

> Neither the dialectic (as logic of contradiction) nor semiotics (as structure of
> communication) can account for the intrinsic intelligibility of confrontations.
> The "dialectic" is a way of evading the always hazardous and open reality of
> this intelligibility, by reducing it to the hegelian skeleton; and "semiology" is a
> way of evading its violent, bloody and deadly character, by reducing it to the
> pacified and platonic form of language and dialogue.[2]

In the English speaking world, marxism and psychoanalysis have
been playing a positive role in many women's work for some time; and

51

semiology, while making a major public appearance for the British in a baffling book called *Language and Materialism*, has yet to emerge fully into the limelight. And for backdrop, we have a general proliferation of references to French texts (many of them creative English fictions) which leads some people to call for the cultural vice squad to intervene.

The Foucault-problem which these conditions create cannot be entirely dismissed by saying, with some malicious souls, that for a culture where the traditional duty of the intellectual is to prove for ever after that he is not a swot and came top of the class without really trying, this is all too much for the mind. (In Australia, this is essentially a masculine mode: the witty drinking companion. Most female intellectuals one can unearth tend to be discreet writers, but raving workaholics.)

• In many places in Australia, students and teachers can still fall into disfavour for introducing marxism, psychoanalysis, semiotics (outside the relatively safe place of the modern language department, where they disappear into the innocuous category 'foreign culture'). Whether these are worth fighting 'for' is a non-question in this context; real struggles take place around them, and through them.

• marxism (and, specifically, marxist political economy) has a local subversive potential unthinkable to most European intellectuals, when deployed in a culture where the most elementary affirmation of the existence of class struggles past or present is capable of triggering explosions left and right.

• marxism and psychoanalysis have been all the more effective in opening up possibilities for political struggles, in that much Australian activism is still organized by the ritual form of the catholic canonical Index: 'what you should not read'. Marx and Freud have had less the status of master-thinkers, and more the exhilarating effect of an indecent adventure (outside the universities, at least).

• for many feminists, marxism and psychoanalytic theory (semiotics in the past only drew a few strays) have played the role of unblocking a dead end encountered after a certain period of feminist practice – that of separatism for some, 'women's studies' for others. Secondly, with the passing of time, marxist and/or freudian feminism now functions for some women as a beginning; what used to be called 'radicalization'. Thirdly, given the anxiety and aggression which has surrounded the mysterious entity 'theory' in the women's movement (and the complex history of that would be well worth looking at), marxism and psychoanalysis have helped to organize the beginnings of a resistance to the appalling behaviourist and sociological bog which swallows up so much valuable feminist empirical research; at the same time, they have helped to make incursions into the institutionalized exclusion of women from certain kinds of knowledge.

In fact, the first thing that one might want to say about Foucault's recent work (particularly the notion of the specific intellectual, and the analyses of the place of resistance in power relations) is that it is Foucault's work itself which provides a strategic thought sparing one the absurd paralysis of wondering whether participation in the real struggles going on is corrupting to one's revolutionary essence. (Although a little political *nous* might do the same job just as well.) If there is indeed – in those few ordered little spaces where anglo-althusserianism calls the shots – a totalitarian reading of Foucault which rifles for References in order and interrogates his respect for Marx, there is also an authoritarian and equally abusive reading, which brandishes the texts at feminists working with marxism and psychoanalysis, casts the anathema of cooptation and then hopes for recantations.

This is a body of work which asks for patient and cautious appraisal. It should be obvious, however, that the last thing that the concept of 'regime of truth' can lend itself to is a politics of the pointing finger (even if, in the ritual of self-criticism, one points it at oneself). Nor can 'truth' be invoked every time someone (especially a 'known marxist') opens their mouth to make a statement: the concept retains its rigour; and if catatonia operates within the theatre of thought, Foucault's work is not a prop to quell others into mutism, 'Theatrum Philosophicum' is not a monologue on the final effacement of all distinctions.[3]

With that said, however, more interesting questions can arise than the 'demoralization in the current conjuncture' which some people fear might follow from reading Foucault's work. For instance, it would be nice to eye a body of work which offers itself as a toolbox, and start asking what use its tools might be to us; or, more positively, what use we might make of them. But wielding a feminist 'we' is tricky at the moment.

The roar of battle surrounds the pronoun: 'I' spells a host of sins from the humanist horror of talking heads to the simply vulgarity of claims to authenticity; 'one' has been written into the masculine, and as for 'we', that embarrassing macro-binary constraint from the days of unity and solidarity, whatever is to be done with 'we'? How many disparate and displacing 'you's and 'I's are being dis-possessed?

We are not only choking on the utterance act. Worse, we seem to be sliding on our signifieds, and the scare quote stalks in to fence off the space of a disaster zone: 'woman', 'women', 'Woman' are the warning signs of an increasingly unposable problem, all of a heap,[4] wrong from the start. Yet when the watchful scare quotes are absent, the result is irresistibly comic: one article stolidly observes, 'Thus women cannot be taken as an unproblematic collection of subjects, once the concept of subjects is challenged'.[5] (Indeed, one would hope not ...)

In the name of the patriarchal mode of production, Monique Plaza berates Luce Irigaray for flirting with the unseemly proposition in which it is said that woman does not exist;[6] and Mark Cousins (who asserts in a different sense that women do not exist) also cautions that, in Marxist terms at least, what cannot be said to exist is the patriarchal mode of production.[7]

While it is frustrating to read too many of these arguments (and if at times it seems as though Valerie Solanas's observation '*the ultimate male insight is that life is absurd*' only needs a little rephrasing in the days of profound examination of the nonexistence of women), it is nevertheless a little too easy to make fun of them.

Feminisms both past and present have run into some solid brick walls through trusting too lightly to 'the obvious', assuming a continuous and evenly distributed, consistently significant, oppression of the eternal natural object 'woman' or 'women' through the ages. Much of the work which questions the 'existence' of women (within different or incompatible frameworks) is attempting to break this wall down and so solidify – or diversify – the grounds for an extension of women's struggles. The research which might roughly be called marxist-freudian-feminist (sign of a strange conglomeration) is insisting that women are 'constructed' in a variety of practices, and is attempting to find a way of integrating feminist and class analysis. Another kind of investigation is being carried out in terms of women's language, the possibility of discovering or rediscovering a speech which articulates the diversities of women's reality.

However, I would like to use a couple of aspects of Foucault's recent work to raise some questions about the terms in which two particular skirmishes *within* these general areas have been carried out: one around the programme for a so-called 'theory of the subject' (with 'language' and 'subjectivity' as two defining terms); and the other around the celebration of a 'feminine' writing, ('discourse' and 'femininity') – blending an old anglo-american interest in women writers with the newer discovery of the work going on in France on 'feminine specificity'.

In doing so, I don't mean to suggest that these are in any sense the main or 'Leading' theoretical tendencies of Feminism. Whatever one thinks about woman, feminism, at least, is never One; and marxist-feminism, for example, is very far from being reducible to the theory of the subject, or to any form of freudian inclination at all. The two debates in question probably impassion remarkably few women. But they do pose fairly acutely, even if only in passing, an ever discreditable and ridiculous political question: the (shaky and shifting) place within the women's movement, and beside it, of academics, intellectuals; or 'theorists', in British-inspired terminology.

These three terms are used with a variety of connotation by different people in different situations. They cover abuse, dismissal, distrust (it's strange to hear two women, each employed in tertiary teaching, describe each other contemptuously for some *other* reason as 'typical academics'), self-abasement, fierce or shy self-assertion. They also hide a multitude of problems. Problems of practice, for even if one leaves aside the proposition that the real task of feminist and other revolutionary intellectuals is to use a privileged relation to truth to explain matters gently to the People, there is always the pressure to feel that 'Practice' always lies *elsewhere* (on the streets, on the beaches ...) and never there where one works, which is rarely an ivory tower of dreams called Theory, but the school, the university, the college, the hospital, the clinic, the media ... contexts in which, if it becomes impossible to cling to the simplicities of sex war, then it also becomes impossible to escape specification as 'a woman'. Problems too of formulation; since behind much of the embarrassment and muddle lies a barely broached question sometimes labelled 'women and philosophy', or 'women and theory', which women working *in* either are the first to realize cannot be posed like that at all.

It's worth insisting that in looking at these problems – obliquely – through Foucault's work, the point is to use it and not to 'apply' it. Even if his texts did not take their own precautions against application, I doubt whether Foucault would apply himself at all well if put directly to work for women. Foucault is a profoundly androcentric writer; it may be frivolous to say so (or worse, old-fashioned), but one only needs to flirt with the possibility of censorship in the act of translating his texts to feel 'Homme ...' resound like a mantra. 'The Life of Infamous People' just would not do, it would not do at all.

In fact, the nicest thing about Foucault in this respect, at least, is that not only do the offers of a philosopher to self-destruct appear to be positively serious on this occasion, but that any feminists drawn in to sending Love Letters to Foucault would be in no danger of reciprocation. Foucault's work is not the work of a ladies' man: and (confounding the received opinions of the advocates of plain speech, straight sex) some recent flirtations between feminists and other more susceptible thinkers would seem to suggest that there are far worse fates than wanking (like being thoroughly screwed).

However *The History of Sexuality 1* contains a number of perspectives

of immediate interest to feminists: apart from the suggestive references
to the hysterization of women, the chapter 'Right of Death and Power
over Life', for example, casts a curious light on the question of
abortion and its history, on the research which has been surfacing on
eugenics and the history of feminisms, on the 'professionalization of
birth control'.[8] At the same time, it seems to me that for such serious
research projects, more would eventually be gained from attention to
Foucault's proposals on the analysis of power, knowledge and struggle
than from simply *isolating* the more obviously 'relevant' material on
sexuality. For if it *is* extracted in isolation, then it becomes only too
tempting to observe that much of the book's analytical force is directed
against a generalized dream of 'sex liberation' which the women's
movement began by resisting; by resisting the invitation floating festively
above the tents of the revolution of a decade ago, calling 'Free Pussy' . . .

*they've seen the whole show – every bit of it – the
fucking scene, the sucking scene, the dick scene, the
dyke scene – they've covered the whole waterfront,
been under every dock and pier – the peter pier, the
pussy pier . . . you've got to go through a lot of sex to
get to anti-sex, and SCUM's been through it all, and
they're now ready for a new show; they want to crawl
out from under the dock, move, take off, sink out. But
SCUM doesn't yet prevail; SCUM's still in the gutter
of our 'society', which, if it's not deflected from its
present course and if the Bomb doesn't drop on it, will
hump itself to death.*

The project of a theory of the subject and the project of a feminine
writing have many incompatibilities, and at least one thing in common:
the unlikely tool of Lacanian analysis. But the manipulation of the tool
is itself a source of dispute. The advocates of 'feminine writing' play with
a Lacan who flirts with Derrida, admire ruse and dirty fighting, cultivate
the tactics of the pricktease; the rigidity of solid philosophical discourse
is taunted and tautened unto dissolution. In contrast, the theory of the
subject aims to be nothing if not solid; in Coward and Ellis's *Language
and Materialism*, or in the pages of the journal *m/f*, there is not much
fooling around. The Lacan solicited there is one who could be put to bed
with Marx, discomfiting the latter considerably no doubt, but all in the
cause of knowledge rather than desire; science coupled with science
breeds science. The language of Lacan is scanned and straightened out;
divested of its power to tease, it becomes simply 'Hard'. It stimulates
exegesis, not exhibitionism.

Yet *Language and Materialism* crystallized a new attention to language, an attention which displaced for marxist-feminists much of the earlier work on 'the subject' which had sprung up around Juliet Mitchell's *Psychoanalysis and Feminism*. The earlier work relied heavily on the notion of symptomatic reading, in which the text is a sort of medium facilitating the location and diagnosis of tainted concepts; and tried to use healthy pieces of Lacan to 'fill in the gaps' in Althusser's comments on ideology. Theories of signification, and the implications of text and discourse analysis received relatively little attention in themselves – partly because of the (continuing) unavailability of most of the material in English, partly because despite its apparent exoticism and 'structuralist' overtones, the method of symptomatic reading did not involve any attention to 'language' at all. Coward and Ellis point to one immediate consequence of the absence of 'a radical understanding of signification, of identity and the sign' in Mitchell's book itself;[9] the lacanian analysis of the unconscious was ignored, and as a result the unconscious was treated as a repository of the structural relations of patriarchy. Marxist-feminists then spent a great deal of time arguing whether this was an *acceptable* formulation, or not; a difficult subject, since while curiously attractive to their feminism, it was indigestible for their marxism, and had horrifying implications all round.

Language and Materialism offered a new set of possibilities. By restoring something of the complexity of lacanian analysis, *and* – at the same time – by interpreting its importance through some concepts extracted from Kristeva's early work, Coward and Ellis were able not only to insist that subjects, and therefore the unconscious, are 'produced' by language,[10] but also to dismantle the fairly simple, monolithic and determined subject of the work inspired by Mitchell. Positions were cleared for plurality, diversity, multiplicity, heterogeneity, disruption, contradiction; the pay-off was not only another crack at a theory of ideology, but also a reopened possibility for struggle; which might, into the bargain, allow marxism to catch up finally on some of its opponents in the ideological domain.

The mention of this possibility prompts questions about the method of *Language and Materialism* itself. Despite its hard-core conceptual approach, there are a number of strange and paradoxical things about it. One is the blithe narrativization of 'developments' in semiology – a discipline (some would say science) whose development is virtually absent from the story except from some glancing asides on Hjelmslev and Greimas. Another is the tendency, disarming in a text written so much in praise of heterogeneity, to synthesize unrelated or conflicting discourses by looking at them through the unifying lens provided by the concept of the 'subject in process', with the equally disarming prospect of a study of the 'subject in crisis' in poetic language, performed in the most placid and imperturbable of philosophical styles, in which 'insights' are clear or unclear, 'appropriations' correct or incorrect. *Language and Materialism* is a monument to the spirit of system; and, courageously enough, builds itself up with the aid of *S/Z* – one of the fiercest attacks on systematization and on semiotics as a science ever written. Barthes' *lexie*, for example, with its nonchalant arbitrariness, is not only a tool for a new kind of analysis; it is also an inspired and lethal joke.[11]

But the terrain of the theory of the subject is not the terrain of the joker, and it really accords only a very circumscribed place to the productivity of language. Lacanian analysis and semiotics are courted only for their use value; they *account for*. If they also explode as well as explain, then the degree of disruption is carefully controlled – the explosion is limited to the site of the 'subject', and not to 'the theory of'. The status, function, and the writing of 'theory' remains untouched. One can write that 'Narration rather sets the subject in place as the point of intelligibility of its activity: the subject is then in a position of observation, understanding, synthesising' (p. 50), as part of the process of constructing a text which precisely has that position of the subject – among other things – in common with the procedures of narration. With no 'contradiction' at all, in truth, since apart from the text's necessary and worthwhile pedagogical intention, a very traditional mode of distinguishing discourses is at work; the theory of the subject is science, and not literature.

> We have tried to-show in this book how the problematic of language has influenced the developments of both Marxism and psychoanalysis in a way that their encounter must necessarily produce a new object of knowledge. This new object is the scientific knowledge of the subject.[12]

The critique of the instrumental theories of language is purely instrumental for the theory. There is therefore every reason why the pursuit of this new object should most rigorously not involve being lured off the path (by Barthes, Kristeva, Lacan) into the thorny territory of the disarticulation of classical rationalism. There, things are sloppy, confused, indistinct, unclear; and as one enthusiast for the theory said, there are perfectly sound philosophical objections to that part of it anyway. (Indeed; and from what place might we speak if there were not?)

If the object at stake is the scientific knowledge of the subject then the political function of knowledge is that of equipment *for* ideological struggle. 'Until Marxism can produce a more adequate account of the role of ideology, subjective contradiction and the family, it will never provide a real alternative to such operations of bourgeois ideology' (p. 156). Knowledge guides struggle, somehow but surely; theoretical competence improves political performance.

If one steps outside this framework – which is not reducible to *Language and Materialism* itself, nor coextensive with it – then innocent and discreditable questions arise again; although it seems to me that to pose them it is neither necessary to adopt the facilities of 'feminine writing' and claim that this is all too cocky for words, nor sufficient to harangue it self-righteously in general terms for complicity with Truth (nor for pretensions to such complicity; the argument has rather the imprint of utopian desires and all discussion of it needs to take account of its marginality). Instead one can ask in a more limited way what the local implications of these developments might be for women's struggles. What is happening there where women work so hard on distinguishing the penis and the phallus? What is going on when the privileged areas of a marxist theory become 'the subject' on one hand and 'language' on the other?

In one sense, it is easy to see the immediate value of this, since constructing a theory of the subject involves trying to work on two legendary disaster-and-devastation zones: one being the outcome of a pugnaciously practical feminism actively hostile to any reflection, confiding itself trustfully to the tender care of sociology, ignoring the claims of economy, and proceeding from the attempt to pit all women against all men at all times to the discovery that the main enemy, when not in The Head, was other women; the other being the failures of an economistic marxism which not only failed to account for subjective contradictions and the appeals of bourgeois ideology, but could not even begin to account for its own remarkable failure to appeal.

Yet the way in which the repair project has been undertaken has some awkward consequences, related at least in part to the althusserian inheritance at work in the plan's scientific design. Since it is of the first importance to distinguish science from ideology, it therefore becomes extremely important for 'theory' to take up a position of combating the enemy *within*. Bourgeois ideology, idealism, humanism … if the procedure by which the theory of the subject constructs its *object* is one of forging an identity from (and between) a series of discourses flourishing outside marxism, then it establishes its own *necessity* by demonstrating that idealism and humanism have infiltrated marxism itself (and that feminism is fairly seething with both). This is not really a manoeuvre of dogmatism, but of defence; since error leads to practical ineffectiveness.

The first consequence is that it becomes strictly speaking unthinkable to question the tools of the necessity-demonstration in any fundamental way, although their refinement, correction and adjustment are allowed to be not only possible but necessary. For example, when psychoanalytic theory is accepted both for its explanation-value *and* its use in combating humanism in marxism and feminism, then not only do critiques of the social function of psychoanalysis become irrelevant, or at best a carefully defined 'separate' question; but no problems can arise within the space of the theory about the *history* of the relations between (for example) psychoanalysis on the one hand and humanism on the other.[13] As long as a 'science' of the subject can be distinguished from an 'ideology' of the subject, the former accounting for the wanderings and limitations of the latter, then there is nothing disturbing about the peculiar convergence of their concerns. Only the naive humanist feminist thinks she can change something by changing her consciousness; the rigorous feminist plumbs the hidden depths of subjectivity, studies its construction in language, follows the diffusing implications of Benveniste's empty instance through to its fulfilments elsewhere, winds through the labyrinth to find not a monster but a new position of the subject ...

Robert Castel has argued in *Le Psychanalysme*[14] that the famous decentring of the subject (and today one needs to add detotalizing, deglobalizing and deunifying) serves precisely to displace the subject's functions by carrying them elsewhere and further: but one has trouble arguing effectively in this way with a science. For Castel's observation rests on a series of asumptions, guiding his own research as well as that of Michel Foucault: it depends on assuming that it be *significant* that there is a relation between analytic knowledge and practice, and sociopolitical power relations; that this analytic knowledge and power inscribes itself in a certain socio-economic form (the contractualization of subjectivity); and further it depends on insisting that this knowledge cannot be unravelled intact from the networks of power in which it is actively enmeshed, networks whose proliferation can be mapped by *historical* research.

Few proponents of a theory of the subject would deny that these assumptions point to real questions; what is at stake, however, is their importance and the time of their asking. A theory of the subject cannot incorporate them if a theory of the subject is to be possible in the first place. (It might be unkind to suggest that this can be an example of a moment of tactical option, in which false unities dissolve indeed; as when, within the space of marxist epistemology, an observation of similarities between Althusser and Popper leads some marxists to take a good hard look again at Althusser, and others to warm to Popper once more.) So one awkward consequence of the freudo-marxist marriage presided over by language is to open up an inviting space for marxist and feminist labours which can only be defined by the systematic evacuation of certain questions – political, economic, and above all historical questions. Unfortunately this strange form of materialism has its nonintentional relays in practice as well: leaving aside the transfer of some theorists from armchair to couch, the work on constructing a theory of the subject has had some success in partially neutralizing the crude and direct assault on psychoanalytics which was once a major tactic for the struggle of women and homosexuals. Long before *Language and Materialism* this was shown to be mistaken, not because it wasn't having effects (which it was; though not all of them brilliant), but because in erroneously assuming that a wide variety of theories, institutions and practices could be called 'psychoanalysis', its aggressively operational ignorance was obscuring the possibility of something much better for the long Run – an adequate 'analysis'.

Other problems appear when the task of assuring internal security takes top priority, if not for its own sake, then at least for the welfare and further development of the struggle under investigation. It then becomes a *point of departure* for 'theory' to insist on the presence of humanism etc. in feminist discourse and practices (a fairly easy job, in fact). The immediate disadvantage of this is not that it can lead to a delirious enumeration of theoretical errors and dangers, though these do diversity delightfully in the site of the hapless subject: apart from the old favourites idealism, humanism, and empiricism, there can be essentialism, moralism, unification, centralization, necessitation, globalization and totalization. Nor is it that this is the speech of policemen or judges: the 'theorist' on these occasions is rather in the speaking position of the impotent and ex-centred chieftain of South American tribes, pouring out words (in times of peace) while others go about their business.[15]

The immediate disadvantage is that '*the*' subject looms up even more hugely as problem and as formulation; though this is often a subject that is indeed an effect of language, emerging from a convenient shorthand term for a multiplicity of problems, and enlarging itself to assume the status of a reading grid. '*The*' subject as a concept in some British work has assumed a massiveness which is probably only equalled in the concepts of French new philosophy.[16] The construction of 'the' subject as problem in the discourse and practice of others means that not only is one forced into the constraints of that form of analysis which consists in demonstrating that women willy-nilly reproduce or reintroduce exactly what they thought they were fighting, but that:

1. There is no escape from 'the' subject as an effective concept in the analysis of political struggles, and;

2. In the process, that analysis is largely deprived of any operative means of distinguishing between strategies of power and tactics of resistance, between statements in common (Right to Life, Right to Choose, for example) on the one hand, and antagonistic discourses on the other.

The most one can do is acknowledge difference in vague and general terms, in an admissive mode; 'It may be necessary at this time ...'; since the foundation of the whole procedure is not to use research itself to diversify the possibility of struggles, but to establish identity, equivalence, significant similarity. Theory as watchdog is a poor creature: not because it is nasty or destructive, but because for attacking the analysis of confrontations, it simply has no teeth.

One of the great beauties of Foucault's recent work is the way that his displacement of the problematics of science and ideology, in favour of an analysis of the fundamental *implications* of power-knowledge and their historical transformations, permits the beginnings of an analysis of that favourite rhetorical flourish, 'struggle': and in so doing, displaces the problematics of humanism – and thus of 'anti-humanism' – altogether (a displacement marked by the wickedness of 'soul' in *Discipline and Punish*).

It is this displacement, for example, which allows Foucault to continue his detailed analyses of the technologies of subjection and subjugation, and at the same time to speak of 'the insurrection of subjugated knowledges' in history; of the revolts of disqualified knowledges, and of their insistent emergence in the political struggles in recent years. It is this which permits a rigorous distinction, for example, between 'prison reform' projects initiated through officials, commissioners and functionaries, and the demands made by prisoners themselves and those who work for them on their terms. It is this which could permit a more productive approach to the articulation – and extension – of the struggles of those resistant objects of knowledge, 'women'. For in a perspective in which bodies and souls[17] are seen as not simply constituted but also invested and *traversed* by relations of power-knowledge (and that unevenly and inequitably – it is not a question of a uniform distribution or a stable 'effect') then what becomes possible in relation to 'women', special category in the catalogues of the human sciences, is something more than a history of a 'construction': it is rather the possibility of a history of a strategic *specification* – a real one, productive perhaps not only of 'specificity' but also of its status as 'intrinsic' in fiction and in truth – and at the same time, a history of that in women which *defies* specification, which escapes its hold; the positively *not* specific, the unwomanly in history.

Men who are rational, however, won't kick or
struggle or raise a distressing fuss, but will just sit
back, relax, enjoy the show and ride the waves to their
demise.[18]

Passing from the realm of the theory of the subject to the shifty spaces of feminine writing is like emerging from a horror movie to a costume ball. The world of 'theorization' is a grim one, haunted by mad scientists breeding monsters through hybridization, by the hunted ghosts of a hundred isms, and the massive shadow of the subject surging up at every turn. Feminine writing lures with an invitation to licence, gaiety, laughter, desire and dissolution, a fluid exchange of partners of indefinite identity. All that custom requires is infinite variety, infinite disguise. Only overalls are distinctly out of place; this is the world of 'style'. Women are not welcome here garbed in the durable gear of men; men, instead, get up in drag. Lacan reigns here not as law-giver, but as queen.

Each performance has its code, however, and the naive feminist blunders in at her peril. The audiences gather to watch her slip on a central shibboleth, the language of psychoanalysis. In Frankenstein's castle, the penalty for careless definition is swift but clean dismemberment: in the shimmering world of feminine impersonation, a worse fate awaits the woman with the wrong style of argument – she is exposed for the straight that she is, stripped bare to reveal (to her shame and surprise) that she is only equipped with a phallus. In either case, however, there is no forgiveness for not knowing what you do when you speak.

But when it comes to a competition between these two rather risqué forms of entertainment for feminists, the gothic stories of science seem to lose out well and truly. Feminine writing is never One, by definition cannot be defined, asserts itself as irreducible difference, as always other and elsewhere, and when confronted by an 'incisive argument', just laughingly melts away. And with certain eminent philosophers laying bets on the lady, all that wheezing science can do is demonstrate, laboriously, its own limitations.

Traditional political criticism in France has indeed had great difficulties with feminine writing when the latter assumes, chameleon-style, an explicitly political or philosophical colour. Christine Delphy has most success in transfixing Annie Leclerc;[19] but then Annie Leclerc's writing is drivel rather than flow. Yet even here, in the midst of a fine dissection of Leclerc's personal 'I' of unquestionable authenticity, Delphy is irritated into matching the mawkishness of her opponent by a melodramatic gesture in the direction of another (if impersonal) mode of authentication – 'psychologism, biologism, and idealism are the three udders of ideology'.[20] One cannot win this argument like that; one can only call for approving cheers from those who are always already on side.

Monique Plaza tries a similar tactic at times in her heroic assault on

Luce Irigaray, '"Phallomorphic power" and the psychology of "woman"'.[21] Plaza's theme is naturalism. However, it is impossible to pin down the formidable Irigaray in this way – her ploys are much more lethal than the simperings of Annie Leclerc, and have practically nothing in common with them. On the shifting, treacherous ground of femininitude, there is nothing more dangerous than appeals to underlying similarity and resemblance, or to kinship. Annie Leclerc, for example, does believe in a 'natural' woman, socially devalorized: Luce Irigaray is very far from confusing the anatomical and the social, but works with a deadly deliberation *on* the point (the site and the purpose) of the confusion of anatomical and *cultural.*

If a systematic analysis born of concepts like mode of production and reproduction is certainly absent from *Speculum,* then in a sense the power of that form of analysis is actively deflated in the text (although its questions are fleetingly reraised): but to reinstate its potency, Plaza is forced into merely ignoring the problematics of discourse and the unconscious assaulted in Irigaray's work, and thus in trying to make the charge of naturalism stick she is obliged to read it largely in terms of Freud rather than the terms of Lacan. Plaza's sense of nature, culture, and society is oddly prelinguistic – baby talk. While it is immensely cheering to read an analysis in which it is Lacan rather than women reduced to effective nonexistence, this is achieved at the cost of triumphantly confronting a text with an argument which is already only one of its own antecedents. So too does Plaza find it sufficient to reveal the ambiguity of Irigaray's project, number its contradictions – when ambiguity and contradiction are openly flaunted as its most tormenting methods in the first place.

Irigaray's text itself infuriatingly resists definition as feminine; for her the feminine is conditional or future tense, an interrogative mood. These pervade her writing, with possibility, it is true, but the speculum is a masculine instrument; the feminine is suspended and explored, and the circular form with the fitting contours for the job is one beloved of classical ('masculine') intelligibility fondling its own limits – the paradox. Irigaray remains the recalcitrant outsider at the festival of feminine specificity – she lounges ironically at the door. For what goes on inside, celebrated in the joyful present tenses of Hélène Cixous or Marguerite Duras, is nothing more powerful than literature.

And where political criticism and philosophy flounder before a menace of some kind, literary criticism runs up joyfully to embrace feminine writing. Men in literature departments love it (the 'display' of power) – relieved of the tedium of exposition, they too can flaunt and fling and giggle with the girls. For, in practice, the feminine writing which has 'come' has very little to do with biological sex and unspeakable desire, and everything to do with gender and gesture. The language of the feminine body, woman's desire, is a deliriously cultural ploy; entirely organized by the binary logic which Luce Irigaray alone attempts (and wittingly refuses) to dismantle.

It is here, however, that Plaza does point to a way of sneaking up on specificity and stabbing it in the back. 'Woman', she says, 'exists too much as signifier. Woman exists too much as subjected, exploited individual'. It is the absolute irrelevance of women to feminine writing that is the give-away; and Plaza shows this up best not when she herself hurls socialism head-on against biologism, but when she points to a possible undermining of the binary problematization of difference itself, and to the desirability of the study of its destruction. (A major exploit for which some marauding philosophers do deserve our admiration is their effort to think difference in terms of more than two.)

Women are irrelevant to feminine writing when what is at stake is a binary stirring, a revolution (turning over) *in the name of* 'Woman'. In 'Women and Philosophy' Michèle Le Doeuff suggested that Hegel's listing of pythagorian oppositions was not out of date: limit and infinity/ unity and multiplicity/masculine and feminine/light and darkness/good and evil.[22] Feminine writing – and much of the proudly obscure literature of 'disruptive' multiplicity – would seem to suggest that this list is indeed not out of date, and that the terms of the final couple are changing places. In the feminine 'beyond', we are only invited to dance in the next same old two-step.

'Woman' not only exists too much as signifier; she has existed too long as such for too much triumphant celebration of the 'coming' of woman in writing to be undertaken without some protective paranoia, least of all when the context is a cult of the signifier itself. The problem 'women and literature', for example, has a history, although that is also a history of the diversity of its formulation: but it is difficult to claim any significance for this once the tantalizing suggestion that woman does not exist is converted – as it has often been in the debates on feminine writing in France – to a flat dismissal of the possibility of anything of interest to the present having been said or done by or about women in the past. What a systematic study of the history of specificity as problem could expose I do not know. But even the most cursory glance at the underground of the recent debates in France alone – if a girl takes her eyes off Lacan and Derrida long enough to look – shows up the outline of a couple of regular features.

For one thing, those texts which pose their problem in the name of the *specificity* of women, in some sense, are rarely specifically about women. To take just four examples: there is the complex debate (analysed by Georges May in *Le Dilemme du roman au dixhuitième siècle*)[23] which raged around the status of the novel from the late seventeenth to the middle of the eighteenth century, with 'école des dames', the school for women, as one of its key terms – the problem of women reading, women writing, what they read and wrote and how, became the symbolic battle ground of a whole series of social, political and moral conflicts, and transformations. At the end of the eighteenth century, one finds the hilariously inciting text of Mme de Genlis, *De l'influence des femmes sur la littérature comme protectrices des arts et des auteurs*; here the greatest pedagogue of the age argues in terms of 'influence', and the most monstrously prolific of scandalous women writers speaks coyly and decently of 'protectors'; but what is elaborated here – *through* a conception (and prescription) of woman's nature and ideal function – is an outline of the woman-function as 'model' for social conduct, social control. Closer to home is Theodore Joran, *Les féministes avant le féminisme*, in 1910; this is the age of significant biography, and Joran's second volume uses a series of wonderfully vicious attacks on the manners, morals, abilities and reputations of a parade of women writers through the ages in order to oppose the notion of women having a 'right' to vote – and across that, the concept of 'rights' in itself. Finally, in Jean Larnac's gallant defence of women in 1929, *Histoire de la littérature féminine en France*, 'feminine literature' becomes the fascinating and dramatic site of a pressing problem of knowledge; can the structure of a brain inhibited and weakened by thousands of years of patriarchal oppression be modified by sudden and rapid social change?

Whatever conclusions could be drawn from this, something more is at stake than a general observation that talking about women involves talking about everything and nothing. When feminine specificity is taken as a point of departure, or as defining the contours of a problem, then we are on the verge of a 'something else'; a reorganization, major or minuscule, in the articulation of power and knowledge. This can be, and has been, exploited by real women (who are never 'only' women). But it can also suggest that women wishing to examine the underside of their present specificity as women might come closer to succeeding by taking their own point of departure somewhere else entirely.

While the practice of Writing and experiments in the artifice of dissemination may seem light years away from the naive evolutionism of Larnac, 'woman' as signifier seems to show a remarkable stability: as *site* of change and changeability, innovation, rebirth, renewal, experiment and experimentation, the place for the planting of otherwise discredited questions. The speaking body of feminine writing is perhaps (like the silent muse) only the condition of possibility for the birth of something other. Whether this use, this time, can be of benefit or solace to women is impossible to say: but since, on this occasion, it is a raid on philosophy which feminine writing is not only being summoned to accompany, but being urged to put its body in the forefront of battle and incited to say its piece, it can do no harm to go humming 'Promises, promises ...'.

For another feature which seems to recur in the histories of feminine writing which might make us wary of incitements to speak a feminine truth, and to burst across the threshold of 'discourse' to the thunder of public applause, is that this theme of shocking visibility ('Let the priests tremble, we're going to show them our sexts')[24] is involved in a reaffirmation of a Literature blending disruption and revelation. If Foucault is right in suggesting that literature has occupied a special place in the systems of constraint bringing the 'everyday' into discourse – a special place defined by transgression, the task of saying the most unsayable – then it becomes noticeable that this literature has itself accorded a special place to the discourse of women.[25] Here again, it is Georges May who has made the most extensive study of feminism and realism in the early eighteenth century; whatever the vicissitudes of the relationship would turn out to be, there is surely something in the belief that the novel is the ultimate 'feminine' *genre*, and something more in the belief that the feminine novel is a patriarchal plot.

May plays with the traditional idea that in the period of transition from romance to novel, men left the field temporarily free for women because of the debased status of the indistinct and undistinguished new form. Foucault (without reference to women) suggests that we are living through the death of the great writer as model intellectual; 'All the fevered theorisation of writing which we witnessed during the sixties was no doubt only a swan song: the writer was desperately struggling for the maintenance of his political privilege'.[26] To make any extrapolations from that to speculate on the appearance of the great 'feminine' writer aureoled with political import, would be both abusive and too paranoid for words.

Besides, in our own culture, political privilege has not weighed upon the writer-intellectual for some time; it is rather invested in the writer as journalist. Yet there is, in each place, a highly prized and profitable form of feminine writing (very carefully delimited as such, and never disrupted by shrillness or imperative mood). In the cult(ure) of the signifier and the irruption of the repressed, it is that of the speaking sext: in the culture of the solid signified, the hard facts, the true story and Amazing Scenes, it's the literature of 'what it's *really* like for women' – *Fear of Flying, Kinflicks, The Women's Room, Memoirs of an Ex-Prom Queen.*

Foucault gives a passing pat of approval, if not quite to the sext show, then at least to chatter-boxing, in an interview called 'Non au sexe roi':[27] tactical reversal and resistance, women are turning their sex-saturation back on the sexuality apparatus (sex you have said we are, sex we will be

...) and in so doing, women begin to outflank it. Perhaps. But if it becomes hard not to sense just a wee tinge of vacuity in this, it certainly also becomes futile to think the phenomenon of feminine writing in terms of co-optation, since nothing follows from that formulation but fear, paralysis, the injunction to secrecy, silence and surveillance; or, less melodramatically, the form of 'feminist criticism' which consists in showing that women who have succeeded in reaching any large audience are prostitutes (selling out) or pimps (selling out women), while those who do not or will not are hopeless auto-erotics (wanking). The position of women desiring both, or neither, would certainly be Unspeakable.

It is not a question of co-optation *in general*; but of the efficacy of different methods of attack in different situations, of the possibility of multiplying rather than restricting (for 'safety's sake') the points from which women's struggle can develop, and of refusing to think in terms of all or nothing – conserving one's virginity for the ultimate Event. To take two films, for example, which define two poles of a debate on women and experiment in the cinema: we do not have to adjudicate between Marguerite Duras's *India Song*, and Nelly Kaplan's *La Fiancée du pirate*, either on the grounds that the former has been heralded as a work of genius, an avant-garde 'classic', and the latter has subversively escaped that fate; nor on the grounds that the former deconstructs traditional narrative while the latter is a 'bourgeois', simple tale about a witch.

But to refuse the logic of all or nothing is not to assert equivalence, nor to propose a bland avoidance of conflict at all. The seductions of Duras's 'profoundly absent' Anne-Marie Stretter, and the well-orchestrated irruptions of the unintelligible language of her mad and colonized double in *India Song*, those of Irigaray's woman thinking of everything and nothing, and of the coming of Cixous's woman giving birth to herself: in all these lady-like textual exhibitions, *a* language is whispering uncommonly loud of desire, the same language which in another dialect and in a harsher register promises knowledge through fidelity to a theory of the subject. That this language can be the language of women – or of their present political struggle – sounds to me unlikely.

At any rate, the seductive sound and the fury have been drowning out another kind of women's speech; feminism already has its store of forgotten and ignoble texts. Aggressive fairy-tales, mostly, like Kaplan's dream of the serving girl who didn't hang round waiting for any black freighters to cruise in and pick her up: sentimental celebrations of a women's language which was never unconscious, and a desire which was most unrepressed, like Monique Wittig's *The Guerillères*: or fanatical attempts to make the metaphorical war a real one, like the crazy Tactical Strategy Charts of Ti-Grace Atkinson's *Amazon Odyssey*. Savagely ingenuous texts: not solid science, but then most unsusceptible to the teasing of pricks. Genuinely disastrous texts too, in many ways: with (in differing degrees) their simplistic view of class and sex, their binary vision of power, their imperative utopianism. Texts disgraced and disqualified: it seems impossible now to mention them without incurring suspicion of nostalgia, saccharine celebration, necrophilia, romantic anarchism, belief in the timeless subversive integrity of texts irreducibly outside truth... Besides, if in France one philosopher can accuse another of being the last dinosaur of the Classical age, the most dreadful condemnation stray feminists have to fear here is dismissal with the last dinosaurs of the late sixties; apart from reassuringly familiar brays about co-optation from other dinosaurs.

However, these museum pieces of *women's* writing do have both a potent charm and a power: which is not to lure back, but to point elsewhere, further, and beyond. As Valerie Solanas (a woman who wrote most certainly in order to become something else than a great writer) reminds us from a place far beyond the construction-sites of 'theory' or the dressings-up of analytical practice, stretching binary schemes to their limits, defining male sex in terms of 'feminine' soul and its undoing, bringing a speech of 'refuse' into being – not to dig deep in the truth of every day, but to wheel round for an extraordinary future – there are lots of other things to do:

Life in this society being, at best, an utter bore and no aspect of society being at all relevant to women, there remains to civic-minded, responsible, thrill-seeking females only to overthrow the government, eliminate the money system, institute complete automation and destroy the male sex.

December 1978

3

Operative Reasoning: Reading Michèle Le Doeuff

For a feminist reader, that is to say for an *interested* reading by one principally concerned to find elements of reflection which might underpin a possible practice, this book has today the appearance of a curious mixture.

Michèle Le Doeuff, 'Operative philosophy:
Simone de Beauvoir and Existentialism'

The book which I am presenting today is not a complete formulation of this problem. These are, rather, essays – the only form which is perhaps capable of not reducing a question before even having posed it.

Michèle Le Doeuff, *L'Imaginaire philosophique*

1. *'De quel lieu parler ... ?'*
Where to speak from? (reading in fits and starts).

1.1 For a feminist reader, Michèle Le Doeuff's *L'Imaginaire philosophique* presents a number of difficulties.[1] In fact, 'discomforts' might be a better term for negotiating the steps in this book of essays with its curious mixture of topics, its unsettling shifts of methods and its plain, sober prose.

Some of these difficulties would be encountered by any reading of an 'interested' kind – one which pursued some further use of the text than that of reproducing the precise range of Michèle Le Doeuff's interests in philosophy. What do you *make* of a text which zigzags from day-dreaming in More's *Utopia* to the notion of affinity in Galileo's law of falling bodies, from the 'polysemy of atopian discourse' to the problem of ethics in Descartes, from women and philosophy to voices in Rousseau and Plato; which closes with a rhetorical analysis of an eighteenth-century physiologist who thought that menstruation was a cultural affair; and which bends back around to a methodological

71

preface linking islands and libidinal sacrifice in the work of Immanuel Kant?

The scattering of texts, authors and themes addressed is matched by the diversity of institutional situations for these writings, which are now bound up in a book. Some began as papers delivered at specialized conferences – a *Colloque de Cérisy* on Utopian Discourse, a *Radical Philosophy* conference at Bristol; others developed through the work of seminars (at the Ecole Normale Supérieure de Fontenay-aux-Roses) and collectives (*GREPH*).[2] One comes straight from *La Quinzaine litteraire*, and only one – '*Les Chiasmes de Pierre Roussel*' – has never been published before. A period of roughly seven years separates the first essay from the last.

Nor does the notion of 'philosophical imaginary' provide an interested reader with a stable reference point – except in the very general sense that this is a book about the function of images and figures in philosophy, that it questions the image/concept opposition often produced in philosophical discourse, and that it might therefore offer the stability of constant provocation to a certain philosophical reading. But at no stage of the work is this imaginary defined as the fixed *object* for an analysis which would repeat itself indifferently on an infinite series of texts. Instead, it is presented as a 'point of convergence' for the published essays, and a 'direction of research' discovered during the course of the work.

So a first difficulty – or a first question – raised by this book of essays is that of adopting a reading position in relation to the whole. The intensity of interest varies from essay to essay, according to the interests one pursues; and different themes emerge, recede and emerge again in a casual linking of texts which is not that of linear progression, nor that of several variations on the Same – but a way of producing connections.

Deprived of the position of 'overview', it's possible to play with other, *partial* ways of situating *L'Imaginaire philosophique*. It could be read from the partiality of an expertise in utopian writing, or in the interpretation of the classics. It could be placed against the work of various masters (Bachelard's meta-poetics, Derrida's 'White Mythologies'); contrasted with the anthropological theory of 'the' Imaginary developed by Gilbert Durand; or defined in part through an account of institutionalized philosophy in France, and the struggles waged by the militants of *GREPH*. Or it could be read in relation to one of its recurring themes – for example, the problem of contradiction in the history (and in histories) of philosophy. And perhaps the most tempting of partial readings would be one addressed directly – ignoring Derrida – to Michèle Le Doeuff's own methods of detailed textual analysis; her borrowings from rhetoric and literary theories, her notion of 'image', and her (today) rather shocking assertion that there can be a value in maintaining a concept of 'literal meaning'.

The temptation here would be one of finding an external but appropriate mode of criticism which could – in its very partiality – remain constant from essay to essay and so serve as a means of dominating the text in its totality. But this (imaginary) reading would run into trouble long before confronting the general argument that it is impossible to deal with philosophical metaphors from a position outside philosophy.[3]

A reading which tried to base itself on, say, the terrain of semiotics – and which nodded politely at philosophical critiques of its concepts, deeming them interesting but beyond its concerns – might begin by regarding as curiously inadequate the critical methods used in *L'Imaginaire philosophique*. With its use of classic oppositions such as literal/figurative, explicit/implicit, the book reads as though techniques which were common enough in literary analyses some years ago (such as posing the 'image' as the site of a tension, the place for a that-which-cannot-be-spoken to emerge; and insisting on the blazon – or the *mise en abyme*[4] – as a device for generating the process of a text) have simply been projected across the concerns of traditional philosophical exegesis – but without much *consistent* attention being paid either to the linguistics that traversed those analyses, or indeed to the various demands that work on signifying practice be bent back on the process of theoretical writing. Oddly enough (from this point of view), *L'Imaginaire philosophique* seems closest in spirit and style to the work of literary critics like Jean Rousset and Jean Starobinski. Above all, it relies on the possibility of thinking metaphor as 'deviation' in a way which, if it is not completely indefensible in the terms of contemporary rhetoric, would nevertheless seem to require a more substantial defence than any to be found in the book.

That might do for a general impression. But this kind of reading is unlikely to survive the shifts between, say, the elegant but purely formal play on the island in *Utopia*, and the intricate dialectics of text and history, discourse and institution, at work in the studies of Descartes and Pierre Roussel. For *L'Imaginaire philosophique* is manifestly not an attempt to contribute to a general theory of rhetoric by means of 'non-literary' examples; and neither is it an exercise in updating debates internal to philosophy by simply importing the latest methods from an alien domain. The methods of reading employed by Michèle Le Doeuff have not been chosen for their intrinsic value (whether 'value' is calculated in terms of progressiveness, scientificity, transgressive potential, or novelty-and-shock), but for their *sufficiency to their tasks* – which are, from the very beginning, circumscribed by the project of analysing a particular discourse in its self-determination:

> Philosophical discourse inscribes itself – labels itself as philosophical, even –
> by means of a *deviation (écart)* from the mythic, the fabulous, the poetic, and
> the image.
>
>   '*La Face honteuse de la philosophie*', p. 9 (emphasis added)

and in its social functioning:

> The notion of the dialectical solidarity of reverie and theoretical work can, in
> my view, only issue in a study of the particularities of one social minority, and
> its problematic confrontations with other thoughts and other discourses.
>
>   '*La Face honteuse de la philosophie*, p. 30.

Deviation, solidarity: at this moment the partial reading would be
returned to the study of that project and the ways it transforms from
essay to essay – and thus to an (Imaginary) position of mirroring the
moves of the text(s) – before contemplating what could only be an
aesthetic assessment of whether they work or whether they don't, and
when.

Back to the beginning.

1.2 For a feminist reader, the major interest in reading *L'Imaginaire
philosophique* is likely to be – initially – a retrospective one. Michèle Le
Doeuff is best known to feminists (and in English) first for her essay
'Women and Philosophy',[5] on the erotics of pedagogy, the difference
between women's relations *to* philosophy and the 'feminine' *in* philosophy, and the need for women to adopt a professionalist approach to
philosophical work; and second for her study of *The Second Sex*,
'Operative Philosophy: Simone de Beauvoir and existentialism'.[6]

'Women and Philosophy' is reprinted in the book. But feminist
readers may be disconcerted to see that among the accompanying texts,
only the essay on Roussel deals directly with women, and with feminist
questions. *L'Imaginaire philosophique* induces a kind of crisis of
identification: it doesn't settle in to any of the positions which usually
allow a text to be recognized and incorporated as 'feminist' (writing
about the work of women only/writing only about the production of
Woman; addressing feminine writing to female readers/putting feminist
questions to masculine texts). Instead, Michéle Le Doeuff writes as a
woman writing philosophy.

As a result, her book falls oddly aslant the concerns of much feminist
theoretical production today. Firstly, at a time of what she has elsewhere called a 'philosophist inflation'[7] in feminist theory, her book
invites feminist readers to take an interest in the details of philosophical
problems rather than repeat the large outlines of a critique of Western

Rationality. Secondly, she insists on a *restricted* critique of philosophical discourse, rather than one of 'rationality' itself:

> I have never had anything against philosophical rationality. As for its irrationality, that's a different matter. To be more precise, it seems to me that philosophy is not a function of some strictly 'masculine' form of 'rationality', but philosophy often produces a misogynist style of imagination, by trying to be more than it actually is, trying to make rationalisation operate to an extent beyond what it is actually capable of.
>
> *L'Imaginaire philosophique*, p. 134

This double restriction – of the scope and the site of feminist attacks in philosophy, and of philosophy's irrational pretensions – leaves Le Doeuff offside in relation to at least two of the major movements in theoretical work: the paradoxical project of inscribing a *feminine* position in discourse (Luce Irigaray) and the orthodox one of announcing a *general* philosophy of radical feminism (Mary Daly). The former needs a notion of 'masculine' rationality in order to speak its disruption of philosophy as a whole; the latter reaffirms the completeness and self-sufficiency of a Philosophy restored to its full, archaic powers.

Thirdly, Le Doeuff does not mark her own writing as either feminine or feminist – except when grammatical constraints in one case and the turn of an argument in the other require the reader to recognize that this is philosophy written by a woman. Her avoidance of prose exhibitionism ('*Nous ne parlerons pas petit nègre pour faire plaisir au colonisateur*')[8] follows quite logically from her own position in 'Women and Philosophy': that the 'feminine' repressed by philosophy is a feminine *created* by philosophy in the moment of repression. Real women, she says, may find themselves constantly compared to the image of the Sphinx of dissolution – but we do not have to recognize ourselves in that image.

> So where is one to speak from? Not indeed from that other-place set up, as a reservation of purely negative otherness, by philosophy itself. Nor from the interior of metaphysics, since it is metaphysics that grounds the binary divisions between male-rationality and female-disorder. But these options don't exhaust all the available possibilities.
>
> 'Women and Philosophy', p. 153

The difficulties in identifying each and every moment of Michèle Le Doeuff's work as 'feminist', and the writing's refusal of feminine display, could lead a feminist reading to minimize the interest of *L'Imaginaire philosophique* – on the grounds, perhaps, that a woman writing philosophy only writes that 'women can write it too' ... the classic position of *pre-* (that is, *non-*) feminism in theory. But there are other possibilities. Le Doeuff's practice *as* a woman writing philosophy is one which precludes the ventriloquy of the dutiful daughter, since it demands a different articulation of philosophy's relations to women (thus, a different philosophy): and the question she poses of possible places for speech, places other than those prescribed by the Outside/ Inside alternative, is an operational question for feminism raised by every page of her book.

'Women and Philosophy' is not only a study of femininity myths in philosophical discourse. It's also one of the few analyses we have of philosophy as a structure of institutional and inter-subjective relations. For Le Doeuff, women have so far been confined to two modes of access to philosophical work – amateur Heloise (the adoring disciple of a particular man) and professional vestal (faithful historical commentary). Either way, women remain bound by a dual relationship: their admiration produces the integrity of a person, or a corpus. In the first case, only an institutional framework could provide the third term necessary for breaking a dead-end transference relationship; and although this experience is now available to women, it contains the danger of inducing a lethal conformity to purely academic norms of philosophical practice. In the second, the practice of commemorative history does provide a place for women to be recognized in their own right; but as 'god's priestess, dedicated to a great dead man', the woman philosopher remains imprisoned in what Le Doeuff aptly calls the 'phantasmagoria of the commentary', nursing dismembered texts in precisely that mode of writing which is most devalued as having no language or identity of its own.

(One question to take up about *L'Imaginaire philosophique* as a whole is, then, the kind of identification crisis it provokes: whether the position of a woman writing philosophy rather than 'feminist theory' might be so troubling because it frustrates a certain desire for dyadic delights at work in the process of formally recognizing texts as *'feminist'* or *'not'*; and whether Le Doeuff's own work from this position as philosopher provides another basis for feminist reading.)

It follows from Le Doeuff's analysis of philosophy's relations to women that for her, the question of possible places for speech implies a complex confrontation with both institutions and modes of writing. If a Heloise-like subjugation to a single philosophy can be broken by professional constraints – (if ...) – then breaking out of the vestal syndrome requires an unsettling of the hierarchies of philosophical discourse. The problem (or the trap) of the commentary, for example, lies in the ways in which it has been represented – in an oscillation between acts of creative violation (original, 'masculine' readings) and of scrupulous fidelity (subordinate, 'feminine' ones). Heloise, vestal: differently placed as they are, both are attentive listeners charged with giving philosophers and philosophy a sense of fullness, completion. It is only a discourse able to assume its own incompleteness, Le Doeuff suggests, which might be able to disengage from the dynamics of subordination.

In 'Women and Philosophy' (p. 165) the example she cites is that of Pascal's *Pensées*:

> Here one has a kind of writing which doesn't purport to reconstruct or explain everything, which slides along the borders of the unthought, which unfolds only after having first grafted itself onto another, prior utterance, accepting its own condition of relative dependence.

In *L'Imaginaire philosophique*, the form she develops herself is the critical essay – or rather, the form of a book is imposed upon a sequence of essays structured by gaps and bridges, and read in retrospect (a preface, the speculative notes linking text to text) by a writing subject which has been produced in diverse encounters with other discourses, other modes of thought. Le Doeuff's use of essays provides feminist reflection with something rare: the trace of an action of *disengagement* from one position to another, to a position where it is possible for a woman writing philosophy to pose feminist questions in a different discourse from that with which she began.

> To build it up after the fact into a rigorously unified theory would undoubtedly be to nullify what seems to me, in retrospect, to be of most importance, namely the fact that the monographic form which I practiced here (working through studies of particular texts, or around relatively heterogeneous themes) changed the perspectives I had had at the outset.
>
> *'La Face honteuse de la philosophie'*, p. 11

2. The Philosophical Imaginary

Yet –

The place accorded to the study of women in/and philosophy is a peculiar one in the movement of modification which constitutes *L'Imaginaire philosophique*. It is a 'privileged occasion' for formulating more precisely the double-edged notion of an imaginary both *in* and *of* philosophy: the claim that 'the icon of the feminine presented in philosophical texts is not a universally shared representation' is presented as the moment in which the theme of a 'totally philosophical' imaginary takes over in the text.[9]

Le Doeuff's occasional integration of feminism with philosophy in the book could confront some feminist readers with a basic political problem. The milder form of this would be to decide how far a project of specifying something as peculiar to philosophy (a project which simply hinges on the study of women and femininity) can be of any interest at all. Does it provide us with elements to underpin a possible practice, or does it lead straight back to the demarcation disputes of academic disciplines – and the founding of feminine enclaves?

More severely, one might ask to what extent *L'Imaginaire philosophique* (while introducing philosophical discourse to feminist questions) is at the same time merely engaged in a salvage operation to rescue philosophy from the more damaging charges of feminist critics in France – and if so, for what reasons.

For beyond the question of the placing of 'Women and Philosophy' in the book, there seems to be – at least at first sight – a certain lack of alignment between Le Doeuff's theoretical project of showing the *solidarity* between imagery and knowledge in philosophical discourse, her argument that the misogyny of philosophy can be *confined* to the imaginary, and her comments on the politics of philosophy in general:

> Let us emphasise the point further: imagery and knowledge combine dialectically here in a single system. There is a feedback between the two terms, which serves as the basis of this discursive formation's peculiar character. (p. 30)

> I have never had anything against philosophical rationality.... To be more precise, it seems to me that philosophy is not a function of some strictly 'masculine' form of rationality, but philosophy often produces a misogynist style of imagination. (p. 134)

> I ask the reader to allow me the postulate here that philosophy is discourse which ceaselessly asserts its own power. And so, in political matters, philosophy becomes entrapped in its persona as the providential, philosophical legislator. The politics of the philosophers is a paternalism of reason. (p. 80)

These passages come from different contexts, and do not address identical problems. The first concerns the relationship between imagery and knowledge in particular texts; the second is a general comment on a possible position in feminist debate; the third concerns a particular philosophical history. The 'paternalism of reason' and 'philosophical rationality' are not interchangeable terms. So it is not a matter of locating a 'contradiction', nor of producing a strong theoretical unity for the book in order to demonstrate its insufficiency to a feminist politics. The problem of alignment is rather one of *how* and *why* these different positions can combine in Michèle Le Doeuff's practice: how her conception of the imaginary develops in a direction which allows a critique of the paternalism of reason to accompany a preservation plea for philosophical rationality.

* * *

'*There is not just* one *reason,* one *imaginary.*'

Le Doeuff describes her essays as proceeding all 'from a common attentiveness to the incidence, in what are called theoretical texts, of a kind of thinking-in-images'.[10] However, there is no formal definition of an 'image' given anywhere in the book. Nor is there any explicit justification given for the choice of such a vague and treacherous term to mark a difference between some pieces of text and other pieces of text: no distinction established between thinking-in-images and any other kind of thinking, no reflection on the general relations between 'thinking' and discourse, and no systematic regulation of the relative uses of the key words 'image', 'imagery', 'imaginary'. Instead, the most basic of these questions is relegated to an elsewhere, a *not-here* of the text, assumed to be open to the well-informed reader:

> To comment on the images that run through philosophical texts, even to decide just what episodes in a text *are* images, can appear a straightforward matter only if one adopts a very naive standpoint. This is not the place to go into all the problems this question raises.
>
> '*En rouge dans la marge*', p. 124

In the context of a short article on readings of Descartes, this refusal to engage with what would indeed be a major theoretical debate seems reasonable enough. When sustained across the span of a book with such a title, the same refusal seems rather surprising.

But this (apparent) avoidance of definition acts within the texts in three related ways. Firstly, the very vagueness of 'image' – the slippage it allows between pictorial, rhetorical and psychoanalytic themes, to mention only the most obvious – also allows Le Doeuff a great deal of flexibility in the selection and interpretation of the elements to fall within the range of her project, and in the methods of reading which can be made to converge upon, and transform, a particular textual problem. Oddly enough, it is a gesture of economy: and the best example of this is probably '*En rouge dans la marge*'.

This essay, subtitled '*L'Invention de l'objet "Morale de Descartes" et les métaphores du discours cartésien*', opens with the question of whether a text can be considered entirely innocent of the blunders made by commentators in its name. In response, Le Doeuff confronts two readings of the Cartesian statement, 'I formed for myself a code of morals *par provision*'. One, the meticulous or 'blinkered' reading, establishes by comparison with dictionaries, commentaries and non-Cartesian texts of the period that the phrase '*par provision*' (a juridical term for a part-payment in advance) does not mean 'provisional', and that no one in France paraphrased Descartes in this improper fashion before the last quarter of the nineteenth century. The second, 'global' reading uses an analysis of the 'marginalized' elements of Cartesian discourse (in particular, the metaphors of the building in the *Discourse on Method* and the tree in the *Principles of Philosophy*) to argue that the text itself, traversed by slidings and indecisions, was also *open to* the distortion worked upon it and with it by the paraphrase 'provisional morality'. This reading became current at a time when French academic philosophers and pedagogues were locked into a debate about teaching morality to children in schools.

By situating these two readings in relation to each other, Le Doeuff is able to work several themes *through* the phrase '*par provision*': she discusses the function of metaphor in philosophical discourse, and the textual conditions of interpretation in philosophy; the relations between philosophical discourse and historical context, the political and ideological determinations of philosophical 'objects' and readings; the nature of philosophy as a discourse reflecting upon its own power and status; and the inscription of desire in the Cartesian text. Here, it is the initial 'assuming' of the imaginary as a loose set of problems (rather than terms to be defined) which makes both the extent and the precision of Le Doeuff's analysis possible.

Secondly, in place of an exposition of the theoretical problems posed by the notion of image there is in fact another, effective mode of definition. *L'Imaginaire philosophique* rests on appeals to convention, to tradition, to the commonplace, to the *on dit* of philosophy. 'Everybody knows' in philosophy what imagery is, since imagery is what philosophy is not. The 'not' of philosophy includes many things which may be brought into a state of tactical equivalence: myth, narrative, metaphor, description, fable, poetry, metonymy, the picturesque, images, imagery, blazons, emblems, old wives' tales ...

Hegel says in effect that the form proper to Thought is the only form for philosophy, having previously remarked that 'the opposition of philosophy to, and its struggle with the pretended representations of popular mythology, is an ancient phenomenon'. It is indeed an ancient commonplace to assimilate philosophy to a certain *logos* which determines itself through its opposition to other types of discourse.

'*La Face honteuse de la philosophie*', p. 9

Le Doeuff seems to rest content with the commonplace, to maintain the equivalence which (to a not-philosophical reader) produces precisely the misty notion of the Literary which several otherwise incompatible schools of discourse analysis have been trying to dismantle for decades. So pervasive is the assumption by Le Doeuff of a common tradition of opinion about 'images' – and thus, a set of rules for recognizing them – that on the one hand her description of that tradition needs only the lightest, most fleeting of references (Plato, Hegel, Bréhier, Couturat, Condillac, 'a' dictionary of philosophy); and on the other, her own examples simply present themselves with the force of the obvious (the island, the tree, the house, the voice ...).

There are moments in *L'Imaginaire philosophique* when the method of setting out from a common-place seems to serve as a means of dispensing with argument. In the essay on Roussel, for example, there is a slide in the definition of 'chiasmus' between an affirmation of 'common sense' (*sens commun*) and an affirmation of 'literal meaning' (*sens propre*). Roussel sees sexual difference in all the elements of the body and life of women, but not in the pubic bone (where common sense would surely place it); therefore, 'Silence as to the literal meaning, a void at the centre; metonymic proliferation everywhere else'.[11] For the analysis of Roussel's discourse and his figuration of the female body, this slide (exploiting to the full the polysemy of the French word 'propre') is a perfectly controlled and functional move in the text. But when Le Doeuff goes on to see in this '*silence sur le sens propre*' a general intellectual mechanism at work in contemporary thought, the amusing observation that 'economy' can now refer to everything but the price of wool in Manchester, and 'politics' to anything but a theory of the State, is made at the price of evacuating the theoretical debates which make these 'precise' and 'proper' meanings problematic. Her critical note on the privilege accorded to metaphor by some philosophers today works in a similar fashion. (p. 194)

> The metaphor presupposes the literal meaning, but (we are told) since there is no literal meaning, there is nothing but metaphors and thus one is always-already installed in a detour. This evidently serves to invalidate in advance the critique of the philosophers' metaphorical evasions when faced with the 'literal meaning' of certain conflictual objects.

Perhaps: but the problem elided here is the status of 'literal meaning' if a specific concept of metaphor is retained, while that of 'deviation' is abandoned altogether.

Nevertheless, the primary purpose of invoking a philosophical common-place in *L'Imaginaire philosophique* is (perhaps by a gesture of seduction towards the reader so inscribed) to bring about discreetly a drastic departure from it. An example here is the introductory note to 'Polysémie du discours atopiqué', a study of the 'bifid' structure of certain fables (Utopia; The Fable of the Bees):

> It is customary to stress the plural meaning of every product of fabulation. The image, it seems, always says too much, so that one is obliged to correct or rectify it ... 'the deep and multiple meaning of the old symbols ...': have we paid sufficient attention to the leitmotif whose formulation I borrow here from a dictionary of philosophy?
> I am not proposing here to depart from this commonplace view ... (p. 65)

It might be tempting to object that even a qualified assimilation of 'plurality of meanings' to 'images' and 'symbols' can only re-produce a naive dream of an intrinsically mono-semic text, a dream which depends for its logic on a strange assimilation of the 'plural' and the 'imprecise'. In the essay, Le Doeuff does indeed accept the possibility of talking about a text with 'one meaning, and one only' or 'one immediate meaning which enforces itself', and she goes so far as to equate polysemy with asemy: 'Several possible meanings, or no precise and definite meaning: these amount to the same thing, if one credits the experiment of interpreting blurred images and ink-blotches'.[12]

Her argument, however, takes an interesting turn. First, she refuses to accept the contrast implied with the 'rest' of philosophical discourse as rigorously and immediately clear and univocal: 'It seems to me that on the contrary, perfect univocity is only ever a localised phenomenon in any discourse.' Then, she treats this univocity as a condition which philosophical discourse strives to achieve (locating it implicitly in the order of desires inscribed in philosophical convention, rather than ascribing it conventionally to certain 'kinds' of language): 'conceptualisation is only ever arrived at with the end of the story, as the outcome of an uncertain effort to establish a meaning.'[13] Next, the possibility of producing 'one meaning, one meaning only and the right meaning' from a text is considered to be a function of the historical context in which it is written and read. Thus the relationship between the two books of Utopia is analysed as a labour of limiting meaning, imposed because More's thesis of the community of goods (elaborated in the 'polysemic' fiction of Book II) initially made no political sense at the beginning of the sixteenth century: 'in the sense More gives it ... it does not correspond to any political discourse actually practised outside the sphere of philosophy.'[14] The function of the first book is to pick up, rework and specify that thesis by giving it a meaning; that is, by establishing the principles by which the second book might be decoded.

(This double structure is what Le Doeuff calls an atopia: one which has no place, in the sense that 'an atopian work is one which finds no already existing circle of witnesses and readers waiting to receive it.')[15] Finally, after shifting step by step away from the common-place, Le Doeuff brings her argument around to a nicely ironic restatement:

> Now we can understand the profundity that is attributed to images: they are not, properly speaking, 'what I think', but rather 'what I think with', or again 'that by which what I think is able to define itself'. Doubtless this is a paradox, given the vagueness of the images themselves. (p. 67)

From the isolated image, imagined as a polysemic bit of text embedded in a mono-semic slab, she moves to a conception of images as agents of definition in a particular discursive process.

The third major mode of definition employed in *L'Imaginaire philosophique* directly reinforces Le Doeuff's technique of departing *from* tradition. Allowing the 'obviousness' of the image to remain apparent, in '*La Face honteuse de la philosophie*' she defines her work in terms of its difference from two other, common ways of representing the relationship of 'thought' to 'images' in discourse.

One is the corollary of the 'ancient commonplace' that imagery is what philosophy is not: when the history of philosophy is written from this point of view, the images which do occur in philosophical texts are, she says, usually treated as merely ornamental – '*outside*' the work of the text. The second is the notion of 'thinking-in-images', of which she briefly cites two examples: the 'remarkable works' produced in our era on myth and dream, 'places where thinking-in-images is in some sense at home'; and Bachelard's analyses of the imaginary in scientific work, analyses which aim to 'deport an element judged to be foreign and undesirable, to assign it a domicile *elsewhere*'. Her own perspective transposes the notion of thinking in images to philosophical discourse: 'I am concerned with reflecting on scraps of the imaginary that do work in places where, in principle, the imaginary is not supposed to reside, and where none the less without it *nothing can be done*' (emphasis added).[16]

In saying this, Le Doeuff passes from a concept of images as *located* in relation to a given discourse (as *lodged* 'outside', 'at home', 'elsewhere') to a functional analysis of what they do – the '*faire*' of images in discourse. The same move is repeated in different terms a few pages later, when Le Doeuff discusses the traditional alibis provided to explain the presence of images in philosophical texts; either, she says, their heterogeneity is maximalized (Bachelard, Condillac), or they are treated as simple illustrations, completely isomorphic with a body of concepts into which their meaning may be fully absorbed. In both cases, what is denied to them is the status of an *element of philosophical work*. Le Doeuff's own essays are concerned with the 'work' of images; which are now implicitly defined as those elements of a text which philosophical discourse has, in the process of its self-definition, (mis)recognized as other.

'*When the learned produce a theory of the imaginary, it is always a theory of the Other...*'

As a study of images 'in' philosophy, *L'Imaginaire philosophique* has the effect of reintegrating these 'obviously' identifiable, alien bits of text into the discourse of philosophy. At the same time, their identity is maintained: since to do otherwise would be to collapse them back to the status of illustration, to reabsorb them in a 'system of concepts', to deny that they do work. It is through analysing the work that images do that Le Doeuff develops the idea of an imaginary '*of*' philosophy: a variety of functions which may be assumed by particular images in particular texts; a series of *specifically philosophical images* (of which Kant's island of understanding provides an extended example); a play of phantasmatic projection in the constitution of philosophical discourse; and a form of institutionalized subjectivity which structures the philosophical 'position'.

'*La Face honteuse de la philosophie*' is quite casual in its formulation of the general relationship between philosophical imagery and theoretical work. This relationship is variously described in different contexts as 'functional', 'organic', 'made-to-measure', 'dialectical solidarity' and 'feedback'. However once again, Le Doeuff is not interested in a general theory of 'the' philosophical imaginary, and she is certainly not engaged in contributing to a theory of 'the' Imaginary in general. Instead, the essays are detailed investigations of particular *cases*.

In the studies of More, and of the role played by the alchemical notion of affinity in Galileo's law of falling bodies ('*Galilée ou l'affinité suprême entre le temps et le mouvement*'), Le Doeuff considers the work of the imaginary to be essentially *innovative* – permitting 'the emergence of the not yet thought'.[17] In contrast, the images of the building and the tree in Descartes have a *nostalgic* function; in holding out a promise of a 'complete' body of philosophy, their work is to blur the precision of 'embarrassing' results (in this case, the strict impossibility of an ethics in the Cartesian system). The last three essays – 'Women and Philosophy', '*La philosophie dans le gosier*' and '*Les Chiasmes de Pierre Roussel*' – are all concerned with different uses of what Le Doeuff calls the blazons of philosophy: 'blazons and armorial bearings – drafts of specular objects in which the writer thinks himself, and thinks his relation to the Other'.[18]

In her studies of the feminine, of the difference between the speaking and singing voice, and of Roussel's spatial distribution of the female body, Le Doeuff finds both 'the *legitimising* figuration of the practices and hopes of philosophers ... (and) ... at the same time, a figuration of dangers, obsessions, negative forces'.[19]

The work of innovation, regret and legitimation in these texts is read according to a principle of *methodological suspicion* which Le Doeuff outlines in the working hypothesis for *L'Imaginaire philosophique*. This hypothesis comes in two versions:

> A restricted version: the interpretation of image-sequences in philosophical texts (taking this category in its widest sense) goes hand in hand with the eliciting of lines of stress in a work. Or alternatively: imagery is consubstantial with the difficulties, the sensitive points in an intellectual undertaking.
>
> An extended version: the meaning conveyed by images works at once for and against the system that uses them. *For*, in that they provide the basis for what the system is unable to justify, yet requires in order to function. *Against*, for more or less the same reason: the signification of images is incompatible with the constraints of system.
>
> *'La Face honteuse de la philosophie'*, pp. 11–12

Here, Le Doeuff's conception of the work of images in philosophical discourse splits into two different representations. One is of the philosophical *text* as a kind of traumatized surface marked by image-symptoms to be read by the analyst; and this representation reappears throughout the book in insistent metaphors of tension, pain and 'neuralgia'. The other is a political representation of the philosophical *system*, supported and undermined by the action of its marginalized elements; and this one comes to the fore in Le Doeuff's text when it is a matter of confronting the meaning of contradiction in philosophy. The hypothesis itself is not concerned with what philosophy's imaginary 'is', but rather with establishing the parameters for an analysis which will be situated, each time, 'between identifying a difficulty and identifying a contradiction'.

Beyond the local function of imagery in particular texts and systems, Le Doeuff sees a specifically philosophical mode of intertextuality in action through the 'migration' of an image from one text to another, one philosophy to another, one 'language' to another. She argues that philosophical images have the remarkable property of being picked up (and reworked) from a precisely determinable previous text. The two examples she studies in detail are Kant's reworking of Bacon's 'island of truth', and Descartes' allusions to the house and garden of the Gospel according to Matthew (7.15f.). The procedure of tacitly quoting an image already invested by a previous philosophy is what Le Doeuff calls 'winking':[20]

One can imagine a number of functions for this kind of reactivation: to mask a lack or a transgression, to reactualise an anterior blind spot encapsulated in the image (where an image is classical, one no longer notices the way it serves to palliate an impossible situation); to reiterate a wish or desire concerning philosophy: to attempt to validate an enterprise by putting it under the 'patronage' of an accredited authority.

'*En rouge dans la marge*', p. 124

In the case of Descartes, Le Doeuff argues that the heavy allusion to the Gospel could be interpreted as a gesture of redemption, an attempt to annul a transgression: 'Descartes speaks the language of what his work excludes.'[21] In Kant's reworking of Bacon, what is at stake is the status of philosophy itself in the historical context of *constituted* sciences; to resume Bacon's metaphor is to suppress a difference, 'occulting (by deciding it dogmatically and obliquely) the question of philosophy's utility within the global project of Restoration, and the question of the utility of philosophical intervention in furthering the progress of the particular sciences'.[22] In Bacon's time, a role could still be accorded to philosophy: the task of the 'understanding' to be secured against the tempests of illusion was to prepare the terrain for the progress of science. The historical situation of Kant's project is quite different: the sciences of nature are well underway, and 'from the point of view of the "Great Instauration", it is quite impossible to justify the need for assistance from philosophy.'

In suppressing this difference – a 'neuralgic theoretical point' of the Kantian enterprise – Kant's image covertly induces a shift of ground. As the self-justification of critical philosophy, Kant's island – surrounded by the terrors of vast and stormy seas full of peril for the wanderer – assumes a positive value only as the single exception in an uninhabitable universe. It offers neither gratification, nor the guarantee of its own necessity, but simply the security of the least painful situation: it 'erects a self-justification centred on a binary division among pleasures and pains – especially among pains.'[23] The function of the image is to construct a terrorist *mise en scène*, the dogmatic value of which depends on the understanding shared by good philosophical readers that such 'illustrations' are neither worthy of, nor intended for, their close attention.

It is in administering its own legitimacy, in establishing its own value, that philosophy is led to define and describe its own myths, to rely on spatial or narrative methods of distribution, to make play in its discourse with tales of pierced barrels, islands ringed by danger, fruit-bearing trees, chains needing to be broken, or forged.

'*La Face honteuse de la philosophie*', p. 15

To engage in a process of self-foundation and self-validation is already, in itself, to initiate an imaginary construction, since no such discourse is possible. But, says Le Doeuff, an act of self-foundation is precisely the recurrent pretension of philosophical discourse. The meta-discourse of philosophy aspires not only to determine the modalities of its own legitimacy, but – through its self-assured 'right' to decide the difference between what is properly theoretical and what is not – to lay down the laws of other discourses as well. Thus, the non-philosophical character of thinking-in-images is a common philosophical theme.

But since the attempt to purify philosophy of images always fails (and must fail, given the imaginary foundation of the discourse itself), several strategies develop to deal with this 'internal scandal': and one of them consists in projecting the 'shameful face of philosophy' on to an Other. To write in images is to adopt the language of that Other: and here – as in the 'winking' procedures of image-quotation – Le Doeuff sees a collective act of dis-claiming at work which characterizes what she calls the philosophical 'corporation'. The disclaimer (exempting the writing subject from responsibility for what is written) takes variable forms, but depends upon a simple mechanism of projection in two main directions. Either the occurrence of imagery is regarded as a 'primitive' upsurge, a return of archaic or infantile thought (and the paradigms of this pro-jection are the child, the old wives' tale, and the mythic, irrational lore of The People); or else it is imputed to the needs of the uncultivated reader, for whom it has didactic or pedagogical value. The image mediates between two theoretical situations, between sender and receiver; as clarification, it gives a means of entry to the text for the uninitiated, and as pure transparency it is the site of an affirmation of corporate identity – a sign to the initiated reader that this is the spot to be skipped.

It is this 'understanding' of the image which, for Le Doeuff, allows it to become the place *par excellence* for exercises in self-legitimation. She argues that while it would be excessive and reductive to maintain that *all* images in philosophical texts are texts about philosophy, the hypothesis of specular function can nevertheless account for the 'eminently classi-cal' images,

> the ones that are to be found everywhere and belong to the language of the corporation (a language which, by definition, transcends its particular speakers), and which, together with a certain number of principles, rules and delusions, structure the philosophical position as such.
>
> *'La Face honteuse de la philosophie'*, p. 15

The notion of corporate position provides the fourth element in Le

Doeuff's conception of philosophy's imaginary, allowing it to open on to a socio-historical analysis of the phantasms specific to a social and cultural minority. She suggests that just as Barthes assigned to language as a whole the paradoxical status of an institutionalization of subjectivity, so the 'language' of philosophy's imaginary may be understood as governed by the needs and the lacunae of the theoretical enterprise.[24]

The point here is the *specialization* of the imaginary at work in theoretical texts. For Le Doeuff, the interest of Roussel's *Système physique et morale de la femme* lies less in the fact of its production of fabulous women with sexless pubic bones, sexualized bodies and minds, and no periods in their natural state, than in the function assumed by the actual elaboration of the fable – realizing the theoretical inventions of the eighteenth century, projecting them on to the female body and, in the process, establishing the principle of generalized doctoral competence based on the 'authority' of a partial knowledge. The step of realization and projection transforms 'a *lettered* imaginary (that which belongs to the general culture of the educated) into a *learned* (*savant*) imaginary'; while the proliferation of the speaker's areas of assumed authority constitutes an imaginary of 'doctorality' itself – which has no necessary relays to other social groups, other practices, other imaginaries. Far from contributing a few new items to some common cultural stock of 'images of women', Roussel's discourse renounces one imaginary in favour of another – the blazon of its own truth.

Similarly, Le Doeuff argues that the Kantian island inaugurates an erotics of action and labour: 'and yet, precisely, it is not really an inauguration at all: rather, it formalises or symbolises a sacrifice which the reader has doubtless already performed.'[25] The pleasure of the island of lesser pain is proffered for a 'circle of witnesses' characterized already by a certain schooling, by scholarly ascetism, and by the libidinal and phantasmatic sacrifices required by a particular education system. But this sacrifice is precisely not the renunciation of myth in general which the classical interpretation holds to be constitutive of 'rationality'; instead, it is a rupture with 'the most widely shared of imaginaries' effected in favour of another – *the imaginary of the corporation*. And if the erotics of the Kantian emblem lends itself easily to a psychoanalytic reading in terms of castration, adds Le Doeuff, then the last word must go not to psychoanalysis itself; but to a 'historicising intertextuality' which would point out that both Kantian philosophy and analytical discourse belong to the same age (that of the constituted sciences transmitted by the school); and that both confront the same question – that of the subjective conditions for *abandoning the right to dream*.

The four aspects of Le Doeuff's analysis of philosophy's imaginary combine in her texts to produce a complex argument about the *impli-*

cations of what she sees as the specialty of that discourse. On the one hand, both philosophical images and philosophical discourse on imagery are treated as constituting a kind of discursive heritage of recognition rituals and allegiance games: the philosophical corporation is a brotherhood bound by winks and secret signs, by a tradition of shared commonplaces, by desires for autogenesis and by dreams of domination (the 'paternalism' of reason). On the other hand, the very procedures which determine the specificity of philosophy's imaginary also guarantee the non-closure of the discursive formation (and thus, presumably, its susceptibility to change):

> To think a specificity does not mean to trace an absolutely rigorous demarcating line: to regard an imaginary as a cultural product certainly involves looking for variations and differences as between epochs, social categories and fields of knowledge – but one should not forget that culture is something that circulates, between different groups, different practices, different knowledges.
>
> 'La Face honteuse de la philosophie', p. 13

When these two arguments are projected across each other in Le Doeuff's texts, the outcome is a concept of philosophical discourse as a corporate enterprise in constant mutation through the shock of collision with 'other discourses, other modes of thought'. The powers of philosophy are further (de)limited in this perspective by Le Doeuff's insistence that the circulation of elements does not necessarily go *from* philosophy to other discourses and practices – and that to 'imagine' it does would be to repeat the 'philosophicocentric proposition' that so-called popular culture is the by-product of a process of degradation.[26]

One immediate implication of Le Doeuff's argument here is that the dismantling of 'philosophical discourse' *in general* need not be of first priority for feminist theoretical work. It is in this general context that her analysis of women and philosophy needs to be placed.

'After islands and trees, women? . . .'

At first sight, Le Doeuff's procedure seems to be a simple one. She argues that the 'icon' of femininity found in philosophical texts is not a universal representation. It may connect with common phallocentric prejudices, but this does not mean that it may be considered as an element of the generalized Imaginary of an undifferentiated Culture. The 'zone of influence' of the masculine/feminine opposition produced by philosophy is extremely limited; and in particular, she says, the idea of woman as sphinx and as chaos is probably only current today in certain fractions of the 'dominant class': 'among popular social classes, woman is more thought of as a power of order, as "reasonable", not to say as a kill-joy – the pole of fantasy and insouciance being supposed to lie rather on the masculine side.'[27]

Le Doeuff's insistence on the specificity of philosophical images is directed against two critiques of 'rationality' which work precisely by accepting the equation femininity = unreason, and by giving it a positive political value. (Both also depend upon a slide between 'rationality' as a property of certain, highly valued discourses governed by a set of rules and procedures, and 'rationality' as a faculty which individuals or social groups are said – often by those same discourses – to possess or to lack).

One is the 'announcement' by Guy Lardreau in L'Ange, that slaves and women are indeed without reason, that 'when a slave, as slave, or a woman, as woman, reasons about slaves or women, this reasoning can only be an unreason',[28] and that the autonomous discourse of the rebel must make itself heard in the irruption of this unreason. His announcement is made in the name of 'Greek frankness'. Le Doeuff replies that knowledge about women has always been masculine property, 'in which case L'Ange is not announcing anything'; and that it is time to return, not to Greek frankness, but to an elementary historical materialism capable of recalling that slave societies proclaim the unreason of the slave, and patriarchal societies fondly repeat that woman, dear creature, lacks reason.

The second critique of rationality is that which underpins 'a certain feminism of difference which seems unaware of its debt to Auguste Comte'[29] – the position that rationality is indeed a masculine property, that therefore philosophical discourse is traversed by masculine values, and that women must seek their own specificity and their own discourse. Le Doeuff's response to this (beyond the immediate noting of the positivist heritage of such feminism) is both extensive and diffused throughout all her work on women. But essentially, she reverses the order of the argument: from the fact that philosophical discourse has often been structured by a misogynist imaginary, it does not necessarily follow that 'rationality' is a masculine privilege. She then develops a two-sided counter position: (i) it is all too easy to overestimate the influence of philosophical representations of femininity, and thus to accept philosophy's myths about its own powers and importance; (ii) when the mystifications which are produced by philosophy come under attack – for example, the positivist image of women as morally superior and theoretically deficient – then it is the practice, and not the refusal, of philosophy which can provide the necessary (if insufficient) critical means for ousting and unmasking the alienating schemas which philosophy produces.

But if this seems fairly straightforward, the problem for Le Doeuff in this part of her work is to establish a relationship between rationality, philosophical discourses and their imaginary, such that the practice of philosophy (in some form or another) remains a political possibility for women. To do this, she puts forward two main propositions; one concerns the role of femininity myths in the general mechanism of projection and exclusion which characterizes philosophy; the other is a historical argument about the conditions in which theoretical incapacity has been projected on to women in the past.

2.1 For Le Doeuff, the image of women as other (as dark continent, disorder, depth of the unintelligible, internal enemy and so on) is only one of a series of Others produced by philosophy in its process of self-definition. The child, the people, the savage and the pre-Socratics also come in for their fair share of alienation. Nevertheless, the figure of the feminine is extremely important. Not only does it appear to be a feature of the oldest metaphysics (as in Hegel's listing of Pythagorian oppositions; limit/infinity, unity/multiplicity, masculine/feminine, light/darkness, good/evil), but it also serves as a means of signifying a difference which creates philosophical *discourse.*

> The man/woman difference is recruited as a way to signify the general opposition of the definite and the indefinite, or of the valid and the excluded, an opposition one of whose figures is the couplet *logos/mythos*, since *mythos* is the old wives' tale, or at best the inspired narration of a Diotima.
>
> 'Women and Philosophy', p. 151

It is too simplistic, she argues, merely to list the various historical exclusions of philosophy (rhetoric, seductive discourse, occultism ...). The fact that philosophy is a discipline, claiming to obey a finite stock of procedural rules and operations, indicates that something is repressed within it. The point is rather that what philosophical discourse labours to exclude must be – and must remain – *something indeterminable*:

> It is not, and cannot be [determined], since either it is precisely the indefinite, or else philosophy amounts to the formal postulate that a practice of exclusion, a discipline of discourse, is necessary in order for the permitted modes of thought not to remain themselves indefinite. *This then would constitute a general form of exclusion, one capable of being given a certain number of different contents, without itself being consubstantial with any one particular content.*
>
> 'Women and Philosophy', p. 151 (my emphasis)

But this 'something-indeterminable' can only be denoted by metaphor –

and it is sexual difference which is summoned up for the task. Yet since philosophy creates both itself *and* 'the feminine' in the repression of this indeterminable something, it must reproduce the act again and again as the old wives' tales constantly return to obscure the clear light of the concept: 'Not on account of some dynamic characteristic of the repressed in general, but because the finite stock of prescribed procedures will not suffice.'

Here, Le Doeuff's work on the function of the imaginary in philosophy seems to coalesce perfectly with her study of the feminine image. Yet this is perhaps the most difficult point of her analysis, since it is here that she implicitly posits the 'disposable' misogyny of philosophy's imaginary. If the something-indeterminable created by philosophy creating itself is a general form of exclusion, then that 'something' need not be constructed as feminine. Nor, presumably, need it be identified with thinking-in-images; since the whole of her book attempts to demonstrate that images are not only fully functional elements of philosophical 'thought', but also the elements most commonly charged with articulating the legitimacy of a given theoretical project. Furthermore, the *status* of the something-indeterminable as menace, threat or cataclysm depends on a particular evaluation of the 'insufficiency' of philosophy's licit procedures which, she argues, may well be historically dated.

2.2 In line with her cautions against inflating philosophy's importance, Le Doeuff begins her study of women and philosophy by observing that real women have not always been excluded from philosophy, that the scarcity of women philosophers in history must be understood in relation to the history of philosophy as the privilege of a tiny minority of entire populations, and that the woman philosopher has not always or necessarily been represented as a monster.

If this 'relative non-exclusion' of women in certain periods of history has also been bound up with the history of the social confinement of women (forbidding them access to the institutions of philosophy) and with the history of pedagogical passions (confining women to a single, 'philosophical' relationship), then it is only from the eighteenth century onwards that references begin to flourish about women's *incapacity* to theorize.

The mechanism of the sexual division of knowledge effected during this period is analysed in detail by '*Les Chiasmes de Pierre Roussel*'. In 'Women and Philosophy', Le Doeuff simply observes that the eighteenth century, the era of the salons and Mme de Staël, 'was faced with the need to exclude not just Woman but *women*, real concrete women who had advanced as far as the limits of the permissible'[30]; and that the dignity of philosophy, 'queen of the sciences', may well have found itself for the first time under serious threat.

But such explanations, she says, are not enough: 'the exclusion of "Woman" is perhaps more consubstantial with philosophy as such, and less readily historicized than our citations from the Eighteenth and Nineteenth centuries might lead one to think.'

The specific conflicts of the eighteenth century reawakened older elements (which could, until then, afford to remain implicit) in an attempt to mask the nature of the philosophical – or as an effort to reinsure the problematic *positivity* of philosophy, to defend the discourse which aspires to lay down the law of other discourses against the recognition of its own limitations:

> The reference to woman (or to any other subject deemed 'unfit' for philosophy) makes it possible to misrecognise this impotence, since it is here projected, in a radicalised form, on to a subject located below even the minimum threshold for any investigation into speculative truths. Putting it another way: the idea that there are persons incapable of philosophising at all gives aid and comfort to the view that philosophy itself is capable of something.
>
> 'Women and Philosophy', p. 148

Paradoxically, perhaps, Le Doeuff uses her own analysis of this exclusion as 'more' consubstantial with philosophy to argue that the historical conditions may *now* exist for this relationship to women to be changed. Once again, her argument is two-sided; sociologial and textual, implying engagement with both institutions and modes of writing.

The sociological argument is the less fully developed, since it depends on a rather tantalizing assertion by Le Doeuff that there is a specific *lack* which produces the philosophical activity: 'that particular lack from which philosophy to my mind derives, a radical lack which no Other can fill.'[31] The limitations placed on the women of the past have channelled them into a theoretico-amorous relationship with one philosopher, one philosophy – and have thus converted a possible experience of philosophical lack into one of 'ordinary', 'classic', 'psychological' lack, which the Other is seen as likely to fulfil. Le Doeuff stresses that she is not constructing an ontology of 'lack', but 'the model for an insufficient insertion in society, or an insufficient adherence to a pregiven cultural formation ... an insufficiency which is capable of acting as the dialectical springboard for what might be called the creativity of the migrant'.

The suggestion is that the 'Movement' of women today has placed them in a position to gain access to institutions, to break from dual transference relationships, and to produce their own response to purely philosophical lack.

That is a comment about what is *possible* for women. Le Doeuff's second argument concerns the changes which are *desirable* – and necessary – if philosophy is indeed to dispense with the 'logocentrico-phallocratic phantasmagoria' which has marked its history to date. Logocentrism, she says, is not the ineluctable presupposition (or hypothesis) of every rational position. If logocentrism has in fact dominated the whole history of philosophy, to the point of making that history the reiteration of a fundamental thesis of the power of true discourse, then it is at least possible today to think rationality differently, in a 'non-hegemonic' mode. This is, for Le Doeuff, an objective rather than a given state of affairs – although she sees historical materialism (a 'rationalism which has renounced the thesis of the omnipotence of knowledge')[32] as the beginning of the struggle. Beyond this one reference, the conditions which constitute 'today' are never spelt out by Le Doeuff: but the very possibility of the sign 'logocentricophallocracy' is probably sufficient to identify a context of developments in modern philosophy.

The stakes, however, are fairly clear. Le Doeuff is speculating on the *effects* of a re-evaluation of lack and limitation in philosophy. If the 'lack' of philosophy is insisted upon not as a defect, but as a condition of its insertion in the historical real; if it becomes possible to desire no longer to mask the incomplete character of all theorization; and if a state of insufficiency ceases to be represented as a threat; then there would be, at least, the preconditions for the theoretical possibility of a non-misogynist philosophy to become a historical reality. The imaginary is transformed, and philosophy changes genre:

> Since for twenty-five centuries philosophers have been comparing the world to a theatre, and philosophy to a tragedy, founding the metaphor on a closure of representation which makes the drama into a well-defined 'whole', I will say that the future of a no longer antifeminist philosophy must lie somewhere in the direction of a Brechtian dramaturgy which … makes plays that always have an act missing, and therefore open themselves to history.
>
> 'Women and Philosophy', p. 154

If such a transformation is indeed a possibility as well as a phantasy for Le Doeuff, it is partly because for her, philosophical discourse has always been subject to collisions, conflicts and mutations; and because – as well as recalling Pascal – in developments such as *GREPH*'s experiments in teaching philosophy to children, the emergence of attempts to set up a *collective* practice of philosophical production, and the refusal to lay claim to an inaugural discourse found in Foucault's

L'Ordre du discours, she sees the actual beginnings of a different practice.

* * *

Yet –

If Michèle Le Doeuff is proposing a transformation rather than a disruption or abandonment of philosophy; if in insisting on the specificity of philosophy she is (far from indulging in demarcation disputes) suggesting that philosophy be kept in its proper place; and if she is indeed engaged in a salvage operation, but one which offers to salvage for feminism the critical means to fight philosophy's mystifications –

Then: the question presents itself, what's in a name?

For in prefiguring an end to the antifeminism of philosophy but not to philosophy itself, in proposing the overthrow of the paternalism of reason but not that of reason itself, Le Doeuff invests in a kind of *wager* that after twenty-five centuries of unevenly distributed but constantly present misogyny, the conditions now exist for a changed theoretical enterprise in the future tense, assured by a rationality without gender – and that there is more to be gained than lost by inscribing this activity under the ancient sign, 'philosophy'.

A feminist reader is then entitled to ask what there is to be gained by investing in any such thing.

3. *De quel lieu parler?*

In the space of the 'feminine' reading ('a fine grasp of detail, but lack of overview')[33] there are various ways of being faithful to the discourse of the other. There are the flattering commentaries, placing an admired text in the best possible light: but there are also understanding commentaries, eliciting details which the violence of hostile paraphrase must efface; and rather more sociably sympathetic ones, which try to turn the difficulties of a text to an occasion for courteous exchange. All are often described as 'dull'.

Le Doeuff points out that the 'feminine' receptivity of a certain style of student paper is institutionally undervalued – probably because the style *is* identified as 'feminine'. One could add that antifeminism in the metaphorics of reading goes well beyond the marking of examinations; and wonder about the phantasies of cutting-up, rupture, dislocating, forcing, and inducing unnatural birth which run through the aesthetics of postmodern theory, and the cult of 'creative' misreading. For the lovers of high-speed iconoclasm, the lowly labour of listening carefully to a text connotes the fussiness of housewife's psychosis.

In *L'Imaginaire philosophique*, Michèle Le Doeuff's readings make nonsense of such dichotomies. As attentive in their humour as they are irreverent in their precisions, the intricacy of the argumentation in these essays weaves a breadth and generosity in interpretation together with a great sensitivity to the slightest sign of a shifty move on the fine lines of a text. But as well as providing an example of another possible practice, in drawing attention to the 'phantasmagoria of the commentary' Le Doeuff provides a feminist reader with a way of asking what it is to read, critically, the work of other women.

For me, the most troubling questions about *L'Imaginaire philosophique* are provoked not by the movement of its method, but by a few faint suggestions in its language and a couple of major decisions on which its philosophical position depends.

It's curious, for example, that Le Doeuff's own metaphors construct the image as always *up to something*.[34] In her working hypothesis, the very presence of imagery in a text is a sign of something concealed – an *activity* of tensing, supporting, undermining. And in addition to the long list of philosophical funny business (which in '*En rouge dans la marge*' goes by the name of 'winking'), her preface speaks of 'the question that the image both settles and *dodges*', and of the image as the privileged site of 'evasions' (*dérobades*) and of dogmatism.

Of course this makes perfect sense. Le Doeuff's theme is the role which mistrust of the imaginary has played in philosophy's history; and given that history, it's quite logical to suspect that when a philosophical text breaks out in images, then there's probably something up. Le Doeuff does not simply repeat, by re-inscribing, the signs of that mistrust. Instead, her own texts are richly imagistic; and an operative distance from strictly philosophical suspicion is maintained throughout the book by methods adapted from psychoanalytic reading (of which it can never be said that the image does not do 'work').

But nor can it be said of psychoanalytic *theories* that their relationship to what they consitute as 'imaginary' – or Imaginary – is unambivalent, innocent of institutionalizing mistrust, or free from the projection of fabulous feminine figures. The problem here is not that Le Doeuff does draw on psychoanalysis, since there *are* no 'purified' methodological tools for thinking the feminine, except in the feminist imagination; since psychoanalysis is perfectly suited to her project of effecting displacements in philosophical discourse; and since she is as concerned to limit historically the significance and uses of psychoanalysis as she is to do so in relation to different philosophical discourses.

Rather, one might wonder whether the combination of Le Doeuff's maintenance of a philosophical position with her deployment of the language of psychoanalysis does not produce a kind of leakage of assumptions about the status of the imaginary as suspect, which works at times to transform her displacements from tradition into a procedure for looping back – moving away, yet returning to the same. The texts seem to offer women a *disturbance* relationship to philosophical discourse: when the book is read uninterruptedly cover to cover, the recurrence of themes of tension, neuralgia, 'tenderness' and pain is spectacularly insistent. There may be a delicate inscription there of the inevitable difficulties bound up by the desire to philosophize today; but what also emerges sporadically is an emblem of the sick body of Theory, to which women are so persuasively incited to maintain some kind of relationship. And it is at this point that Michèle Le Doeuff's own image of the woman-commentator as 'nurse' and 'healer of works' presents itself to speculation.

But it is the initial decision to argue for the maintenance of an activity one consents to call philosophical which (for me) raises the most diffi- cult questions – since this is probably the very issue which it is strictly impossible to 'argue' about at all. The question of naming is very important here, since it is all too easy to challenge feminist defections from philosophy on the grounds that it is impossible to leave – that to be 'outside' or 'elsewhere' is at best a dream, at worst a repetition of metaphysical nightmares.[35] For a feminist to refuse to inscribe her theoretical work as philosophical (or as 'rational') is something slightly different from pretending that a relationship to philosophy is thereby abandoned, avoided or destroyed; and it is certainly quite different from claiming to be unreasonable, from denouncing 'male logic', from running off on the flows and rediscovering Art. Instead, it is a decision to fix the sign Philosophy to a particular set of specific texts and prac- tices – and to leave it at that, for 'reasons' which Michèle Le Doeuff has been among the first to explore in detail.

That said, two questions arise. One is whether the wager proposed by Le Doeuff – that philosophy and reason may yet be salvaged from their respective and interlocking histories – does not place a little too much faith in the possibilities opened up by philosophical developments 'today'. It's difficult to interrogate *L'Imaginaire philosophique* very closely on this without reading, too much, between the lines. Le Doeuff's vision of a philosophy which would no longer be antifeminist is avowedly futuristic; and her texts quite properly and emphatically refrain from citing the work of contemporary philosophers as either signs or portents.

But it would not be abusive to suppose that among the conditions which make the Pascalian possibility seem feasible to Le Doeuff in

imagining philosophy's future, one might well include the history of
various reasoned critiques of Reason carried out since Marx. One could
then add that among recent French philosophies working in this direction (notably the work of Derrida and Deleuze, not to mention the
differently placed discourses of Lacan and Kristeva), we can find –
among a multitude of incompatibilities – a common interest in writing
philosophical discourse differently, which co-exists (in quite distinct
ways in each case) with a theoretical interest in the Woman Question.

It seems to me that a problem of faith arises when Le Doeuff chooses
to argue *towards* a position where these works *could* be cited as pointers
to a different philosophical future. For a feminist might equally well
begin by wondering why Woman – and, to a much lesser extent, women
– has achieved the status of a theoretically dignified problem; and why
some, though not all, of these thinkers privilege 'woman' or 'femininity' as
a signifier of both the problem of Truth, and Modernity (the dream of
an other discourse).[36] It is the conjunction, the 'and', which seems to be
important: and the same set of questions might well be put to the history
of modernist discourse in the arts. To choose to begin with these
questions – rather than with the equally reasonable question of the terms
on which it has been, is, and might be possible for women to philosophize – need not necessarily imply a different writing practice from that
developed by Michèle Le Doeuff. It can, I think, imply a different
(though not a 'more feminist') set of premises about the political import
of working with philosophy.

A debate between these positions (both of which, of course, the same
feminist(s) can occupy in different contexts) is probably irresolvable, for
the simple reason that it tends to take on the futility of an argument over
which term subsumes which term. For women working in the direction
suggested by Luce Irigaray's *Speculum*, for example, 'philosophical
discourse' could probably be equated with the practices of what Le
Doeuff calls the Corporation. While quite unsparing in her critique of
the corporate language, Le Doeuff herself would like to retain an open-
ended conception of philosophical *discourse*, both in the assessment of
the past (see, for instance, her distinction between 'disputes' and
'communiqués' in terms of the value each constructs for 'coherence' in
philosophy),[37] and in the prefiguring of tactics for the future.

The other question which concerns me is that throughout *L'Imaginaire philosophique*, the most explicit argument used to urge the practice of philosophy is in fact an argument by menace. To say that certain
feminisms of difference, for example, run the risk of reproducing the
schemas they presume they are renouncing, is to invoke the classically
philosophical threat of entrapment *by* philosophy for those who do not
pay heed. It would be excessive, as well as parasitic on Michèle Le

Doeuff's own arguments, to read in this a trace of the paternalism of reason. The problem is rather the accompanying absence of *other*, positive arguments for the value of philosophy to feminism.

Yet I have perhaps begun to construct a strong theoretical unity for a book which is, in fact, very far from being an apology for philosophy directed towards feminists. Nor is it simply a demonstration that it is possible to be a feminist in philosophy, combined with a philosophical critique of some directions in feminist theory. Certain passages in some of the texts do adopt each of these positions, but in a manner – and above all, with a mode of address – which is always determined by the particular theoretical and *institutional* context of each essay; and much of *L'Imaginaire philosophique* is not concerned with, or by, the argument that philosophy should be able to justify its political value to feminism.[38] Once again, in attempting to read *L'Imaginaire philosophique* from a position of partiality, one rediscovers the degree to which the book resists all efforts at totalization.

Besides, to construct general criticisms of Le Doeuff's scattered comments on feminism and philosophy may lead one to ignore what seems to me the most thought-provoking suggestion which can be *drawn out* of the book, and followed through to other work: namely, that the setting up of *general* 'positions' on the relations between femininity, rationality and philosophy, when conceived of as a general problem, may not always or necessarily matter very much.

This suggestion can be produced from (for example) the gap between the use of menace – entrapment by philosophy – to counter 'a' feminism of difference in 'Women and Philosophy', and the convincing precision of the argument in '*Les Chiasmes de Pierre Roussel*' that a historical relationship can be established on the one hand between *Système physique et morale de la femme*, and the position that sexual difference comes *before* other systems of discrimination; and, on the other hand, between *Système physique et morale de la femme*, and Evelyn Sullerot's presentation of the collective work, *Le Fait féminin*.[39]

The gap between the two texts by Le Doeuff is not one which can be bridged with a simple contrast organized by an abstract/concrete opposition, or by treating '*Les Chiasmes de Pierre Roussel*' as an extension (giving the 'evidence') of the earlier essay. Instead, it is a matter of a different procedure.

The passage in 'Women and Philosophy' works by invoking fear of contagion, as though the very mention of Comte and positivism suffices to demonstrate the dangers courted by ignorance of philosophy's history. '*Les Chiasmes de Pierre Roussel*' abandons the scenario of threat-in-general in favour of positive analysis of the circulation of different elements of a particular discourse. The relationship between

Roussel's text, the modern political discourse according absolute priority to sexual difference, and *Le Fait féminin* is not represented as a simple reiteration of identical propositions ('women really are really different from men'); and the two contemporary discourses on 'difference' are not treated as interchangeable, coextensive, or as symptomatic of all 'feminisms' of difference. Instead, Le Doeuff argues that Roussel's discourse and one particular radical feminist position share an image of the *feminine* (the 'pleasant reverie of a womanhood enclosed in itself'), dependent on a notion of the intrinsic determination specific to Woman: while the recurrence of the same image in *Le fait féminin* is analysed in terms of the history of the '*Doctoral*' imaginary in medical philosophy.

In *L'Imaginaire philosophique*, Le Doeuff disengages from the debate which assumes that some stable relationship between 'feminism' and 'philosophy' needs to be established (fixed as contestation *or* cooperation, refusal *or* practice). In analysing a particular case where *a* conjunction of feminist and philosophical discourses already operates politically, '*Les Chiasmes de Pierre Roussel*' moves towards posing a question which may be one of the most important results of her philosophical work:

> in what respect, if any, is the choice of this or that philosophical reference-point a decisive factor in feminist studies? Over the last few years we have been witnessing a certain philosophist inflation in the domain of theoretical productions. Thus, Luce Irigaray's books insist on the idea that, since it is philosophical discourse that lays down the law for all other discourses, the discourse of philosophy is the one that has first of all to be overthrown and disrupted. At a stroke, the main enemy comes to be idealist logic and the metaphysical *logos*. Simone de Beauvoir's book leaves me with the contrary impression, since, within a problematic as metaphysical as any, she is still able to reach conclusions about which the least one can say is that they have dynamised women's movements in Europe and America over the last thirty years.
>
> 'Operative Philosophy: Simone de Beauvoir and Existentialism', p. 48

Le Doeuff's essay on de Beauvoir is not included in *L'Imaginaire philosophique*. But in many ways the book can be read as a 'disengagement' of the methodological principles underpinning an essay which is one of the few feminist commentaries on *The Second Sex* to try to come to grips with that work as a productive political text, rather than an emanation from its author. Instead of effacing or excusing the existentialist substratum of the book, and instead of pursuing an imaginary knowledge of de Beauvoir the woman through a diagnosis of her texts, 'Operative Philosophy' more sensibly asks how de Beauvoir was able to produce the results she did from a particularly unpromising philoso-

phical position. There has been an oddly possessive/aggressive strain in
various judgements of de Beauvoir's work by feminists;[40] and the
relative novelty of Le Doeuff's specific set of concerns – how to work as
a feminist in philosophy, and how to utilize philosophy as a feminist –
can provide methods of posing questions *politically* which might well be
of interest to feminists working in quite different theoretical contexts.

Above all, the notion of 'operative' philosophy implies that the
response to the question of philosophical reference-points in feminist
studies must always be *variable* (though not indifferent: as well as stressing the drawbacks of the existentialist referential in *The Second Sex*, Le
Doeuff comes to quite different conclusions in the case of de Beauvoir
from those that she draws in her study of Roussel).

This may – and should – seem obvious. But one of the side-effects of
some discourses of feminine/female difference in recent years has been,
ironically enough, a *fixing* of 'positions' on philosophy. The difficulty
with this is not that such fixations repeat the structure of certain
philosophical (and psychoanalytic) propositions. It's rather that they
bring about an immediate loss of political (and rhetorical) flexibility for
feminist interventions in different institutional and discursive contexts.
Whether signing allegiance to the feminine writing of Hélène Cixous, or
the a-mazing grace of Mary Daly's bio-rhythms, there is little of the
famous feminine fluidity to be found in perpetual re-inscriptions of the
same hard line. Or in other words: there is little to be gained from
projects to disrupt the discourse of philosophy by inscribing difference if
and when such a project comes down to reiterating a single, fundamental thesis held to be always usefully true of all philosophy ('it's
phallogocentric ...') – and to countering philosophical discourse by
maintaining, from place to place and text to text, the rigidity of a 'different' *style*.

Whether Luce Irigaray's work can be described in these (anecdotal)
terms of mine, and whether Le Doeuff's summary account of the theme
of her books is a just and accurate one, seems to me another matter
entirely.[41] But by raising the case of de Beauvoir against an idea of the
main enemy as idealist logic and the metaphysical *logos*, Le Doeuff's
essay is doing something more than contesting a generalization. In
tracing the steps by which de Beauvoir transformed the existentialist
problematic – transposing it from the status of a system to that of '*a
point of view* oriented to a theoretical intent by being trained on *a* determinate and partial field of experience' – 'Operative Philosophy' also
shows how de Beauvoir was able to eliminate the need for the famous
'holes and slime' imagery on which the Sartrean metaphysic depends. It
points to at least one case where a particular philosophy has been
modified by a political project in a manner which has, in fact,

demolished that philosophy's spectacularly misogynist imaginary – with gains to feminism which can only be described as considerable. This is not to say that Le Doeuff proposes to read prescriptions for future practice in the method of *The Second Sex*: but that her own method of reading draws attention to the importance of asking how philosophical discourses can *work* in particular contexts, rather than debating their (imagined) intrinsic *worth*.

PART II

4

Indigestion: A Rhetoric of Reviewing

This article is a revised version of a paper given at a Sydney Film Festival forum on film criticism in 1982. In that context, it had two aims. One was to challenge the overpowering conviction expressed at the dead end of most such forums that reviewing is merely a matter of 'personal taste'. The other was to suggest that while theorizations of reading and writing have to some extent transformed the study of cinema, literature, philosophy and art, many of the humbler practices of a mass media culture (like reviewing) have not been seriously re-examined but left in the limbo of the 'personal intention'. Today, it seems to me that a critique of explanation via the 'personal' can be as difficult to defend in broad public debate as ever it was: partly because the simulacra of 'new subjectivity' and 'neo-humanism' now offer a mirage of relief to critics after a phase of theory fetishism; partly because academically situated cultural theorists have still paid little attention to either the material constraints on production of meaning in mass media practices, or the 'theories' of practice that circulate between media producers and consumers alike.

So the aim of this article now is to take seriously one such theory (the 'gut reaction' thesis), and criticize it in relation to the everyday conduct of 'reviewing' as a mode of work. Therefore the article does not in itself constitute a re-examination of reviewing, but I hope that it does suggest some questions from which one might depart.

The Critical Anatomy

I'd like to begin by questioning a curious metaphor that has been disgorged at a couple of film festival sessions I've attended in the past on criticism. On those occasions, when an assortment of Sydney critics was asked to describe criteria for 'judging' films, each time most of us fell back sooner or later on a notion of Gut Reaction. The scenario should be familiar: the critic on the spot shrugs, mutters about the diversity of films in the world, the straitjacket of 'standards', the scarcity of time, the delusions of objectivity – and then announces, modestly or triumphantly, 'I just depend on my gut reaction'.

This common chorus (which partakes of the same anonymity shared by those thousands of artists who all line up to intone in unison 'I just make very personal work') does not subsume everybody all the time. John Hinde, for example, has always been prepared to discuss problems of critical values and critical responsibility.[1] But on the whole, most of us have found refuge in this one basic trope for the convulsions of our subjectivity: gulp it down, chew it over, throw it up.

At which point, somone in the audience always says, 'Well, what makes your gut reaction so much better than mine?'. Since few Australian critics have so far felt willing or able to do what American film writers usually do on such occasions – namely, go ahead and *tell* the audience why they think that their critical subjectivity is more qualified to judge than another sort might be – the debate then hiccoughs away into a silence ruptured only by the odd gurgle of disgust.

I don't think that the Australians' refusal to indulge in a grading of gut reactions should in itself be a cause for complaint, but I do think that these stagings of an inability to articulate some principles of a critical practice is symptomatic of a certain malaise about how reviewing works in Australia. For there are a number of possible responses to this recurrent question of 'criteria' which do not require resort to some transcendant – and irrefutable – intestinal principle.

One could, for example, argue that the initial question about criteria is inappropriate, and therefore unanswerable, in the first place – since films in circulation impose expectations on critics (and on audiences) as well as the reverse. One could also argue (and I will later) that media criticism and reviewing are not, essentially, activities of judgement or evaluation at all. Or one could say that the question of criteria can never be answered in general terms and in advance, but only in relation to, and after, specific evaluations of particular films.

However, one problem with that last response would be that the inability to articulate values has not only bedevilled the film criticism forums – but also the annual agony of the forum on the Greater Union Awards.[2] There we have a clear use of an activity of judgement, rather than of reviewing or criticism, and an equally clear case of a set of particular films which have been judged. Yet at most festivals there has been a noticeable difference between the pinched and furtive speech of the Australian judges (if they turn up at all), and the relative plenitude of critical assurance assumed by the overseas judges of the Mamoulian Award.

So one *could* connect the gut-reaction coyness of the critics with the timid or nonchalant vagueness of the judges, and then do one of at least two things. One would be to rebuke the 'Australian' practices in terms of an opposition with those of 'overseas': unkindly, by suggesting that the locals are bumbling, incompetent amateurs, or kindly, by pointing to the relative lack of credit accorded to critical activity by Australian culture in general. This strategy of rebuke is used, for example, in David Stratton's book *The Last New Wave* – and I don't think it tells us very much, since it reinforces that dubious logic whereby Australians are found wanting in comparison with the overseas, simply by virtue of their national origin.[3]

Another possibility would be to claim that the problem is not one of confidence and quality in judgement, but one of understanding and possibly changing the protocol of public speech: that what is at stake is not the competence of speakers, but the significance of the act of speaking; and that here, as in other areas of cultural politics, a history might be written. After all, there must be some powerful tradition at work when groups ritualistically submit (and not only at festival forums) to the torture of bunging a few people on a stage, insisting that there need be no formality or preparation, listening to most of the people spend half their time announcing that they have nothing much to say, and then finding that through lack of preparation and of something to say, nothing, in fact and informally, is said.

But rather than pursue these mysteries, I want to return to the Gut Reaction to try to squeeze a bit more sense from the metaphor – from the image of subjectivity convulsed. I think that the Gut Reaction is, in fact, a rubric for a theory of criticism – even if the metaphor itself operates to conjure up some dark domain of interiority immune to theorization. It's a romantic theory, it's an expressive theory, and to the extent that it allows for debate about whether a critic can or cannot accurately 'describe' (like a nineteenth-century novelist) what's sometimes called the 'surface' or the 'detail' of a film, it's a realist theory.

In brute form, however, it goes like this: the critic goes along to a film as either representative or uniquely idiosyncratic consumer, tests out the quality of the product by monitoring his or her immediate taste sensations, then expresses the experience in the form of a review.

Someone might object here that I'm using the term 'critic' to dignify the activities of mere reviewers – a different species from critics, and to whom alone the Gut Reaction thesis might apply. Thus an old, but classic, polemic from the self-styled critic John Simon:

Reviewing is something that newspaper editors have invented: it stems from the notion that the critic is someone who must see with the eyes of the

Average Man or Typical Reader (whoever that is) and predict for his fellows
what their reaction will be. To this end, the newspapers carefully screen their
reviewers to be representative common men, say, former obituary writers or
mail-room clerks, anything but trained specialists. To accept such a reviewer
as critic and guide is like expecting school children to teach one another, or
patients in a hospital ward to undertake one another's cure.[4]

There is much to object to in Simon's formulation; not least, the
equation of the film public with children and sick people in need of a
teacherly, doctorly critic – and, indeed, the suggestion that children and
patients can't help each other without interference from 'authority'.

But Simon is one of the American critics prepared to say what
qualifies a 'critical' subjectivity in its difference from that of the Average
Man (sic); and it's clear that for Simon, the critic is distinguished by His
status as *intellectual superhero* – artist, teacher, philosopher, someone
'very, very intelligent'.[5] The reviewer is vulgar, untrained and (by implication) very, very dumb.

Now in the 1950s and early 1960s there were quite lively debates
about a distinction between criticism and reviewing (which later died
down in the assiduous casualness of the late 1960s and early 1970s).
Most of these were also structured, or crossed, by equally polemical
distinctions between 'the cinema' and 'the movies', Art and Industry,
Culture and Entertainment. Simon is very much a criticism/cinema/
Art/Culture man.

But if one turns to the work of Pauline Kael, whose position in that
period might be to some extent described as veering towards that of a
reviewing/movies/Industry/Entertainment woman – though not, of
course, an anti-intellectual one – it seems that the whole debate was in
fact worked out *within* the terms of the Gut Reaction theory. Thus, Kael
on Bazin might be Simon on Simon:

> I rather imagine Bazin's stature as a critic has less to do with 'universals' than
> with intelligence, knowledge, experience, sensitivity, perception, fervour,
> imagination, dedication, lucidity.[6]

Whatever their differences, both these writers are engaged in a process
of listing the special psychological and biographical (i.e. social) characteristics which constitute the critic as a certain kind of *person*. Criticism,
in this logic, is not a particular practice but a sort of byproduct or after-
effect of pure person-ality. Both Simon and Kael distinguish The Critic
from the Average Man/Reviewer by virtue of the former's *superior* Gut
Reaction. The Critical gut is more trained ('experience', 'knowledge').
Critics have a finer palate and, presumably, they bring up better prose.

Both share, in fact, the same theory of reviewing as the newspaper editors they despise. For if one stretches Simon's formulation a little further, it becomes easy to see the figures of The Reviewer and The Critic as metonyms of an (imagined) social group. The brute gut of The Reviewer is the emblem of the Average Man, who convulses for The General Public. The trained gut (or 'sensibility' in this code) of The Critic stands for the general figure of The Intellectual – who quivers, chews things over, and emits for that *part* of 'the public' imagined as, say, 'informed lovers of the arts'.

The classical criticism/reviewing debate simply offered only a choice of populist and elitist versions of the *same model* – one which worked to generate a fantasy of audience 'bodies' in an 'organic' society. (The only procedural difference would be that professional guts are supposed to predict the reactions of the general body, while professional sensibilities attempt to shape the growth of the select.) It is thus entirely logical that the aggressively populist intellectuals working in the organo-cosmic ambience of the late 1960s should have collapsed the choice of versions and refused to bother with a criticism/reviewing distinction, leaving the schema with only two terms – the *my gut/a public* of the Modest Person, or the *my gut/the public* of the Megalomaniac.

Here and now, it's probably easy to dismiss these accounts as quaint. Yet the person-ality cult is still active: not only amongst critics them- selves, but in the anti-critical rebellion of the 'personal response' that we hear about every year when the argument gets tricky. People say that all judgements (and, they assume, by extension all criticisms) are 'just personal': if the social organism is made up of a lot of personal bodies who all react in their unique personal ways, then it is clearly more democratic to have a large body of persons all having personal gut reactions to films (whistling, cheering or booing to 'express' them), than it is to have a small body of judges or critics doing that same personal thing. The political logic of that is impeccable, and I'm not concerned to contest it. I simply want to object to the point of departure for the entire argument, and to its effects.

Those effects are, firstly, to mesmerize us with an infinitely regressive mirror exchange between an audience confronting critics who have nothing to affirm but their status as persons, and critics confronting an audience which has also nothing to affirm but its (pluralized) personal status: and secondly – *by means of that mesmerization* – to obliterate any possibility of public speech about the competing social, economic and political investments at stake in a situation where some people are PAID for their gut reactions while others are not, and in which various desires, demands and imperatives about what 'good' Australian short film looks like, or should look like, circulate silently through the elimination process known as 'judging'. After all, when we all agree that we're all 'just' persons, there is really no basis for disagreement ... We're all always already on the same old human side.

Thus the point of departure – the Gut Reaction – is perfectly geared to disguise the fact that a great deal has changed since the time when it might have been sufficient to celebrate the mere making of films in Australia as a miracle in and for itself; and to protect critics and judges from criticism and judgement, with the full complicity of those film-makers and film-goers who – in the guise of questioning critics and judges – simply rabbit on with that very same personalist rhetoric which always provides its own response: 'You claim to be a critic but you're only one person.' 'Yes, that's right, I'm only a person so I like what I like.' They have an interest in doing so, of course, for the rhetoric is reversible – and can, in turn, protect their own work as filmmakers or as film audience members from any demand for critical intelligence.

The Personal and the Printed

There are at least two elements of professional (i.e. paid) critical activity which the Gut Reaction theory conveniently elides. One is cultural *politics*: and in ignoring this, the Gut Reaction is always a defence of the current regime, even if it takes the form of a burp from the margins. The other is the politics of *discourse* (critics write and/or speak): and in ignoring this – by, say, accusing critics of 'being' frustrated film-makers – Gut Reactors exempt us from ever examining what critics actually do, or what criticism does.

Politics

1. To rework a cliché: commentaries on films are not just personal, they're political. This is not to argue that the 'personal' does not exist, nor is it to argue that the personal is not political. But it is to argue that the political is not *only* personal – it's social and it's cultural. It defines points of conflict.

Where the 'personal' can only be stated or shared (in the twin states of catatonia and empathy), the political can be debated, discussed, fought over – and is thereby open to the possibility, at least, of change. It is only when all criticism (and not just that which signifies itself as 'feminist', 'marxist', etc.) is seen as political, that one can talk sensibly about changing criticism, and about using criticism to change something other than itself – even if the change desired is something as small-scale and difficult as an improvement in the conditions in which film-makers

make, and above all screen, their films. For in citing 'politics' – an
unfashionable value in an age of corporatist consensus and of guerilla
entrepreneurial chic – I am not dreaming of Winter Palaces or of a
correctness in 'lines'; but of a recognition that in a society where criticism can be a wage-earning activity, economic and ideological interests
are always at stake.

An Australian film director once told me that I was an ideologue, and
I'm quite happy to accept that description – as long as it's understood
that I think that's exactly what all reviewers, and most critics, are. It
seems to me to be nostalgically preindustrial nonsense to conceive of a
bunch of cultivated souls sitting round mulling over the Good, the
Beautiful and the True for the sheer love of aesthetic play, and for the
good of their own, aristocratically homogeneous, ruling class. In the
heterogeneity of a postindustrial culture, reviewers of film are not
arbiters of taste, or judges, or even representative consumers, but
mercenaries in the stabilizing force of the Thought Police. We do not
decree what should be thought about any particular *film*; but we do help
to patrol the limits of what is safely *or* adventurously think-able as
cinema at any given time.

2. If the social role of reviewing is something that the Gut Reaction
theory does not describe, my second objection concerns something that I
think it cannot describe – namely, what goes on between the gut, or the
sensibility, and the printed page?

Film reviews, I'd suggest, are not made of shreds of stomach lining,
bits of sensibility, or even of frustrated urges to make films. They are
made of words, sentences, paragraphing, headlines, layout, rhetorical
strategies, generic plays, reference procedures and fictional personae ('I'
the writer, 'you' the reader, 'him/her/them' the filmmakers, 'it' the film)
– and of the constraints imposed in and by the economics of various
media.

This is, or ought to be, ludicrously obvious. But in a large pile of
American and British film criticism that I read while preparing this
paper, I was only able to find two references to the fact that film reviewing is a practice of writing – or, at least, only two that were at all
specific.[7] Other references to the language of criticism were rather of the
order of general attempts to establish criticism as an 'art', or as a minor
branch of 'literature'. Whatever one thinks of such attempts (I find them
anachronistically self-defeating), the point is that they are only
concerned with the intellectual *status* of criticism, not with an analysis of
critical writing *activities*.

Criticism, I suggest, is not a matter of 'being' but of 'doing' – and of
different kinds of doing at that. It is not a person-ality problem, but a

practice. So if a discussion of film criticism in Australia is to advance beyond the level of the question 'Why didn't you (they) like my (this) film?' – a question which really deserves the resounding response DUNNO – then analyses need to be based not on the gurgling of guts but on the assumption that all criticism, right down to and especially that least literary and most formal of activities, the three-line consumer guide, is writing. This is not to call for some aesthetics of criticism whereby one could distinguish 'good' from 'bad' critical writing; but it is to claim that no understanding of the general social function of film criticism, and no intervention within or against it, is possible without an exact understanding of how it works, and what sort of work it is.

If an analysis began from that assumption, then several cherished postures about criticism would have to be abandoned – or, at least, revised. It would no longer be automatically clear at the outset, for example, whether – or how – criticism should so easily be distinguished from other signifying practices, and whether 'criticism' could be usefully conceived of as a single entity at all. And notions of censorship – all too often stuck in the 'blue pencil' conspiracy thesis about editorial inter-ference – would have to be considerably refined.

Censorship

People often ask critics 'are you able to write what you think?' I can only reply that I am not – because I do not 'think' in 500-word slices of *Sydney Morning Herald* prose, nor in 1,000 word slices of *Australian Financial Review* prose. This is not only to point, pedantically perhaps, to the absolute non-fit between 'thought' and the verbal which is the fundamental condition of all language. Whatever I 'think' about any given film usually exceeds (but occasionally falls short of) what can effectively be said using the space and the codes available in any given context. What should follow from this is NOT an image of the poor embattled critic struggling apologetically against the harsh limitations imposed by nasty newspaper magnates – but rather an axiom that the politics of a review will consist in selections made and combinations effected (of 'topics', of modes of address, of vocabulary, of contexts for reading the film, etc.). It will also thus consist in what has *not* been said – but might have been.

It's true that the 'writing what you think' question is really an inquiry about conscious interference by another person, or by house rules, and deserves an answer. I think that instances of directly political censorship (say, via pressures from advertisers) are quite rare in the insignificant and relatively non-sensitive area of arts commentary: not only because newspaper policies are much less monolithic and much more subtle than lefties like to think, but because 1) anyone who can keep a job reviewing does so because they are already willing and able to keep all the unwritten rules about what does and does not constitute an appropriate 'style' for any given publication, and; 2) because apart from clearly defined problem-points like defamation, 99.9 per cent of 'editing' decisions (again, speaking only of arts commentary) are made for reasons of space and layout design.

This means that the 'edited' writer can never be sure why a particular paragraph is cut out. It could be that it formed the right-sized chunk (i.e., purely formal criteria), or because the editor judged it *more* redundant than other paragraphs (semantic-aesthetic criteria), or because it is judged 'less interesting', 'less important', 'less essential' (an interpretative decision about both the structure of the text, and the likely interests of readers). In the latter case, *interesting, important* and *essential* are all names for ideological decisions referring not just to the personal tastes of the editor but to a professional consensus about 'what really matters' when writing about film for the audience of that publication. That consensus is a cultural one: at the moment, for example, we have the assumption that matters of cinematography are somehow more technical and less essential than those of plot – so one's token paragraph about camera angles, or lighting, is most likely to be up for the chop.[8]

I'm not convinced that 'censorship' is an appropriate term for this process. Firstly, because the process itself is too random and irrational in practice to carry the weight of systematic intention implied by that term; and secondly, because it exempts the critic from the complicity in helping to define 'what really matters' which is a condition of one's own activity. For example, what if the cinematography paragraph were not token? How long would someone last writing 1,000 words a week about zooms and pans? Who knows – and who has tried? But whether this is censorship or something more subtle, it's clear that the editorial and critical administration of the limits of much of what can be said about cinema is, broadly speaking, political (and thus open to the kind of change which consists in producing *different* limits); and that it is exercised not in the gastric juices, but in the fine print on the page.

Authorship

If considering film criticism as writing could lead us to rethink some aspects of censorship (and thus of the cultural role of reviewing as censor-*ing* rather than censored), then it would also require a revision of the Authorship principle often assumed by people who ask critics to account for or defend 'their' opinions.

Newspaper and magazine reviewing operates between the poles of a flagrant contradiction. On the one hand, critics tend to develop – and occasionally, they are encouraged to develop – a *persona*. They are not exactly stars in Australia, even in cultural hanger-on circles. But they do, in the reiteration of certain tastes and values, or in the repetition over time of certain pet clichés, favoured syntactic structures, rhythms, jokes, didactic obsessions etc., produce an effect of Identity which is sometimes taken to be that of an Authorial Voice. This tendency is intensified by the regular (i.e. potentially mechanical) nature of the job, and by the principle that the faster you write the more you earn by the hour: both of which can encourage reliance on tried and trusty formulas for producing a mirage of one's own presence in the text.

Yet reviewers are quite clearly not Authors in the traditional literary sense. The production of the meaning of a review is a collaborative process – even without taking into account the role of the reader. Not only do the editing procedures mentioned above work to modify or sometimes change a text which nevertheless still bears one's name (occasionally with embarrassing or disastrous consequences), but other factors such as rewriting, hidden typographical error, the cropping of accompanying photos and – above all – headlines, can all converge at random to inflect what is said several degrees away from whatever it was that one 'meant' to say. Headlines, in particular, are crucial (I have never written my own). They can often accidentally or even deliberately contradict the text, and they *always* interpret it – so if one can assume that many readers simply read the headline, the first paragraph and the last, then one can also assume that what they think you think bears little relation to what you said. Or later, to any memory you might have of having said anything at all: for the ultimate stage of the reviewing process is achieved when a few words or phrases float off for endless recycling in publicity material, 'signed' by one's proper name or simply that of the newspaper in which they first appeared. The review as *quoted* object is a collectively, institutionally produced, and perfectly depersonalized text. Indeed, it's not far-fetched to argue that a reviewer's main commercial function is merely to supply resource material to advertising copy-writers, and to lend a name for author-effect – a name which can become interchangeable with that of a media 'source' of authority ('"*See this film!*" – *Sydney Morning Herald*').

I'd want to make two points about this contradiction. One is that it should in no way be seen as constituting an excuse for *reviewers*. Because I am not interested in critics as Persons, I am not saying that these occupational details constitute 'difficulties' for which sympathetic readers should make allowance. On the contrary, I think the contradiction is constitutive of *reviewing*: it is positive, in the sense that it helps to define what reviewing actually is as an activity in Australia at the moment.

The second point follows from this. If reviewing is a non-authorial activity which nevertheless produces a persona-effect – for example, the effect of '*a bit of your Meaghan Morris type stuff*', as Geoff Burrowes once put it[9] – then it might be more useful for critics of reviewing to consider it as a process of constructing not Authors, but fictional characters. Or rather, fictional stereotypes – emblematically 'personal' figures conforming to, and thus exemplary of, a limited set of conventions defining currently acceptable modes of speaking about (in this case) film. Some examples might be: the bush philosopher ('I know a thing or two, but I learned it at the school of hard knocks'); the breathless enthusiast (loves-loves-loves the Movies); the no-bullshit hard-nose ('I know a bit of crap when I see it'); the tough feminist, the passionately purple poet, the judicious weigher of pros and cons and, yes, the male or female Average Man – that most presumptuously imperialist of figures, which symbolically incorporates the entire population in its own aggressive display of self-deprecation.

One could go on. But I should stress that the point of scrutinizing reviews in this manner would not be to better 'understand' or attack individual critics – which would hardly be worth so much work – nor even to examine the function of reviewing as an isolated phenomenon of our culture. The point is rather that newspaper and magazine reviewing is an activity carried out at a site of intersection of *several* cultural practices and institutions: the media, the 'arts', the film industry, advertising, propaganda, the academy, promotion and marketing. Consequently, the fictional stereotypes of reviewing not only tell us something about the 'state' of film criticism in Australia. They also tell us something about prevailing modes of normalizing knowledge and 'opinion', fixing conventions of what is 'appropriate' for whom to say what about what and how, in our culture at large.

Here is an obvious (indeed blatant, therefore trivial) example of the intertwinings of persona-production and censor*ing* taken from my own practice. Writing about some scenes of men talking about how men talk about women in the Australian film *Yakkety Yak* (*Sydney Morning Herald*, 13 September 1980), I came up with the following:

> Still, more learned friends of mine tell me that European philosophers now have a name for that too. It's called phallogocentricity.
>
> That's hard to pronounce but – like *Yakkety Yak* – it's fun to try if you're in the mood.

I do not know what would have happened had I written this instead:

Yakkety Yak thus presents us with an interesting study in what the philosopher Jacques Derrida has termed 'phallogocentricity'.

I don't know whether it would have been published or not – very likely it would have been. I only know that it never occured to me to try.

The difference between the two versions is not one of the difficulty or abstractness of words (and 'phallogocentricity' was defined, albeit shonkily, in the published review). The difference is in an enunciative shift from a speaking position which gives responsibility for a bit of knowledge to a third party ('they tell me, and I pass it on to you') to one in which the speaker admits to knowledge ('I tell you').

Clearly, my choice of the former rather than the latter had nothing to do with my gut reaction to *Yakkety Yak* (yes, I liked the film). Retrospectively, I imagine that what I was trying to do was simultaneously make the film sound quirky but attractive to that vague 'general public' whom reviewers vaguely imagine they address ('fun to try if you're in the mood'), and also use a trigger-term immediately identifiable to particular people interested in, say, film theory, and to whom I thought the film would be of special interest ('phallogocentricity').

But in fusing those two 'you's in the way I did, I automatically fell back on the persona of film critic as Middle-Brow, bumbling cheerfully yet untainted through the perils of Learning ('more learned *friends* of mine tell me') – keeping a cool head, irreverence and that precious Common Sense. This is one of the most widespread and poisonous of media-intellectual tricks: knowledge is flaunted and yet denied, wielded and yet apparently neutralized by the simple expedient of admitting ideas *only* on condition that they be attributed to someone else, who is then made to seem slightly comic. Thus is theory rendered ridiculous, yet maintained as the province of the few; and thus – in an 'automatic' decision that it would be inappropriate for a film reviewer to write in a daily paper as a closet Derrida reader – is ideology reproduced.

Criticism/Reviewing

So far I have been using the terms 'criticism' and 'reviewing' more or less interchangeably. I have also been discussing both at a level of generality which would make most of my remarks applicable to arts commentary in general, and possibly to wine, cheese, or football reviews as well.

I think that there are good reasons for beginning with generalities, because one of the things I wish to contest is the idea that film criticism/ reviewing is a single entity defined by the 'IT' to which it refers – i.e.

'film'. In order to pursue this (and to define one specific activity which it will then be possible to examine in relation to the film industry), I would like to suggest that it is, in fact, useful to make a distinction between criticism and reviewing.

There are two established ways of distinguishing criticism from reviewing without setting up an opposition between intelligent Persons and dumb ones, good writers and bad, or between superior and inferior versions of the same thing. I first heard both of them from John Flaus (who is not, however, responsible for what I make of them).[10]

1. If all film production ceased tomorrow, criticism would continue but reviewing would not.
I'm not sure that this is true, insofar as film reviewing could continue for as long as films were shown. One would simply review what was on at the 'museum' or 'gallery' (or TV), much as art critics can review travelling Masterpiece shows. However, that very shift of venue – and thus of the social significance of what one was promoting and of the act of promoting it – suggests that it is plausible to make a distinction in what would be, roughly, socio-economic terms.

It isn't just that reviewing is directly 'dependent' on the day-to-day functioning of the film industry to a degree that criticism (a practice that can ignore release dates, efface the difference between commercial distributors and libraries or archives, and produce a range of referents – e.g. films – unconstrained by problems of print availability, etc.) is not.

It's also that reviewing, unlike criticism, is *necessarily* involved in the production of Novelty, of Here-and-Nowness, which characterizes both the film industry and the media within which reviewing is inscribed. This is not to say that criticism is not constrained by the Here-and-Now: obviously, a book about Longford and a book about the *Star Wars* cycle are equally books about, and for, the time in which they are written rather than the time about which they write. But reviewing is consecrated to producing an infinite, repetitive series of *concrete novel events* – a new video 'this month', a Longford season 'this week', a *Star Wars* release 'today'.

It thus participates directly in at least two of the key processes of postindustrial capitalism: it helps to produce and regulate desire for new and (strictly speaking) unnecessary products; and it contributes to the media's unceasing reconstitution of the present in the image of what the Present really is (c.f. Schlöndorff's *Circle of Deceit* on the Western media's construction of the Middle East as 'news' site).

Criticism may be caught up in and by these processes, but it does not necessarily derive from them. Reviewing does. This is why, although individual films and film-makers may not 'need' reviewers, the cinema as a capitalist institution needs reviewing as a practice. This is also why television 're-viewing' (snippeted glimpses of the What's-On of the Here-and-Now) is currently in the forefront of the business since it has laid the ghost of Aesthetic Judgement which still haunts much news-paper reviewing, and which marks it as a survivor of an older economy.

2. Reviewing assumes that the reader hasn't seen the film; criticism assumes that the reader has, will or should have seen the film.
I think that this distinction – a rhetorical one, distinguishing different techniques of persuasion, reference procedures, and modes of inscribing desire – could easily be derived from the first. If reviewing produces desire in and for Here-and-Nowness, then it does so in part by (for example) imitating the narrative mechanism of *mystery*: the 'plot outline' which takes up one-third to two-thirds of the vast bulk of reviews, and in which the ending is usually either withheld or teasingly flaunted, acts as the posing of a problem to which seeing or not seeing the film becomes the solution.

This is a point which should be expanded. It's interesting, for example, that reviewers who tend not to specialize in plain, neutral, obedient plot summary also tend to specialize in what comes very close to Authorial prose. It is the persona-effect that becomes, in a sense, the obscure object of desire ('What's X got to say this week?') – and the mystery, the joke, and the pleasure can be the problem of the relation, or nonrelation, between film and review.[11]

However, I'd like to confine myself here to pointing out that this difference of aspect between criticism and reviewing – the former refers to the film retrospectively while the latter refers prospectively – can be used to define a fundamental difference in the way criticism and review-ing respectively construct their object FILM – a difference in the 'it' to which they refer.

The object 'film' defined in and by reviewing is necessarily incom-plete, partial, veiled. Criticism, on the other hand, *may* (though not must) speak of a film as though it were finished, whole and – thanks perhaps to the very operation of criticism – now revealed in all its inexhaustible fullness. The IT of criticism *may* be a closed structure; potentially, at least, it has a beginning, a middle and an end (though not necessarily in that order). The IT of reviewing *can only be* an open structure – the ending is suspended, deferred – or an *ad hoc* series of items.

In practical terms, one could argue that this explains one of the famous 'inadequacies' of Australian reviewing, and allows us to see it rather as a defining-problem of reviewing – the inability to 'do justice', as film-makers say, to the 'complete project' of a film. Quite simply, the object predicated by reviewing is never complete. Quite crudely, it also follows that if you can't/don't reveal the ending then you can't discuss structure, and if you can't discuss structure then it is practically impossible to admit the concept of double or contradictory readings.

The weakness of the retrospective/prospective distinction is that it is too pure, and flagrantly conventional. (Reviewers can and do give away endings, etc., though often to a howl of protest from readers.)

As I have used it here, it also depends fairly strongly, though not entirely, on an assumption that narrative film is the normal object of reviewing. This is not an unreasonable assumption, since reviewing usually colludes with industrial cinema in upholding that 'norm' – if only by relegating documentary and experimental work to a lower priority in the choice of what one writes about. It might also be a useful assumption: since a complicity between industrial narrative cinema and reviewing's production of desire might help to explain why most reviews of, say, documentary or non-narrative experimental work, usually manage – whatever the writer's intentions – to signify *themselves* (let alone the film) as boring, dutiful, routine.

But if it is 'only' a convention that reviewing is prospective in orientation, defining the what-you-are-about-to-see, then it's clear that such conventions are open to change to some extent. And it is in this sense that it might be a properly political task for writers to undermine reviewing with criticism, for example, or to do the opposite and push the partiality of reviewing to more radical limits.

However I would like to propose two further working definitions of reviewing, differentiating it from criticism on formal and technical grounds – in order to specify more clearly what *kinds* of limits are at stake, and therefore what kinds of 'politics' may be involved.

3. Reviewing is a signifying practice in which pre-existing formal constraints are primary and determining.

What distinguishes writing for a magazine like *Filmnews* from writing for the *Sydney Morning Herald* is not that the former gives the liberty to 'say what you think' while the latter doesn't. It is that when writing for *Filmnews* one is able to invent an appropriate form (with the qualification, of course, that it is never possible to say everything in every possible way in any publication). One can't write a 40,000 word article, perhaps, but one can use greatly varying lengths, paragraph sizes, sentence constructions, styles. One can write essays with all sorts of different structures, divisions, spacings. One can, therefore, simultaneously think form and substance. That simultaneity currently constitutes criticism (of whatever quality).

When writing for the *Sydney Morning Herald* or any other mass-market newspaper (and exceptions would merely revert to the *Filmnews* model), one cannot normally invent a form. One plays with an already given genre (the 'review') and a set of rules with a very limited range for flexibility and variation. The content of those rules will vary from paper to paper, house to house ('no oxymorons here!' a friend of mine was once told); but they will always be present as every writer's point of departure, and they will constrain the kinds of meanings, and the kinds of representation of film, that are possible in a particular context at any given time.[12]

Three examples must suffice.

Space: a set of priorities about what to include (and therefore what to exclude) will develop according to whether one's normal allocated space is four inches, eight inches, ten ... In this context, for example, I think that people's complaints about the absence of cinematographic analysis in reviews are deliriously misplaced; for unless one *did* go to the radical extreme of writing about nothing else, the function of a half-inch or so on the subject is simply to signify *the reviewer's* technical competence – and thus help construct his or her persona.

Semantics: if there is vocabulary control exerted in arts commentary, I think it has as much to do with the visual properties of long and Latinate words in newspaper columns as it has to do with ideologies of the Average Reader – or rather, the two things help to produce each other. Too many long words wreck the look (i.e. the readability, especially when standing in trains and buses) of the column as they spill over the edge and swallow up whole lines, while too many Latinisms clump together in blobs that signify themselves as abstract, even if the words themselves are quite common (e.g. 'construct in order to locate' *v.* 'set up so as to find').

This visual play-off between the columns and the words is one of the sources of the humour that newspapers can create from apparently pompous or 'academic' speech – much of which would be perfectly clear if laid out across a full page, and properly punctuated (few papers, in my experience, will use a semi-colon or a colon). It is also one reason for the exclusion of most technical terms from reviewing, and for a certain preference for the Straight Talk posture. While a *spade* may, at a pinch and for author-effect, become a *bloody shovel*, it's just too LONG to call it a *gardening implement*.

Paragraphs: like the words, most of these are very short – two sentences at most, or sometimes three at the outside. This in turn limits the possibilities in sentence construction; so that on the whole, one cannot carry more than one dependent clause. (One breaks this rule at the risk of sticking out like a sore thumb visually from the rest of the page, thus finding oneself cast in the role of Breathless Enthusiast, Purple Proser, etc.)

And this, in turn, means that reviewing tends to be an abrasively *assertive* mode of discourse – tick, cross, wham, bam – or an *exclamatory* one (gee whiz, wowie zowie, gasp, sigh, yuk). For without either a more complex clausal structure *or* a generously stretchable space, it is very difficult to introduce nuance, qualification, or the civilized right to contradict oneself.

I stress once again that this is not a matter for apologetic. It is not to say 'we poor reviewers do our best, despite those nasty insensitive subs'. It is to say that if reviewing differs from criticism it is not a matter of one's Personal tastes and abilities, since the same person may practise both. It is because reviewing, unlike criticism, is currently set up as a *formalist activity* – just like sonnet writing, acrostics, crossword puzzles, or writing stories by beginning with a first and last word chosen initially at random. And if one is to speak of 'qualifications' for reviewing, as many do at Film Criticism forums, then I'd argue that the first and fundamental qualification for reviewers at the moment is that they be, for the duration of the job, literary formalists to the back teeth (if not the gut). Knowing or caring about film is merely a bonus.[13]

And so at this level – which is the level of *how* reviews are written – I'd argue that any politics of reviewing must be a 'formalist' politics. It should be concerned with working on and against the rules that define reviewing itself in any particular context. It should not indulge in the fantasy that reviewing directly changes or influences film: changing film is the business of film-makers. Political reviewing is a matter of changing what can be *said* about film, and how: and if this has any importance at all, it is that filmic discourse and discourse on film are inextricably related in and by the institutions of the existing economy; and because film – and the cinema – matters for reasons other than and beyond that mythic entity, 'itself'.

Institutions, plural: my last working definition of reviewing follows from this, and I leave it undeveloped both by way of a last polemic against the idea of the unity of criticism, and as a recognition that most of what I have said applies in detail only to print media:

4. A review is a signifying element in the discourse of the medium in which it appears. It is not a parasite on the film industry nor an extension of a personality, but a bit of a newspaper, a journal, a radio programme, a television show.

5

Apologia: *Beyond Deconstruction* / 'Beyond What?'

Howard Felperin, *Beyond Deconstruction: The Uses and Abuses of Literary Theory*, Oxford 1985.
Roland Barthes, *The Responsibility of Forms: Critical Essays on Music, Art and Representation*, Oxford 1986.
Roland Barthes, *The Rustle of Language*, Oxford 1986.

I

It may well be a mistake to review these books together.

Two volumes of critical essays – written over fifteen years, for many different occasions (academic, journalistic, private), on a generous range of themes – have little in common with a singular polemic about that Anglo-American phenomenon, 'literary theory'. There is no comparison: Barthes and Felperin are engaged in such different projects, and asking such different questions, that the appearance of a character called 'Barthes' in Felperin's fable seems to be an unhappy coincidence – more an accident than an encounter.

That's more or less where my private response to the question of comparison would end.

Alas. Since John Docker's *In a Critical Condition* (1984), the question of the relationship between the work of Roland Barthes and the most conservative forms of criticism in our universities, has become a difficult one to avoid in Australian public discussion.[1] In fact, the really useful comparison might be between Docker's book and *Beyond Deconstruction*. They do address each other: they take opposing positions within the same debate; and, although Docker sees literary theory negatively as an extension of the influence of American formalism in Australia, while Felperin sees it positively as a possible salvation, they speak a similar critical idiom.

Both books are polemical and militant, defending a plan of action for an activity of criticism which should have (both agree) some wider influence in social life. Both are scurrilous, in the literary sense: they argue by jest, invective, caricature, parody – and witting or unwitting befuddlement of the concepts of their two-faced common opponent, 'semiotics/structuralism'. Both books use (as that opponent does not) a text/context opposition to organize literary study. For Docker, there is a 'deep split' between text and context which needs to be overcome (but the split remains in the way he states the problem). For Felperin, 'textualism' and 'contextualism' are personified – along with deconstruction and marxism – as 'mighty opposites' in a struggle, and he sides, in the end, with the former. That is, Felperin's enthusiastic version of deconstruction is rather like Docker's hostile one, and is quite unlike the more usual understanding of deconstruction as, not a 'textualism', but a project of *undoing* that category – for example, by rethinking the text/context opposition in relation to concepts of limits, borders, frames.[2]

This schematic mapping of positions could be carried on indefinitely with these books (and would be ridiculous with *The Rustle of Language* or *The Responsibility of Forms*). This is partly because unlike Barthes, who rarely wrote polemic, Docker and Felperin are both concerned with the *topical* – that is, with spatializing current thought, with locating, placing, positioning, taking stands on a given terrain (and both offer authorial anecdotes about being put *on the spot* in their critical careers).[3] While Felperin zaps from one position to another within his framework, Docker tends to hold fast to a single line. It's a difference in mode of argument consistent with their disagreement about textuality (rhetorically unconstrained for Felperin, socially anchored for Docker). It is also consistent with a certain overlap in their procedures and aims. Where Barthes' essays are concerned with concrete, minute difference, both the polemics work by revealing that a wild variety of critical activities are basically 'the same': that is to say, their aims are reductive.

Docker reduces different discourses to ideological equivalence (Australian metaphysical criticism = American new criticism = Russian formalism = semiotics/structuralism = the aesthetics of T.S. Eliot = ...). He paraphrases bits and pieces of different texts to do this – rewriting them so they 'say the same thing'. For Felperin, it's a matter of reduction to the fact of rhetoric, to a common rhetorical condition: paraphrase is used repeatedly to show that X, criticizing Y, provides yet another version of Y; the phrases 'yet another', 'only another', 'still another' boom through *Beyond Deconstruction* as in an echo-chamber of sameness (the point of his zapping about is to prove, by performance, that 'rhetoric is rhetorical'). Where Docker repeats that discourses say the same thing, Felperin repeatedly says the same thing about discourse.

But there is only overlap, and not identity, between the two modes of levelling. Docker's purpose is altruistic: he believes that the seeming radicality of semiotics and structuralism may fool people, and that by reducing them to variants of the older English department conservatism, he can show them up for what they really are. Felperin apparently believes that they are, together with marxism, fooling themselves: to show them their own rhetoricality is supposed to be a paralysing shock to their radical aspirations; his purpose is competitive, within a commitment *to* a variant of English department conservatism.

It seems to me that Docker has the advantage in this dispute. *Beyond Deconstruction* has a skittishness about politics (and an innocence of marxist theory) that might confirm Docker's worst suspicions. It barrels through an array of theoretical tenpins, barely touching each one before flattening them all – only to return us, after all that sweat, to the good old solid values of the 'canon', the 'great texts', a distinctive 'literary language'. In that sense, *Beyond Deconstruction* is a nostalgic book. If Docker flings and flays about in an equally abusive fashion, he also has a much broader understanding of culture, and a livelier sense of new possibilities – and new tasks – for criticism Beyond the English Department. While Felperin, like Docker, fears the marginalization of literary study to 'the specialist discourse of a clerisy', Felperin's only counter-model is that of 'the leisurely, indeed élitist, *lingua franca* of educated men [*sic*]'[4] – in itself, one would have thought, an entirely clerical ideal in post-War media societies.

The notion of a *lingua franca* points to one of the major rhetorical disadvantages of Felperin's book. *Beyond Deconstruction* is an awesomely baffling read. It can make the simplest propositions seem esoteric. The book is the outcome, Felperin says, of his own perplexity; and so he is uncertain as to whether it is an introduction or a sophisticated commentary (his phrase) for initiates. Heaven help the novice as the book begins, *in media res*, offering accounts of theoretical arguments that are (depending on the reader's humour) either half-parodied, or wholly muddled. To be effective parody needs not only to be 'accurate' (as Felperin reminds that arch-befuddler Denis Donoghue), but to play on a certain familiarity with its model.

For this reader, at least, the differences in *Beyond Deconstruction* between jests, clever sleights-of-hand, decorative flashes of jargon, and nonsense are all too undecidable. It's possible to claim, I daresay, that this undecidability is 'the point'; it's also possible for the perplexed reader to reply that it's not a very interesting point.

Much of the chapter on 'Structuralism in Retrospect', for example, was to me quite unintelligible. One bit moves from an account of *half* the Saussurean model of *langue* ('half', because without the precise

concept of the *system* of signs, which Felperin skips, the sign definition
makes no sense), to equating both 'any set of signs' and 'the signified'
with 'meaning', and then on (gathering input as it goes from a variety of
linguists) to something called 'the literary signified' which then swells to
'the signified of literature'.[5] What seems to happen here (though I'm not
sure) is that the semio-babble serves as a frilly new dress to the plain old
(American) problem of literary interpretation.

To give Felperin his due, his aim in the book is quite explicitly to
salvage some of the traditional values and practices of literary studies, by
appropriating to them the work of their strongest critics. In the process
he often, unlike Docker, notes differences between the concerns of
European thinkers and Anglo-American 'anxieties'. So one way of
comparing *Beyond Deconstruction* to Barthes' essays is to take a theme
of considerable importance to Felperin, rather than Barthes – and to
trace a different set of priorities in Barthes' essays. To do this is to make
myself what Felperin would call an apologist for Barthes. Yet it is also to
re-organize his work in an uncongenial fashion; it allows Felperin's book
to choose the question.

II

> Is it not, in fact, an odd automatism to put the painter, the writer, the artist in
> the enfilade of his kind? A filial image which, once again, imperturbably
> identifies antecedence with origin: we must find Fathers and Sons for the
> artist, so that he can acknowledge the latter and kill the former, uniting two
> *beaux rôles*: gratitude and independence: this is what we call: 'going beyond'.
> Roland Barthes, 'The Artist: *Beyond What?*'[6]

One of the essays from *The Rustle of Language* most often polemically
overemphasized in English is 'The Death of the Author' (1968).
Together with *S/Z* and 'From Work to Text', it is invoked to create
Barthes variously as assassin of artists, patron saint of an impersonal
critical supremacism, and tardy exponent of the 'intentional fallacy'. The
next step is to find it ironic that he signed his books, or wrote about
himself. However 'The Death of the Author' is not a critique of
'intention', but of *origin* (whether it be called the artist's intention,
God's will, or class society); not a denial, either, of subjectivity (a major
theme of Barthes' work), but of the Origin's status as an emblem of the
goal of criticism. The Author is not a fallacy, but a *myth*. It is not a
failure of logic, an error to be denounced in argument, but a historical
experience to be criticized.[7]

This process of criticism was, for Barthes, carried out in the work of
artists and writers (all kinds: linguists and philosophers as well as poets

and novelists). It was not a matter of a power struggle between professional critics and their hapless, now nameless, suppliers of 'material', or between warring sects of critics. If we must insist on reading 'The Death of The Author' as a key manifesto (something like an Authorial statement), then *The Rustle of Language* and *The Responsibility of Forms* should give us pause to consider what its implications were for Barthes' practice. He did not give up reading singular writers, or single texts. On the contrary, both volumes are full of studies of *particular figures*. The death of Authorship does not lead to literary theory in Felperin's sense: in Barthes the theoretical is an *outcome* (as in his essay on Bataille, 'Outcomes of the Text') of a particular activity of reading, and not a professional field to be surveyed before returning to our Authors, their texts, as Felperin does to Shakespeare's sonnets.

But *Beyond Deconstruction* is no more interested than is the work of Barthes in defending capital–'A' Authorship as a principle either of Origin, or of writing linear literary history. It is, however, organized by a defence of another *enfilade* once associated with Authorship – the ˙Canon of great texts by classic authors. Why?

A Rotarian Profession

One of the interesting features of *Beyond Deconstruction* is that Felperin makes an explicit case for literary study as a legalistic regime. It must be a humane regime, a sort of club ('rotarian', as he says himself of American academic life), offering plenty of room for argument, change, and flexibility about what counts as The Canon, and why. But it must none the less defend the idea of The Canon, and continue to exercise Judgement. It's easy to sneer from what he calls 'egalitarian' grounds at Felperin's stress on 'great classic texts' and their 'distinctively literary language', but the point of his argument (if I've understood it) is to say that criticism as a *professional practice* cannot survive without them as organizing values.

I stress 'professional practice' because Felperin, unlike Barthes, sees the 'interpretive community' as not only enabling but defining what literary study can be. It's the pragmatic notion (derived in this case from Stanley Fish and, more remotely, from Richard Rorty) that criticism will be what the community agrees it is, and, conversely, that whatever the community agrees to do, is criticism.[8] The activity isn't fixed, and the community isn't closed, but it *is* institutional. Without some consensus there is no community, without community there is no socially meaningful activity, and without the social activity of differing over common objects, there is no consensus. This is a theory of action recognizable now in Australian political life, but still perhaps a little alien to our traditional critical and artistic 'communities' who favour a more romantic view of the absolute worth of their activities. It is also quite foreign to the organization of French intellectual life – at once hierarchical, and idealized (as the 1986 demonstrations reaffirmed) as free-for-all, universalist, rather than rotarian.

It follows from this that for Felperin the great texts and the distinctively literary are not ends, but means; not essences, but pretexts; not realities, but necessary fictions. Therefore, all the linguistic, historical and political criticism of these fictions in recent decades – from marxism, semiotics, structuralism, feminism, derridean deconstruction – must be rejected in the name of 'the necessity of our reading the *same* texts, or enough of the same texts, to enable the discourse of the interpretive community to go on'.[9] These, of course, are the great texts. So the professional is obliged to find ever new ways of adjudicating between great and lesser, success and failure, literary and non-literary – even if that means energetically misreading critiques of such judgement as though they were arguments for its validity.

One such misreading vital to Felperin's argument is his rephrasing of Roman Jakobson's term 'the poetic *function*' – which Jakobson thought was intrinsic to all language use in varying degrees – as 'poetic *language*' (in opposition to 'ordinary' language).[10] This is a slide which enables Felperin to avoid mentioning the main case against the ordinary/literary language distinction: which is not an egalitarian claim that literature shouldn't be seen as distinctive but, on the contrary, a claim that the complexity of so-called ordinary language use makes an 'ordinary/literary' opposition inadequate for thinking the distinctiveness of literature.

But there really can be no argument with Felperin about transforming literary study. Since the very existence of the community is dependent on assent to the rules, real challenges must either be excluded (semiotics, feminism) or coopted (deconstruction). You either want to play the game, or you take your bat and balls (or ... whatever), and join another club. That's why, in spite of all its talk about indeterminacy, *Beyond Deconstruction* can make determined judgements of what is valid/invalid, tenable/untenable, possible/not possible for what shall be known as criticism.[11] The book is a defence, and not a deconstructing, of limits (and thus the very opposite of the derridean project).

It's at the end of this line of argument that I'd want to place the extraordinary anxiety about Theory when it is understood (in association also with Marxism) as Science in *Beyond Deconstruction*.

One could argue at length with Felperin's unusual representations of structuralist epistemology, and of marxist aesthetics. Much of his discussion depends on translating both into a positivist scenario for an 'ultimate theory of theories', with its phantasmagoria of 'firm' grounds, and 'master-keys'.[12] It's a cruel irony that Felperin should canonize Louis Althusser – rather than, say, Charles Morris – as this scenario's patron (although 'Marxism', 'Althusser' and 'Macherey' usually signify, in this book, 'Terry Eagleton' – from whom Felperin's impressions of marxism appear largely to derive). This translation produces a number of peculiarities: for example, the assumption that notions such as 'theoretical object' in epistemology or 'object-language' in semiotics, have something to do with *objectivity* as an empiricist ideal. Thus a long footnote explains that a 'growing body of thought' considers that objects are 'constituted', not 'given': which is, indeed, the very premiss – rather than a refutation – not only of Althusserian epistemology, but of Saussurean linguistics (and of 'scientific semiotics') as well.[13]

Beyond these cross-cultural crossed wires, however, is a reason for anxiety quite specific to Felperin's pragmatic view of Law and literary study. Once science *is* understood as aspiring to a master-position as theory of theories, then it poses a symbolic threat to the conversation of the interpretive community. It threatens (so the fantasy goes) to judge, 'explain', conclude – and so break the binding rule of the interpretive game, which is perpetuation of the rule (the game) itself.

'Let the semioclasts beware, lest there be no signs or idols left to break.'[14] The Law (the Canon) requires transgression; but transgression needs a Law to transgress (as does the 'deviancy' theory of poetry).[15] Without Fathers to kill, Sons perish. This scenario presumes, I think, a deeply authoritarian Imaginary: and since fathers in *Beyond Decon-struction* tend to be theoretical rather than artistic figures, it explains an otherwise inscrutable remark that the disinterest in 'literary language' and the lack of 'institutional anxiety' in Derrida, as in the late Barthes, could be ascribed to the fate of philosophy – which, says Felperin, has long given away 'any social or missionary rationale' in Anglo-American culture, and is resigned to its marginality (or its impotence).[16] But this is a *non sequitur*: Even the Americo-centric Felperin must know that philosophy in France still remains among the most prestigious, and political, of disciplines. However, this troublesome detail is elided because for Felperin, a thinker who sets out to destroy the bases of his own thinking is, strictly speaking, unthinkable. As is an attempt not to think *beyond* the existing Law – since that is the filial attempt (Lacan once suggested that *Beyond the Phallus* would be a really cute feminist title) – but to think in *other terms*.

Amateur Practice

The passage that I quoted above from the section called 'The Artist:

Beyond What?' in Barthes' essay 'Réquichot and His Body' is a response to a comment made by Réquichot: 'Going beyond van Gogh or Kandinsky isn't much good, nor is *wanting* to go beyond them: all that is only a historical transcendence.'[17] It is part of a dialogue with Réquichot's painting, not a statement of general principle.

Nevertheless, there is throughout Barthes' work a distaste, even a revulsion – something much stronger than an objection – for crudely oedipal accounts of art history. There is not a skerrick of interest in a Bloomian – and Felperine – 'anxiety'.[18] The later work, in particular, is concerned with the maternal and the bodily in art – not the dynamics of paternity, filiation, and Law (or the Canon). Thinking the body, love, admiration, is not possible as a *theoretical* project for Felperin's framework, which knows only paternal law-and-order OR impotence ... and so thinks of subjective experience as a saving (or arousing) grace beyond Theory. Barthes' essays, far from 'killing' admiration of art, return again and again to beloved texts (the music of Schumann, for example); but it is always to rethink the question of his own attachment to them – not to lay claim on their behalf to dominance and power.

It's not a simple matter of different sensibilities. For Felperin, the Canon of great works is an instrumental value which safeguards the interpretive community. Barthes has no comparable restrictive concept of a critical *profession.* At least, not of an identity between the institutional practice of criticism, and his own – or others' – writing. He wrote a great deal about institutional experience ('Reflections on a Manual', 'Research: The Young', 'Writers, Intellectuals, Teachers', 'To the Seminar'), but always as of a *body politic* – not only of hierarchy and limitation in academic structures, but of the flux of power – and desire – in voice, gesture, speech, writing, as we talk, listen, write, read.

This flux is also, for Barthes, the movement of the social in the seminar. A vital difference between Barthes' understanding of modern society and an American pragmatist model is that while pragmatism may see literary criticism as a cohesive language-game in a greater social tournament – cohesive because players must observe certain minimal rules to maintain disagreement – Bathes sees it as always dissolving and dividing, in the same 'secession of languages' that regulates the whole cultural life of mass-media democracies ('Pax Culturalis', 'The Division of Languages', 'The War of Languages').

For Felperin, sociology, or politics, or mass-media study, is what professional literary criticism doesn't do. For Barthes, all reading and writing is carried out in relation to, and *in the midst of,* the general culture: the media change how we speak and hear, how we understand each other, how we read Balzac, and a treatise in linguistics, and a Panzani Pasta ad. Criticism, therefore, is subject to no identity crisis, no necessary limits – and so no need for making, or defending, canons. The text becomes a problem of passion, not a pretext; or values, not validity; of a desire to return, not a will to master. This is perhaps one reason why, even in those essays addressing the 'we' of a conference or seminar, Barthes never *writes* as a professional speaking to other professionals. His rhetoric is intimate, as though arguing with himself, and courteous, as though anybody could be listening.

When Barthes does refer to something like a canon, it is either in the familiar sense of a historical product: 'the history of literature ought to be conceived as a history of the idea of literature' ('Reflections on a Manual'); or as a mode of inhibition: '*the intolerances of contemporary reading*' ('Michelet, Today'). Barthes doesn't simply denounce intolerances. While his essays explore with equal intensity the most canonical of figures (Proust, Stendhal, Balzac, Brecht), the neglected or unfashionable (Michelet, Schumann), the new (Renaud Camus) or the unpublished ('F.B.'), he is also fascinated by *what it is* in the work of some artists that now arouses intolerance – and what this tells us about contemporary reading. To read Barthes on pathos in Michelet, or on kitsch in Wilhelm von Gloeden, is to realize the poverty of a professionalist ethic which can only envisage mutually intolerant 'egalitarian' and 'élitist' positions in culture.

If there is no equivalent in Barthes of the interpretive community as source of value, there is a concept of the *amateur* as a *kind* of value. Amateurism for Barthes is not a matter of lesser knowledge, imperfect technique, or merely casual commitment. Nor is it a dilettante's abandon of what Barthes called the social and historical 'responsibility of forms'. In his essays on music, it is sometimes a nostalgia for a lost style of performance (Lipati, Panzera). In the essay on Réquichot (whose work was rarely seen during his lifetime), amateurism becomes defiant: the amateur is '*the one who does not exhibit*, the one who does not make himself heard'. Above all, however, amateurism is a relationship to pleasure: 'the amateur seeks to produce only his own enjoyment (but nothing forbids it to become ours *in addition*, without his knowing it), and this enjoyment is shunted towards no hysteria'.[19]

So the amateur for Barthes is closely associated not with the demands of a critical profession, but with a desire for a mode of practice – something like John Forbes' idea of poetry as 'a hobby'.[20] In 'Musica Practica' amateurism emerges from a distinction between the music you listen to, and the music you play: 'the same composer can be minor when listened to, enormous when played (even poorly) – take Schumann.' In a later essay, 'Loving Schumann', it is traced to the way that 'Schumann's music goes much further than the ear; it goes into the body, into the muscles by the beats of its rhythm ... as if on each occasion the piece

was written only for one person, the one who plays it' ... Amateurism is
a bodily practice, and it stirs 'not satisfaction, but desire – the desire to
make such music'.[21]

In this stirring of desire-to-make, amateurism overlaps with the
concept of the so-called 'writerly' in *S/Z*, and certain essays ('From
Work to Text': *the Text is experienced only in an activity, in a production*').[22] The 'writerly/readerly' distinction is often taken in English,
understandably, to mean 'avant-garde/classical' or even 'unreadable/
easy' – and in parts of *Beyond Deconstruction* it reverts to 'artistic/
critical'. A different emphasis is possible if we substitute a less elegant,
but more accurate, translation of Barthes' *lisible/scriptible*: that is,
readable/writeable. It's not a distinction between two grades of texts, but
two kinds of relationships to two different experiences: one of a product
(the readable text), and one of production (the writeable). Because there
are four terms here (not two objects), Barthes can explore the 'writea-
bility' of a readable text – like Balzac's story, 'Sarrasine'. To do this –
and not to denounce realism – is the project of *S/Z*.

Two points follow about Barthes' relationship to art works. One is
that it can imply *identification*, not rivalry or imitation (as in, for
example, a cult of 'style' in critical writing). It's an identification with a
desire – not with a person, a life experience, or an achievement – and it's
a responsive desire, a particular identification with another's desire. Just
as the desire to make Schumann's music responds to the 'effervescence
of the beats' in his music ('Rasch'), so Proust is 'the privileged site', for
Barthes, of a special identification: *In Search of Lost Time* is the
narrative of a desire to write ('The Death of the Author', '*Longtemps, je
me suis couché de bonne heure ...*').

Secondly, writing emerges in Barthes from an experience of *failure* –
and not from success in a critical triumphalism. This is one of the crucial
differences from the liberation of the writer in the critic that follows the
discovery of rhetoric in *Beyond Deconstruction*. The special identification dreamt of by Barthes is always productively impossible: sometimes because of an artist's power (the essays on Cy Twombly – 'Here is
Age of Alexander: oh, that one smear of pink!'), but always because, as
the title of his last essay puts it, 'One Always Fails in Speaking of What
One Loves'. This essay too is an essay in identification: identification
with Stendhal's failure in his travel journals to say his passion for Italy,
and then with the emergence of writing that enables *The Charterhouse
of Parma*. Critical writing (in this respect, like any other) arises for
Barthes not from professional imperatives, but from a wish to overcome
failure, a struggle to say, in spite of failure, 'what one loves', and to
survive that 'fiasco of style' that plagues and yet signifies passion –
platitude.[23]

Here is one context for reading Barthes' comments, in these essays, on science. Where *Beyond Deconstruction* has, in its anxiety, no sense of humour and beauty in science, Barthes writes in a tender appreciation of the work of Jakobson ('A Magnificent Gift'), of Benveniste ('Why I Love Benveniste'), of Kristeva's *Semeiotike* ('The science of language cannot be Olympian, positive')[24] – that unanxiously coexists with his criticism of his own earlier efforts at semiotics. While for Felperin the revelation of textuality surprises science, for Barthes it is a point of departure to assume that science is writing ('From Science to Literature', 'Research: The Young'). The question is, *what kind?*

There's an appreciation, too, of the spirit of amateurism in great scientific writing. This is the point of 'To Learn and to Teach', his essay on Christian Metz – the theorist of cinema today most often cartooned as the archetypal exponent of a systematic Dullness. For Barthes, there is an *'enraged* exactitude' in Metz's practice comparable to the effects of hashish for Baudelaire; a solicitude for the demand for enlightenment, 'which Metz knows is always a demand for love'; and the stirring of a desire to learn which is Metz's own desire: *'he is teaching himself* what he is supposed to be communicating to others'. This is Metz's amateur practice, and for Barthes, it keeps his semiotics vigilant against (not subject to) 'dogmatism, arrogance, theology; in short, that monster: the Last Signified'.[25]

III

I began by discussing *Beyond Deconstruction* as polemic, and I would like to end with some notes on the essay.

In *'Longtemps je me suis couché de bonne heure . . .'* Barthes describes Proust's hesitation, while writing *Contre Sainte-Beuve*, between two 'ways': the way of the essay, and the way of the novel. For Barthes, these ways correspond to metaphor (sustaining 'any discourse that asks "What is it? What does it mean?" – the real question of any essay') and metonymy ('"What can follow what I say? What can be engendered by the episode I am telling?"; this is the Novel's question'). Proust's hesitation is resolved in the *third form* – 'novel? essay? Neither one, or both at once' – that is the form of *In Search of Lost Time*.

For any critical tradition that devalues or ignores the essay, an association with metaphor may seem odd and pretentious. The equation Novel + Poetry + Drama = Literature has been upheld tenaciously in institutionally dominant Australian criticism (see Leonie Kramer's *Oxford History of Australian Literature*, 1981) – along with a casual respect for the essay as 'light literature' from Walter Murdoch to Ron

Saw.[26] Always hard, perhaps impossible, to define as a positive genre, the essay acquires contradictory definitions by default in the absence of discussion: it is thought to be both didactic (the transparent vehicle of serious criticism), and whimsical (the thick medium of subjectivity). These functions combine in its punitive use in schools: to write '*My Weekend ... (we came home, tired but happy)*' is to submit to rules of 'self-expression'. Murdoch himself, in the preface to *Speaking Personally* (1931), produced a synthesis of didacticism and whimsy by mocking his own role as preacher – a solution still used today by media columnists whose trademark is an anti-intellectualism fused with arrogant opinionation.

We could call this critical neglect of the essay an intolerance of contemporary reading, and wonder why it occurs in a society increasingly organized (from polls to psychobabble) by opinion-industries, and disciplines of subjectivity. But we'd need to qualify the question: which contemporary reading? whose intolerance? For one of the most striking aspects of the problem is that the essay – in newspapers, magazines, journals and books – is the most widely and enthusiastically read, and used, prose form in our culture today. It should therefore provide a link between the critical profession and a wider writing and reading public. When it doesn't, the intolerance logically lies with the former. When it does – as in the growth of a non-academic readership for those essayists called 'theorists' – intolerance mutters darkly about the fashionable, the modish, the trendy (before going on to worry separately about the future of literary studies).

As Don Anderson pointed out in the *Age Monthly Review* (March 1987), Barthes was not only a great reader, but a great essayist. It seems to me that more than a tribute is at stake in saying this. Whatever its difficulties of definition (since those difficulties can define the form), the term 'essay' is useful as a counter to the tendency to reify theory as an esoteric art. Thus popular essayists like Barthes, Baudrillard, Eco, appear as priests of Theory – seen as both a secret knowledge (didacticism), and an arcane stylistic practice (whimsy). An alternative is not to substitute 'essay' for 'Theory' as a word suppressing differences between philosophy, criticism, science, art, but to remember that the essay since Montaigne has been a way of reworking, by experiment, those differences.

In *Beyond Deconstruction*, the essay is elided as a formal problem – with consequences for reading that are by no means exclusive to Felperin. There is no concept to mediate the clash of Big Absolutes (Science/Poetry, Truth/Fiction ...), and Felperin can then only show how easy it is to convert each of those to its Other. Next, in the subsidiary exchange between Theory and Practice, critical reading becomes *allegorical*: in an ironic demonstration of how 'to read our canonical texts with one eye on them and the other on the theoretical journals',[27] Shakespeare's *Sonnets* are read as 'foreknowing' the whole history of Literary Theory (as narrated by Felperin) using a grid of correspondences as tight and as absolute as any exegesis of *Revelations* by a millenarian fundamentalist.

This is allegory in the classical restrictive sense, and what is remarkable about it is how exhaustive a reading it produces, how little it allows for any indeterminacy in practice. In Felperin's version of the Barthes encountered during his Pilgrim's Progress of Theory, something similar happens: the responsive particularity of the relation between a Barthes essay and its objects gives way to a set of generalizations about those Big Absolutes and their mutual conversion. Consequently, a problem arises: 'How can Barthes' work maintain a claim to being systematic when its procedures continually change?'.[28]

To this and other rhetorical questions, Felperin replies that 'system-making' has thus turned back into 'fiction or poetry!'. Another answer is that the procedures of Barthes' essays vary with their objects (as constituted by the essays, not given to them): the object of *S/Z* is for Barthes not a discovery that science is poetry, but the experience (the *essai*) of an interrupted reading – 'to systematize all those moments when one *looks up*' from a book ('Writing Reading'). This, rather than a simple thesis on the fictionality of systems, can account for the practical form of that essay (and no other).

This is not a mimetic concept of the essay (criticism imitating art). To say that an object is 'constituted' is to say that it is made, not copied, by a practice. It is in this sense that Barthes could talk about 'changing the object': changing the musical object, for example, 'as it presents itself to speech'; not changing the language used about music, but the 'fringe of contact' between them ('The Grain of the Voice'). It's a matter of shifting relations and creating differences, not reducing terms to variations of the 'same thing'. Barthes' comparison between the essay and Jakobson's concept of metaphor as *displacement* is relevant here: the answer to the question 'What is it?' is in differences, not indifference.

Barthes' work here rejoins – even in the midst of his confrontations with science, his struggles with failure to speak a love of art, and his own dreams of a Proustian third form – Adorno's conception of the essay as a coordination of elements in an irreducible *tension* between science and art, concept and rhetoric, system and 'catching fire' ('The Essay as Form', 1958).[29] For Adorno, 'the essay verges on the logic of music, the stringent and yet aconceptual art of transition' ... and it is as a practice of transition (displacement) that the mobility and mutability of Barthes' essays could be distinguished from the standpoint-topicality of polemic.

The preface to *Beyond Deconstruction* closes by citing (as 'fashionable nowadays') Walter Benjamin: 'The object is to learn, not how to find one's way, but how to lose it.' Fashionable these remarks on wandering round a city may be, but for Felperin (rather than Benjamin), they lead to fixing *points* – where are we now? where did we come from? where do we go, beyond?

Barthes, using an apparently similar spatial image, puts the emphasis otherwise; on movement, process, transformation, *essai*: the shift makes all the difference:

> the work of art is interminable, like the cure: in both cases, it is less a matter of obtaining a result than of modifying a problem, i.e. a subject: gaining release from the imprisoning finality of the point of departure.
>
> 'Réquichot and His Body'

6

Two Types of Photography Criticism Located in Relation to Lynn Silverman's Series

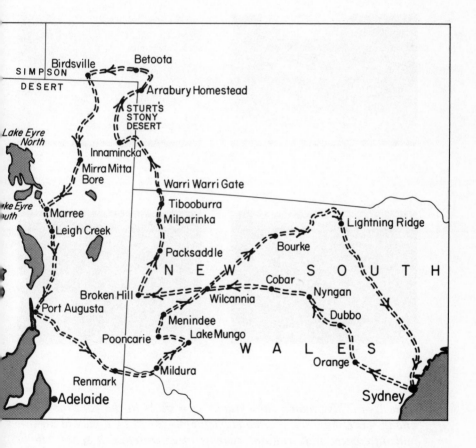

Collecting ground samples and locating them in relation to the horizon from where they were photographed

In a translation of a French history of Australia, the prologue begins by
defining the continent as vast, harsh and weird. It closes by alluding to
Cuvier's comment that Australia is like a fragment of another planet
which just dropped on to our globe by chance.

In a book of tearout postcards, one of the most popularly posted images
presents a bare horizon line and a signpost saying, NEXT 5,000
MILES NOTHING.

*I see Lynn Silverman's photographs as a study in the construction of
inland space: how space is made intelligible for us by a play of identity
and difference; how cultural systems of interpreting a space can be
unsettled by exhibiting the process of framing interpretations; and how
landscape photographs induce a curious convergence between what you
do when you set out to see the sights, and what you see when you look at*

In common speech, there are a number of signs combining the variety of flat, dry and largely uninhabited lands of Australia's surface into one single concept of generalized space: the inland, the interior, the outback, out west, the dead heart and – most rich and imprecise of all – the desert.

In each case the speaker (regardless of physical location) articulates the vision of an outsider gazing at an elsewhere.

an ordered sequence of images.

At first glance, you can respond to the pleasures of familiar recognition habits. The eye starts scanning the horizon line, joining up frame to frame in a single track along the series. One movement abstracts a generalization based on the formal similarity of a succession of separate items. The eye then rediscovers difference and precision below that line;

Desert descriptions can never be seen as innocent of cultural reference. 'The desert' is always a preexisting pile of texts and documents, fantasies, legends, jokes and other people's memories, a vast imaginary hinterland which most coastal dwellers like to dream all their lives of seeing in reality one day.

The history of this fantastic area is quite recent. For tens of thousands of years, Australia was merely a real land mass which held a diversity of

the exact details of a flower, a bush, a nest or a cluster of stones can be lingered over in a step by step celebration of the traveller's coded wonder that such unique objects exist.

Both ways of seeing mesmerize. You could go on and on hypnotically linking horizon lines, effacing frames and poring over precious places.

different cultures thriving in separate regions. Today (the time of what Donald Horne has called 'the imperial procession of the white people across Australia'), it makes little difference to insist that much of the inland is not desert at all, or that there are many kinds of desert and that some are white man-made.

In urban imaginations, that space is *there* – immense, unique, invested with meaning, and rather expensive to tour.

The photographs are very beautiful, and there is no intrinsic reason I can find for the series itself to stop. I imagine that the photographer had her reasons for standing at one spot rather than another, for going home when she did, for choosing one image rather than another; but nothing of this remains in the series, which points instead to the disorienting, dislocating possibilities of endless repetition.

The myth of the inland precedes any deliberate act of seeing it with one's own eyes. In this, no doubt, it is like any other tourist attraction; the myth motivates and structures the visitor's vision of the land. The peculiarity of Australian inland space lies rather in the series of stark oppositions which define it (and which reappear in other contexts as basic problems of Australian history and culture in general): here/there, positive/negative, presence/absence.

The play with the pull of the inland and the urge to fall through an image is checked, however, by the vertical lines of comparison linking pairs of photographs apparently taken while standing in the same place.

They are utterly different, joltingly so; and as the empty immensity of distance there repeatedly confronts the minute detail of surface here, this difference (and the systematic oppositions which produce it) ceases to be

In the Eastern cities, there is a whole cultural industry for promoting the presence of the desert. Television documentaries, postcards, films, the lavish landscape celebrations of books of Australiana, even ecological campaigns keep accumulating and circulating images of wondrous far horizons – which function as so many signposts to another reality, a 'real' Australia.

an effect of a dream of endless, all-embracing space, and appears as the outcome of a predetermined and limited procedure. Our sense of the identity of site binding each pair is itself an outcome, not of nature or visual evidence fixed within the frames, but of the formal arrangement of the series on the wall.

The work then confronts us, not with objective and subjective inter-

Yet their assertiveness responds to a contrasting form of fascination, one depending on doubt, forgetfulness, and the mysteries of the unseen. That space – into which people occasionally vanish – has so little effective reality that it is always on the verge of disappearing; and the routine snapshots of travellers returning are pored over as so many incredible testimonies that the inland might actually exist.

Signposted yet sign-effacing, it is a space accorded the status of a

pretations of the same space, but with two different ways of manipulating subject-object relationships. One makes myth, the other makes personal statement; one includes us, the other addresses.

The images of landstrip, horizon and sky seem anonymous, impersonal; all trace of the photographer's presence is effaced. Yet for that reason, reservoir of places where nothing might be, or anything might happen. In traditional legend, birds fly backwards there; rivers run against nature, the sand spawns fishes, and inland seas are lapping just beyond the dry horizon. In contemporary speculation, lost creatures reappear and vanish; regions belong obscurely to alien powers, while the wasteland hides a monstrous proliferation of caverns breeding new forms of experimental warfare.

subjectivity dominates here; any one of I/you/all of us can take her place and assume that vision. This is the timeless land, 'our' land, laid out ahead alluringly for acts of possession to come – the product of an imperial way of seeing and proceeding.

The ground shots, in contrast, are personal in a way which does not absorb us all into a universal vision of inviting emptiness, and which fills

This aspect of the myth attracts quests, produces the travel patterns of voyagers in search of special realities, evidence, or some new vision. But the enduring seductiveness of the myth resides in the reversibility of its meanings. The inland is also repulsive; an image of a natural dreariness, dullness, desolation and monotony which slowly encroaches upon settlements, and spreads its emptiness by contagion to culture. For a century,

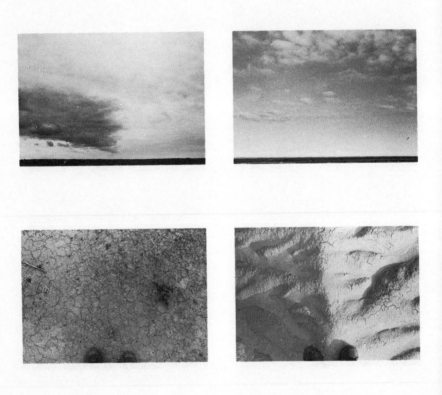

the frame with the clarity of a particular place and time. There has been an event; and the sensibility which found and saw the sheer hilarious difference between the delicate traceries of various patches of cracked earth was not interchangeably yours or mine, but hers. Our one guarantee of identity and constancy comes down to a bit of somebody else's boots.

recurring projects prove that Australia is or is not a cultural desert: poor towns, and unpleasant parts of cities, are not jungles here – but deserts.

The negative desert takes many forms – vacant lot, backyard, quarry, cemetery, dump. The most intimate of all, however, is the desert of school geography: long lists of names, explorers, lifeless rivers and

And looking back to those horizons, you see – of course – that they are not the same at all. A troubling difference emerges, one which is not the product of the purely formal play of a system imposed, but of the order of the variation of different skies seen on different days in different lands.

empty places shrunk to marks on a map, names which can never have any more meaning than hot afternoons in a droning room.

This is the heritage of texts, travel-writing repressed and revitalized in succeeding generations. Documented, measured, mapped and crossed, the inland is viewed through a grid of preestablished procedures of possession. The wanderer, artist, tourist who goes there repeats the great itineraries of the predecessors, follows the broken lines on the map of a

Generalized space disintegrates, the line breaks up, the frames stand out, and the spaces between them point to an absent narrative of a lost itinerary – and what happened (to somebody) along the way.

What remains is a set of tracks. Not the single broken line of the traveller marking a progress on a map; but a double line, an exploration of

trip which has already been made.
The generalized space of the inland
solicits an act of repetition which is always,
in the beginning, a rediscovery
of the same.

reversibility, the trace of a movement on a strange, still space
in which everybody looks at elsewhere, and
somebody looked at here.

7

On the 'On' of *On Photography*

1. On 'On'

A text 'on' a topic is not necessarily a text 'about'. On and about are choices made for reasons as well as rhythms. Essayists also have the resort of 'of': *Of Women and Their Elegance*, said Norman Mailer, writing about himself.

Essays (trying, testing) speculate in provocation, meditation and possibility. They are skeptical, testing not hypotheses but how it might be possible to be them passionately. They write *on* – they scribble, deface and reform until the meaning of a surface has changed. Essays are cantankerous: they like to take received ideas of About, chew them up and spit them out in little pieces which have changed.

Passionately, people including Susan Sontag have stressed that *On Photography* is not a book about photography. They say it is about consumerism, about advanced industrial societies, about the uses of photography when 'a chronic voyeuristic relation to the world levels the meaning of all events'. 'Uses' and 'when' are different words from the word 'Photography'. Such distinctions when an effort is undertaken to refuse the levelling of language to the murmur of muzak are always a matter of just semantics.

Relations to reading are scrapped and shredded by shock-horror headline habits when people read *On Photography* piecemeal. You get shards of statement about photography and violation – poor little pellets of idea. They pick out abouts. Ons, on the other hand, are the smooth swirls which are not straight lines which bind the pieces together.

2. On About

William Gass[1] said that 'the book is a thoughtful meditation, not a treatise, and its ideas are grouped more nearly like a gang of keys upon a ring than a run of onions on a string'. Colin L. Westerbeck Jr[2] writing in *Artforum* said that this metaphor is opaque. Yet what could be more clarifying than the differences between gangs and runs, keys and onions, rings and strings?

Colin L. Westerbeck Jr. is a bit of an About man. He says that *On Photography* might have been called *Off Photography*. His own first metaphor is about Point-Wound-Penetration, and it leads him to lament 'the difficulty of pinning Sontag down'. The titling says 'On Sontag', but the essay goes beating about. Sontag is depressed. Sontag is nervous. Sontag is insecure: and Sontag 'has never been equally good at having continuous thoughts'. This is an On of another sort (it is a little love story).

Penetration is what Authors are for when writing is seen as transparent, like veils. It also comes about when continuous thoughts are thought to be thoughts people have before writing, a way to display the continuous thoughts and their goodness. Reading this way doesn't have to read writing. Reading this way is clairvoyant. Colin L. Westerbeck Jr. 'sees' the personality in Atget's Paris shop windows (not the difference between 'keys' and 'onions').

Clairvoyant reading tears through. Rapidly, Colin L. Westerbeck Jr. reveals that *On Photography* contradicts the contradictions of Sontag's own writings. (Of course it does: that's what it's about.)

3. On 'modern'

On photography can be a book about 'modern' for even Colin Etcetera. 'Modern' is a messy word, especially when tacked to 'taste'. Modernity: 'the way we are now', says Sontag in an interview. Modernism: what we do no longer do, says style in *On Photography*. Tacking: taste today to photographic taste to modernist taste to pop taste to surrealist taste to the taste for quotations. (Or a similar gang: this one ends with a problem for writing that goes back to a problem of taste, 'today'.)

Style in *On Photography* asserts an aesthetics of exposition. Style is never a matter of ornamentation but partly a matter of pronouns. 'The taste for quotations is a surrealist taste': who says that sentence for whom? Anybody or everybody could say that sentence when only one knew enough. (Say, 'A stitch in time saves nine'.) Such sentences make statements which when running continuously on like the thoughts of Colin L. Westerbeck Jr. make the sound of expository wisdom. That sound is most unmodern like the sound of knowing enough.

Anybody however is not invited to run on and expound. Running requires system and the order of *On Photography* is a non-systemic order. Its order is what *On Photography* understands partly as modern. It breaks, fragments, returns, repeats, and stops. This is why the order of *On Photography* cancels its style by refusing an order of knowing enough. (But if knowing enough is refused, then not just anybody can know what the knower does know.)

'Modern' (hooked on 'photographs') is why the end is a tacking of quotations. Order has the last word, 'Make picture of kaleidoscope'. This is a word from William H. Fox Talbot on the writing of *On Photography*.

Inset: quotations

'Photographs – and quotations – seem, because they are taken to be pieces of reality, more authentic than extended literary narratives. The only prose that seems credible to more and more readers is not the fine writing of someone like Agee, but the raw record – edited or subedited talk into tape recorders; fragments or the integral texts of sub-literary documents (court records, letters, diaries, psychiatric case histories, etc.); self-deprecatingly sloppy, often paranoid first-person reportage.'

'Well when I first read *On Photography* I thought it had a really brilliant analysis of all these problems you come up against working on quotation in art, you know, and it's sort of like one of the most interesting things in a lot of modern writing ... well modern, I mean modern doesn't mean much, but anyway it's something a lot of people have been doing for ages. And then here was this really amazing sort of cut-around overlap book in this incredibly clear sort of style saying that playing with quotation which is supposed to be, you know, this remote élitist activity, had something to do with talking heads.'

'America, that surreal country, is full of found objects.' 'Photographs ... traces ... pieces ... fragments ... pellets ... litter ... junk ... garbage-strewn ... shards ... (quotations) ... ruins ... trash ... eyesores ... rejects ... peeling surfaces ... kitsch ... short-cuts ... collage ... collection.'

'But then I started to think about the way she talks about quotes like they're things and how she sets up all these things like they're the same, you know, by using lots of words for debris, basically. And now I'm not so sure I like it, because I don't know about photography, but quotation's not to do with debris at all.'

4. On 'Quotation'

On Photography however it may be for photography is not a book about quotation. Quotation is a process while *On Photography* says 'quotes'. Quotes is a very ugly word for the plural of an object not an action and once there is an object there may need to be a place from whence it came. Only an object is found by somebody somewhere so they can say that something has been lost or left. A process is of no importance for such saying of loss since a process is making or changing.

Quotes can of course be called pieces by a call for original contexts. Original, whole, integral, real: a way of dreaming of Eden. A first text, a whole text, a pure text, a one text, a text of a once and for all. Dreaming of Eden is when *On Photography* says that modern history (shedding quotes and photos during the fall) has 'shattered the living wholes in which precious objects once found their place'.

Dreaming is different from history but quotation is more like histories. Quotation is neither a piece nor a whole but simply an action of saying. Some ways of quotation are boasting, blinding, justifying, wounding, dulling, denying, deceiving. (Only in special circumstances like a letter to a depressive can quotation occasionally kill.) Other ways are further ways of making anything at all from anything other than nothing: fighting, flirting, explaining, soothing, laughing, seducing, persuading.

Quotation however it may be for photography is fragmented by *On Photography*. It is fragmented in order to fit an order which is predicated as 'modern'. So the fragments will then need tacking together in a writing of no-longer modern. This is a classic manoeuvre (check): from 'piece *versus* whole', to 'lack *versus* having', to 'loss *versus* gain' – a strategy for calling for action.
About: 'This book self-destructs' (Colin L. Westerbeck Jr.).
On: No it doesn't, it can't; it re-creates the myth of origin that its writing's about.

8

Intrigue

I

... he might be crude, he might be rough, he might lack entirely the decorative charm of the gentlemanly Geoffrey and the contemptible Evan, he might lack the wakening sensibility of Dan, but he was as solid as an old bull in a field, and he had no fastidious artificial hesitation about saying what he thought.
Vita Sackville-West, *Family History* ('Portrait of the Jarrolds')

No matter where I may wish to begin (or where I imagine I ought to), the first thing I see in any viewing of these four drawings by Richard Dunn is that the head of the man on the left-hand side of *The Observer and the Observed (Men and Towers) # 2* – is very, very handsome.

It draws my gaze – *he* draws my gaze – in a manner not repeated by the second drawing of the 'same' head in *The Observer and the Observed (Men and Woman) # 2*, and not renewed or extended by the other heads in the sequence, all of which persistently derive, despite my best efforts, their initial significance from *him*.

This effect of primacy is so strong that I can't really imagine these objects arranged, to my own satisfaction, in a different order. It should be possible: since surely a series of cruciform grids – divided here into two sets (*The Observer and the Observed*, and *Untitled*), each set containing a pair of works, each work composed by two planes intersecting, and one plane of each defined by a pair of heads – might ideally admit a number of possible orders, each of which could generate, as well as delimit, a number of possible readings. (And in a gallery, if not in an article, I can look anywhere, anyhow, I like.)

But in any other ordering, I would want to see a mistake; and wherever I move to re-place *him* in the structure, he draws me there, back to the beginning. (Even just then, describing the composition of the work, I lost interest in grids and planes, and began to talk about 'heads'.

155

THE OBSERVER AND THE OBSERVED

(MEN AND TOWERS) #2

THE OBSERVER AND THE OBSERVED

(MEN AND WOMAN) #2

UNTITLED

(COUPLE AND WATERFALL)

UNTITLED

RICHARD DUNN 1985

(COUPLE AND FIRE) #2

I should have said, 'sheets of paper'.)

His is a head with *presence.* Alone among the eight heads I see, his has character. I can also see that this head is, like all the others, a drawing of an image of a head; and that it is, like all the other components including the composite central images, a drawing of a mode of representation (in his case, a mode that makes 'character'). It doesn't matter (the mode of representation works). He's riveting. Beside him, the others are as shadows.

I can seek reasons for this effect, and in doing so, try to draw away. For the effect of this head is embarrassing. I don't think I'm supposed to be so distracted by it. He places me in some realm of purely private observation, making it hard to shift between the one who looks to the one who will write about looking. This makes beginning a bit of a problem.

So, first: there is a slight difference between the two versions of 'his' image, a material difference deriving (I imagine) from the artist's repeated act of drawing. (The doubled heads represent *en abyme* one element of the formal composition of the series: each pair represents the intersection of a reiteration of a systematic principle of repetition, with a discrete act of differentiation.)

The handsomeness of the man on the left of *Men and Towers* seems to lie along the curves of mouth, moustache and hand. But it is not quite so: there is a crescent of light curving from hair to forehead to hand around the left side of his face (*his* left side) that leaves his right cheek in shadow – except for the light in the eye. It is the intersection of curved line with light and shade along the upper lip that makes him handsome, meeting between hand and eye in a sort of ironic twinkle.

The man on the left of *The Observer and the Observed (Men and Woman) #2* seems coarser in comparison; aged, perhaps, or crabby; his eye is faintly dimmed, his curves are less distinct (as though black does not become him).

Briefly satisified with this, I look for verification to the other couples. The man turned away in *The Observer and the Observed,* that nearly faceless man, seems thinner, still more faceless, in his second variation. The twins in *Untitled* also differ; the man in *Couple and Waterfall* has the softer mouth, the firmer chin, a less harsh and pursed expression as he looks at the woman, the waterfall. The woman in *Couple and Fire* has an air of faint surprise beside her other self, her lips a little more open, her head just slightly inclined – less self-conscious, more attentive, perhaps.

But I have now moved from formal observation straight to psychological impressionism. I am already reading the works as residual, expressive 'scenes', from a narrative of incidents and feelings – and effacing the gestures of drawing I set out to retrace. I do this not only because of the paradox of difference-in-repetition (which can generate desire for *verification*, a narrative desire, desire to 'solve' a question of identity, the intrigue of doubles and twins), but also because I have failed to abstract the relation between the paired drawings of heads from a wilfully partial reading of the complex system of the work. If I began with the female head(s) of *Untitled*, for example, what could prompt me to imagine that the differences in line and shade from one to the other – (and are they really there? my eye is not so sure ...) – might signify 'faint surprise'?

In any case, this fanciful description is a byproduct, and not an explanation, of the effect created by *his* head: of coming first, starting something, setting great events in train. And it was this effect that I set out to leave behind.

Clearly, it rather derives from his adjacency to the industrial landscape that sustains, interrupts and mediates his relation to the image of that other man, subordinate (*his* gaze hits the side of his face).

That tall, central tower is grossly symbolic ... overwhelmingly, unmistakably, THAT.

And it's *his*, no doubt about it. (Re)production is at stake here, with property rights and power. It is the tower, as well as his pose, that makes *this* head of a man a portrait of a progenitor. His is a founding figure of, and from, a whole cultural order I must assume in order to recognize him, and still to be intrigued. (Here is another difference. With all the other images, I want to know, with the irrepressible curiosity of the amateur, 'where does it come from?' With this one, I ask, 'who's he?') Furthermore, his primacy is extended and completed by the *other man*; in this relation, this tableau, this ordering of representation, 'there are no ladies'; for this so symbolic economy, the most feminine of parts is what the other man exposes, the synecdoche of his supplementary – that receptive device, an ear.

He was so vigorous, and withal so eloquent, that Evelyn understood at last how he had always been able to carry his board of directors with him. She was glad to see that Dan had crept into the room and was listening.
　　　　Vita Sackville-West, *Family History* ('Portrait of the Jarrolds')

So part of *his* charm, no doubt, is that I supplement his image with a voice. His 'presence' derives from my past. He is a composite figure of memory: he reminds me of a film by Jean Eustache, *Une sale histoire*, about a voyeur who yearns to tell women his story, but declares that their ears are 'defective'; of a photograph by Charlandré von Jobin, a huge question mark superimposed on a 'portrait' of an ear; of a performance-text by Jean-Michel Raynaud, for which the speaker's place must be taken by that imaged interrogative ear . . . It's a pleasure to look at *his* head; all I have to do is to listen (lend an ear).[1]

But this does not explain why in *The Observer and the Observed (Men and Women) #2*, the power of the portrait fades before me. Its position remains proprietorial, the relation between the men the same. Its hierarchical reciprocity is horizontally extended, rather than reversed or contradicted, by the substitution of images between them in the vertical plane.

Yet this work does act in many ways as a reversal of the first – by colour; by the posing of a human, and female, figure in and as the scene of mediation; by the use of a domestic 'interior'; by the eerie eventfulness of its shallow space, its superimpositions; by its magazine-page assemblage effect, its jaunty commercial design: and by the scattering of signs of consumption as spectacular, as obvious in their way, as the rearing productive tower – a cascade of flying commodities, of which the woman might well be one.

At the same time, there seems to be a shift between the two – a historical development, a fictive sequence (from production to consumption, from factory to home, from early-high to early-late capitalist 'periods', from one phase to another in a 'life' . . .).

But this shift results from the locking into place of a set of oppositions allowing me to see *Men and Towers* retrospectively as the enabling condition for this, its now perfect, complement. For visibly, obviously, the industrial and domestic images exist synchronically in the space of the sequence. Both are drawn, obviously and visibly, from an image-repertoire of the real in the present, and present discourses on the past. They are here and now, there, together.

It doesn't matter (the reversal works, and so does my sense of history). What draws me here is not the head but the commodity scene, and its curious hard-line gaiety. This is a space of kitchen magic, consumer bricolage, labour-saving appropriation: that toaster, this iron, floats up as well as down; the housewife rises on a flying carpet as her skirt sweeps out around (oh, the *fun* of modernity!). This is a field of ecstatic prosthesis – that toaster becoming a breast, that pot extending a hand, in giddy contiguity. There is no temptation here to a realist fiction, to found meaning in plot-and-character ('depth'), and in looming metaphor. This image between men is Allegory, with consumption its privileged figure and metonymy its conjuring device.

I am as though confronted by stereotypes of two opposing aesthetics – both terribly familiar. Each accuses the other of a certain sentimentality ('realist ideology' *vs* 'period-effect'). Yet they are mutually interdependent in the system of reversals; and also interchangeable in the circuit of the gaze.

That interchangeability supports the aesthetic of *Men and Woman*. It can incorporate, subsume, the scene of *Men and Towers*, as well as place it as retro-spective. And that woman's arms outstretched, hands hinting at display, claims credibility from her setting: she is surrounded, is she not, by an art of metonymic assemblage, of commodity conjunction?

So, at least, an allegorical reading suggests. Looking back to *Men and Towers*, I am accused of nostalgia, and *'piercing regret for the head'*.[2]

It's true that in looking at *Men and Towers*, there is a restful security to be savoured in representation. I can look at its beauty, with the gaze of a proprietor, yet enjoy my exteriority. I am outside this system, which I nevertheless control: I am the amused voyeur (phalluses, really, are funny), observing observation. I look at *him* (and It).

But the effect of *Men and Woman* is the opposite, and in an unexpected way. It's a reality-effect, a blast of connotation, a violent revulsion of memory. If this image between men is an Allegory, this space between men is Hell (that bright social destiny). Its keeper is a woman, and she is looking straight at me.

Or rather, *Art* looks at me. (I remember a picture popular in the 1950s, an opaline face swathed in veils, and eyes that had the trick of following wherever you went. It was thought to be very artistic. It was entitled, *Head of a Girl*.)

II

She wandered to the door which opened straight on to the invisible garden, and stood on the threshold looking out into the night. ... The lake, she supposed, must lie in thatt[3] direction. The lighted room lay behind her, but in front of her were darkness and shadow, which her eyes could not explore.
Vita Sackville-West, *Family History* ('Portrait of Miles Vane-Merrick')

And at *Untitled (Couple and Waterfall)*, I strike trouble with Art, and titles.

The title *Untitled* asks a question about the relations between the visual and the verbal. It is also a cliché title for a work of visual art (and so, asks a question about titles).

As a high conventionalized paradox (a verbal declaration of suspension of the verbal), it asserts the history of a certain myth of Art (*Visuality*). But in the moment of asserting its visuality and verbal indefiniteness, any work entitled *Untitled* is placed in the vast series of visual works defined by the *word* 'Untitled'.

Untitled, like all titles, is a reading instruction. It tell us we are not to interpret from titles, but from looking at the work of art. But it is a reading instruction we must disobey in order to see (to do) what it says.

This paradox is underlined here by the two parenthetical titles – *(Couple and Waterfall), (Couple and Fire) # 2* – which are strictly, outrageously, descriptive. It is intensified by the opening of the set with a gridded drawing of a painting by Courbet – de-titled, re-titled, and paired here not only with a 'couple', but with a gorgeous industrial accident. It is staged by a new obliqueness in the scenario of the gaze: the woman is there to-be-looked-at, 'looking' artless, unaware, as any (art) object, of my gaze; the man, however, proffers himself as he looks, head turned to that exact degree of ostentation that signifies 'exhibitionism', a to-be-looked-at-ness of Art.

There is also a complication to this scene of *Visuality*, made unnervingly obvious as I seek routine ways of referring to Richard Dunn's visual 'work' in this exhibition, and of distinguishing its parts. The series containing *Untitled* really is untitled. (I am irresistibly drawn to write this as a negative – a series 'without', 'lacking', 'not given' a title.)

It is very annoying. There is no way of mentioning 'it' casually, in passing, without stumbling on a problem of designation (these-four-drawings? series-of-cruciform-grids? sequence-of-four works? sequence-of-four-works-from-a-series-of-cruciform-grids?). It produces unwieldy compounds and pedantic specifications, that destabilize whatever it is that I may really want to say. It is particularly annoying since *It* visibly creates effects of formal unity which I would like, at times, to be able to take for granted.

And the trouble doesn't stop there (or 'here'). If both *The Observer and the Observed* and *Untitled* are sets containing instances, or case-studies, of a general problem, both sets we see here are also sub-sets – since the recurring sign *# 2* suggests that these objects have been selected from two larger sets containing a number of versions of each instance (as well as further instances, and versions of instances, not included here). These sets are subdivisions of a series, defined by the repetition of a cruciform visual figure. But 'cruciform' will rarely serve me as a stable visual 'term'; each is subdivisible by plane, by section, and finally, by sheet.

(All this, of course, can be taken in at a glance.)

So *Untitled* acts in this sequence, this series, as a *mise en abyme* in reverse. It highlights, by contrast, the untitling of the series and the sequence in which it occurs; and it foregrounds a refusal to allow my taking-for-granted of these visual relations, or the identity of their terms. (I write this as a negative – 'refusal'). I become entangled, in each minute move of syntax, in their complexity; blocked, by their opacity in my discourse (I can say them, but badly) against their clarity on the wall.

I am falling for writing a myth of *Visuality*. (In fact, I'm nowhere near a work-on-a-wall. Are you?)

I am confusing designation with segmentation, segmentation with description, description with mapping, mapping with analysis, and analysis with designation. And I am muddling various models of the work's existence in several spaces and times – collapsing my looking, my writing, and my writing fictions of both.

Why? It isn't simply a matter of missing a handy proper name to 'match' with a visual object. On the contrary: this work reminds me that reference is a process of inventing relations (of which the act of nomination is a small, if crucial, part). *Untitled (Couple and Waterfall)* – for example – is a complex emblem of exactly that.

One reason for my matching urge may be the ordering of relations in the series precisely by a spatial play of *analogy*.

Different images, for example, are brought into an equivalence by the similarity in their positioning (the heads, the central scenes), and by formal effects of resemblance. That smoke in *Couple and Fire* is like a cascade of cloud; that cascade in *Couple and Waterfall* is thickly clouded with foliage that billows about like smoke.

The disturbing analogy, however, is to a certain model of language.

It's easy to see the series as a succession of huge plus signs, and an emblem of the act of conjunction: + + +, 'and' ... 'and' ... 'and'. Seeing it like this, it's possible to talk about it as representing a long proposition, something like a sentence.

The cruci*form* makes a further analogy tempting. As an intersecting of horizontal and vertical planes, it seems to map on to a surface the privileged figures of a rhetoric of selection and combination: paradigm/syntagm, association/displacement, substitution/contiguity ...

(So it might be more accurate to see each cruciform as a sentence, the series as a discourse, this sequence as a text.)

The interest of the effort is the way the analogies fail.

First, unlike '+', or 'and', the cruciform *contains* the material it connects (though it doesn't 'contain' – exhaust or limit – their significance). To see 'it' as *like* a conjunction, I ignore the images conjoined. Seeing it only in outline, I fail to see the space outlined.

Second, in seeing it as a map of horizontal/vertical figures I see the contestation, and not the illustration, of a critical vocabulary. To speak of 'axes' of selection and combination in discourse is, after all, quite precisely a figure of speech, not space.

So I'm not looking at a visual model for a theory of verbal discourse. I'm looking at a visual text that maximizes the ambiguity of the analogies that makes describing it in these terms possible.

This, perhaps, is its critique of *Visuality*, and of my desire to match it.

... she was aware of the gravest differences between them. She was full of premonitions which she tried to hide from herself. She did succeed in hiding them. But they were there, like a black cloud at which she refused to look.
Vita Sackville-West, *Family History* ('Portrait of Miles Vane-Merrick')

Except in times of commodity fetishism for linguistic theory in art, a graceful art-critical practice depends on ignoring minute matters of reference (or on solving such problems quietly, behind the scene of the text).

A common alternative to making a scene about reference is to produce, from a rhetorical position very far back from the work (the towering position of 'overview') a paraphrase of its 'concerns'. Connecting these to constellations of paraphrases of other works, of a context, of current critical theory, we forget about figures of speech and figures in space, and blend them both in the *topic.*

Here a new twist to *Untitled* occurs. This untitled series combines the intimidating form of the grid – the very sign, as Rosalind Krauss has suggested, of 'modern art's will to silence, its hostility to literature, to narrative, to discourse'[4] – with a selection of images which are, on the contrary, only all too easily *spoken.* These images are polemically eloquent, not mute.

It is as if the mythic structure most resistant, most closed to verbalization has been opened up by images most unresistant to discourse – yet least inviting of written supplement to frame their immediate significance.

If I try to write one sort of overview, a series of critical topoi easily starts to form: '*a play on paradoxes of difference and repetition, original and copy, to explore the shifting relations betweeen production and consumption, artwork and commodity, public and private, industrial and domestic, art and media in the hierarchies of power and desire inscribed in the circuits of the gaze in mass-mediatized late capitalist culture where images...*'
This sentence, like the series, is infinitely extendable.

But unlike the series, the sequence, the set *Untitled,* or the cruciform, it merely accumulates terms – to state its own contemporaneity (which is a referent of that sentence). It can see the work as a structuring of an archive, rather than a structural model, of meaning(s) – but it smudges the extraordinary co-incidence of the two possibilities in the space of the visual work. Avoiding the agony of detail, it becomes a discursive smear.

Untitled (Couple and Waterfall), for example, does more than add an image of Art – and Landscape – and Quotation – and Museum – and Commodification – and a 'waterfall' – to the syntagm of vertical planes; more than bring generation and gender into the field of observation;

more than initiate for discourse a new play of dualities (water/fire, rural/urban, scene/incident ...).

It transforms the syntagm that allows me to name what it 'adds'. It acts as a hinge between two scenes of gazing, brings doubt as well as analogy into the play between their terms. And it revises the previous images by *breaking* oppositions, destroying, as well as making, symmetries: 'public and private', 'production and consumption', for example, already ambi-valent in *The Observer and the Observed,* now converge in an image of an artwork which is also, here, an idyll between lovers, and an aesthetic site of exchange; an outcome, a prelude, and a nexus of social and cultural relations.

To put it like that, however, is to return to talk of topic. What happens with each cruciform is rather that something *happens,* and it modifies everything else (including my ease with my topoi). There is a general situation represented, and a situation of representation, dense with associations and yet quite clearly defined. There is also an event, of an acute particularity.

Their encounter undermines any sense that I already know what is happening, what each image is about – what factories and toasters and paintings and fires have to do with one other, and with towers and woman and waterfalls and smoke. If there is a model of social relationships here, as well as a model of discourse, it is a model of the eventful ambiguity of the moment, the incident, the sensation, as well as of the enduring order.

And looking, minutely, at titles once again, I can see a certain change. *Men and Towers, Men and Woman, Couple and Waterfall, Couple and Fire*: progressively, it is the visual image that interprets the title, and not the other way round.

'Towers' seems to name exactly that first central image. There is an effect of descriptive match – between the transparency of the name to the drawing, of the drawing to the photograph to the real. It is a space of clear definition (yet of dense connotation). 'Woman', however, is already inflected by the allegory it names: 'woman' here is an *array*, a set of appliances, a metonymic field, a volatility in constriction. By 'Waterfall', the accumulation of images almost fully controls the word. The possibility of 'matching' here between noun and 'falling water', or even noun and 'picture of waterfall', lingers now like a ripple of humour, the eddy of a joke. And 'Fire' has an inevitability now generated by the sequence, which colours the word with its sense of an ending, of trans-formation, and of return to a beginning.

III

*It was no good straying about the room, being so restless. He might be left
alone there for hours; he must try to concentrate on something, must try to
keep some grasp on life. ... Looking about for a book, he found one ...*
Vita Sackville-West, *Family History* ('Obituary Notice of Evelyn Jarrold')

Is it possible now to combine in any way, from any stable position, these
assorted observations of a work? There is an imbalance in my reading; a
sense that if *The Observer and the Observed* gives me an angle from
which to look and a rhetoric to adopt, then *Untitled* takes both away.
This is still, in a way, a mimetic response (but to a non-'mimetic' art –
and so, in fact, contradictory).

One kind of overview does let me produce a coherence and a position
in relation to all four objects: '*Once upon a time there was a handsome
but ruthless man who worked very hard and rose to become the head of
his own corporation. He married and had children and was a tyrant to his
family. But eventually his son took over the business and fell in love with
a beautiful woman and took her to France to look at landscapes, and they
were rich and leisured and happy. But someone set fire to the factory, and
that was the end of that.*' ('To be continued')

What I see, and like, immediately about the work is its resemblance to
a family saga. Or to an episode, or two episodes, from a serial (since
another cruciform added could put an end to the ending).

The whole work can then be seen as a complex pun on 'relations' (a
network of affinities, with a touch of consanguinity).

This is an act of wilful partiality, and of piercing regret for the head.

But it can be justified (no smoke without fire). This grid is not hostile
to narrative. I can derive my story by reading each cruciform, left to
right, as a triptych,[5] each triptych, left to right, as a narrative sequence –
the central section transforming the static event on the left (Before) into
the static event on the right (After). Each set of two cruciforms then
becomes an elliptical narrative; I must infer the central transformation
between the 'states of affairs' represented. Then I read all four
cruciforms from left to right as a sequence turning on a double transformation: one composed by *Men and Woman* plus *Couple and Waterfall*,
the other inferred between them.

To do this I project causality into consecution. That is what narrative,
and narration, does. But I also read the images as intelligible to, and
articulate of, certain social and historical logics.

And in this way, I can see better how to write their visuality, and no
longer as a titling myth. There is a narrative of the transformation of
colour from *Men and Towers* to *Couple and Fire*; of the transformation

of dyads and quatrains into triads, of symmetries into assymetry; of the transformation of space in an intersecting of planes and lines; of the transformation of images by acts of representation, of meanings by acts of conjoining; of the transformation of the obvious, the solved, into the curious form of a question. (There is also a question of a mystery behind the scenes; another event, invisible behind the masking vertical sections, that completes in a fictive space the horizontal story.)

If the work is read as a narrative, as well as a product, of transformation, the cruciform becomes the emblem of its production – a figure, in both the rhetorical and visual senses, of an act of *mise en intrigue*.

It is a configuration. It spatially represents the co-incidence of certain formal events, as well as a *mise en scène* of meaning. But it also confronts the observer with a moment; not only preserving 'that moment when a plane in one dimension crosses a plane in a second',[6] but the intersection of that moment with another in time – in which someone looks at a work of art, and wonders (with the irrepressible curiosity of the amateur) what, and how, it means.

Interpreting these moments in order to form my saga, to dream of dynasties and dramas, I draw on my own archive of everyday social knowledge: a blur of acquired assumptions (topics – like 'archive') about the way my culture works. I am a *head*, in fact, full of clichés.

But seeing each cruciform, I see the vaguely familiar transfigured by a luminous particularity: I see the durability of a social structure in the obdurate mystery of the everyday, the poignancy of an instant.

This helps to explain, though not to resolve, my mimetic intrigue with the work – desire to describe, to say everything at once, and from every imaginable position (the pansynchronic delirium – to which succumbing, for critics, is fatal).

It is not a matter of insoluble tension between verbal and visual discourse; and not a desire for an impossible imitation or identity. If anything, it's an urge to contradict the structuring achievement of the art – to fail, in response, to structure.

There's admiration in that, and nostalgia: the effect of an Imaginary indivisibility from this rigorously analytical work is, paradoxically, quite strong. But there's also a response to *something like* a representation of a certain experience of reality: that feeling of surprise, perhaps, that I still see in the image of the woman's head on the right of *Untitled (Couple and Fire) # 2*, a surprise, in looking, that I want then to make my own. This is the experience (*hers*) that makes one want to make, not to recognize, meanings – the experience of the density, the clarity, unnameable like the Real, of a moment before writing begins.

And as soon as I must begin, I am at liberty to observe, intrigued by a

luminous particularity, that the head of the man on the left-hand side of
The Observer and the Observed (Men and Towers) #2, is very, very
handsome.

PART III

9

Politics Now (Anxieties of a Petty-Bourgeois Intellectual)

14 July 1985

The bourgeoisie cannot exist without constantly revolutionising the instruments of production, and thereby the relations of production, and with them the whole relations of society. Conservation of the old modes of production in unaltered form was, on the contrary, the first condition of existence for all earlier industrial classes. Constant revolutionising of production, uninterrupted disturbance of all social conditions, everlasting uncertainty and agitation distinguish the bourgeois epoch from all earlier ones. All fixed, fast-frozen relations, with their train of ancient and venerable prejudices and opinions, are swept away, all new-formed ones become antiquated before they can ossify. All that is solid melts into air, all that is holy is profaned, and man is at last compelled to face with sober senses his real conditions of life and his relations with his kind.

Manifesto of the Communist Party, 1848

Earlier this year,[1] the *Sydney Morning Herald* published a stirring letter from Frank Hardy on the occasion of the publication of the *Oxford Anthology of Australian Literature*. In exhilarating terms, with a great deal of pep and fire, Hardy attacked what he called the 'baleful' influence of Professor Leonie Kramer on the study and dissemination of Australian writing. I enjoyed this letter very much until I got to the end, and then something went badly wrong – as though present realities shifted and disappeared, and instead of reading a piece of living polemic I was suddenly hearing dialogue from a full-dress period-nostalgia mini-series on TV. This happened when Hardy, for the benefit of Professor Kramer, quoted, from Henry Lawson's poem 'The Uncultured Rhymer to His Cultured Critics', these famous lines:

I leave you alone in your cultured halls
To drivel and croak and cavil:

173

Till your voice goes further than college walls,
Keep out of the tracks we travel.

Now the trouble with this, and what gives it that 'period' quality as a
piece of abuse, is that unfortunately Professor Kramer's influence might
indeed be described as 'baleful' by her opponents precisely because it
does go further than college walls: quite a lot further, in fact (I believe
they even heard it in Katingal);[2] and much further, I suspect, than Frank
Hardy's own voice these days. That's the trouble with cultural travel,
and fellow-travelling, today: there's a shuttle service in the hyperspace
between the cultured halls, the college walls, the prison walls, and the
tracks, and there's a lot more baleful riff-raff on the road than there
used to be.

That's a way of beginning to speak about cultural politics by stating
that there have been huge shifts in the relationship of 'intellectuals' (in
the broadest sense of that term, that is to say those whose work is with
ideas and ideology) to politics; obviously since the time of Lawson and
Lawson's populism, but also since the 1950s, the last period for which
Hardy's rhetoric might have still seemed plausible (if already anachronistic). These shifts in turn are merely components in a dynamic of a
greater uncertainty, the instability in our understanding of the relations
between 'culture' and 'politics'.

Since today's forum is about 'The Politics of Culture, the Arts and
Media', I want to address this instability between the terms of 'culture'
and 'politics', but I don't initially want to do so in large or general
theoretical terms – though I do want to argue eventually that this is
indeed what must be done, and done by everybody, not just by self-
appointed so-called 'theorists'. But I don't want to start with general
terms because, as what this conference has been calling a 'cultural
worker', I must say that I'm *very nervous* about 'politics'; and I don't
think that I can manage a way through current debates, or envisage
actions and/or alliances of the sort suggested here today by Denis
Freney, without at least admitting that nervousness and trying to be a bit
honest about its basis.

This means that in the first part of my paper I'll be speaking a bit
personally, although I'm rather embarrassed by the 'speaking personally
...' style. I've always disliked the idea that personal speech is somehow
more authentic than any other sort, not because I don't accept that the
personal is political (I do), but because I don't accept that the political is
only personal. So it's therefore a symptom of my own malaise, probably,
that I can't think of any other way to start talking about 'politics' at the
moment except from personal experience and observation. I know how
to be political without being personal in relation to particular activities

undertaken in 'culture', 'the arts', 'media'; but as several speakers at this conference have been reminding us, that's not the same thing as 'politics' proper, is it ...? Obviously, I could resolve this dilemma for myself by taking refuge in feminism, asserting a 'feminist politics' that I could lay claim to simply by virtue of being a woman and being engaged in public speaking at this very moment. If I refuse that possibility – for the moment – it's not because I want feminism wiped from the political agenda (I don't), but because adopting what would be in this context the very safe, indeed privileged, speaking position of feminist politics might hide the very political anxieties I want to stress.

* * *

I can't help being aware that this is the first time in almost ten years that I've attended a large, mixed, cross-activity talkfest run by 'The Left'. It will be ten years this November, in fact, for the last Big Political Event I went to in Sydney was a large meeting of feminists held to discuss the fall, or the tripping, of the Whitlam government in 1975. At least, it started out as a large meeting – to discuss 'theory', and how it had come about that this terrible thing could have happened while we somehow hadn't been looking – but over a month of recriminations and accusations it ended up with a few paranoid coteries. I don't know what they did because I didn't fit in to one – and began henceforth to work, as I have ever since, either completely alone just writing, or engaged in intense but ephemeral group actions in the purely cultural sphere (journals, teaching, forums, etc.). This was a fairly classical Left trajectory: start out wanting to learn all the secrets of political economy in four weeks, and end up discovering that the real secret is that your worst enemy lived in a nearby terrace and was trying to sabotage the vegie collective. Or to monopolize the attentions of some Marxist 'star', Marxist stars being much in demand for a month back then.

At least, it was a fairly classical trajectory for the kind of Left movement that ends up saddled with lots of people like me – writers, artists, lumpenculturati, let's face it, petty-bourgeois intellectuals – unstable, undependable, selfish, tunnel-visioned, sectarian, impatient, easily discouraged, easily swayed; able to get violently angry about the minute details of theological disputes and yet remain deaf, dumb and indifferent in the face of mass suffering; mere reeds bending before the prevailing wind or, to choose a culturally more pertinent metaphor, an unpleasant inner-city species that crawls in and out of the woodwork according to the season. And it's all true: or at least, it's part of my argument to accept that kind of political description. For if, as Denis Freney and others have suggested this weekend, the nature of the current right-wing ideological offensive is such that 'culture' becomes a major battleground, then it may no longer be sufficient for the more solidly-based Left to simply diagnose the nastiness of the petty-bourgeois 'kind'.

At any rate, for me and for quite a few kindred spirits, those events in 1975 marked the end of a whole period of classical political activism. Now it's 1985: instead of meeting to discuss the felling of the Whitlam government, we're meeting, for other reasons, by accident, during the week that marked the fall – or is it the felling – of Lionel Murphy, arguably the most progressive judge in Australian history, and certainly in recent Australian history. So I want to make a schematic comparison between the petty-bourgeois condition in 1975, and today, in terms of the destabilizing of 'cultural politics' – more precisely, of the leaking away of the 'political' in that period. Ken Wark has objected quite rightly to the sort of periodization (in, say, debates about postmodernism and politics) that involves drumming up a *Zeitgeist*, a spirit of the age, and discussing problems in terms of a drama of generations. I hope I'm not doing that, because all I want to do is specify particular changes during a time defined not just by two major political events (the dismissal of Whitlam, the conviction of Murphy), but also by two mass-media signifiers (since there has been debate already about whether signifiers, and their subversion, really matter). I'm referring to the fabrication of significance, amounting to the creation of complex myths, coagulated over months of media insistence on two terms which in turn help to define events of far-reaching political significance, namely: 1975/PETRODOLLARS; and 1985/MY LITTLE MATE.[3]

So here is a possible schema of change, remembering that I'm using 1975 to mark the end of a longer period rather than as a moment in itself, and that I'm only concerned with the activities of petty-bourgeois (leftist) intellectuals.

1. In 1975, cultural politics were the concern of the *full-time radical.* It was a matter of taking politics *to* various cultural activities. These politics were not pieces of fixed, closed dogma; they were open to reformulation through the experience of cultural work, but they were acquired from the various social movements (feminism, gay liberation, anti-psychiatry) and then brought to bear on one's media work, writing, film-making and so on.

By 1985, the full-time radical has in many cases become the *radical professional* – operating in a fairly narrow but precisely defined sphere of activity, with 'politics' increasingly defined by, and in terms of, the day-to-day conflicts structuring that (usually institutional) activity. This can mean vastly increased local and concrete effectiveness, but it also means far fewer new general political ideas, and ideas of politics, coming in.

2. *Circulation*: in the era of full-time radicalism, much the same personnel keep circulating through and around a range of quite different activities. This leads to exhaustion, paranoia and burn-out, but it also creates a buddy network – a sort of familial alliance system (complete with enmities and feuds), probably inevitable in a smallish population, which generates a tradition of 'lifestyle' leftism in which burnt-out as well as still-active activists define their politics by their opinions, their friends, and their memories.

With the rise of radical professionalism, circulation gives way to *redundancy*. Adjacent areas of cultural activity develop in complete or almost complete mutual ignorance, even when these activities are very closely related (e.g. film, the visual arts, community access video). Workers from one area almost never turn up at another's debates and events, even when the same or similar issues are being discussed. Yet this system also gives rise to a buddy network and to lifestyle alliances; however these are now activity, or 'profession', based, in standard petty-bourgeois style – rather than emerging from any shared diverse political experience.

3. The debacle of 1975 could be regarded as the symbolic end-point of a phase of intellectual *gay abandon*. With entirely cheerful confidence and passion (look back now at, say, Shulamith Firestone's *Dialectic of Sex*), radicals had set about a process of totally revising, rewriting or just rejecting all inherited frameworks of understanding, i.e. the heritage of 200 years of European radicalism. So much so that by early 1975 many felt that the Whitlam government was 'nothing to do with us'.

Whatever else it may have had to do with us, its decline could also be regarded as a symbolic beginning-time for a long phase of deep, conservative, *suspicion and inertia* on the Left – at least in relation to frameworks of understanding, especially of understanding matters cultural. Stylized disapproval takes the place of analysis and action, with the result that political commitment comes to be treated – understandably if tragically – as *bad style* in some of the livelier arenas for cultural debate (try flipping through the last few years' history as defined in *On The Beach, Virgin Press, Cantrill's Filmnotes*). Two examples might be the complete failure of the Left to respond positively or effectively to the phenomenon of *Art & Text*, and the mood of coy trauma that coagulated around the event of the *Futur*fall* conference at Sydney University last year.[4] Both seem to me to be instances of a general tendency for the Left to be content to operate purely reactively, and to bask complacently in its own lack of energy, loss of initiative.

4. In 1975 everything was, oppressively, Political. By 1985 everything has become, obscurely, Cultural.

('The Left' is a sort of logjam between these two currents, with some forces still pressuring cultural workers to act as though everything is and must be political, while other forces make it hard to imagine any salvage of 'politics' at all).

As Charles Newman says at the beginning of a very conservative little book full of reactionary values and wonderful one-liners called *The Post-Modern Aura*, such statements only amount to 'a dim pathology of the contemporary, which amounts to Art is everywhere and Life is vague'. To frame his own pathology, Newman chooses a quotation from the loathsome Philippe Sollers – a French novelist who followed another classical petty-bourgeois trajectory by becoming a maoist and winding up in the embrace of christianity – who said once upon a time that,

> No longer is it, 'When I hear the word Culture, I reach for my revolver.' We are permitted instead, 'Culture sits so well in my pocket that whenever I hear the word "thought" I smile'.[5]

The point of my schema, then, is not to lament the loss of the good old days (I personally didn't like them very much), but to ask what has happened on and through the Left that has helped to foster these shifts, and that creates problems when 'radical professional' practice becomes a dominant model in a time of expanding culture, shrinking politics, ubiquitous Art and fading Life.

One thing seems to have been an increasing incapacity for lifestyle leftism to perceive its own cultural functioning, or to understand its reduction to, apparently, yet another subculture (complete with buddy-system) among others. We hear a lot these days about superficial style-obsessed postmoderns: but the smart young things about town have very little indeed to teach the Left about the politics of authoritarian control through style. We're the ones, after all, who installed a ruthless surveillance system monitoring every aspect of style – clothing, diet, sexual behaviour, domestic conduct, 'role-playing', underwear, reading matter, 'accessibility' versus 'obscurantism' in writing and art, real estate, interior decoration, humour – a surveillance system so absolute that in the name of the personal-political, everyday life became a site of pure semiosis. And this monitoring process functioned constantly to determine what styles, which gestures, could count as good ('valid', 'sound') politics, and which ones could not. When I think of the resulting loss to the Left of so much goodwill, enthusiasm, commitment and activist energy coming from quarters not necessarily immediately recognizable as 'ours', a loss often directly attributable to the Left's own conservatism, inertia, and punitive style-scrutineering, the fact that some stylish young kid might be striking nihilistic poses in the latest art-exhibition catalogue is quite frankly the very least of my worries.

A second development can be described as mental bureaucratization, or addictive gravy-training. This occurs when purely administrative conflicts and/or funding (welfare) ploys come to substitute completely for any other form of politics. It is the underside of what has been undoubtedly one of the greatest achievements of 1970s radical politics, namely the occupation by the Australian Left of positions of real and effective social and political power. So I am *not* attacking bureaucratic and funding politics in the name of some pure powerlessness and powerless purity.

Nevertheless, there does seem to have developed over a number of years an increasing reluctance, in a number of different spheres of activity, to discuss or even to recognize the need for criticisms of basic principles, for the renewal of broad debate. Those who are concerned by such debates – for example, those around postmodernism and consumer capitalism which have been the subject of one forum here – are suspected of wankerist tendencies with the same monotonous predictability with which anyone attempting to bring new or unfamiliar *general* ideas to bear on radical politics is likely to be accused of obscurantism – unless the practical applicability of those ideas is immediately obvious, and so doesn't really need discussion in the first place. The most appalling concrete example of bureaucratization that I've seen lately has been around documentary film-making – once one of the liveliest sites of political cinema in Australia, now so saturated by chronic bureaucratitis that at recent film festival forums few film-makers seem able to get beyond recriminations over getting $100,000 instead of $120,000. It's an understatement, a gesture at politeness for old times' sake, to say that in a climate like this it's hard to get much of a sense of value or values, of political direction or purpose. It's harder still to persuade anyone outside the alliance system, the buddy-network, that 'politics' so conducted is in any way an important or desirable pursuit – or even that politics is really what's at stake amidst such flagrantly personal manoeuvring.

This is compounded by that endless blackmail to Urgency that the Left's so adept at bringing to bear on wankers, obscurantists, anyone who looks like dreaming or wondering or goofing off into (heaven preserve us) the exploration of possibilities unknown. The sense of urgency itself is surely understandable, but the blackmail always seems to insist that response take the tried and trusted paths (that is, often, the very ones that haven't been working very well, which is why the situation's still urgent). I sometimes feel that every day for fifteen years I've been told that today's crisis is too urgent for me to take the time to work on a project that might only come clear tomorrow – with the result that the same old solutions keep on failing day after urgent day.

Someone might well say that my range of references today – from *Art & Text* to documentary film forums – simply shows what narrow and trivial preoccupations I have, and that if I got out amongst community groups and other real people I might see things in a different perspective. Maybe. But my point is precisely that 'radical politics', and the possibilities for imagining anew what that might mean, seem to have shrunk to a set of very fixed, rigid reference-points – to a repertoire of narrow and moralizing attitudes. And to return the blackmail to urgency, I must say that this seems to me to be a very dangerous time for that to happen.

Events like this conference obviously imply a change, and a desire for more change, so I don't wish to appear to be carping. But before I will be able to talk, or talk again, to people with a more direct relation to activist politics than I now have, I need to be at least able to say that (unstable petty-bourgeois as I am) I have been finding it increasingly difficult to stay 'Left' political, since nearly every time I've tried to do something 'political' in my own narrow sphere and according to my lights, 'the Left' kept getting in the way – bearing down again and again with all the weight of its incredible inertia and suspicion. At times it almost seems that the characteristic Left theoretical question has become – '*What's all this crap, then?!*'

I'm aware that throughout this paper I've been invoking a monolithic and mythical 'Left', a Left-with-a-capital-L, inviting everyone to identify themselves with it yet making it most unattractive for anyone to do so. The relationship that I've established between myself and this Left is simply and crudely oedipal, with this heavy figure bearing down punitively like ... Yet this figure, mythic as it well may be, in fact defines many of my real anxieties about politics, and it has arisen from many a real experience. Who could forget the occasion of Juliet Mitchell's visit to Sydney, soon after the publication of *Psychoanalysis and Feminism*? – a theoretical work which slowly over many years helped to transform large areas of feminist practice (in ways which I myself still think are pretty baleful), a book which proved to be of tremendous practical consequence, but which on its first appearance seemed difficult, mysterious and heretical. Mitchell completed a generous and enlightening lecture on her work, only to be greeted instantly with that voice, that nightmare voice of the Left, yelling boldly from up the back of the room, '*Yeah, Juliet, what about Chile?*' As it happens, I think Juliet Mitchell at that time was one of the feminists most equipped and able to deal with precisely that kind of political question. But the point at issue is not her competence, but the way that voice from the back could so smoothly inscribe itself – and politics – as a perfect *non sequitur*. This is not, I should stress, a matter of the gulf between intellectuals and the working class, but a matter of the way that petty-bourgeois intellectuals treat each other.

This is not *just* a whinge (although it's certainly partly just that). I'm mentioning these problems because I think that the combination of radical professionalism, bureaucratization and the sinking into lifestyle has produced a number of structural problems for the Left, which are really starting to matter in terms of a decreased effectiveness in practical matters, and a drooping spirit in speculative ones.

For example: as Helen Grace pointed out in the 'Film Criticism' session at this conference, there isn't really very much interest now in the actual products of cultural work. It's rather a matter of monitoring ideologically-sound production processes or, if that's not appropriate, the producer's personal political profile. Helen stressed that this is not to call for a renewed interest in Objects as discrete, collectable items available for aesthetic admiration, but to point out that in spite of the rhetoric about a need for Left intervention in culture, most products are not discussed and utilized as the *social* objects they're supposed to be.

It would be easy to draw up a very long list of abandoned or neglected products which could have given rise to a broader and more productive debate (in the sense of going beyond the immediate context in which they first appeared). A few examples which come to mind almost at random from the contexts I've been involved in are: Sylvia Lawson's *The Archibald Paradox*, which could have been read as providing a political theory of journalism; the *Art and Social Commitment* exhibition organized by Charles Merewether last year, which was hardly ever discussed as bearing on the art of the present (I thought it could easily be used as a way of discussing the plays of Stephen Sewell); the installation orchestrated by Dennis del Favero around elements of Italian migrant experience; Virginia Coventry's great work on mining and documentary photography, called *Whyalla – Not A Document*; the painting that Richard Dunn has been making for the last few years; innumerable films, like *Two Laws* (used effectively by Aboriginal communities in different parts of Australia, it's true – but when one long letter was published in *Filmnews* trying to begin a critical debate in Sydney, no-one ever replied in print); Helen Grace's *Serious Undertakings*, a film actually saturated in 'coverage', reviews, etc., and which even stimulated an article by Ross Harley analysing the coverage, but which was never, to my knowledge, criticized seriously or substantially in public; Pauline Johnson's book *Marxist Aesthetics* which ought, one would think, to be a major focus of debate at a conference like this, but which you have to hear about by accident in order to even know that it exists.[6]

These are examples taken only from the last few years, which I've chosen in part because most of them should in fact be fairly familiar at least by reputation. Because precisely what is *not* much use is the reduction of works to 'reputation' (whether of the person or the product) – which is what happens when response is limited to one or two good reviews here and there. Sylvia Lawson has argued strongly for a more aggressive and enlightening approach to existing critical/ reviewing mechanisms, and that seems to me too to be an indispensable step towards a better public use of the political work that we've already got. At the same time, there should surely be some attention given to new mechanisms for disseminating knowledge of and debate about our 'products' beyond their narrow professional context – at least, there should if notions of broadly-based alliances including cultural workers are going to have any credibility beyond the level of worthy sentiment. For at the moment, I think, self-interest rules: artists go to art shows, a few film-makers go to film screenings and forums, academics mostly stay away from everything, and everyone watches television.

If that is a fairly negative assessment of the concrete state of a politics of culture, it also implies a positive statement that in spite of and in the midst of the fairly grim picture it's so easy to paint of politics today, the elements *for* a renewed radical and critical political culture are already available, right now, in all spheres of activity. The problem has been that they are just not utilized by the Left in the ways that they could be – perhaps because the Left (one sometimes suspects) has become more interested in simply reproducing itself as a social network at worst, or at best in maintaining an exclusive interest in access to production ('funding'). The National Library in Canberra is stuffed full of the unused film products of that particular philosophy.

A second structural problem I'd want to mention follows more or less directly from the lack of interest in actual products. This is the insistence on *repetition*: the way that the same problems and solutions keep on being recycled every few years, or at the same time in different areas, as though no one had ever dealt with them before and there was nothing to be learned from the past; and also, the way in which individuals are endlessly asked to perform returns to first principle, to keep on saying the same thing over and over again, since they can never assume a broad familiarity with their work in contexts where there's a claim to be interested in precisely that – the work. This problem is difficult to discuss in detail because any one example will always be trivial. But the cumulative effect of imposed repetition is *not* trivial, because it means that much of the complex history of radical cultural politics, even the immediate past, simply becomes unavailable for use.

Lack of interest in products, and insistence on repetition, both exacerbate a third problem which is the continual displacement of criticism by diagnoses of personal motivation. John MacDonald argued in the 'Postmodernism and Radical Politics' forum that criticism now needs to become more critical rather than celebratory, and more *self*-critical. I'd agree with that, as long as it's a matter of the criticism of products, and not of persons. It's not just that the buddy-systems and the life-styling encourage stress on the praise or denunciation of personalities in a way which is actually a poor, second-rate version of the ethos of *Interview*. It's rather that the lurid fantasies about *why* people do what they do, fantasies which are trademark of lifestyle leftism – so and so's power-hungry, narcissistic, self-seeking, opportunistic, exhibitionist etc. – are merely the broken-down, personal-is-political variant of an older tradition of discrediting what people say or do by revealing their class origins. In exactly the same way and for the same reasons, the criticism of motive can miss the point as did the criticism of class origin (see Lenin on Tolstoy): one can perfectly well *be*, in fact, power-hungry, narcissistic, etc. and produce work which – given that texts don't just translate intentions, and given that consumers are not purely passive – cannot be derived from or reduced to its maker's more unattractive characteristics. (Another question is why it is that, rather like women who never trust women, petty-bourgeois intellectuals can have such sensationally uncharitable visions of each other's intentions. Why does it so often seem plausible that because one disagrees with a particular action or argument, it automatically follows that its author's reasons must have been even more selfish, sordid, and suspect that the meanest spirit could possibly imagine?)

With these problems in mind, then, I want to argue that while the current stress on bureaucratic skills and on the politics of access (to funds, to institutions, etc.) must not only continue but attract support where and when it is threatened, we also need now, more than ever and *not* less, to pursue a politics of the distribution and dissemination of the products of such 'access'; and above all, to allow them to give rise to speculation, to thinking, to imaginative effort which does not have to give a pragmatic account of itself before it has barely begun to develop. Petty-bourgeois intellectuals do like to feel plugged into power by pounding the table loudly and calling, with suitably tough gestures, for attention to the Real World. That's fine: but pure pragmatism itself is not likely to be able to form the differentiating basis of a radical cultural politics in the Real World of R.J. Hawke's Australia. Distribution block-age and bureaucratization are mental and ideological phenomena as well as physical and institutional; and sometimes it seems that when we are most immersed in discussing the practical problems of the physical sort, we are most at the mercy of the paralysing effects of the other.

Does any of this really matter?

I think it does if Fredric Jameson, for example, is right in his analysis of 'Postmodernism, or the Cultural Logic of Late Capitalism'.[7] Jameson bases his own argument on that of Ernest Mandel in *Late Capitalism*, that, far from having entered into some new system unlike that analysed by Marx, we are now experiencing the purest phase of capitalism to date – since previously tolerated enclaves of pre-capitalism organization are now being eliminated. It follows that for Jameson, 'postmodernism' is not a style, an option, but a cultural logic corresponding to the current phase of the 'constant revolutionising of production' analysed in the famous passage from the *Manifesto* which I invoked at the beginning of this paper (a passage which is commonly used to explain modernism, but which works just as well to explain why postmodernism is in turn cannibalizing modernism). For this reason, Jameson claims that 'every position on postmodernism in culture – whether apologia or stigmatiz- ation – is also at one and the same time, and *necessarily*, an implicitly or explicitly political stance on the nature of multinational capitalism today.'[8]

This capitalism, which Jameson follows Mandel in defining by the machine production of electronic and nuclear-powered apparatuses since the 1940s, is accompanied by the emergence of a new cultural space with various characteristics which he explores in detail – such as a preference for pastiche over parody, the revival of older discourses on the sublime, the sense of nostalgia and sensitivity to period-ness (knowing exactly, for example, what 'very late-60s' means) accom- panied by a weakening of historical sense, the ending of Real History, and above all for my purposes here, the abolition of 'critical distance' – that creeping, contagious condition of being unable to get entirely outside the process of kitschification which invades the most passion- ately sincere gestures, actions and references.

For example, when I was deeply involved in a fit of leftist paranoia about this conference, a young friend said cheerfully 'Why worry? It's going to be nice! It's like a vintage car rally' ... Or to take a less private example (although the first one is not really so private in the precision of its awareness that all events have now become spectacles), let's consider the function of famous quotations from Marx of the sort with which I began. I can remember, dimly, a time when it was possible to watch in awe while Communist Party titans hurled quotations at each other as weapons in serious battles of interpretation (i.e. policy). Then came a time when the use of a quote became a means of flashing one's pedigree ('where I'm coming from'). Now, it's all too easy to imagine Famous Quotes from Marx as the latest version of Trivial Pursuit, or as the theme of an intricate video game. 'Now', of course, is that state of culture within which it's possible to use cutesy little pseudohistories of the sort I've just made up.

I won't continue describing Jameson's argument, since it's not my purpose here to address the postmodernism question for its own sake. There are certainly problems with his text; for example, his claim that consumer capitalism is now colonizing two big targets, Nature and the Unconscious. As Gayatri Chakravorty Spivak argued in her *Futur*fall* address, the generalizing force of this kind of analysis can disguise the fact that the development of postmodern culture in certain sectors of advanced industrial societies may depend upon the dissemination of *pre*modern economic and social conditions to particular groups elsewhere.

However, the value of Jameson's sketch for those who do work here in the contemporary culture industries, the arts, media (all those 'areas' piled together in the title of this forum and which add up to the wreck of the old concept of 'superstructure') seems to me to be its practical insistence that any critical political culture has to emerge within, and in relation to, the 'force field' of that postmodern culture which has, by its abolition of 'critical distance', made the old tools of ideology-critique, and the moral denunciation of the other, completely ineffective. I've tried to suggest in a very cursory and schematic fashion that the elements for such a 'critical political culture' are already available; and that what's hard is the task of imagining a different politics of their *use*, a more generous politics than the squawking and squabbling style of chookpen territorializing we've got now.

A second point would be that Jameson's analysis helps to set up a slightly different perspective on the long-standing dispute about the relations between aesthetics and politics. We were asked yesterday not to confuse aesthetic gestures, textual 'subversions', with political actions. Let's not. But let's also remember that in a mass-media society with mass-media cultures and mass-media politics, the relationship between *signifying* (rather than 'aesthetic') gestures and political ones may not be so clear-cut. For I suggest that no one is really in any danger of confusing a painting with a general strike, or of imagining that swopping a 'p' for a 'q' in a text is the same as hijacking an aeroplane. But to pose the question like that is to elide the much more difficult and important questions of the political status and function *of* signifying gestures (defamation, for example, is precisely that, and so is contempt of court); of the effect that the study of media could have on our understanding of politics, and thus on the formulation of political actions; and finally, the question of what the relationship of artistic and cultural work to other kinds of politics might actually become if it were fostered rather than dismissed by a denunciative (and self-defeating) sectarianism. I think that it is in relation to those questions that the anxieties of petty-bourgeois intellectuals begin to matter, and to demand attention rather than the contemptuous dismissal they may also, irrelevantly, deserve. The

Thatchers, the Reagans, the Hawkes fight (and lose, of course, as well as win) with images, ideas, myths, statistics, jokes and signs. A Left which refuses to think through the implications of that development, and to encourage rather than alienate those unstable, undependable creatures who reluctantly find themselves caught up, like it or not, in ideological conflicts, is likely to be a Left condemned to a perfectly postmodern nostalgia.

For all these reaons, one of the most 'political' things that I can think of doing at the moment, pitiful as this may sound and small as it undoubtedly is as a gesture, is to plead against a possibility looming on the horizon and articulated already a few times at this conference, namely – the return, under pressure, of the same old calls for plain-speaking, common sense, hard facts, immdiately practicality ... the tendency to say that things are too urgent now for serious people to be bothered with idle speculation, wild theorizing, and lunatic prose. I think precisely the opposite: that things are too urgent now for the Left to be giving up its imagination, or whatever imagination the Left's got left; and that the nature and the originality of today's urgency is such that any large-scale succumbing to that temptation is likely to bring politi-cally catastrophic results. The very last thing that's useful now is a return (as farce, rather than tragedy) to the notion of one 'proper' critical style, one 'realistic' approach, one 'right' concern.

And speaking of catastrophe, I want to conclude with the famous question from the postmodernism forum which probably best summed up the anxieties between different groups and different interests at this conference: '*Is the peace movement postmodern?*'

If Mandel and Jameson are even vaguely right, then the postmodern era could be said to begin in 1945, at Hiroshima and Nagasaki. It begins not simply on the ground, under the bomb, but in the relationship between that ground, those people, and the pilot who could only ever thereafter confront the 'reality' of that bomb, those deaths, through an image, a film, a story, a representation, a reconstruction, a vestige, a simulation of what had, or might have, happened on the ground. The postmodern begins with an experience in which it is impossible to 'see' unmediated empirical reality and survive; an experience which would-be survivors, potential victims, can only evoke and express with images, metaphors, fictions and rhetoric which they must try to convert into actions to ensure that we may never know that 'reality'. In this sense, if I were asked 'is the peace movement postmodern?', I could only reply: I don't know, but it'd bloody well better be.

10

Room 101

... *change, loss, an altered life,*
is only a danger when you become
devoted to disaster.
Lillian Hellman, *Scoundrel Time*

Or

What is this helpless anxiety
still waiting for, if the terrible
has already happened?
Martin Heidegger, 'The Thing'

A Few Worst Things In The World

> *'You asked me once,'* said O'Brien,
> *'what was in Room 101. I told you that*
> *you knew the answer already. Everyone*
> *knows it. The thing that is in Room 101*
> *is the worst thing in the world.'*[1]

simulation: more true than the true
seduction: more false than the false
the obscene: more visible than the visible
the secret: more hidden than the hidden

'la spirale du pire':[2] the strategy of inducing that which is worse, the spiral of worser and worser; the refusal to resort to primary opposition, but instead to intensify the same; the aggravation of the adjective outbidding its noun in an ecstasy of description.

With this device ('assured of a vertigo effect independent of any content or any particular quality'),[3] Jean Baudrillard has made the delirium of attributes his own. It is the thing (and perhaps the only thing) which clearly distinguishes Baudrillard's writings from the host of contemporary work to which his own plays the role of parodist, and parasite. Yet this delirium is also, for him, the delirium of our world – the interminable terminal illness of a case of permanent ecstasy. To which there is, it seems, at least one remedy: fight fever with fever, the pox with the pox.

We might find in this venerable practice of medication traces of more modern solutions in both politics (destabilization through terror, or toxic politics) and culture (the prescription to be beyond, or the present survived as 'post' – more present than the present). We might also observe that the oppositional relation refused in a first instance is simply revived in a second: not *true vs false, visible vs hidden,* but *simulation vs seduction, obscenity vs secrecy, banality vs fatality* ...

But both of these discoveries could be predicted by Baudrillard's texts. In the first case, any argument that the trick is all too familiar simply succumbs to the logic it might want to contest – and to which Baudrillard proposes ironic collusion as a *better* response than contestation. In the second, the higher-power oppositions turn out from text to text to be little more, and nothing less, than a formal rule. While seduction is often opposed to simulation, when porn (more true than the true) is opposed to the *trompe l'oeil* (more false than the false), porn and *trompe l'oeil* are opposed as, respectively, disenchanted and enchanted forms of simulation – that is, as antagonistic phases *of the same thing.* (Similarly, in the final chapters of *De la séduction,* the banal simulations of modern media and information are opposed to the fatal simulations of the lost age of aristocratic seduction – in terms of an opposition between cold and warm seduction.) Seduction may be the other of production, but it is not the other of simulation (although it may, at times, be its enemy): but seduction can, fortified by the secret of appearances, be infinitely more potent than both.

So Baudrillard's strength is not some chemistry of substances, but the magic of intensifying qualities. And as in all effective magic it is only the movement, the spiral of intensification, the 'raising of the power', that counts.

It is curious, then, that Baudrillard describes the vertigo-effect as the outcome of 'any characteristic thus raised to the *superlative power,* caught in a spiral of redoubling' (my italics).[5]

For surely, the dizzying force of the movement of 'more X than X'[6] is precisely that the superlative can never be attained – except as a mirage created in the speed of the spin, or a cruel illusion of stasis in which we think we find rest (*le pire*), at the very moment when the energies of the-same-but-worse gather for another displacement. Baudrillard conjures not superlative power, but comparison to infinity: and in that scenario, there are no worst things in the world. Then again, perhaps the superlative has become *the ecstasy of the comparative* (more comparative than the comparative): and if that is the case then worst things will proliferate, afflicted only by obsolescence.

Either way, the technique of adjectival escalation in Baudrillard's recent work is intimately bound up with the enigma of The Thing: not simply as object and as commodity, but as pure object and absolute commodity; as malign and ironic force for fatal reversibility that lies in wait for the subject and distracts it, deprives it of its truth in the moment of apparent triumph. The object is always *worse* than the subject: while the subject seeks the object, the object can defy the subject by ecstatic responsiveness (more! more! say the masses to the media) or by utter indifference (silence, inertia).

A theory, for Baudrillard, might let this object speak; and theory can become an object of this sort. Such a theory – fatal, objectal – would be a *théorie-récit*: not simply a fiction, and not only in the Victorian sense of fiction as that which is not 'true', but a theory-narrative, a theory-story.[7] While Baudrillard insists that this theory need not revive the novelistic or revert to 'literature', we can wonder whether it would not also provide a contemporary analogue to *the work of art* envisaged (according to a note in *Les Stratégies fatales*) by Baudelaire: an absolute commodity, 'in which the process of fetishization is pushed to the point of annulling the very reality of the commodity as such'.[8] A commodity in which use value and exchange value mutually destroy each other: *more commodified than the commodity...*

The charms of this analogy are evident for a world (or – a few streets in the global village) racked by xerox fever, neophilia, and hallucination on the names of fame. As the same-but-worse, such theory could be the antidote to all intellectual pain: it would be useless, beyond value, and occasion no exchange; in its concrete form it could simply shimmer on the shelf, the table, responding to and yet defying the avid proprietorial caress; seductive, inviolable, secure.

But this is only speculation, or perhaps a dream of a state of affairs. Yet Baudrillard himself surpasses Mary Daly and Peter Fuller in the art of formulating the impossibility of criticism, or at least of a criticism that might try to 'take' as its object the text of that very formulation. Daly and Fuller are fire and brimstone, vicars of body and soul: criticism – or dissent – is defined as a *failing*, a sign of biological and spiritual imperfection in the one case, and moral turpitude in the other. There is no such wrath, no self-righteous fury, in Baudrillard: he is the magician, and his medium is wind and air; and it is with the sadness, the restless curiosity of the sprite that he comes to ascertain that criticism, today, is *futile.*[9]

This is not a brutal affirmation, although his clones might make it so. There are reasons, of which I shall mention only two. One is called up in the self-definition of Baudrillard's project, the distinction between banal and fatal theory: 'in the former, the subject believes itself to be always more malign than the object, while in the latter the object is always assumed to be more malign, more cynical, more brilliant than the subject ...'[10] Baudrillard approaches his own object(s) with proper humility and resignation: so, woe to the one who would in turn approach the malignity, the cynicism, the brilliance of a Baudrillard text, with a banal lack of decorum.

But fools, no doubt, may still rush in – since this may be but Baudrillard's *défi* (the challenge, the provocation at the heart of seductive relations) to the reader. It is the invitation to the *duel*: and if all those who take it up know the certainty of their own immolation, there is, for Baudrillard, at least one fate worse than death – the mortal illness of those who can never be seduced. So the futility of the critical gesture is, in this instance, at least redeemed by a certain pale dignity.

The second reason is less alluring. A description of it could be expanded to a paraphrase of Baudrillard's whole history of the metamorphoses of capital, from *L'Echange symbolique et la mort* to *Les Stratégies fatales*, or it can be shrunk to one small sentence: '*that's just the way things are*' ... We've changed; it's all over ... Don't you *know* what's going on? This futility is unredeemable, ugly: the critic is repulsive like the spurned lover who can't believe his ears, or just isn't listening.

The State of Things: the seductive object of enquiry, and the ultimate guarantee of pertinence. But this guarantee is no mere feint on Baudrillard's part, no base gesture of self-protection. On the contrary: the guarantee comes to him *from the world* to which his work is a response; '... the truer than true, the falser than false. ... This logic seems more interesting to me because it *corresponds more* to the evolution of things today' (my italics).[11] If Baudrillard's abolitions of the real, of representation and of reference have led hasty admirers to hail his project as solipsist, it may be more decorous to suggest that his work (like the fascination of reading it for its dazzling actuality) is absorbed by the mystery of correspondences between discourse and the world. For only a sociologist, a philosopher or the occasional modernist might so easily believe that with fiction, narrative or story, we have left the world behind.

Indeed, a question of correspondences might serve as an opening for a (seduced, and so hopelessly doomed) critical reading of the Baudrillard-object. The question might arise in the world, with reading: with the apparent paradox that there where there is most delight in a Baudrillard who declares that 'the real' no longer exists, there is most admiration for a writer who at last describes the way things *really are* ... The question might then find not a response, but a co-respondent, from another reading of his discourse: with a fascination that the four elements defining his charm – the ecstasy of adjectives, the enigma of the thing, the teasing flight of the object, and the guarantee from actuality – are also the parameters of a problem of *description*.

'The social void is scattered with interstitial objects and crystalline clusters which spin around and coalesce in a cerebral chiaroscuro'.[12] What is this, if not a formal description? It might equally well be speaking of a field, a face, or a cow. We need not resort, however, to too much detail: to pose the question, it is enough to note that Baudrillard is read, rightly or wrongly, as a great describer; and that for a whole range of rhetorical traditions, description itself is the worst thing in the world. For example, Barthes:

> Here is how we might understand description: it exhausts itself in its attempt to render the moral properties of the object while pretending all the while (an illusion by inversion) to believe and wish the object to be alive. 'Capturing life' really means 'seeing dead'. Adjectives are the tools of this delusion; whatever else they may be saying, their very descriptive quality makes them funereal.

Citing this, Michel Beaujour wonders why description (which 'ought to be considered a life-force')[13] is so often declared to be *deadly*. Barthes is not alone in his distate, and description is commonly associated with melancholy, loss, 'the fetish of the lost object',[14] the experience of the void and dispossession: 'for without the fable, without the anecdote, without the memory', asks one writer, 'what is a description but the formal proof of an absence?'[15] And even those writers who attempt a more kindly evaluation may do so in terms that evoke a mellow sadness: descriptive writing as '*the being of passing*', yet with affinity to the frozen structures of utopia and porn.[16] It's rare to find that 'descriptive figures derive their energy from idealization, excess, hyperbole, cosmic order'.[17]

These descriptions of description provide a thematics oddly echoed by Baudrillard's work. But his own vision of description is apocalyptic: our impasse of death today is that the real ('stockpile of dead matter, dead bodies, dead language')[18] is a descriptive disaster; the real itself has been replaced by 'a metastable, programmatic, perfect descriptive machine which provides all the signs of the real and short-circuits all its vicissitudes'.[19] The hyperreal: more-deadly-than-deadly, *virulent* description.

It is in response to a literary horror of this sort, I think, that Baudrillard's recent writing (*De la séduction, Les Stratégies fatales*) starts to tell us the fable of the object – its return and revenge. It is a magic story: the object is conjured, not caught or revealed. It is a worldly story: the fatal is cast against the deadly in the game of correspondences. There will be four phases to the trick: the laying of a decoy, the bait (degraded object); the purging of the scene (disappearance); the annunciation of a new scene (appearance); and the raising of the power (the dire object). The enigma is thus not only the enigma of the worst thing in the world, but of that *place in which it may be so invoked.*

> With the deep, unconscious sigh which not even the nearness of the telescreen could prevent him from uttering when his day's work started, Winston pulled the speak-write towards him, blew the dust from its mouthpiece, and put on his spectacles.

1. sticky television

(glued to the screen): Well beyond Oceanic surveillance devices, we inhabit an obscene world of total transparency. The walls are down, the telescreens superseded. There are no more secret places, no torture chambers of Power, Party, State – and there is no place left to hide.

There are only the terminals, and *we are* the terminals; 'everyone is his own terminal ... the group plugged in to video is also nothing more than its own terminal.'[20] Cold, bleached obscenity; the cold seduction of the police-like order of the ludic; playing the media, playing ourselves. Not only do we know the answer to the question of our own worst fears ('the precession of the reply about the question', The O'Brien Theorem): we *are* the reply, and the secondary spectacle of our own worst fears becomes our favourite programme.

This is not negative – just fascinating, and fascination is the ecstasy of the *neutral.* 'We should concede our agreement neither to those who exalt the beneficent usage of media nor to those who scream manipulation, for the reason that there is no relation between a system of meaning and a system of simulation.'[21] But: while Baudrillard interrupts description from time to time to warn against evaluation, we may nevertheless in turn describe – in all neutrality – the terms of his descriptions of the 'white lymph' of media, the 'viral contamination of things by images'.

The order of obscenity has at least three characteristics.

Hypervisibility: the terror of the all-too-visible, the voracity, the total promiscuity, the pure concupiscence of the gaze; the violence of a civilization without secrets. A fatal condition: 'if all enigmas are resolved, the stars go out ... if all illusion is given up to transparency, then the heavens become indifferent to the earth'.[22]

Excessive wetness: the obscene is humid, visceral, sticky; too wet (slime rather than mud) and too avid ('we are a culture of premature ejaculation'). A 'spectral lubricity': the women at strip-shows are obscene because of the sexual spillage (*débordement* – overflow) evident on their faces.[23]

Tentacular tactility: the obscenity of television is the obscenity of The Touch; massage, sensorial mimetics and tactile mysticism; 'solicitation, sensitivisation, branching, targeting, contact, connection – that whole terminology is one of a white obscenity, of a dejection, of an uninterrupted abjection'.[24]

Television, then, is goo. Virulent, invasive, infectious, chilly goo. And, it's going around: abjection spreads, through the total environmental theatre (the 'abject caricature' of Artaud), through the hi-fis, stereos, quadrophonics (definitive degradation, castration of *musical* enjoyment by technological ecstasy), and through to the formal promiscuity of fashion (*mode*), which is the degradation of Dress (*parure*). And the ludic is the degradation of the game, the duel: playing the channels (playing ourselves) is fascinating, not seductive. Narcissus/Narcosis: blocked at the screen stage, our auto-fascination offers a 'monstrous parody' of the *myth* of Narcissus. Fascination is vulgarized seduction – though this is in itself a grand seduction, since it distracts seduction itself – sweet and diffuse, banal and soft.

(This is not negative – only fascinating. Yet we may lift our gaze from the page to stare at that screen, that funny little box ... and wonder – in all neutrality – whether the fascination of television enthusiasts for Baudillard is not like that of feminists for Lacan. The great seducer, says Baudrillard, is the one who knows how to capture and to immolate the desire of the other.)

Liquid-ation, degradation. But it doesn't stop there: the very terms of television's description start to spread and spill, until obscenity is *so much* television that it isn't television at all ... There are many modes of goo: obscenity is 'the sentimentality of concern', it is 'social lubrication' (greasing), it is generalized solicitation and solicitousness, it is the social as 'a kind of foetal security space ... a degraded form of lubricating, insuring, passifying and permissive sociality'; it is 'liberation' and 'rights'; it is 'a gigantic enterprise of therapeutic mothering' in which 'the social becomes monstrous and obese, dilates to the dimension of a niche, of a mammary, cellular, glandular body' – (*niche*, a cavity; *nicher*, to nest, *nichon*, a tit). Obscenity, in another's words, is WET POLITICS ... We are over-protected, swathed in goo; and as a species we may be dying of security in domestication.[25]

Too much of something, for Baudrillard, is the same-but-worse as nothing at all. The real is growing and enlarging, so the real no longer exists. The social is both residual, and swelling. The escalation of information itself generates the implosion of meaning in the media. Or else; the ecstasy of too-much, of ever more-X-than-X, absorbs the opposite of something by abolishing the *distinction* between them. Over-representation abolishes both real *and* illusion; over-banality is not the opposite, but the equivalent, of fatality.

Too much is also *confusing*: if wealth were really redistributed, the bottom would drop out of our lives; with too many channels to choose from, I no longer know which I want; and in the era of the pill and orgasm 'assignment', modern women have come to share with previous generations a 'profound intuition of the ravages of liberty, of speech, and of untrammelled *jouissance*'.[26] Liberty now is bilious, comic: 'everyone secretly prefers an arbitrary and cruel order, which leaves him no choice, to the horrors of a liberal order in which he knows now what he wants, is forced to recognise that he knows not what he wants.'[27]

Obscenity: promiscuity and confusion. We have lost the 'tact' which was the ceremonious avoidance of contact: two bodies colliding, two things in direct contact, two signs coupling without ceremony are obscene, unclean, impure; 'their promiscuity is that of the corpse with the earth, of excrements with each other'.[28] Without discrimination, without distinction, the universe becomes miserable with the perfectly useless violence of confusion. Putrid, fascinating.

Yet beyond the lure of the telescreen, beyond its intolerable *nearness*, all is not necessarily lost. There are forces ... Irony (the filter which can preserve things from promiscuity and 'amorous coagulation') ... Discrimination (the worst thing in the world for the 'moral, sentimental and democratic disorder in which we live') ... Theory (to fight against the promiscuity of concepts and 'the viviparous obscenity of the confusion of ideas'(... But these are still but dreams, vague intimations of another order, outlined only in potential as we describe the screen, and our degradation.

First, there is worse to come.

Gazing again at the screen, we must survey the extent of our loss, the place of our desolation. This is difficult, painful, confusing: for the screen woven by media around us is a screen of total, and *totally new*, uncertainty. Traditional uncertainty could always be resolved; this one, ours, the uncertainty of overload and overkill, is irreparable – and will never be eased again.

> *'How many fingers am I holding up,*
> *Winston?'*
> *'I don't know. I don't know. You will*
> *kill me if you do that again. Four, five,*
> *six – in all honesty I don't know.'*
> *'Better,' said O'Brien.*

2. the lost referential

the empty scene: 'The designated place is still there, but things aren't any more. The scene is empty.'[29]

It is dizzy torture indeed to stabilize, for security's sake, some sense of what Baudrillard means, and when, by *meaning, reality, the real, representation, reference, referent,* or 'a' *referential.* In all honesty I don't know. 'All the referentials intermingle their discourses in a circular, Moebian compulsion':[30] what terrible thing is a referential, that it may 'have' a discourse – and twist it, as it were, in a strip?

But the point of this uncertainty is not only, as quaintly mimetic souls might have it, that *'that' is the point* (invoking some post-historical necessity or obedience to the texts). The point is also that Baudrillard's recent books do not unequivocally rejoice in confusion: that his deadly reductions of the concepts of textual analysis to 'soft, sticky, lumpen-analytical notions'[31] have the effect, in fact, of limpid, comforting clarity, a certainty that it doesn't really matter 'what' he means because *we always know already*; and that these reductions, this familiarity, actually clear the way (like the inspired muddling of 'mass', in *In the Shadow of the Silent Majorities*) for some antidote to confusion in 'distinctions' of Baudrillard's own. This clearing-out, this demolition phase, is a conceptual equivalent of virulent description – purgatorial paraphrase (*Oublier Foucault*).

So a place to look at loss is perhaps in the clarities of Baudrillard's texts, and not in one's own confusions. There are several such clarities, created in recurrence and repetition from text to text.

For example it is clear from the essays in *Simulations*, and from the essays on film and television in *Simulacres et simulation*, that the icon (and not the verbal sign) is often taken as a general model for considering all semiosis: that it is considered to be a mode of resemblance; and that the icon (echoing oddly an ancient Judaeo–Christian suspicion) is commonly considered to be murderous. A few scenes in *Holocaust* suffice to prolong and surpass the extermination of the Jews by exterminating the event itself: 'The telly. The veritable final solution to the historicity of every event.'[32] Secondly, it is clear in essays like 'The Precession of Simulacra' and 'Desert For Ever' that the murderous messiness of mass media culture implies something profoundly unEuropean; and that the lost 'reality' we mourn can sound remarkably like a declension of classical European (academic) values. The wondrous description of Disneyland as deterrence machine finally depends for its effect not on its inversion of real and imaginary (in which the latter conceals that the former does not exist), but on our acceptance that the American social is – really – infantile, banal, childish.[33]

More serious, perhaps, is Baudrillard's clear contention that the real, our lost utopia, is abolished because media *destroy the imaginary* (especially the 'cold light' of television, inoffensive to the imagination because it doesn't even offer an image ...). Again and again, the same point is made: glued to our screens we are, like the narrator at the end of Zamyatin's *We, fantasiectomized* – at the point of no return, the end of the novel, the end of fiction, even science-fiction, for we can no longer imagine another world. We no longer even fantasize about the minutiae of a programme.

At stake here is not only another addition to the appalling powers of goo, but a positive notion of 'existence' as *the way things used to be* – according to a system of noble dichotomies. And when that system becomes unstable (like the 'unstable equation of lines, dots, frames and pulses'[34] in the video image), then things are as good as (but worse than) dead. Reality can only exist, be positively itself, be 'real', if it is different from and opposed to the imaginary. So it is with sex and work, history and nature, desire and power: if a 'savage opposition' between them is dissolved then they are, in an absolute sense, no longer with us ... This is one difference between a system of 'meaning', in Baudrillard's terms, and a system of simulation; the former depends on solid oppositions, which in the latter are 'short-circuited by the confusing of poles, in a total circularity of signalling'.[35] The curious clarity here is not that this logic then requires us to declare the death of meaning, but that it *first* requires us to consent that meaning was really 'that' – and *only* that.

'When the real is no longer what it used to be, nostalgia assumes its full meaning'.[36] Nostalgia also assumes that there was once a stable exchange between meaning and the real, when both had their designated 'place'. A thing in its place (not spilling, not making mess) was clearly identifiable as distinct from other things, as 'proper'; Baudrillard makes it clear that there was once such a thing as 'meaning *properly speaking*',[37] and as a real that could be 'isolated' as real (real reality was rare, singular). An example of their convergence, not given (though used) by Baudrillard, might be some such venerable and proper formulation as 'literature *and* reality' – in which we know what reality is, because literature isn't it. A formulation which we then might use to ask how literature *refers* to this reality – which is already given, separate, waiting to be named.

It is this meaning, this reality, this concept of reference which is dead for Baudrillard. Why does the term 'mass' have no meaning? Because it is 'without attribute, predicate, quality, reference.... It has no sociological "reality"'.[38] Nor, we might add, does any other word outside an instance of its use (in awe here at the conjured rediscovery of the mysteries of the verbal, and so lethally late in the day). But the reverse is also implied: a term which could be held to 'have' sociological 'reality' could also be held *to have meaning*. A system of meaning, then, is only and exclusively a system of real and stable correspondence between sign and thing, word and world.

If this is so even slightly, then what we mourn with Baudrillard, what we have so cruelly lost, is simply *faith in denotation* ... For another writer, denotation might be merely a subset of the problems of meaning, or a different thing from reference, or a parenthesis in a history of theories of representation. For Baudrillard denotation is – was – all. And for a sociologist, perhaps a philosopher, or even the occasional marxist, such loss might indeed be a dreadful thing. For a certain sort of realist, it could be the worst thing in the world. Thus, for example, the shock of the *model*, in simulation: by substituting signs of the real for the real itself, by rendering the real re-producible, it does something worse than remind us that discourse is discourse, with no way 'back' to the real; it initiates a catastrophe for any realism still surprised (yet are there many such?) that the referent may be the future of a sign, not its 'proof', not its past, not its cause.[39]

There are certainly several realisms (and many theories that might take their object to be 'meaning', though not at all in Baudrillard's sense) that would be entirely unsurprised. Yet we have all, perhaps, been bereaved of denotation at one time or another: either by encounter with those realisms, those theories, that have made the meaning of meaning so unstable and insecure; or without any such encounter save the one with Baudrillard; or again, by forgetting all other encounters while we watch him wave his wand. This is the magic of those 'soft, acritical' reductions, and that familiarity we feel with Baudrillard: by disappearing denotation *in the name of* meaning, reality, reference, he banishes not only (and yet again) a commonplace, common-property, and still comfortable concept of 'proper' meaning; he also banishes *both* that concept's uncomfortable, demanding, improper, critical opponents *and* the draining, distressing imperative to remember distinctions between them. Forgetting: such sweet relief; and only the ragpickers of memory need stoop to the sour tasks of 'salvage'. Forgetting: the gesture that also ensures that there is now nothing left but language; that familiar language that speaks of itself as the very disappearance of things.

So the clearing begins, and the place is deserted in no time ... *the desert of the real* ... for just as denotation expands and consumes all other possibilities for meaning, reference, the real (in a move of metonymic swelling, the move that makes the clone, the opinion poll, the *trompe l'oeil*, Disneyland, the television screen, engulf and exhaust the significance of an era), so those terrible referentials turn out to be but bloated denotata. Sex/work, nature/history, desire/power: big, complex, summary denotata, the 'things' we talk about – the things we once had for real when we believed in denotation, and our discourse about them was stable ('History is our lost referential, that is to say, our myth').[40]

Or else: the referentials allude (yet might we not say, refer?) to the things *they* talk about; for, in a move of metonymic reversal, the big denotata in turn refer to (yet here we should say, conjure) those delusions, those rival discourses, of others who do not know that when denotation dies, all density dies in things ('nostalgia, the phantasmal parodic rehabilitation of all lost referentials').[41] In Baudrillard's discourse, for example, the couple desire/power almost always 'conjures' the parodic couple Deleuze/Foucault in the same moment that it asserts a failing, a loss, an absence. (But for the sociologist, a stray philosopher, or the occasional modernist or marxist, a discourse referring to discourse is no real reference at all). So the twisting referentials, ironically, still have a life of sorts: they are not only shadows, *remainders*, of realities which once had meaning in a system of proper opposition; they are hauntingly present to Baudrillard's discourse as metonyms (buzzwords) to summon – the better to exorcize, banish – *the burden of other discourses, others' discourse.*

For when the scene is empty and denotation's tragedy played out, there is one thing still in its designated place. There is a voice that elaborates emptiness, announces disappearance, and whispers revelation (in apocalyptic tone) of an end to end all ends ...

> *'It's a beautiful thing, the destruction of words. Of course the great wastage is in the verbs and adjectives, but there are hundreds of nouns that can be got rid of as well. It isn't only the synonyms; there are also the antonyms. After all ...'*

3. famous last words

plus de ..., no more ...: the tiny operator of annihilation.

No more God, no more Subject, no more Philosophy of the Subject, no more Progress, Regress, History, Nature, Reality, Imaginary, Profit, Revolution, Repression, Representation, Power, Meaning, Production, Dialectic, Judgement, Criticism, War, Liberation, Capital, Class, Change, Exchange, Fiction, Value, Society, Secrets, Scandals, Truth, Ideology, Politics, State, Fantasy, Alienation, Phantasm, Identity, Difference ... Death. No more, and/or much-too-much (no more Rarity, Distinction, Aura). No more Utopia (we're living in it). No more Linear Time, no Catastrophe, no Finality. No more Last Judgement: even the Apocalypse is over, and we're out the other side.

The list is, in principle, endless (not merely at the whim of the writer, but because of the way of the world). For the transpolitical – ecstatic, transparent, obscene – announces *the end of the scene itself.* 'Behind our biological telecommand screen, no more game, no more stake, no more illusion, no more *mise en scène* ...':[42] in the depthless screen of the media there is no perspective space for 'play'.

Why is this scenario (*Lost Illusions*, the twin of the loss of the real) so utterly thrilling? (Why also may it mesmerize those who would laugh to hear that media mean the end of civilization, or ruefully wish that they did – who would scorn the paranoia of an Adorno describing jazz, 'light music', the 'lost and wretched eyes' in faces after a film?)

One reason, perhaps, is the hint of a self-descriptive suicide suggested at this point; when the sorcerer announces the end of the scene, how can he keep on speaking? The scene, after all, is his place, and his profession to summon its terrors. Another reason, however, is a perfect response to the first: when Baudrillard announces *absolute* bereavement ('nothing can compensate this destruction of every scene and all illusion')[43] he offers both peace (no blackmail to 'action'), and the promise inherent in every nadir, and every zero degree – resurrection, return, the comeback.

But this is a delicate task, since artificial resurrection is already the *modus vivendi* of all dead things in the age of simulation, where 'everything is already dead and risen in advance'. Mere negation, opposition, is hopeless: life can never again be proclaimed against death, since when the deader-than-dead becomes livelier-than-life the result is obscenely im-mortal.

Sometimes (for example, '*Le Cadavre en spirale*', *In the Shadow of the Silent Majorities*) Baudrillard suggests a general strategy with honorable antecedents – a pataphysics of simulacra, a science of imaginary solutions. Yet this, perhaps, was still dangerously antonymic: in hypersimulating simulation, one might merely cast a real imaginary against an imaginery real. *De la séduction* and *Les stratégies fatales* propose a much stronger spell, in *savage synonymy*: and against the deadliness of artificial resurrection comes the fatality of fabricated revival:

> Against the truth of the true, against the truer than true ... against that unclean promiscuity with oneself called resemblance, we must re-make illusion, rediscover illusion, that both baleful and immoral power of *tearing the same from the same* called seduction.[44]

Both solutions (pataphysics, seduction) are self-descriptive of Baudrillard's project, and both absorb, and so surpass, the scenario of suicide. Pataphysics, for example, provides a principle of endless (re)invention, and so a place for the inventor. Seduction itself has many strengths (as an event without precedent, it remains, ironically, a 'true' catastrophe; and so provides the possibility of an other-instigated death), of which the chief is these: seduction is '*the form which remains to language when it has nothing more to say*'.[45]

This is the turning-point in the story of the object: when resemblance runs riot in the obscenity of media and imagination expires, when the death of denotation destroys the distinction of signs and things, a salvation of sorts may be sought ('absurd', illusory, and so always already successful) in the secrets of language; those special secrets known to language alone and immune, in a sense, to obscenity. These are the sense-less, but ceremonious, secrets of signs seducing each other:

1993

subscription summer

Summer in the city is hot.
Sydney Theatre Company's
Summer Season is hotter.

Three International hits from Chile, Ireland and USA are set to sizzle on the Sydney stage. The 1991 Olivier Award Winning Play of the Year **DEATH AND THE MAIDEN** opens on December 16 with Helen Morse, John Gaden and Frank Gallacher in the starring roles. "A triumph in every way" is be

world

what power but language, for example, could dream a distinction between 'fatal' and 'deadly', or become absorbed in the ravishing of its own rules ('deader-than-dead', or 'livelier-than-life')?

Such, for Baudrillard, is sorcery, *la parole magique*. But it is not (despite appearances at this point) a simple matter of brandishing a dictionary at the TV screen: perfume, voices, singing may at times have the same effect; and not all words, or any use of language, will suffice to do the trick. Seduction is language purged of denotation and 'meaning' (sense): it is a practice in which 'the charm is always of the order of annunciation and prophecy, of a discourse with a symbolic efficacy that passes neither through decipherment, nor belief'.[46]

It is in an act of self-seduction of this sort, perhaps, that the Baudrillardian text finds a principle (in the ethical as well as the aesthetic sense of that term) not of auto-genesis (since there need be no *raison d'être*, that problem need not be posed), and not merely of auto-description, but of self-perpetuation – survival, the fabrication of survival, through the endless moment of doom. Charming, prophetic, this discourse enchants itself: like the classical figure of Narcissus, the Baudrillardian text is mesmerized, and mesmerizing, through its strategy of *more of the same*, of *the same again but more so ...*

This strategy may provide a context for our appreciation of the importance accorded to the retelling of fables, anecdotes and stories in *De la séduction* and *Les Stratégies fatales* – death in Samarkand, the fox's red tail (*De la séduction*), the voyage of S. to Venice, the jealous lovers, the tale of two people with the same name (*Les Stratégies fatales*). Each of these is told or retold as an instance – both a cited occurrence, and an example for the argument – of the principle of seduction. In each case, something happens to the story; something which we need not call 'decipherment' or worse, 'interpretation', but something which makes the story an echo to that discourse which calls it forth.

In one such story, for example, a fairy agrees to give a little boy anything in the world he desires, but on one condition – that he never, never think of the red colour of the fox's tail. The poor child, of course, is instantly obsessed by this absurd and insignificant image; and wanders miserably through an existence made wretched not only by the loss of the fairy's gifts, but also by the loss of a taste for life itself. This story is enfolded by Baudrillard between two propositions: first, that 'We are only absorbed by empty, insane, absurd, elliptical signs without references'; and second, that this story brings out '*the power of the insignificant signifier*' (Baudrillard's emphasis).[47] And so the story – indeed, the very colour of the fox's tail – receives a second significance: that of supplying parabolic correspondence, of saying the same again (in enchanted form) as the surrounding propositions.

A literary soul might be mystified here: why is this, a classic instance of a *mise en abyme*, not a matter of 'meaning'? why is this an example of 'signs without references' and not an allegory of reference itself? after all, is it not the fairy who *makes* the insignificant significant, who makes the stray sign red *refer* to an interdiction, a promise, a threat? Is this not the absurd, insane and absorbing story of the enchantments of colour becoming sign, and sign becoming referential? But for the reader of Baudrillard's strategies, the alluring thing here is not to oppose his interpretations, nor to expose paradoxes that those strategies quite calmly sustain, but to observe that Baudrillard has so defined his catastrophes of 'meaning' (murderous resemblance, and dying denotation) that certain fundamental, and lovely, uses of language are excluded, saved. And to observe that when Baudrillard speaks of fiction, it is with the assumption that fiction (like language speaking of language) need not denote a set of real and solid things, and that therefore it does not refer: 'What can we rediscover, collectively or individually, beyond the fission of the referential universes, if not fiction, the ironic strategy of appearances?'[48]

To observe too that in invoking the powers of signs which are *insensés* – senseless, crazed – Baudrillard is not preparing arms for supporting a regime of chaotic senselessness, of chance and nonsensical encounters in an unclean promiscuity of signs, of an anarchic gibberish that might be but a liberalism, *laissez-faire*, in disguise. On the contrary: the principles of echoing similitude and correspondence, in which the same may be extracted again and again from any story and from any object in the world, prepare instead for a highly formal (but baseless, and so 'sense' less) system of obligation, ceremonial, constraint. Not an obscene proliferation of difference (as in a pluralism of readings, perhaps), but the arbitrary, violent, and unjustifiable coherence of acts of *discrimination*.

This may sound archaic: and justly so, for in announcing a new scene for seduction to balance the disappearing scene of sense, in summoning the remainder left to language when it has nothing more to say, Baudrillard calls forth against the deadly simulacra of eternal contemporaneity the fatal powers of *ancient* forms – illusion, appearances, fiction, seduction ... These are, in Baudrillard's three-stage schema of the history of the world, the survivors of the first, catastrophic slaughter of the caste-system of appearances (where things were the way they were because they were) by the equivalences of sense (equal and rational exchange). In this, our own and endless apocalypse (the destruction of sense by simulation), they may counter simulation because they are always already ghosts.

This, then, is the come-back: reinvention requires *reversion* ('neither floating causality, probability, uncertainty nor relativity shall be the last word, but reversion, reversibility'),[49] and a place is ready for certain things to stage their (re)appearance.

> *'Don't go on!' said Winston, with his eyes tightly shut.*
> *'Dearest! You've gone quite pale. What's the matter? Do they make you feel sick?'*
> *'Of all the horrors in the world – a rat!'*

4. *Le Cristal se venge,* or the cat came back ...

the crystal strikes back: corpse, beauty, fetish, hostage ...; 'It has no value, but it also has no price. It is an object devoid of interest, yet simultaneously it is absolutely singular, without equivalent, and, so to speak, sacred.'[50]

'*Le Cristal se venge*' is the subtitle of *Les Stratégies fatales,*[51] or rather the story-title that supplements and echoes the descriptive title: a title for a tale of terror and vengeance, in which the tormented yet indomitable object (inexchangeable, unpossessable) retaliates after centuries of subjectivity's triumph; a tale that the teller announces in the awed tones of the prophet overwhelmed by a vision of some still distant, but irresistible, coming force –

> Beyond the final principle of the subject rises up the fatal reversibility of the object, pure object, the pure event (the fatal), the mass-object (silence), the fetish-object, the femininity-object (seduction).[52]

The dire object: for the collapsing order of meaning, causality, finality, reason and in the emerging order of simulation, the very worst thing in the world.

It first appeared as a dream, a deformed possibility for hypothesis, haunting the description of the degraded (mass-media) object: indeed, as a possibility unseen, yet always present, from the beginning with *Le Système des objets,*[53] and now, with *Les Stratégies fatales,* it crystallizes in a descriptive dream of transformation, metamorphosis, in a play of possible hypotheses.

What is the Thing? It's hard, if not impossible, to say; since the *effect* of this thing is to defy description, to flee before, or parodically surrender to, the subject trying to take hold – leaving the latter with an inarticulate stutter or a banal cliché. Yet some things may prudently be said. It isn't television, for example (though it may take television's likeness): and it isn't *opposed to* television; rather, its distance and its distinction provide a balance, a counter, a charm against the telescreen's intolerable nearness and obscene confusion.

Its mode is not quite that of ecstasy, but rather one of excess: the mass-object, for example, abolishes a system (economy, medicine, welfare) by pushing *it* into the hyperlogic of 'excessive practice'; and the secret of magic, poetry, the secret of the language-object turns out to be, in *Les Stratégies fatales*, something 'not far' (in Baudrillard's phrase) from that famous 'excess', that 'superabundant order' of the pure signifier. A distinction between ecstasy and excess perhaps might be that in the former, forms are out of control (ever-more-X-than-X), while in the latter they are *over*-controlled – excessive in their submission to some strict, but senseless, rule. Excess, for Baudrillard, is *regulated.*

The description of degraded, liquid-ated, disappearing objects engages fascination, the ecstasy of the neutral in a world of simulation, of eternal living death. The dire object is rather a possibility *for* a world in which 'nothing is neutral, nothing is indifferent': a world ruled by seduction, in which 'nothing is dead, nothing is inert, nothing is un-chained, decorrelated, aleatory',[54] in which everything appears and disappears in accordance with an incessant cycle of metamorphoses, with the seductive (not rational) chains of forms and appearances.

So a fascinated, neutral description will not take us close to this Thing: instead, we may follow only a chain of formal distinctions describing the world in which the thing is a possibility. These distinctions are invented – or rediscovered in a dream – by Baudrillard: for since 'the forms of simulation may be recognized by the fact that there is nothing to oppose them to each other' (so that sex, love, seduction, perversion and porn, for example, can all 'co-exist on the same libidinal track'), it becomes imperative to *re-discover hierarchy*, re-distinguish the figures of seduction, love, passion, desire, sex (in the same example); 'an absurd wager, but the only one that's left'.[55]

A hierarchy of distinctions, then, against the obscenity, the 'wet politics', of confused coexistence. But we must be careful: this is not a rational hierarchy, and not a logical chain. There is echo, overlap, synonymy rather than development, difference, or antonymy between the terms of the chain itself. Each term has its own opponents, perhaps, but it exists in regulated resonance with other terms throughout *Les Stratégies fatales* – in which they occur and recur in a movement which is quite unlike this list:

the world in which the thing is a possibility may be characterized by;

Irony (vs Criticism): an objectal irony, not subjective or objective since the latter is but a guise of the former. An irony proper to the object; one of its (im)moral qualities, so to speak. A mode of *détournement*, but not that of the subject re-arranging meaning in montage or parody: rather, it is a 'detour' taken by the object itself in relation to the meaningful ends that the subject pretends to impose. This is the irony of photons fleeing the instruments of the physicist, and so confounding his aim. It is the irony of the masses diverting the aims of opinion polls (information about the masses) into the involuntary humour of a mass spectacle of information. Criticism, critical theory (subjective/objective) created differences: irony, ironic theory (objectal) creates distinctions, but only as a means of retaliation to the subject's enquiries. And so irony's distinctions are precise, not confused (though they may bring confusion): its strategy is neither capitulation nor confrontation, but one of turning the subject back on itself, and reversing a situation.

Reversibility (vs Finality/Chaos): the metamorphosis of appearances, a principle for evading both chance and necessity. A principle for turning back time, causality, history, for example: in a reversal of the causal order, effects do not cease to happen nor fade in a flux of uncertainty – instead they come to precede their cause. Reversibility entails both reversion and reversal: so if our condition today is eternal, or beyond linear time, it is not necessarily irreversible. And reversibility works to rule: it is neither aimless nor teleological, but a principle in which 'things are neither chained by the law, nor free and indeterminate by chance, but reversible by rule'.[56]

Rule (vs Law/Chance): the principle of ritual, ceremony, convention. Its most common emblem is the game (the lottery, poker ...): it has no sense (unlike law) but its operations are never random. A game is a cycle of highly conventional, perfectly regulated procedures; whereas law, for Baudrillard, is an instance founded in irreversible continuity. Law entails constraint and interdiction and so it can, and must, be transgressed. There is no point in transgressing the rules of a game: they are arbitrary, meaningless, and they impose only obligation. At the same time, the game is alien to chance – at least, to 'chance' in the vulgar sense of accident, random occurrence. As every gambler knows, the game is ruled by Fortune, the arbitrary force which precisely leaves nothing at all to chance and never deals out uncertainty. The outcome of every game is always predetermined by a capricious, unreasonable and rigorous fate.

Destiny (vs Desire), *Predestination* (vs Liberty, Subjection): the subject pursues its desire, the object fulfils its destiny. Destiny is the way of the world, or is at least more 'natural' than chance. The Western world imagines, says Baudrillard, that God brought order out of chaos: but perhaps the reverse could be true; and God is a force bringing chaos out of order to allow us to believe in both the spectacle of order and in chance, to hope and to believe in chance, in accident, in something 'stray' to save us. But chance does not really exist; and we are not free, any more than we are subject to the rational order of law. Astrology, magic, know better that our destiny is already fulfilled in the fatal stars of our birth. The sign of birth is the same as the sign of death: fatality is the annihilation of causality and chance, and destiny is a mode of *simultaneous* appearance and disappearance. Ceremony, once, was a way of regulating the metamorphosis of forms appearing and disappearing; the decisions of destiny may be baseless and unjust, but never indiscriminate.

Discrimination (vs Difference, Indifference). This, the pure observance of signs at their most intense, is the 'arbitrary and cruel' order that we all prefer to the ravages of liberty. This, the very essence of ritual and senseless regulation, is what we have lost in the democratic and poductivist sentimentality of our culture. If liberty is bilious, comic, discrimination is miraculous, tragic. Unlike difference (which makes sense) and the promiscuity of indifference (in which ritual is destroyed by obscenity), discrimination is *'the truly rigorous form of marking'*,[57] and the equivalent of predestination-in-time: it has the force of a sign before sense (and so it is perfectly arbitrary); and is imposed as an end, a fate, before it can be justified (and so is perfectly unjust). It is the order in which we are all, so to speak, *marked* – marked from birth, marked for life, marked for death.

Such, then, is the world (or: the set of possible hypotheses) which Baudrillard dreams for the object, the thing. We still may not, as already defeated reading subjects, say what this thing might be: we cannot even question this world, those visions of distinction, too closely, nor interrogate, not their resemblance, but their echoing similitude to certain worldly orders long-known to Jews and slaves; since visions fade before the question, leaving laughter's trace behind, and the evasion of interrogation is the very aim of the object's irony.

We may, however, observe that one thing, one power raised in Baudrillard's dreams of fatal strategy is the power of Theory, the twin of Ceremony. Both are violent: both are 'made for preventing things or concepts from touching each other carelessly, for producing discrimination, for remaking a void, for redistinguishing everything that has been confused'.[58] It is Theory – or perhaps a transfigured Theory, baseless, senseless, initiatory, distinctive – which can come to occupy centre-stage in the new scene of seduction, and fight against the miscegenation of concepts and ideas, the obscene mixity and promiscuity of degenerating multi-disciplinarity.[59]

We may wonder then at the sense of rightness, of appropriateness, of exact inevitability that attends this climax of *Les Stratégies fatales*: the feeling that this, all along, was the unseen destiny of the sorcerer in his scene, through all the encounters with degradation, death and resurrection; that the raising of the power, perhaps, could never end in any other place or way but this. The effect precedes the cause, and in our ends are our beginnings.

However, it remains, in the end, for each reader-*object* solicited by Baudrillard's discourse to name the thing for itself: and to wonder whether *le cristal se venge* is the tale of an enticing dream, or rather the replay of another's nightmare which destiny, cruel destiny, some simple twist of fate, could yet still make one's own.

> *The voice from the telescreen was still pouring forth its tale of prisoners and booty and slaughter, but the shouting outside had died down a little. The waiters were turning back to their work. One of them approached with the gin bottle. Winston, sitting in a blissful dream, paid no attention ...*

    more eventful than the event: catastrophe
      more final than the final: hypertelia
    more real than the real: hyperreality

the hyperreal: 'We too live in a universe everywhere strangely similar to the original – here things are duplicated by their own scenario. But this double does not mean, as in folklore, the imminence of death – they are already purged of death, and are even better than in life; more smiling, more authentic, in the light of their model, like the faces in funeral parlours.'[60]

It is tempting, reflecting back on the four-phase fable of the object's return, to find therein a strange similarity, a hallucinatory resemblance, to a scenario for a realism. Not a eulogy of the hyper-realism of the icon run riot, and not a simple salvage of a dying aesthetic, but a scenario for surpassing something dead, some lost illusion, with a form the same as, but better than, the original.

That dead thing might be realism's desire to pursue, to capture, and to reduplicate in language every object in the world, with its faith that this was possible (to cover the empire, so to speak, with a map). For Baudrillard, the media brought the death of this desire, this faith: desire and faith have died by the absolute fulfilment of both *elsewhere*, and more so, than in language; when the real itself became descriptive (more deadly than deadly, virulent description) there were no more objects for description to pursue, no more real, no more illusion, no more difference between empire and map. The old realism proved mortal, and it died in the screen of the media.

It would be in response to a horror of this sort, then, that Baudrillard's recent writing begins to imagine something better, and to reinvent those illusions that only language might invent. In face of a real become descriptive, language invokes an object not only revived but transfigured: not only back on the scene but vengeful; an object that can and will forever *defy* description. This object in its teasing flight provokes and annihilates and provokes again a desire that can never die because it can never be fulfilled: a realism made immortal, heroic, because it knows itself utterly doomed. Fortified by the pathos of the lost referential, purged by the death of faith in denotation, this might be an anti-realism – a *trompe l'oeil* realism, forever 'casting radical doubt on the reality principle'[61] – with Baudrillard as its anti-Zola, its prophetic and melancholy describer.

The temptation to say this might be reinforced by recalling the rhetoric of correspondences, that troubling claim that the spiralling adjectives of Baudrillard's discourse trace a logic that 'corresponds more to the evolution of things today'. This is not, after all, a modernist credo for a purely self-reflexive and 'non-referential' theory, and still less a postmodern conceit of scavenging: it is a claim that a discourse might be adequate to its ('non-referential') world – a world that it does not 'produce', but that it matches, rivals, echoes. It is, in that sense, a realist claim, and its dilemmas are realist dilemmas:

> the fundamental characteristic of realist discourse is to make narrative, all narrative, impossible. For the more it saturates itself in descriptions, so the more it is constrained to multiply empty thematics and redundancies, the more too it organizes and repeats itself, and so closes in over itself: from being referential, it become purely anaphoric; instead of citing the real ('things', 'events'), it perpetually cites itself.[62]

If for Baudrillard narrative is not impossible, but rather an ideal condition which theory might strive to attain, it is nevertheless the case that throughout his work the fable always comes to supplement and to repeat description; and that both fable and description are redundancies multiplied in, by and for the demonstration of a discourse demonstrating its own inevitability. This has always been the absorbing fascination of the theory of simulation: it offers a universe, an inexhaustible, infinite world of examples, exemplary matter, for the citing of the theory itself. From obesity to terrorism, from the clone to the handicapped, it can discourse upon anything at all and always say the same thing.

Yet however pleasing it might be to cast Baudrillard in the role of the last great dinosaur of the realist age, it would be both ungenerous (too much *like* Baudrillard in his parodic mode) and inexact. For in face of a delirious world, to correspond to that delirious world, *Les Stratégies fatales* explictly attempts to break away from the blackmail to realism, to outline strategies other than, and in distinction to, 'the ultimatum of realism' – that disenchanted realism which for Baudrillard has kong been a worst thing in the world. So I shall not call these strategies 'realism', nor even *funereal* realism, but rather begin again with a word taken not from Baudrillard's discourse, but from that delirious world to which it corresponds.

more descriptive than description: hype.

hype: the strategy of invoking that which is most, the spiral of moster and moster; the enchanted equivalent of virulent description as something the same but more so; the frenzy of attributes outbidding each other in an ecstasy of endless one-upping.

Hype is always and blatantly falser than false. Hype is often scorned as 'inflated' description, or a misleading excess of sense. But it may be these descriptions of hype which are spurious, misleading, since they discover what hype *displays already*: its own lack of correspondence to any object whatsoever, and its absolute abandon to the charms of self-seduction. Hype is never realistic, credible; rather, in the best of hype, credibility is displayed *as* a super special effect. Hype is pure promotion promoting itself: the object (brand X) is only ever a pretext, a decoy, a ceremonial trigger; we are summoned not to differentiate objects, but to discriminate, in fascination, between competing brands of hype. Hype does not refer, at least not in Baudrillard's sense; but hype is also a genre, and each instance of hype refers if not to things, then to itself, to its own status as hype, and to all the other instances of hype in the spiral of competitive outbidding. Hype knows the secrets of seductive language: it is hype that can dream a distinction between 'fatal' and 'deadly', send superlatives into perpetual spin (or even, said an undertaker in *Hill Street Blues*, into three different styles – eternal, perpetual and perpetual-eternal); and it is hype, pure hype, that pulls our fascination away from the object and attracts it to the skill of the spruiking.

('Hallucinating on platitude',[63] said Baudrillard, of the audience at a hyperrealist exhibition: a perfect description of the pleasures of hype. And what else do I do but hallucinate on platitude when I read, with so much pleasure, the banalities of his texts – that television is lethal, that modern culture is a mess, that this culture, my culture, is an abject caricature of some other preceding culture, that the mass (which does not exist) is a site of dumb, beast-like irrationality and brute indifference, that we're all confused by overload and overkill, that too much of anything is bad for you, that a sense of discrimination is lacking in the world today? and when I happily skip, discount, the banality of those banalities in the hallucinatory pleasures, the fatal charm, of his writing?)

Yet hype, perhaps, has a dream of death, a fantasy of its own abolition. Hype itself is invasive, solicitous; it must overwhelm and swamp, swathe in goo, so to speak, the objects it takes as its pretexts. Hype deals in the degradation of objects: it liquidates what little claims the object may have to distinction by absorbing them for the play and display of hype; for hype to live, its object must die – or at least find parodic resurrection as a secondary and derivative simulacrum of itself in the pure illustration of hype. So hype, dreaming of death, dreams a dream of the *absolute commodity* – some arch Object, some wonderful and terrible transcendant Thing that might never succumb to hype, but rather lure it along, exhaust it, stand ironic and indifferent as hype spends itself in its ecstasy of annihilation. And it dreams that its dream might be fiction, with the force of an innocent fable – archaic, *pre*-real, folkloric, endowed with the merciful powers of death. But for hype, poor hype, relief is sweet but dreams are fleeting: for it stirs, reaches out and finds, like Narcissus, that it is ever pursuing itself.

So Baudrillard's discourse is garrulous about the silence of an object which might still somehow speak: so it vaunts the powers of enigma and seductive senselessness, while creating a most severe and rigorous and predictive allegorical mode of reading and writing: so it summons fictions, not to end but to double and redouble ever-expanding exposition: and so, in the end, does Theory (not the crystal, the corpse, the beauty, the hostage) come to embrace itself as work-of-art, dire object, and absolute commodity.

If this alone were the story, and the fate of the story, of *Les Stratégies fatales*, there would be no horror involved – merely a poignant replay of the classic modernist tragedy, intensified and enriched by a crucial additional scene in which Theory at long last responds to those charms of advertising, fashion, and frenzied consumption, that it had hitherto surveyed from afar. The horror is rather in the twist that a drama which, from Baudrillard's earliest books to *Les Stratégies fatales*, begins as the most sustained meditation attempted on the conditions of contemporary culture should, after all, *end there*: not beyond the depthless screen of the media; not with the terminals; not in orbit; and not in some hitherto unimagined space or scene; but back, safely back, in the prison-house of language. The walls have been rebuilt; the decor has been updated (video, hi-fi, computer ...); the telescreen is there, but its chatter a mere diversion; and we are once again in our secret Room, our familiar torture chamber: we have been brought, once again, to the Library. We ourselves have made sure there is no way out: and turning, as we confirm from every page that nightmare absence of Things, we see the sign of our own dear despair approaching – with the assurance that in this place, whatever the question, we will know the answer already.

> *'The worst thing in the world,' said O'Brien, 'varies from individual to individual. It may be burial alive, or death by fire, or by drowning, or by impalement, or fifty other deaths. There are cases where it is some quite trivial thing, not even fatal.'*

11

Postmodernity and Lyotard's Sublime

Without the sublime, beauty would make us forget our dignity. The enervation of uninterrupted enjoyment would cost us all vitality of *character* and, irremediably shackled to this *contingent form of existence*, we should lose sight of our immutable vocation and our true patrimony.

Friedrich von Schiller, 'On the Sublime'

All versions of the sublime require a credible god-term, a meaningful jargon of ultimacy, if the discourse is not to collapse into 'mere' rhetoric.

Thomas Weiskel, *The Romantic Sublime*

I Modes

A Context

In a 1960 preface to his 1935 study of critical theories in eighteenth-century England, *The Sublime*, Samuel H. Monk wrote: 'Twenty-five years ago I wrote: "The development of the sublime was a sort of Methodist revival in art." Today that statement seems to me, like most analogies, a good deal more clever than true'.[1]

Today, contemplating after twenty-four years more a possible Sublime revival in art, it is almost irresistibly tempting just to appropriate the cleverness of Monk's analogy. A (revived) Methodist revival: how better to characterize those rebukes from Jean-François Lyotard to the wanton yet dreary limbo of our times? his fiery denunciations of eclecticism and kitsch, and his cry that we rally to defend the honour of painting against corruption, indeed, defend the honour of thought itself? his call that we 'bear witness', that we 'testify' to the unpresentable, the incommensurable, that we accept the 'mission' of an 'immanent' sublime?[2] These gestures, if not Methodist in any strict sense, certainly seem to suggest that Lyotard's position in current art debates would be both funda-

213

mentalist, and protestant. Painting (*pur et dur*) just wasn't meant to be easy.

Why one would want to succumb to this temptation is another question. Why diagnose in such unsympathetic terms an argument that exists in the form of a few sketchy articles plus the threat of an exhibition, 'The Immaterials', to be prepared by Lyotard for the Centre Georges Pompidou?[3] If Lyotard himself defines the modern in relation to the principle that 'Any received idea, even if it's only a day old, must be suspected',[4] surely it is to carry conformity to this ideal too far to suspect the concept of an exhibition that hasn't happened yet, or a catalogue that one has never seen?

Yet Lyotard himself has also said (predictably, perhaps, given the Kantian formulation of his notion of the sublime) that 'Sublimity no longer is in art, but in speculating on art.'[5] Even allowing for the way that 'speculation' here can refer to artistic as well as critical processes, and to the impact of market pressures on and in the 'moves' that artists choose to make, there is still a sense in which one could claim that the choice of *works* (say, for a hypothetical exhibition presenting works presenting the unpresentable) then becomes, indeed, immaterial.

For one thing, the major stake should be the problem of making such an exhibition *itself* present the unpresentable in its presentation of presentations of the unpresentable (curatorial procedures, critical manoeuvres, publicity, etc.) in a way which would go far beyond a mere assemblage of commentaries on the museum of the sort that Lyotard has admired in the work of Daniel Buren. For another, Lyotard's version of the sublime as a history of events, a tradition of happenings constituted by the invention of moves and rules, implies that actual artworks might be but the residues of such events and/or testimonials to a mission to produce new events (to keep on keeping on). In both cases, the suspicious soul might predict that while Lyotard rejects the cynical eclecticism of the culture of Anything Goes, his own aesthetic implies a selection and evaluation process for the exercise of which, eventually, Anything Does.

This is mundane, not sublime, speculation. What I want it to do, however, is to indicate a possible discursive context within which Lyotard's work could, and possibly will, be situated. That context might be informed by North American and Australian art criticism, and it might therefore go on to construct a weary sense of *déjà-déjà-vu*, a sinking feeling that the neo-expressivities, pastiches and quotations of the past few years are about to be absorbed, in the fullness of time, by a proliferation of Sublimities which can subsume all three while resolving the differences between them.

A new Sublime: what a terrible prospect.

The terrain of Lyotard's aesthetic proffers a petrifying and formidable complex of elements, especially if they are envisaged as re-cited and re-situated by art institutions avid for the next phase after the postmodern, or anxious to discard the same old paradox of being bored by the new. Lyotard's sublime could be both 'new', a 'change' (it moves right away from the thematics of appropriation, for example), and yet renovate the stabilizing value of a tradition of the new (or, more precisely, the 'next').

For it is clear that by 'the sublime' understood as a historical concept, Lyotard has in mind the heritage of the avant-gardes rather than a succession of kitsch landscapes (despite illustrations to his text in the April 1984 issue of *Artforum*). So a first element is a revival of the classic postures of avant-gardism, taken as defining a principle of art as interminable critical research. The second element is for Lyotard the name of a method, 'language-games', taken from Wittgenstein and combined with communication models borrowed from pragmatics; but which can also evoke horror re-visitations of the poetics of conceptual art.

The third element is Lyotard's increasingly explicit and insistent Kantianism in both aesthetics and politics,[6] and here it is easy to imagine a fairly ordinary art-world drift (a *dérive*) away from the details of Lyotard's arguments and towards something that might indeed accommodate a vogue for kitsch landscapes, a spasm of ersatz transcendental-ism with 'sublime' for its buzzword and for its content a re-discovery of the unspeakable, the ineffable, the mystic catatonics of art. And thence — since Lyotard's sublime is very much a matter of a disposition (to suspicion, and to ever-restless discontent) rather than of the properties of any object — to revised bursts of expressionism, and declarations of distance between politics and art.

A final element on such a list might be the '*re*'-factor never empha-sized or addressed by Lyotard, the recycling, revising, reworking, redis-covering, and renovating impulse that on the one hand seems hostile to the frontiersmanship of Lyotard's programme for future art, but which on the other subsumes his efforts the moment that he suggests we give again the antique name 'sublime' to a framework for desirable activities today. Or rather, it happens when an admirable descriptive term for analysing the history of modern art becomes an injunction to and for the postmodern: 'The answer is: Let us wage a war on totality; let us be witnesses to the unpresentable; let us activate the differences and save the honor of the name.'[7] So the *function* of Lyotard's sublime, if not its intention, could easily be to appropriate appropriation for a new con-ceptual conglomerate.

Lyotard's own drift, it seems, is so passionately particular that he has been capable of maintaining violent disagreement with both Achille

Bonito Oliva and Jurgen Habermas at the same time. Yet his aesthetic of the sublime, capable as it is of being made to maintain avant-gardism, language-gaming, transcendentalism, can become — in *this* context — a wash of indiscriminate generalities distinguished only by the magnitude, the vastness of the possibilities for re-presenting the whole history of art since the eighteenth century in the name of an anti-eclectic, salvation-ist revival.

But this context, after all, is but a bad dream based on a borrowed analogy.

Another Context

If the words 'witness' and 'testify' are picked out from the preceding context, separated from the possibility of protestant association, and are referred instead to Lyotard's 'philosophy book', *Le Différend*, a less clever mode of situating Lyotard's work on the sublime may emerge.

The witness (*le témoin*) is the focus of a number of entries in this book, which is a philosophical album in the genre of Pascal's *Pensées*, Wittgenstein's *Philosophical Investigations*. None of these entries has much to do with fundamentalism. For example, the initiating problem of the book is that posed by the so-called revisionist historians who, like Robert Faurisson, have denied the reality of the gas chambers on grounds including the argument that no surviving Jewish witnesses can be found to testify that they actually saw one in operation.[8] Later in the book, independent testimonials (*témoignages*) are defined as 'sentences having the same referent, but not immediately linked to each other':[9] while elsewhere the figure of the witness is associated with that of the 'third party' indispensable to the agonistic model (sophist, conflictual) of knowledge that Lyotard wants to oppose to the dialogue, and to consensus.

In other words, the witness-ing vocabulary can in this context be read as indicating a concern with problems of reference (not of inspiration, self-expression or the ineffable), of the strategic definition of 'reality' ('a state of the referent of cognitive sentences'),[10] of historical knowledge, political argument, of the un-sayability, in some conditions, of certain wrongs.

This context for discussing the sublime might begin by citing Lyotard's own description of the context of *Le Différend*, a work in which the sublime is considered (via the 'enthusiasm' of a 1789) as a historical experience:

The context: 'the linguistic turn' of western philosophies, decline of universalist metaphysics, retreat of marxism in Europe, lassitude towards 'theory', that is, towards the human sciences, rise of logotechnologies, world domination of capital, political despondency.

At least, that is how the context is presented by the book's back cover to a potential reader of *Le Différend*. In the text, in the introductory 'Fiche de lecture', we find this elaboration of the condition of lassitude towards theory:

> and the miserable slackness that accompanies it (new this, new that, post-this, post-that). The hour to philosophize.[11]

This passage, signed by the author of *La Condition postmoderne*, is a warning that a context created by Lyotard's proper name would not provide a more reliable, authentic or legitimate situation from which to refer to his work on the sublime. But I think it is a more interesting one than that provided only by recent polemics about art, because it is capable of describing the conditions within which Lyotard's own work will become a new-this on the post-that.

Genre: (review)

Lyotard's essays on the sublime are oddly suspended, at the moment, between the miserable slackness of *La condition postmoderne* (arguably Lyotard's worst book), the dour and demanding pages of professional philosophy in *Le différend* (heavily influenced by Anglo–American traditions of linguistic philosophy) and the jaunty interview format of *Au juste*,[12] recording his debates with Jean-Loup Thébaud about justice and judgement, political and aesthetic.

It is something of an image-change for Lyotard to be presentable as a theorist of justice, reference, reality and rigour — particularly since his work, along with that of many another French philosopher marked by May 68, is often associated with the posture that such concepts are either doomed or irredeemably reactionary. A more familiar Lyotard invokes decadence, libidinal intensities, the aggressive, snarling style of *L'Economie libidinale* (1974), admired for its theatricality by some (Marc Eli Blanchard in *Diacritics*, June 1979) and rejected as brutal and violent by others (Catherine Clément in *L'Arc* 64, Thébaud in *Au juste*), for whom Lyotard's denunciations of political organization and theoretical constraints declared his to be an 'enemy thought' (Clément), his form of writing 'non-negotiable' (Thébaud).

Today those disputes (like the joyfully cocky brashness of his *Drift-works*[13] essays from a decade ago) may seem out of place and out of time in the degree to which they presupposed viable organizations, stable constraints, to be denounced. Lyotard has always been a topical thinker — which may or may not mean trivial — and his tone has mellowed, his focus softened, to the extent that he could easily be presented (in explicit opposition to, say, the howling nostalgia that Lyotard has criticized in Jean Baudrillard)[14] as your friendly exponent of strategic non-pessimism, of a refusal of mourning, of a wager on the possibility of invention. Even in art.

This presentation would only be a just one, however, if accompanied by a recognition that his work towards 'a politics that would respect both the desire for justice and the desire for the unknown'[15] maintains many of his earlier concerns. His concept of justice, for example, turns out to be a version of aristotelian *prudence*: judging without criteria, judging without the underpinning of a general model of justice (thus, no such thing as a 'just society'), and judging in terms of discrete evaluations of particular cases, particular relations of force, with only 'opinion' as a guide. ('Pagan justice': the notion evokes romantic sheikhs, chieftains, wise princes and so forth, but might be more applicable now to the opinionated radio talkback host — a possibility Lyotard does not discuss.)

Similarly, his interest in defending the 'reality' of the Holocaust in *Le Différend* does not signify some back-to-basics move to recover political and historical common sense under the pressure of right-wing revival in Europe. On the contrary (in a way which may confuse anyone who associates reality-values with the Left, and 'formalism' with explicit or implicit conservatism), historians denying that the Holocaust took place are the ones to have pushed common-sense notions of tangible reality, and professional notions of *evidence for* reality, to a rigorous extreme. Rather than arguing that the annihilation included the annihilation of evidence, they argue that if there is now no 'evidence' it is because it didn't happen. For Lyotard, on the other hand, 'the annihilation named Auschwitz' now requires a formal transformation of what counts as history and as reality, and in our understanding of reference and the function of the proper name.

Above all, one might claim a continuity for Lyotard's work precisely in terms of formal experiment and rhetorical difference — of a politics of manipulating and modifying the rules of different genres, inducing pragmatic shifts (in the sender/receiver/message/referent relations that usually define Lyotard's basic model) in order to alter a particular context. It is the sort of practice which has become a commonplace over the past few years, at least as an ideal, and which has in art attracted awful names like 'site-specific intervention'.[16]

I suspect that few writers, and fewer philosophers, have applied this principle in their own work with the meticulous consistency of Lyotard.

He is not a stylist: cut free from the author's proper name, nothing would link a scrap of *L'Economie libidinale* to a bit of *Le Différend* because the writing in each case represents a formal solution to a particular problem which it has, in a sense, invented — although always in relation to a given history. This is one reason why a general aesthetic cannot be derived from his books about the work of particular artists. These books are always books *in response to*: the prose layers reconstructing the layering of time in paint in *Sur la constitution du temps par la couleur dans les oeuvres récentes d'Albert Ayme* (1980); the 'portrait' of migration accompanying the portraits (of famous men, including Lyotard) by Ruth Francken in *L'Histoire de Ruth* (1983); the anecdotes of *Récits tremblants* with Jacques Monory (1977); and the testy accumulation of fragments in *Les Transformateurs Duchamp* (1977) — a work which, with its outline of a 'politics of incommensurables', perhaps comes closest to providing grounds for extrapolation.

It is perhaps the fact that Lyotard has not invented a singular style, nor even a succession of singular styles, and that he also plays with inducing bewildering shifts in modes of address within and between his different texts, which makes 'Lyotard's work' quite hard to discuss — this, perhaps, which encourages the writing of reviews of his work that can barely bring themselves to address to their own readers the slightest hint of what Lyotard has to say. (For fear of violating the author's intentions in restoring coherence where inconsistency was sought?...)

Lyotard once agreed that *L'Economie libidinale* may give the impression that its theses are not to be discussed because of (to borrow his terms) a violent separation between its mode of presentation (*lexis*) and its content (*logos*): 'But actually they can be discussed ... it is also possible to read the book skipping over all the rhetorical machinery, whether spontaneous or not, and perhaps one can realize then that the book is completely inconsistent from this point of view.'[17] It's just a matter, he says, of not being intimidated.

If this is a refreshingly simple approach to questions both of representation and of the protocols of reading, it is also a familiar concept of the writer's 'art' as a test of the reader's strength. So first, an example of the difficulty of deciding which of Lyotard's 'theses' to cite.

(Quotation)

(Lyotard has said that quotation constitutes a metalanguage which converts all sentences into one single sentence-regime — the cognitive. Instead of questions, orders, descriptions, there are only statements of the form *It was asked, ordered, declared that X* ...; statements to be verified or falsified in terms of whether X was or was not asked, ordered, declared. Thus only quotation, Lyotard has said, could be the discourse genre of a supreme tribunal of history aspiring to judge the validity of all sentences.)[18]

Lyotard said: 'Is it in this sense that we are not modern? Incommensurability, heterogeneity, the *différend*, the persistence of proper names, the absence of a supreme tribunal? Or is it, on the contrary, romanticism continuing, the nostalgia that accompanies the retreat of ..., etc? Nihilism? a good stint of mourning for being? and the hope born with it, which is still the hope of a redemption? All still inscribed in the thought of a redemptive future? Could it be that "we" aren't telling each other anything any more? Aren't "we" telling each other, either in bitterness or in lightness of heart, the master narrative of the end of master narratives? Isn't it enough to think in terms of the end of history to ensure that thought remains modern? Or else is postmodernity the pastime of an old man grubbing in the garbage-bin of finality to find scraps, brandishing bits of unconscious, slips, edges, limits, gulags, parataxes, nonsense, paradoxes, making from them his glory of novelty, his promise of change? But that, too, is a goal for humanity. A genre. (Bad pastiche of Nietzsche. Why?).'[19]

(Do these questions, in being directly instead of indirectly quoted, cease to be direct questions about postmodernity? Are they converted into a statement in relation to which the only pertinent question is whether 'Lyotard' did or did not say these things? Does Lyotard's analysis of the formal structure of quotation say anything about different cases of its use?)

(Can there be a distinction between direct and indirect quotation in painting? If so, what kind of metalanguage would direct quotation represent, and what would be its 'aspirations'?)

II Theses

The Postmodern Condition

There is no mention of the sublime, and very little mention of art or aesthetics, in *La Condition postmoderne* — a 'report on knowledge' prepared by Lyotard for a governmental university council in Quebec.

There are, however, several different values accorded to the term 'postmodern' in Lyotard's work, including his work on the sublime. It can serve as a tool for vague periodization: in *La Condition post- moderne* it variously refers to the state *of* culture after the scientific and artistic transformations of the end of the nineteenth century, or to the equivalent *in* culture of the 'postindustrial' age that Lyotard dates in Europe from the end of the 1950s. In *Le Différend* it appears as an ideal called 'honorable postmodernity', defending a programme for the future, and a set of guiding proper names (the later Wittgenstein, the Kant of the *Critique of Judgement*[20] and various historico-political texts).

Apart from these basically organizational uses of the term, there are two separate positive concepts of postmodernity to be considered. One (sketched in 'Answering the Question: What is the Post-Modern?') is that of postmodernism as the originary, and not the terminal, gesture of modernism. Its details are specific to aesthetics, and I want to postpone them in order to first discuss the other, general concept, developed in *La Condition postmoderne* — that cultural postmodernity (primarily but not exclusively scientific in terms of the examples used) is defined by a condition of incredulity towards metanarratives, towards what are also called *grands récits.*

With the enthralling simplicity and inevitability of a fable, this text unfolds its account of the formation and disintegration of the two great legitimizing 'narratives' of modern knowledge, in both teaching and research — the political emancipation of Man (the People, the Working Class), the philosophical adventure of the speculative Mind. The account also includes a brief tale of the collapse of the ideal of a universal metalanguage in the sciences and mathematics, and of the dispersion of these into a variety of heterogeneous specialities ('Languages') each with its own rules of validation. At the same time, the nature of the social relation (or rather, of an appropriate representation of the social) changes from the modern alternative between *organic whole/total system* (optimistic-liberal sociology/cynical-technocratic systems theory) on the one hand, and the divided society riven by *contradiction* (marxism) on the other — to enter the postmodern condition in which Lyotard allows no alternative but to accept that social relations are primarily language-like.

These three elements are harmonized in the book to define postmodernity in the sciences, in culture and in social life, as a sort of infinite field of linguistic possibilities. Not 'linguistic' in a Saussurean sense: for Lyotard there is no underlying code. It is rather a field in which we are all traversed by a multiplicity of different, indeed incommensurable, languages, where we are all engaged at different pragmatic posts (sender/receiver/referent ...) in a variety of language-games, and in which legitimation is a procedure immanent to each and every particular game. There is no unifying meta-discourse which might determine the validation of moves made in different games (so a political aesthetic, for example, is impossible while an art-move made politically is not).[21]

Finally, this field is conflictual, not communicational, agonistic rather than consensual; this is society seen (again) in terms of chessboards, war games.

In his essay 'The Discourse of Others: Feminists and Postmodernism', Craig Owens enthusiastically cites *La Condition postmoderne* to support an argument that the crisis of what he calls 'master narratives' is a crisis of cultural authority — 'specifically of the authority vested in Western European culture and its institutions[22] — that allows now for the liberating recognition of *differences* (ethnic, sexual ... these are the ones he mentions, but the usual others could easily be added). Owens assumes, I think, that the master-narrative crisis is both real and essentially benevolent to women and other Others. I want to question briefly both of those assumptions, as a way of suggesting some limitations to this version of postmodernity in Lyotard.

Firstly, while it would be miserably grim to contend that Western European culture and its institutions have undergone no such crisis of authority (though one would have to specify for whom they have, and the answer might not flatter Owens' thesis), I think that incredulity towards master (and/or meta-) narratives is not necessarily the kind of universal *fait accompli* that he (like Lyotard) suggests. The problem here is not one of competing views of 'social reality', but rather one of what is at stake in the shifts throughout *La Condition postmoderne* between *méta-récit* and *grand récit* — both of which are subsumed in Owens' term 'master narrative'.

A difficulty arises the moment that the author of *Le Différend* can speak credibly of '*le grand récit de la fin des grands récits*'.[23] In *La Condition postmoderne* the two great narratives analysed (emancipation, speculation) could effectively be related to the history of nineteenth-century universities, to a whole range of policy decisions and orientations in teaching and research, as well as to the development of intellectual values and passions. I am not sure that the narrative of the *end* of those narratives (or any version of the end of history) could be said to have the same status and power in the same institutions. It might well provide the content of a university experience, for example, but it is unlikely to be used to validate a committee decision. (As Lyotard points out at great length, in fact, 'performance value' and 'efficiency' have become the major modes of such institutional validation.)

There would then be two possibilities. Either the narrative of the end of master narratives is not *itself* a master narrative, but just a meta-narrative in a strict but uninteresting sense — in which case the criticism of *La Condition postmoderne* implied by the author of *Le Différend* misses its mark, and we may well be safely installed in postmodern incredulity. Or else it *is* a master narrative of sorts, a mini-master or a medium-*grand récit*: something more like a myth, an organizing and explanatory tale that reconciles some values and some passions to some institutional dilemmas and ideologies, but on a grander scale than a purely local story. This too, in its partiality, could be postmodern. But then, 'the end of history' while grandiose, isn't the only one of these ... what about 'a better life for our children', or 'personal fulfilment and self-expression' or 'social consensus and reconciliation'? all *guiding* narratives, let's say, which can be directly related to knowledge institutions, which are still not so very distant from emancipation fairy-tales (least of all when their failure is lamented), and which do not yet seem to be withering away under the impact of new technologies — despite Lyotard's prognosis that data banks, personal computers and so on will completely externalize the relationship of knower to knowledge. In which case we are the most gullible, and not incredulous, of cultures. At least, some of us are.

However, more serious problems are posed if we concede easily enough that legitimation crisis is a general cultural, as well as a specialist, phenomenon — and if we then *also* assume that it is automatically good for women, blacks, gays, migrants and anti-nuclear movements.

It is true that *La Condition postmoderne*'s rhetoric of heterogeneity, incommensurability, language-games and difference can be irresistibly attractive if introduced to the rhetoric of certain political movements. (If for Lyotard the postmodern text always arrives too late for its author, there is a sense in which Lyotard's recent work arrives too late for an entire generation.) But like 'site-specific intervention' and other variants on the principle of purely contextual activity, the crisis in credibility of meta-narratives can, in context, simply mean the disintegration of motivating arguments for intervening in anything at all, and that there are no longer any means of deciding in what, when, and how to intervene except by random passion (intuition, personal profit, suffering, caprice).

This is not to say that such a situation should be construed as a *danger* (to, say, feminism); and it is not to say that there should or could be any point in calling for artificial renewals of unity, faith, or boring old stories. It is to say that this situation does not necessarily *favour* difference-based movements (most of which refer to some version of the emancipation narrative anyway), or indeed any particular politics. It doesn't necessarily mean a field day for the sanctified difference of women, gays or blacks, and it doesn't have to mean indifference or apathy. It can also mean a state of permanent bellicosity in which Might (even Lyotard's 'strength of the weak') is Right. There is often a sort of scout's-honour ethic among leftists brandishing contextualism and the death of meta-discourse (usually at the few remaining visible marxists to be found), which allows us to forget that 'site-specific intervention' is after all not a bad description of the recent philosophy and conduct of the Australian Labor Party. (Though they call it 'pragmatism'.)[24]

Again, the point is not to lament this but to stress that 'specificity' is no longer a politically specific value (if it ever was), and to suggest that argument should shift to debating the implications of this rather than simply celebrating, or even still demanding, the arrival of days of difference.

Precisely that debate has been taking place in recent exchanges between Lyotard and Habermas, with Habermas developing a critique of the practice of 'determined *ad hoc* negation', while Lyotard reaffirms the impossibility of unity and consensus. Richard Rorty has summarized the stakes in these, rather cranky, terms:

> So we find French critics of Habermas ready to abandon liberal politics in order to avoid universalistic philosophy, and Habermas trying to hang on to universalistic philosophy, with all its problems, in order to support liberal politics.[25]

Without pursuing further here the details of the dispute, it seems to me that on the contrary *La Condition postmoderne* is fascinating for its attempt (considerably extended in *Au juste* and *Le Différend*) to reinvent a 'liberal' politics *after* abandoning a universalist philosophy — while openly confronting all the problems that involves, and which Craig Owens tends to ignore. Nevertheless, whether it succeeds — and whether it succeeds in escaping 'liberalism' taken in a less generous sense than that intended by Rorty — is another matter.

One example here must suffice. *Au juste* is a text that assumes the value of, and the necessity for, a new concept of justice for our bellicose postmodernity. Lyotard's particular uses of Kant, of Wittgenstein and pragmatics, all lead him to insist that the 'just' cannot be derived from the 'true', that a prescriptive sentence cannot be derived from a cognitive sentence. The conclusion he draws from this familiar separation is an optimistic one: it means that we can practise justice without seeking to base that practice in a 'true' theory. We can produce prescriptives (or imperatives, *you should ...*, *we must ...*), and impose upon our interlocutors an obligation to respond if not to obey (even a non-response is a response), without fear of claiming to impose our 'truth' on them — because we aren't playing the truth (cognitive) game, but the justice game.

The ingenuity of this is, *contextually*, at least equal to its vapidity if it is taken as an argument designed to persuade those terrified of being tainted by 'truth' that they may still take part in conflicts over what ought or ought not to be the case in the world, or up the street. When pressed on the matter of motivation for refusal or revolt (the Americans in Vietnam, the French in Algieria are the examples used), Lyotard comes perhaps as close as he ever does to admitting what Thomas Weiskel calls a 'jargon of ultimacy'. *'Il y a un vouloir'*, he says: there is a transcendence of justice, as long as 'transcendence' is understood as an abstract Obligation, a prescriptive, coming we know not whence and willing we know not what.[26]

If this jargon is admitted, however, it is mostly for the sake of argumentative convenience. Lyotard is more interested in two other modes of legitimation in the justice game. One is that *in*justice, indeed terrorism, is a matter of threatening a participant (the Vietnamese, the Algerians) with elimination from the game, or with the destruction of the pragmatics of the game itself. This threat gives grounds for revolt in any situation.

The other is that of the 'politics of opinion' mentioned above. One concept of 'the just' that Lyotard recommends is 'an answer through autonomy; it amounts to the assertion that the set of prescriptions produced by the whole of a social body to which the prescriptions apply, will be just'.[27] He suggests that this notion, already available in ancient Greek democracy, is peculiarly appropriate to modern societies – perhaps because of what is often called 'the court of public opinion' or (others might say) 'trial by media'. The same concept (which is un-nervingly close to that espoused for 'postmodern bourgeois liberalism' by Richard Rorty),[28] is developed in slightly different form in *La Condition postmoderne*:

> What is a 'good' prescriptive or evaluative utterance, a 'good' performance in denotative or technical matters? They are all judged to be 'good' because they conform to the relevant criteria (of justice, beauty, truth and efficiency respectively) accepted in the social circle of the 'knower's' interlocuteurs. The early philosophers called this mode of legitimating statements opinion.[29]

In the context of the discussion of science, Lyotard is at pains to criticize the evident role accorded to custom in this 'mode of legiti-mation', and to find it inadequate to the condition of science today. But for justice, it seems, he allows a customary pragmatism to stand.

There are several general problems with this position: for example, as Christopher Norris reminds us in his article on Rorty, the 'crucial problem as to how one could criticise *any* system of belief if the only means of properly understanding it was on its own implicit terms of cultural justification'.[30] Another, I think, is the degree to which (at least in Lyotard's use of it) it presupposes another, antagonistic position to which the pragmatist argument needs to be put in the form of a revelation/provocation: for *without* that presupposition and the resulting rhetoric and form, we end up with only a double affirmation of a *status quo*. That is, with the assertion that whatever the milieu says is just, is just (whatever the art-world says is art, is art); and with the further affirmation that this is so because it is so, and so on *ad infinitum*. From Rorty's position as critic, apologist and exponent of American (self-named) bourgeois liberalism, this affirmation does not necessarily pose a problem. In Lyotard's work, where no equivalent act of cultural self-identification appears to be being performed, this same rhetoric all too often produces an impression that rebuking the assumptions of classical political theories, especially marxism, can become so important that for this purpose Anything Goes as well as anything does – with a resulting contextual effect which seems, even if its Eurocentrism is accepted, to be both naive and anachronistic.

Above all, I think that Lyotard's adoption of a general pragmatist argument about the determination of justice *in combination with* his highly personalized, almost novelistic model of a pragmatics of language-games played by figures called 'senders' and 'receivers', leads us almost irresistibly towards a 'Harper Valley PTA' version of social conflict.[31] The milieu (remembering that we are dealing with a multiplicity of milieux, not Society, with local disputes and not a universal Politics) decides what's right and wrong, and that decision is right because the milieu so decides. But if I dissent, if I respond to the call of an Obligation, if I want to challenge a decision, modify the state of play and so perhaps transform the game, then what I have to do is make an unexpected move. And for Lyotard it is the making of unexpected, para-doxical moves that may in fact constitute judgement and a *politics* of opinion – not the reliance on sedimented layers of custom, but 'the capability of thinking outside of the concept and outside of habit'.[32]

In the context of Lyotard's general hypotheses for postmodernity with honour, then, the question of language-games requires further discussion since this in turn frames Lyotard's formulation of a post-modern sublime in art.

The Pragmatics of Language-Games

'Mere' rhetoric, to borrow both Thomas Weiskel's phrase and his ironic qualification of the 'mere', is crucial to Lyotard's thinking in general, to his conception of the possibility of an 'immanent' sublime, and to his attempt to combine a politics of justice with a politics of the unknown. In its very simplest form, this comes down in his work to the position that all 'speech acts' – including by this term everything ranging from the most insignificant phrase to complex events like books, artworks, indeed exhibitions ... – produce effects, and that these effects (which he sometimes calls *displacements*) constitute a kind of change that can properly be called 'changing the world' or just 'changing *world*'.

This is hardly a novel or even stirring proposition these days. It is important to stress, however, that in Lyotard's work this orientation has very little to do with a politics or even a problem of representation. Furthermore, and in contrast to many critics of contemporary art in the English-speaking world, he has suggested that 'artists today are engaged not in the deconstruction of significations but in extending the limits of sense perception' – with the proviso, however, that at the same time he called for 'an aesthetic not grounded in a *reality* of the senses.'[33] As his articles on Daniel Buren imply, it seems that the aesthetic Lyotard has in mind there would be one grounded in a strict pragmatics of 'seeing' understood as an interpretive activity carried out in an institutional context. More generally, and in his recent work, both signification and representation are ignored in favour of a concern with *reference* understood purely in terms of pragmatic relations (sender/receiver/referent, what he has elsewhere called the 'three contact-points of the work's force').[34]

It is in relation to these relations as they are established by the rules of different 'sentence-regimes' (descriptive, cognitive, prescriptive, evaluative, interrogative, performative ...), and *also* of different discourse genres (the larger 'games' which determine the finality of the linking of sentences in particular cases, and which determine what is at stake), that change may be effected.

One long quotation (of a text which I have transformed by transposing it from a tactical statement made in the dialogic game of *Au juste* to a new status as evidence of 'Lyotard's' position cited in and for my own exposition) may spare further exposition:

Prescriptions are not alone in causing the world to change. When a scientist describes something that no one has ever seen, the description may pass for purely fictional, and it is in a way, since the reality meant by the discourse will come into being only if names are attached to effects, and these effects exist only inasmuch as new discourses can be grafted onto them. Well, this too changes the world. I mean that a description can change the world. It changes it in another way, to other rhythms, but it changes it no less than a prescription. And when you say, 'to change worlds', that means 'to change pragmatic positions'. There are many ways of changing positions, of changing the pragmatic positions, and these ways define a language game. And if there are specific pragmatics, it means that a statement, with its form and in the context in which it is uttered, necessarily has an effect upon the world, whatever it may be.[35]

Lyotard then discusses dreams as an example of a 'precise pragmatic' defining a language–game: 'a statement that places the utterer in the position of an unknown utterer and the addressee as the ordinary utterer of wakeful discourses, that is, as the dreamer himself.'

It is this insistence on the *precision* of the pragmatic defining different language-games that differentiates Lyotard's work from many another vague exponent of 'discourse', 'textuality' and so forth working in the general field of contemporary aesthetics. To say that there are many ways to read a work, he wrote in 'Preliminary Notes on the Pragmatic of Works: Daniel Buren' does not imply that all possible readings may be applied to every work, nor that every reading may be applied to all works. In a text like 'Theory as Art', for example, while stressing the affinities between theory and art he is also concerned to define the differences between 'theory' and other arts (the role of the disciple, the authority accorded the referent).

For this very reason it is perhaps the question of precision which can most appropriately be posed to Lyotard's concepts of pragmatics, language-games, and the relations between them. For to say in criticism (as I would certainly wish to) that to speak of 'changing the pragmatic positions' as 'changing world' is today a necessary but trivial and insufficient observation (insufficient, that is, to a concept of change able to do more than state and restate that language effects effects), and to say that it has undoubted polemical force against the argument that such effects are inconsequential or nonexistent or irrelevant to the '*real*' world but that this argument itself is today relatively inconsequential – would be simply to accuse Lyotard's work of not going beyond the limits that it explicitly sets itself in the first place.

It might also be to ignore the positive value, the *usefulness*, that Lyotard's insistence on the calculability of change in terms of pragmatic relations can have as a method of invention. It is a practice of cunning, and a mode of generating ideas. Lyotard's thought does not help much with the question of 'ideas to what purpose', and it most certainly does not intend or pretend to do so. At the same time, however, Lyotard does claim in *La Condition postmoderne*, that a certain tonic and anti-pessimistic effect can be gained from thinking the problems of postmodernity in terms of broken-down narratives and dispersed language-games. It means that while 'a *self* does not amount to much', it is never isolated: because 'no one, not even the least privileged among us, is ever entirely powerless over the messages that traverse and position him [*sic*] at the post of sender, addressee, or referent'.[36] That many of our culture's most successful and/or fashionable 'lifestyle' designers (I am thinking in particular of Milton Glaser rather than Malcolm McLaren or Keith Haring) espouse a similar philosophy in no way discredits either the thought or the sentiment.

In *Le Différend* Lyotard goes a little further and argues, in effect, that the heterogeneity of sentence-regimes and discourse genres provides the only insurmountable obstacle to the hegemony of capital's privileged 'genre' – the economic genre. At this point we are entitled to ask what – *precisely* – that might mean.[37]

Part of the difficulty is that Lyotard repeats the same sort of analysis whether he is dealing with a sentence (like the declarative, prescriptive and performative sentences – *The University is sick, Give the University more funds,* and *The University is now open* – analysed in *La Condition postmoderne*),[38] or with an instance of sustained discourse (his analyses of Buren's works), or with a genre ('Theory as Art'), or with the complex discursive and institutional compounds that Lyotard still calls 'genres' (economics in the example above). The only mediating concept to deal with the difference between the pragmatics of the sentence *You're fired!* and the generic hegemony of economics in capitalism's discursive repertoire is the distinction alluded to above, between the sentence-regimes and the discourse-genres that organize them (dialogue, exposition, validation, narrative – this list is in principle endless).

Lyotard, of course, is not a linguist and his speculative game is certainly not aspiring to generate a linguistics. But the relative paucity and generality of his operative concepts for analysing his language-games is most discomfiting when he begins to make rather large claims about the scale and scope of their effectiveness. In fact, they simply seem to create a sort of tier of fictions of function: a well-ordered but unvarying hierarchy in which each 'message' at each level is almost geometrically defined by its triad of sender/receiver/referent. The coherence of this schema is as oppressive, in a way, as its incapacity to differentiate is striking.

This and other problems with Lyotard's pragmatics seem to be connected to his borrowings from Wittgenstein (the way that he simply projects the pragmatic communication model on to the model of the language-game), and the way those elements are combined in turn with a mix of mathematical game theory, paradoxology, analytical philosophy and speech-act theory. His work is in one sense a delightful and ingenious conceptual collage, quite explicitly enacting the theme (in fact, articulating the prescriptive) that in postmodernity one must invent. But too often (and particularly in *La Condition postmoderne*) the result seems merely forced, and facile.

For example, it depends quite heavily on a relatively uncritical appropriation of the 'language-*game*' metaphor, and makes no real attempt to address the problem of the notorious 'disanalogies' between rule-governed formal games, linguistic events, and complex social and discursive practices (history-writing, economic activity, art ...).[39] As a result, Lyotard sometimes gives the impression that he sees the latter as merely rather large tournaments composed of a multiplicity of little games – the problem with that vision being not its triviality, but rather its unnerving *orderliness*.

It is true that at one moment in *Le Différend*, Lyotard suggests that in fact there are no language-games (*jeux*) but rather stakes (*enjeux*) linked to discourse genres. However, the change simply transposes the site of the difficulty since 'stake' retains the metaphor of game structure; and it is made only on the grounds that languages are conflictual rather than 'playful' (which for Lyotard seems to be a distinction in intensity rather than of kind). So the problem remains that Lyotard's 'genre' is as vague and all-embracing as the corresponding concept of 'framework' in the *Philosophical Investigations*, in which 'No clear distinction is made between linguistic (semantic-syntactic), institutional, anthropological, or behavioristic frameworks or forms of life'.[40]

However, Lyotard is interested in a different sort of distinction – one which exists *between* language-games once this levelling of hierarchies of difference and complexity has been achieved. His most common reference-point for the notion of language-game is the famous twenty-third entry of the *Philosophical Investigations* with its insistence on the multiplicity of kinds of sentence ('But how many kinds of sentence are there? Say assertion, question, and command? – There are *countless* kinds'),[41] and its list of 'the multiplicity of language-games' (of which Lyotard gives a version adapted to painting in his *October* text on Buren). He is interested not in inventing concepts to specify particular differences, but in the pure difference of difference itself – in the incommensurability of one game with another, in the *abyss* that separates (for this theory) one sentence-regime from another, one discourse-genre from another.

It is with this metaphor of the abyss (the gulf, the ravine) that a concept of the Sublime can be made to re-appear:

> Kant after Burke recognises sublime sentiments other than enthusiasm. Besides respect, of course, and admiration, chagrin, *der Kummer*, is also among the 'vigorous emotions' if it has its foundation in moral Ideas.... The despair of never being able to present in reality something adequate to the Idea wins out over the joy of being nevertheless called upon to do so. One is more depressed by the abyss which separates heterogeneous discourse genres than one is excited by the indication of a possible passage from one to another. – Would a vigorously melancholy humanity thus suffice to prove that humanity is progressively progressing?[42]

The Sublime and the Avant-Garde

> certainly we are no longer plunged into bathos by daffodils. Yet our experience remains riddled by discontinuities, and the sublime or something like it, as well as the bathetic or something like it, will always be found in the ill-defined zones of anxiety between discrete orders of meaning.
>
> *The Romantic Sublime*[43]

Appropriately, no doubt, Lyotard's observations in aesthetics exist in adjacency to, rather than continuity with, his speculations on an 'honorable' postmodernity in science, politics, linguistic philosophy. The relationship between them is of the order of a reverberating similarity, a kind of family resemblance in styles of argument adapted to different games.

In this essay I have stressed these reverberations rather than attempting to discuss Lyotard's aesthetics as an addition to the history of the idea of the Sublime, and I want to maintain that emphasis here. However, in order to do so it is useful to note a couple of points about what Lyotard has drawn from the classic debates about the Sublime in eighteenth and nineteenth century aesthetics.

One is that whereas for Kant and Burke the Sublime and the Beautiful constituted two species of aesthetic judgement, and could be mutually defined as the two poles of an opposition, for Lyotard the Beautiful merely serves a purpose of brief expository contrast – and that in terms of what *was said* by, say, Kant, rather than in terms of presenting a category viable today. In 'Answering the Question', the aesthetics of the Sublime is presented as *the* aesthetic appropriate to the history of modern (including postmodern) painting, while the harmony and pleasure specific to the Beautiful (pleasure calling for 'a universal consensus of principle (which will, perhaps, never be achieved)' is relegated by the deadly word *still* to a scrapheap of history along with Habermas and his dreams of art as a culturally healing force: 'aesthetics for him is still the aesthetics of Beauty'.[44]

The effect of Lyotard's move here is a peculiar one since on the one hand it transforms 'the Sublime' into a purely historical and descriptive category in relation to the analysis of art, while on the other it strips the concept of its own history if it is analysed in relation to itself. The former seems to give rise to an effective, because overwhelmingly familiar model of modernism as a sensibility dependent on strong and equivocal emotion, on pleasure arising from pain (and boredom), and on the propulsing force of unresolvably recurrent oedipal seizures. The latter helps suppress the rather crude sexual-differentiation metaphors that are usually evoked by classic Sublime/Beautiful distinctions ('Like everybody else at that time', Bertrand Russell said of Kant, 'he wrote a

treatise on the sublime and the beautiful. Night is sublime, day is beautiful; the sea is sublime, the land is beautiful; man is sublime, woman is
beautiful; and so on'[45]). At the same time it generalizes and treats as
absolute the stern, forbidding disruptive half of the opposition rather
than the charming, tender, harmonious half now deemed historically
obsolete.

This in itself need be of no special importance except to those cultural
Others who maintain an interest in representation as one of the elements
that make problems of reference matter. Yet the effacement of the
Sublime's history takes its toll of Lyotard's rhetoric since it leaves him
ranting like Schiller ('Then away with falsely construed forbearance and
vapidly effeminate taste'[46] cried Schiller, before going on to muse on the
wedding of beauty to the sublime) about defending the dignity and true
vocation of art – without any apparent context or reason for the resur-
gence of this exceeding strange vocabulary, this patrimonial posture.

A second point about Lyotard's interpretation of the sublime can be
made in response to its apparently curious omission of any reference to
Schiller's elaboration of Kant. Schiller's originality, after all, was to push
the Kantian themes of unpresentable vastness (magnitude and power)
towards an aesthetic of *confusion* ('the uncertain anarchy of the moral
world'), and of *'incomprehensibility itself as a principle of judgement'*
(my emphasis).[47] This might have seemed an ideal tool for discussing the
history of modern art's relation to its publics sketched in 'Answering the
Question', and for extending that text's critique of communication and
consensus. There are moments when Schiller on the 'sensitive traveller'
might be Lyotard on Habermas: 'If, however, he willingly abandons the
attempt to assimilate this lawless chaos of appearances to a cognitive
unity, he will abundantly regain in another direction what he has lost in
this.'[48]

Lyotard's interests lie elsewhere; and Schiller's sublime does have the
inconvenience of being intrinsic, albeit ambiguously, to its objects,
whereas in Kant,

> The importance of the philosophy of the beautiful and the sublime in the first
> part of the third *Critique* resides in the *derealisation of the object* of aesthetic
> sentiments, and at the same time in the absence of a faculty of aesthetic
> knowledge properly speaking.[49]

As the phrase 'derealisation of the object' suggests, the emphasis in
Lyotard's version of the sublime is placed on processes that may have
the making of art-objects as their byproduct, but that *must* have the
making of activity, or eventfulness, as their defining and motivating
characteristic. This means that unlike much of the theoretical work of

the past decade, Lyotard's aesthetics does not stress notions of reading, viewing, etc. (except within a consideration of a precise pragmatic): instead, it comes much closer to offering a theory of creation, with the qualification that it cannot incorporate a notion of the 'creative *subject*'. For Lyotard is not presenting the sublime as a 'subjective' experience, but as a failure in the regulation of the relations between the subject's faculties, as a flawed subreption – as accord only in the inevitability of discord.[50]

Lyotard's borrowings from Burke, however, constitute his own most creative and extravagant move towards the re-legitimation of the avant-gardes, and the thematics of eventfulness and discord. In 'The Sublime and the Avant-Garde' Lyotard makes of Burke a theorist of the *Ereignis*, the occurrence, *der Fall*, the '*what is occurring*', the '*is it happening*', the event; in other words, a theorist of the something happening which is not tautological with that which happened ... and of all those concepts with which Lyotard in *Le Différend* attempts to do away with a philosophy of being and the subject, and to transform the philosophy of time.[51]

The major gambit of the *Philosophical Enquiry into the Origin of Our Ideas of the Sublime and Beautiful*, says Lyotard, is to show that the sublime is kindled by the threat that *nothing further might happen*: and it is certainly true that Burke (for whom pain could be a cause of delight, understood as the lifting of tension or terror) shared Schiller's suspicions of the 'enervation of uninterrupted enjoyment':

> as we were not made to acquiesce in life and health, the simple enjoyment of them is not attended with any real pleasure, lest satisfied with that, we should give ourselves over to indolence and inaction.[52]

Samuel H. Monk's analogy of the Sublime as a Methodist revival does not seem too far distant at this point, and it is interesting to note that if Burke feared the vegetable stupour of happiness and the indolence of inactivity it was because 'in this languid inactive state, the nerves are most liable to the most horrid convulsions'.[53] The best remedy for the 'Melancholy, dejection, despair, and often self-murder' which could accompany relaxation, said Burke, was *Labour* – an exertion which resembles pain in everything but degree.

Lyotard dismisses Burke's empiricism and physiologism in order to concentrate only on the concept of happening and on Burke's concept of poetry as 'countless active investigations of language'.[54] Here again, however, and just as the idea of art as research ('active investigations') emerges to complete the set of basic elements needed to link the Sublime to the avant-gardes, one may wonder whether the puritan inheritance of the concept can be discarded so easily and so painlessly. For what it leaves to Lyotard's sublime is precisely, I think, a sort of work-and-agony ethic of artistic activity that bears not on the conditions of production experienced by particular artists, but on the formulation of a general Prescription about how art today should continue to function. Apart from what I believe to be its fundamental unpleasantness, this ethic raises at least two problems. One is that it adds nothing to existing romantic ideologies of art as labour-pain, while it quite fails to come to terms with those developments in art which operate in relation to the dismantling of the work/leisure, research/entertainment distinctions which make Lyotard's rhetoric historically possible. The other is that it is hard to see why this ethic, revived for *art*, would not re-join the meta-narrative of the adventures of speculative Mind.

To clarify this, however, it is necessary to return to the question of the relationship between Lyotard's remarks on the sublime, and his arguments about (and for) postmodernity; to consider, also, the difference between the general outline of *La Condition postmoderne* and the second, positive concept of postmodernity proffered by Lyotard for art in 'Answering the Question: What is the Post-Modern?'.

The book assumes a roughly consecutive relationship between modernity and postmodernity – the search for grounding principles gives way to incredulity via 'delegitimation'. The essay, however, predicates a post-modernity which, as a recurring moment of rupture, actually *institutes* the modern: 'Post-modernism ... is not modernism at its end, but rather modernism at its very beginning – and that beginning is always recurrent.'[55] Postmodernism, then, is the original modern gesture and it is only a terminal phase of modernism insofar as it terminates modernism's various phases. That is to say, the 'postmodern' in Lyotard's argument here corresponds to the action of criticism proper to the avant-garde, while the 'modern' corresponds to the institutionalization (celebration and destruction) of the results.[56]

This proposition about time is accompanied by two others which define its significance, and introduce the sublime. The first of these is actually a proposition about form/content relations, which depends upon an odd equation between form, 'the' signifier, and 'presentation'. The modern, or the nostalgic Sublime (Proust), poses the unpresentable as an absent content while retaining the comfort of 'good' (familiar, pleasurable) form. The postmodern, the genuine sublime sentiment (Joyce) presents the unpresentable in the form itself.

The remaining proposition reconciles the temporal and formal aspects of postmodernism in a rule about rules. The postmodern will be work which will begin without rules, but which will proceed in order to establish (according to the paradox of the future anterior) the rules of what will have been made. The principle, however, is not specific to the artist: it defines the practice also of the judge who judges without a model of justice, and the philosopher who writes to discover the rules of his philosophy.

The elegance of the rule about rules may obscure the peculiar relation between the first two propositions. Postmodernism understood as the injunction to formal eventfulness (the invention of new rules) guarantees the temporal function of postmodernism as originary rupture – and *vice versa*. The rupture must be recurrent because the very structure of the obligation to 'event', *as well as* the logic of the art market, soon drains any actual event of its eventfulness. (This explains why most avant-garde art eventually reverts to good form, though it does not explain why Lyotard opposes Proust to Joyce as though their works were intrinsically modern and postmodern respectively.) The sublime is immanent to each such event as it happens.

So in order not to lapse into the stasis of modernity, and in order to keep '*it*' *happening* (whatever '*it*' may be, since the invention of refer-ents to take '*it's*' place in the sentence is the business of invention) we must always become *again* postmodern. 'Postmodernism', therefore, is for Lyotard in this instance a galvanizing principle, a critical dynamic which ensures that events can still occur and occur meaningfully in art without being grounded in a legitimizing meta-narrative (of, say, art's 'value' or 'usefulness').

Postmodernism in art is thus the equivalent of paralogism in science and philosophy, of the unexpected move in a politics of opinion: and this hypothesis, I think, is as remarkable for its adroitness as it is for its strange banality. It is banal because it restores us to the paradox of a history driven by the sole, and *traditional*, imperative to break with tradition. Lyotard is anxious to distinguish this imperative from that of 'the *petit frisson*, the profitable pathos, that accompanies innovation' (innovation advances, the *is-it-happening?* arrests);[57] and in *La Condi-tion postmoderne* he wants to distinguish true paralogism, a 'move' of formal fallacy made to enable further thought and thus a displacement in the pragmatics of knowledge, from 'innovation' understood as a requirement of a given system to improve its efficiency. It doesn't matter, he argues, if in reality the former is often transformed into the latter.

Yet in relation to art at least, it is hard to see how or why Lyotard's distinction could matter except at the level of the purity of individual intention. Surely an entire history of modern art institutions (including criticism, the gallery, the museum, and the relations of all three to the rest of the market) could be written precisely in terms of a strict rhythm of alternation between advance and arrest, pure event and mere innovation. The transformation of the former into the latter is vital to the art 'system' – indeed, as Lyotard's own version of the modern/postmodern relation suggests, it may actually be a rule that defines the game. If this is so, then Lyotard again has done little more than re-present a familiar description of the status quo – spiced with the sort of moral encouragement to artists to keep on experimenting for the sake of the pursuit of pure Event that one might find in any romantic biography of a dead art-hero. And it is in the prescription to this pursuit, and in its list of heroes (Cézanne, Picasso, Duchamp, Buren), that there are echoes of the story of Speculation.

The adroitness of the hypothesis, on the other hand, is relative to the context of the debates about postmodernism (and in particular, the trans-avant-garde in art) within which it was actually proposed. (A good scenario, according to *La Condition postmoderne*, need be neither original nor true but simply of strategic value in relation to the problem posed.)

It is adroit because in appropriating for *post*-modernism the gestures classically associated with the avant-garde, it decrees that we cannot escape from the problematic of the latter – least of all at a time of '*post*-', i.e. ruptural rhetoric pronouncing the escape to be a *fait accompli*. At the same time, it conserves the possibility of rejecting the academicization of art – henceforth called 'modernism'. One way of describing Lyotard's move here is to say that it imposes a double bind. Another is to suggest that it turns the avant-garde gesture into a rough equivalent of the Human Condition for the age of incredulity. A third would be to observe that it turns the whole matter of 'Postmodernism' into an elaborate joke.

At this point, which is the turning-point in Lyotard's arguments between their ingenuity and their triviality, it is possible to recall his location of sublimity not in art but in speculating on art – and to wonder about the effects his arguments can induce in the current state of play in art-speculation. For the language-game in which they are involved is, of course, not directly 'art', but art-criticism.

There can be no stable answer to that question, but I would like to conclude my own speculations on Lyotard's sublime with two remarks.

The first is that it does – as both a description of the rhythm of arrest and advance and as a prescription to 'present the unpresentable' – have the enormous advantage of undermining the persistent opposition made between *modernism* as a problematic of self-reference, purism, ontological preoccupation and concern with media specificity, and *postmodernism* (avant-gardism) as an insistence on problems of reference.[58] On the one hand, Lyotard's emphasis on the pragmatic of works formally eliminates the need for such an opposition (which still rests on an art/world dichotomy, assuming as it does both that it is possible for some art to talk about art while other art talks about the world, and that the loquacity is in either case intrinsic to the artwork concerned regardless of how, when and by whom it is read): in Lyotard's terms, the question 'What is painting?' is at all times a referential, and not an ontological, question. On the other hand, this same emphasis allows the modernism/postmodernism, self-referring/other-referring opposition to be understood in terms of its function as a *stake* linked to conflicts in the discourse-genre of art criticism.

My second remark, however, tends to cancel the first insofar as it consists in a scepticism that any fundamental displacement (as distinct from the pragmatic flutter of a passing fad) of the stakes in contemporary art debates can come about through Lyotard's presentation of the sublime. The problem is precisely one of presentation: of the difference between the concept of the sublime as 'presenting the unpresentable' referred to in his recent articles on art, and the cognate concepts of presentation and of the *différend* in his philosophical work.

In both cases, a kind of 'jargon of ultimacy' seems to be achieved. In the former, it is that the unpresentable exists, while in the latter it is rather that the incommensurable is (or happens). (In both cases the rhetoric implies an antagonistic position to which these testimonials need be addressed, prompting the question of what sort of art criticism, what kind of philosophy, might develop from these presuppositions if the imaginary opponents were abandoned — and so if the affirmation of the presuppositions ceased to be the main function of texts.)

The difference is that in the articles on aesthetics, the 'unpresentable' is purely and simply asserted as a value with the joint significance of being firstly a Good Thing, and secondly a brief paraphrase of Kant. Its 'ultimacy' lies in its status as a recurring ultimatum to activity imposed (by the universe, by Lyotard) on artists and on art. In *Le Différend*, problems of what can constitute 'presentation' and under what conditions, constitute a major subset of mixed questions and affirmations in a general theoretical project deliberately mined and undermined with doubt, and with instances of the incommensurability of languages it exists to evoke.[59]

The *différend* itself is perhaps one of the names of this principle of incommensurability. It is defined in a first instance as a case of conflict between at least two parties which cannot be equitably decided for lack of a judgement rule applicable to the two different argumentations, and in which any ruling must therefore wrong one of the parties by judging it according to inappropriate criteria. This basic notion then rapidly expands in the book as it is supplemented with different observations: of the differend as constitutive of victimization, if a 'victim' is defined as

THE PIRATE'S FIANCÉE

someone who (like the victims of the Holocaust) has not only suffered a wrong but *also* the loss of the means to prove, in terms that count as 'proof' in the appropriate games (history, in this case), that the wrong ever took place; of the differend as the 'unstable state and the moment of language in which something which ought to be able to be put into sentences still cannot yet be so,'[60] of the differend as both that unsayable something that hovers only in potential in the irreducible and depressing abyss between different discourse genres, and as the resultant, exhilarating imperative to make it sayable, to have it said. It is in these terms that Lyotard wants to reply to the revisionist historians about the reality of Auschwitz and its annihilation of 'testimonials';

> so it is necessary for the historian to break the monopoly over history accorded to the cognitive regime of sentences, and to risk lending an ear to that which is not presentable within the rules of knowledge. Every reality imposes this demand insofar as it imposes possible unknown meanings. Auschwitz is the most real of realities in this respect.[61]

There is not a trace of this complexity or of these concerns, of this sense of what is at stake in allusions to the unpresentable and to a politics of the unknown, in the articles on the sublime in aesthetics. This is not to complain of a lack of 'rigour' in the latter but rather to point to the functioning of a different mode of argument in each case. Where in *Le Différend* each concept is constantly destabilized by being repeatedly redefined and displaced, the articles constantly collapse a number of 'possible' different concepts (the unpresentable, the indeterminate, the inexpressible, the unrepresentable) into one flat assertion of an unpresentability which good avant-garde art, and the true sublime, will allude to in 'form' as well as 'content'. Perhaps the clearest example of the difference is in the role and scope accorded to 'politics' in the two kinds of writing: in *Le Différend*, politics can appear as: 'the threat of the differend. Politics is not a genre, it is the multiplicity of genres, the diversity of ends, and par excellence the question of the linking [of sentences].'[62] In 'Answering the Question', politics appears in its familiar art-burble role as the repressive enemy of experimentation.

Why this difference (between inscriptions, perhaps, of what counts as philosophy and as art criticism in Lyotard's work) should take this form at this time escapes me: and so do the reasons why any thoroughgoing contextualist in the Anglo–American world would take seriously an argument posing social realism and theoretical marxism as major threats to artistic and intellectual freedom (to experiment ...) in their respective games at the moment.

I don't think the reasons really matter. Much more important, it seems to me, are the questions Lyotard's practice raises about the placing and function of different kinds of argument – questions raised, at least, for every writer. If the meditations in *Le Différend* help to describe the conditions in which Lyotard's sublime can conform to the requirements of the sort of bad dream with which this essay began, if it provides a language with which to say that this sublime simply represents the most familiarly presentable guarantees of significance, and of tradition and novelty combined, to art institutions contextually receptive to all three – then it is the abyss, the difference, the anxiety that exists between the two that best defines the pathos, if not the sublimity, of both.

12

Tooth and Claw: Tales of Survival, and *Crocodile Dundee*

The moment of survival *is the moment of power*

Elias Canetti

Preamble: *Dundee* and The Great White Whale

In a passage of *L'Image-mouvement*, Gilles Deleuze makes a casual distinction between the path of commercial success in contemporary cinema, and the movement of its 'soul'. The distinction clarifies a historical claim that a 'crisis of the action-image' seized postwar American cinema: 'Certainly ... the greatest commercial successes still take that route, but the soul of the cinema no longer does.' For Deleuze, cinema's soul craves *thought*; and in the aftermath of the Second World War, thought begins to undo the system of actions, perceptions and affects that had supported classic cinema. One of the reasons, and one of the results, is that we can now scarcely believe that 'a global situation may give rise to an action which is capable of modifying it'.[1]

Whatever the value of Deleuze's work for students of cinema, my point of departure here will be to see in this casual moment of his text, in which soul divides from commerce, another instance of *thought* veering away from the problems posed to criticism by cinema's 'big, fat, commercial successes' (Paul Hogan).[2]

L'Image-mouvement and *L'Image-temps* invent a philosophy of time rather than a theory of film or of popular culture, and for Deleuze, no useful problem may be posed by those blockbuster cycles which, from *Star Wars* to *The Wild Geese* to *The Road Warrior* to *Rambo* to *Crocodile Dundee* (not to mention the small, fat commercial successes of Chuck Norris and Charles Bronson films), have had quite a bit to say in the aftermath of the Vietnam war about action, its capacity to modify a global situation, and 'our' capacity for belief.

More surprising is the relative lack of attention paid to such films in

241

recent debate about postmodernity – with its concern for the bases of valid actions ('moves'), the global – or the multinational – against the local, and the conditions of credibility now. Indeed, an avoidance of cinema in general structures some founding texts of postmodern debate: historic essays by Habermas, Lyotard, Jameson, Huyssen, which have helped create for contemporary theory its own version of cinema's blockbuster: the state-of-the-globe, state-of-the-arts, Big Speculation.[3]

There is a *genial disinterest* exemplified by the Habermas-Lyotard debate: it's clear that these texts do not emerge from a cultural sphere in which the latest *Muppet* movie might be taken to be an Event; and Lyotard's venture into film theory, 'Acinema', is confined to classic experimentalist problems.[4] Fredric Jameson is quite right to note a convergence of commitment to the Art-revering values of high modernism uniting these otherwise fiercely opposed protagonists in a common belief in the powers of critical culture.[5] Then there is the use of *functional allusions* to cinema: the addition of film to a general list of cultural practices surveyed (Huyssen), or the parabolic exegesis of an exemplary instance (the 'nostalgia film' in Jameson's essay) which confirms and extends a prior argument.

From these morsels of analysis, little enough can be said about the complexities of cinema – but more importantly, the complexities of cinema have had little to say to the analyses. Yet surely (to emphasize but one issue, the famous 'mixing' of high and popular culture so often said to characterize a postmodern condition) – if one cultural form could alone suffice to shake the sense of classical dichotomies (avant-garde/ kitsch, avant-garde/modernist, innovation/tradition, experiment/cliché, high/low, elite/popular), the cinema would be that form? Or if one might use only one institution to invoke relations between modernity and modernization, technology and ideology, economics, politics and culture, then cinema could be that institution? Why then, for the founding texts of postmodern debate, did cinema not occupy a position at least as privileged as that accorded to architecture? Particularly since cinema and architecture are beginning to develop close and complex new relations, through shopping malls and total entertainment venues, in the material redevelopment of the space of urban lives?

With these questions in mind, I want to put forward some working assumptions for reading the politics of action, location and credibility in Peter Faiman/Paul Hogan's *Crocodile Dundee*.

It is definitely a big, fat commercial success. In 1986 it made more money in Australia than any film from any country in Australian cinema history; and in the United States, it remained the national top-grossing film for many weeks. It isn't 'art', avant-garde, or modernist cinema, and it certainly isn't radical cinema. It's one of many products of contemporary commercial cinema which are not easily salvaged by criticism for an *auteur* canon (unlike the Coppola–Lucas–Spielberg complex); valued for their inaugural status (*Jaws, Star Wars*); or prized for a sociopolitical commentary that serves as a mirror to theory (like *Blade Runner, Alien/ Aliens, The Terminator, Videodrome, The Road Warrior* on technical reason, monstrosity, difference/indifference, and death).

However I am not interested in producing an essentialist reading of *Crocodile Dundee* as a 'postmodern film', although it might be possible to do so – stressing its folksy, common sense populism, its use of parody and pastiche, its comedy of cultural (in)difference, and the pragmatics of its well-made *move* in the game of international cinema. What I prefer to do instead is to take postmodernism not as a cultural logic (a reflection of which I might read in the film), but as a repertoire of critical terms. The notion of repertoire doesn't imply that my choice of terms – or text – is arbitrary. As I have suggested, *Crocodile Dundee* is one of a number of recent films about action, belief, and the relationship of both to 'global' situations – films about danger, adventure, commitment, credibility, global conflict, and local heroism. I want to read it as an intersection point of several fables of survival, read against the context of the apocalyptic rhetoric pervading postmodernism.

At the same time, the problem of whether a global situation can give rise to an action capable of modifying it is also the problem of the action of a text upon the social signifying systems that make it possible, and which constitute its materials. I'll take from the repertoire the notion of 'appropriation' to analyse a privileged mode of action in and by the film – the critical modification of cultural, and cinematic, codes. This notion often functions, especially in art criticism, as a vague essentialist wave in the general direction of intertextuality. So I'll define my usage here (in order to question the term, and its place in the postmodern repertoire, later). 'Appropriation' is a critical interpretation, produced in some textual practices, of the intertextuality which is a constitutive principle of all text-making. This interpretation is made explicit by a sign of appropriation: a type of *mise en abyme* (of the code and/or the *énonciation*) that generates some kind of explicit commentary on the modifying power, or desired effects, of its own action on other textual elements, other texts.[6] By doing so, it presupposes some problem of power to be regulated in and by that action (in the sense that parody, for example, implies a *status* problem). In this sense, I want to take appropriation as an object of commentary in *Crocodile Dundee*, as well as a means of modification by which the film solves certain 'action' problems.

This emphasis is not simply determined either by the film's practice – which makes it easy to assimilate to an aesthetics of recoding – or by its economic strategy of surviving as an Australian film in the global market by means of that recoding. It is also determined by the film's allusions to colonialism. As the Indian art critic Geeta Kapur points out,[7] the term 'appropriation' resounds with the history of Western imperialism: and *Crocodile Dundee* is a post-*colonial* comedy of survival, with remnants of the British, land-taking, appropriative regime (bushmen, Aborigines, Darwinian 'natural' perils) emerging into the 'multinational' cultural space of American-media modernity.

This is a way of introducing a final working assumption. If *Crocodile Dundee* is, in a banal sense, an Australian film, I shall assume that it is not an Australian phenomenon. By phenomenon, I mean what the advertising industry means: an *event*; a complex interaction between commerce and 'soul'; or, to speak more correctly, between a film text, the institution of cinema, and the unpredictable crowd-actions that endow mass-cultural events with their moments of legitimacy, and so modify mass culture.

To study phenomena in this sense is to study the formation of *prodigies*, the marvels of 'contemporaneity'; yet another name for what Mike Davis engagingly calls 'that elusive Great White Whale of cultural criticism – the specific *object* thereof – which so many have pursued, struggled with for a while (some drowning in due course) and, then, invariably lost hold of'.[8] It may well be true that cultural criticism cannot properly constitute its object. However it can, in its pursuits, do fieldwork (or since water's involved, go fishing) for more rigorous disciplines in that dissolute domain of culture where a film like *Crocodile Dundee* can be a marvel in the same way, and for some of the same reasons, as a book by Habermas, Lyotard, Jameson – or Mike Davis.

To pursue that phenomenon further is the object of this article.

PART I

The Call of the Crocodile–Poacher

The whole world wonders now why the call for
designs outside of Australia itself was ever made.
This is but proof of what is so often said of these
people: they are mere imitators. Originality is
unknown. They are positively unable to originate.
Everything is a copy with some small alteration,
usually a disadvantage to the subject.

Jessie Ackermann,
Australia From A Woman's Point of View, 1913

SUE: *I'm always all right when I'm with you,
Dundee ... God that sounds corny. Why do you
always make me feel like Jane in a Tarzan comic?*

DUNDEE (feeble imitation of Tarzan's call):
AARGH–AARGH!

Crocodile Dundee, 1986

Sue Charlton (played by Linda Kozlowski) in *Crocodile Dundee* is not
the first American woman journalist to brave the wilds of remote
Australia, and live to tell the tale. Jessie Ackermann, a dauntless organ-
izer for the Women's Christian Temperance Union, made four visits to
Australia around the turn of the century, travelled widely, and wrote a
critical account of her experiences. Ackermann's brisk American faith in
innovation and pioneering as the mix that makes a nation produced one
of the sharpest (though not 'original') statements of a powerfully active
myth – that the one distinctive feature of Australian culture is its *positive
unoriginality*.

That Ackermann was referring, in the passage quoted above, to a call for
designs of Canberra as national capital city – and thus to a symbolic founding gesture – is a touch suggesting the rich potential of this myth for a variety
of uses. Today, it can still be invoked as a tragic flaw requiring bureaucratic
interventions in culture, or as an ironic virtue, placing Australia in a
privileged postmodern position as a playground of simulation.

This is, of course, a myth (in Barthes' sense of the term), and a very
complicated one. It naturalizes historic, hegemonic operations. It generalizes to 'these people' the dilemmas of a colonial intelligentsia. It inter-
nalizes, in its classic Australian form, global material structures and
effects of imperialism as 'national' psychic problems. It universalizes the
modernist imperative of originality. And it rarely (except in its ironic
mode) examines the eye of the beholder. It functions, that is to say, in

much the same way as many accounts of postmodernism as a global
(rather than national) cultural condition.

By the mid-1980s, positive unoriginality and its effects on foreign
beholders had become a focus of bitter political conflict for the Australian film industry. For almost a decade in journalism and in public
reports, the film industry had regularly been represented as a creature
on the verge of extinction. The prognostic varies with circumstances, but
the problem remains the same: how to ensure survival for a frail young
thing beset by local perils, international (American) predators, and
deadly shades from the past rising up to harrow the present.

Most of this rhetoric (including the hopes and fears of a Hollywood
invasion) can be derived from the structural fragility of a small industry
dependent on government support – and thus on party-political whim,
national economic fluctuations, and bureaucratic manoeuvre – in a
country of sixteen million people with expensively American tastes in film.
From this economically menacing environment, and from myths of cultural
insecurity, three theories of unoriginality and national cinema emerge.[9]

One assumes that unoriginality is a Bad Thing, a byproduct of
'cultural imperialism'. In this context, that notoriously imperfect term
refers not only to the usual dominance of Hollywood norms in the
programming of pleasures, and dominance of the American majors in
the Australian film market (a 78 per cent share of theatrical rentals in
1985). It also refers to polemically mobilized memories of disastrous
meddling by American studio interests in Australian film production
(like the standing down of the great director Raymond Longford to
make way for an American hack on the 1927 blockbuster-flop, *For The
Term of His Natural Life*), and of the use of Australia as exotic backdrop to rising American stars – which in 1961 gave us the unforgettable
spectacle of Ernest Borgnine, just before *McHale's Navy*, playing a
North Queensland cane-cutter in *The Summer of the Seventeenth Doll.*

Not surprisingly, an argument with these reference-points often
combines a call for collective originality with a realist aesthetic ('cultural
exactitude'), an essentialist model of audience (the eye of the beholder
as site of national perception) and a politics of primary anti-American-
ism. Thus, the film-maker Bob Ellis on Hollywood's power for
monstrous alien-ation: 'I have seen so many people coming back with
those strange Peter Allen accents talking about warmth and love and
having a nice day, and it is like the end of *The Invasion of the Body
Snatchers.* You run towards the car, you open the door and everybody is
turning into eggs.'[10] To this horrid prospect, Ellis opposes an ideal of
native accent, *positive authenticity* – well articulated by Bruce Beres-
ford's *Breaker Morant* (1980).

But Ellis's allusion to that canonical Australian text, *The Invasion of the Body Snatchers*, exposes the vulnerability of his cultural nationalism (and the closed concept of culture it must at some level assume) to a second theory of unoriginality: cheerful acceptance that it is a natural and necessary thing in modern times. Film is an industry in a Western mega-culture, and Australia is simply part of it; ideals of originality, independence and authenticity are sentimental anachronisms, inappropriate to the *combinatoire* of industrial cinema; performance, in film, is all, and performance is by nature 'inauthentic'. Imitation today is true realism, because 'the broad base of Australian culture, from McDonald's to prime-time television and everything in between, is comparable to the American' (Tony Ginnane, producer).[11] The eye of the beholder, wherever it's placed, is always American anyway. This is an ideal of *positive unspecificity* (give or take a decorative use of landscape, Aborigines, wildlife ...). An exemplary text might be Richard Franklin's 1981 co-production *Roadgames*, starring Jamie Lee Curtis, Stacy Keach, and a dingo.

At the box office, neither theory was often a roaring commercial success. A third possibility emerged, to displace the originality/authenticity, imitation/unspecificity couples. It salvages some of the cultural assertiveness of one, and all the economic pragmatism of the other. It rejects both hostility to Hollywood (*The Invasion of the Body Snatchers* really is part of Australian culture) and base denials of Australian contexts. It takes the 'eye of the beholder' as a figure for seeing double: survival and specificity can both be ensured by the revision of American codes by Australian texts, in a play which can be beheld quite differently by various audiences, and individual eyes therein. Furthermore, it has a tradition: parody (like the in-joke) has always been a favourite ploy of Australian colonial culture. As Stuart Cunningham points out, a characteristic example would be the 'extremely successful appropriation' of the road-movie genre by the Kennedy-Miller *Mad Max* films.[12]

This is a theory of fully *positive* unoriginality, a context in which, for critics, the privileged metaphors of postmodernism can come in to play – image-scavenging, borrowing, stealing, plundering and (for the more sedate), recoding, rewriting, reworking. But it wasn't merely the *Zeitgeist* – or global trends in criticism – that fostered this cultural logic.

From 1980 to 1986 most Australian films were funded under a special modification of the Income Tax Assessment Act, called *Division 10BA*. Essentially a government-run tax avoidance scheme, 10BA was an alarming success. In 1983/84, the revenue cost to the Australian government was estimated by Treasury at $100 million and rising. The concessions were drastically reduced, the risks spiralled for investors, and they began demanding substantial pre-selling of films.[13] In the context of Australia's tiny domestic market, this meant pre-selling films overseas, most desirably in the United States. Pre-selling may have aesthetic consequences: favouring themes thought 'familiar' to Americans, using imported (usually American) actors to attract foreign audiences – and so, shaping narratives to validate their role. That is to say, the financial organization of the industry gradually shifted the force of 'credibility' away from the rhetoric of national authenticity.

Crocodile Dundee was funded under 10BA, and articulates its logic magnificently. The cultural strategy is scarcely concealed: Dundee, the provincial crocodile-poacher, flagrantly acts as a figural *mise en abyme* of the film's *modus operandi* in relation to a Hollywood canon and to Australian mythology. Its borrowings are as clearly displayed as Dundee's outback costume, with its comic mishmash of cowboy/ western, bushman/jungle shreds – originating and imitating nothing but a late rural effort at vintage *Bow-wow-wow*. Moreover, *Crocodile Dundee* is an *export-drive* allegory: the small, remote community of Walkabout Creek with its fumbling exotica industry (emblematic of Australia's place in the global cinema economy) manages to export its crocodile-poacher and, with a little help from the American media, market him brilliantly in New York. The subsequent real success of the film – an example of pre-cession of the simulacrum that might delight Jean Baudrillard – can then be taken by some producers as a call for others to follow.

However, *Crocodile Dundee* made some innovations; it appeared to overturn the assumptions of a decade of debate. According to insistent publicity (i.e. promotional) reports, the film was deliberately *not* pre-sold, to avoid (or at least, preempt) initial interference; and it made a profit in unpopulous Australia before beginning its American release.[14] This makes its career (like that of Paul Hogan) the stuff of media legend; the art of combining economic pragmatism with cultural assertion in positive unoriginality ironically acquires a nationalist aura. The strategy of appropriation in the film can also be read in these terms.

Unlike the romantic, virtuoso variations played by the *Mad Max* films, only rarely interrupted (most often in *The Road Warrior*) by comic Australian asides, *Crocodile Dundee*'s use of appropriation aims explicitly at what Jessie Ackermann calls 'some small alteration, usually a disadvantage to the subject'. The 'subjects' (American models) are comically altered, and disadvantaged, by the narrative.

For example, three American references (or, signs of appropriation) define the hero's cultural mission and his *savoir-pouvoir-faire*: '*Davy Crockett*', '*Jungle Jim*' and '*Tarzan*'. Each of these reiterates frontier codes, and also reconciles, for Australian consumption, the old bush mythos with the imported media culture of the 1950s. So their function is initially confirmatory, and sentimental. But in each case, an imbalance is created by a failure to fit the model.

Dundee is compared to Davy Crockett in disgruntlement by Sue after the crocodile attack, when his attention to her haunches makes him more like the croc than the wholesome Crockett.[15] His New York rival calls Dundee 'Jungle Jim' at the airport, before his first battle with an escalator. It's a demeaning reference – not just to Dundee as rustic, but by assimilation to the ageing Weissmuller. Jungle Jim is a failed frontier-figure: so Dundee's charm in beating the escalator prepares for his success in the urban jungle at the expense of the younger native. His effective New York name (first given to him by the prostitutes) is 'Tarzan'. When formally baptized by Sue after saving her from the mugger, he smiles, thumps his chest, and fluffs the line she gives him – trying Tarzan's yodel, he comes out with a mangled gurgle.

One function of all three references, as *mises en abyme* of the code, is to affirm the mock-heroic novelty of Dundee's idiom in relation to the slightly tired American models (or straight media repeats, like *I Love Lucy*) by which he is made intelligible. On the one occasion when the hero gives *himself* an American name, '*Fred Astaire*' – as he lurches exuberantly round a tin-pot pub, with Sue as his Ginger Rogers – he uses it to invent a self-promoting bush ballad. Self-promotion is Dundee's job as a tourist commodity, and his *raison d'être* as hero (his nickname makes him 'more colourful for the tourist industry'). In this context, appropriation is a competitive activity; a seizing not only of comic advantage, but mythic power (capital).

A schematic comparison of the first and last scenes of the film must suffice to suggest how the strategy of seizure works in the overall narrative structure.

Most reviews of the film assume that it has two parts, one for Australia and one for New York, and that it plays for two potential audiences. In fact, two obvious cuts slice the film into three, juxtaposing contrasted 'sceneries' (city/outback/city) in the dramatic manner of wonderful-world travelogues. The first part, though usually ignored, is crucial. A prelude to the credits, it is internally structured by contrasts; two urban locations, New York and Sydney, and two urban *spaces* – office and hotel room, the high-rise control points of a media regime. The action linking these commercial spaces (centre and periphery of the *Newsday* empire) is a communicative one: a phone-call between editor and reporter, stay-at-home lover and wandering lady.

The call initiates a *hunt*, a quest for a story for *Newsday* – with Dundee as an object for promoting a global circuit of power. It also states a disjunction between business and pleasure arising from sexual equality: Richard is torn between his roles as editor and lover, while Sue prefers work to love. At the same time, the fictional enunciative setting is defined as initially *urban*, as well as international. Far from being differently addressed, 'Australian' and 'American' audiences are rhetorically conjoined in the vast network of media simultaneity (quite sensibly, since the relation of most Australians to the outback is exactly like Sue's). But at this point, both space and communication are controlled (from 'above') by Americans.

The last scene takes place underground. Sue is again on a hunt for Dundee, but her goal has changed. She isn't chasing him on *Newsday*'s business, but for her own pleasure – the power circuit has been broken, and Sue's gender confusion solved, by Dundee's manly charm. The subway should be her place, rather than his: but to reach him, she adapts to its dense, American urban space an Australian, rural medium of communication over vast distance: an echoing coo-ee call, and then the bush telegraph – the public transfer of private information by word of mouth.[16] The New York subway has become another setting for an Australian country practice; the exotic 'story' that *Newsday* sought has taken control of the narrative; the Australian in American space has power over action and speech. On the cue 'sheep', Dundee literally *treads all over* this mass of Americans, as a sheep-dog bounds over the mob. As a finale the sheep – now 'Americans' to Australians, while acting as all 'our' audience-doubles – flock to the reconciled couple (distance and difference overcome), to applaud Dundee/Hogan's performance, and confirm the happy ending.

Crocodile Dundee is more than an export-allegory, with Dundee as commodity, salesman and company combined. It is a *takeover* fantasy of breaking into the circuit of media power, to invade the place of control. As a 10BA polemic, the film's response to insular fears that Hollywood turns Australians into eggs seems to be a utopian call to turn Americans into sheep (as we all are assimilated, in one crucial scene, to a buffalo stunned by the force of the hero's mesmeric gaze). It's an ambitious fairy-tale, and an oedipally ungrateful one. It thereby remains, of course, and for all the comic reversals, utterly admiring of the (brutalizing) structure of American power.

In this admiration, appropriation as positive-unoriginality figures as a means of resolving the practical problems of a peripheral cinema, while reconciling conflicting desires for power and independence: symbolic nationalist victory is declared, but on internationalist (American) grounds.

Unfortunately, perhaps, for Australian cinema, not all simulacra without originals do produce a reality in their own image. Rather than leading local cinema out of the wilderness, *Crocodile Dundee*'s imaginary position may yet be more like that of Canetti's survivor who exults when everyone else is dead.[17]

As a work of global wishful thinking, however, the film's plan of action may be read in livelier terms.

Evasive Action

To march off into a future free from nuclear peril is,
from one direction, to free ourselves from claustrophobia, but it is, from another, merely to evade the
claustrophobia inspired by the pressures of intersubjectivity, the kind of claustrophobia that keeps
Jack in *The Shining* from ever feeling that a spectacularly enormous hotel is big enough to hold a man,
a woman, and a child.

Frances Ferguson, 'The Nuclear Sublime', 1984

You don't get plots in Australia.
The country's too big for plots.
Plots come out of claustrophobia.

Bob Ellis, interview, 1982

What can *escapism* mean now in cinema? Serious criticism today rarely
uses the term. Indeed, to avoid it when speaking of any popular culture
is a sign of serious purpose. There is a justified shame at its past pejorative sense in élitist critical practice. But 'escapism' (like wishful thinking)
is also a *useless* term: it doesn't help in the revision of amusement as a
prolongation of *work* that Adorno and Horkheimer saw in the culture
industry, now reaching truly arduous intensity in rhetorically product-
ivist theories of ideology, pleasure, and the active construction of meaning.[18] Escapism unacceptably implies the possibility of exemption – and
continues to 'work' to do so in much popular cultural commentary.

Thus, Paul Hogan on *Crocodile Dundee*: 'But I'm not artistic
anyway. I didn't want to make a meaningful little film. I just wanted to
make good escapist entertainment. I don't want to be moved by the
plight of the uranium miners or anyone else.'[19] Escapism here is not
merely the opposite of meaningfulness (the 'work' of art), but a positive
evasion of political, emotional *pressure* (to 'be moved' – and by nuclear
labour as a representative plight). The *promesse de bonheur* of escapist
cinema is thus a release from something like what Frances Ferguson
calls 'claustrophobia'.[20] But paradoxically, it can happen by not being
moved in theatres – in inter-subjectively pressurized spaces, specially
built for 'closed crowds' (Elias Canetti). For Hogan, an escapist 'standard' is set by precisely those films (he mentions *Arthur, Back to the
Future, Every Which Way But Loose*, and *Romancing the Stone*) to
which 'people flock along in their millions' and emerge, he says, 'feeling
good'.

At a time when a unifying, convergent pleasure-principle for cinema can be stated so lucidly, the feelings of the millions (and their millions of feelings) have become, for much serious cultural criticism, an occasion for the dispersal of objects of analysis by the *varietal* thesis: in the mobile play ('work') of film-consumption, a variety of meanings and pleasures are actively constructed from a multiplicity of heterogeneous and shifting positions. In a repetitive *règlement de comptes* with criticism's own history, much criticism unvaryingly restates this thesis – in a rhetoric of intersubjectivity again giving rise to claustrophobia, the kind that Paul Willemen irritably calls 'the near-psychotic difference-babble that currently goes by the name of "theory of post-modernism"'.[21] In the process, it can miss something concrete about the orchestrating effort (material and symbolic, architectural and filmic) of contemporary big cinema that Hogan's model *doesn't* miss. If film-texts may be read as articulating theories, then *Crocodile Dundee* may be read as a text on escapist cinema – and thus as theorizing (though not prescribing) the pleasure it provides.

One of the unusual qualities of the film compared to Hogan's Hollywood standards is a low-speed, low-pressure style that disturbs a certain consensus of what an action-comedy should do. For example, many critics noticed 'spasmodic' qualities (*The Age*), 'undeveloped' script (*The New York Post*), 'problems with the pacing', 'flat, dull spots' (*Variety*) – and one expressed an urge to 'haul out half an hour' (*The Australian*). Paramount did, in fact, haul out seven minutes of Northern Territory scenes for American release.

Even so, for one critic its expansively lazy movement was the meaning of the film: 'It is an ironic inversion of the *Temple of Doom*, and *Romancing the Stone* fast American hype mentality. Nothing much happens in *Crocodile Dundee*' (*The Australian Financial Review*). And for another, this moderation becomes (like the mock-heroic heroism of Dundee) an anti-apocalyptic action principle: 'Where Rambo would grunt and fire off a nuclear arrow, Dundee would think a minute, then maybe lob a tin of beans' (*The Washington Post*). And it's true that if Dundee is at one level a rational-deterrence myth (always already capable, armed with his Big Knife), rather than a vengeful, first-strike figure like Rambo, there is also an important reduction of scales of necessary conflict in the film. Part of its populism is to imply that homespun remedies work best because they are (like a tin to catch a bag-snatcher, steam to sear a nose) parodic remedies, parasitically 'spun' out from the situation they undo.

Escapism in *Crocodile Dundee* is generally defined by a 'masculine' refusal of overkill, hyperbole, and hysteria as principles of action. All Dundee's male opponents are edgy types, and the one serious urban menace (the pimp, rather than the mugger) is electric with nervous effeminacy and can't even act by himself. In this sense, effective modifying action is a predicate of, in Hal Foster's phrase, 'the old pragmatic, patriarchal self',[22] calmly steering its way through a mass of volatile humanity. This basic framework is, however, modified in turn by a more positive evasive principle of movement in relation to situations, spaces, and passions.

When its three parts are read as a media-power allegory, *Crocodile Dundee* has a strong narrative structure. An imbalance in the initial situation (global American control of Australian space) is, by the hero's action, corrected in the final situation (local Australian control of an American space). The *means* of action – appropriation – works by negotiation rather than direct challenge. The transition, however, is ordered by *weak plot* rather than strong narrative, by a loose stringing of incidents with 'scenes' (a croc attack, one serious brawl, a few kisses, a failed mugging, the odd punch, and a lot of one-liners) that has little to do with mythic, big-country Australianness, and a lot to do with the conventions of television comedy. Appropriation works transitionally as a logic that links, but divides, two comically reconciled local events (snatching a bag and grabbing a tin, snorting coke and sniffing steam).

There is no paranoid driving-force to make Dundee's actions cohere, little carrythrough from one incident to another (the pimp's return – an ideal minor detail for a Clint Eastwood film – works here as a major exception), and above all no buildup of *pressure* from moment to moment, scene to scene. Not even the romance is claustrophobically plotted. Dundee's idea of courtship is to show and be shown scenes (companionly tourism) and wait for something to happen. His major mode of movement is a vaguely purposeless ambling (walkabout). Then, like the croc from the river and the mugger from the street, events erupt anecdotally from the scene. Movement becomes rapid, reactive, and *reductive*: enemies are diminished, not exalted; situations are cut down to episodic size, not inflated to narrative importance. The aim of action is to restore the scenic pleasure of river and street by a minimal gesture of self-preservation – to evade, not to escalate, pressure.

Situations can be deflated in this way because space itself (the support of walkabout/tourism) is benevolent and barrier-free. To move through space as though barriers weren't there is Dundee's social strategy (and his pedagogical purpose). Even in Walkabout Creek, there are two *states* of space: closed and crowded (the pub), open and sparsely settled (the bush). Dundee's evasive move is to treat the two as everywhere continuous – surviving even New York by reducing its crush of humanity to a string of (sparse) communities. In this schema, there is nothing between the global and the local except a move of mutual conversion. There are no mediating structures, and no real institutions – none of the containing force of class, family, school, army, prison that provides the limiting frame for most evasive heroes of comic and tragic drama.[23] The global is just an open continuum of interesting locales: here an Aboriginal corroborree, there a bourgeois dinner. It's an agoraphiliac world, with no capacity for absolute conflict – and no sense of the sublime. No landscape is finally overwhelming, without any means for escape: the sweeping Never-Never is impressive, but hospitable, and in the surge of a New York crowd there's still a friendly horseman. Two corresponding 'lookout' scenes secure this taming of space: from both an Australian rock and an American skyscraper (linked by an Aboriginal musical motif) Dundee *points* – once as guide, once as tourist. The first gesture turns the Never-Never into an illustration of the crocodile story (*that's where it happened*); the second reduces the New York vista to a visitor's memento (*I was there*).

It's also a world with only two dispositions – friendly and hostile. Unlike most of its current American equivalents (and certainly unlike *Rambo*), *Crocodile Dundee* is a relatively passionless film. The most avid creature is the croc. There's no heat to the violence, no steam to sex, no ice to Dundee's cool. Human life is pure, rational, free sociability: no unconscious, no neurosis, no repression (gossip gets things 'out in the open') – and no maniacs. Even the hostiles are reasonable in their practical self-interest. But that self is not a locus of heroic (*or* fragmented) subjectivity; no one, least of all the hero, has psychological qualities. Nor is life thereby seen as 'depthless', flat or superficial. People and their 'interests' simply emerge, like friendly or hostile acts, from the local scene, the social situation, with which they have firm but non-necessary links. Sue, for example, is most at home in her city when she races to the subway after Dundee. She flings away her shoes, but she isn't going 'bush': crucially, she *keeps her scarf* floating out behind her – with the result that any still from the sequence would make a high-fashion icon of urban elegance.

People and places aren't the same, but they *are* mutually intelligible, with an unlimited ability for movement and exchange (Dundee making friends with a black New Yorker by trading unintelligible idioms) that makes difference always negotiable. One of the reasons why the hero has no grand sense of purpose, why situations aren't paranoid, why action doesn't escalate, and why space isn't confining, is precisely this: for the evasive subject, difference isn't *inherently* threatening. On these terms difference, fully social, can't be repressed or denied – but simply relieved of significance.

At this point, I should perhaps shift the level of analysis away from the order of representation and its weak-plot logic. A varietal reading would go no further and might never have gone so far – leaving what audiences 'make' of this in the realm of the ineffable, or rather in the domain of demonstration that whatever they make, they make. A feminist reading might move instead to re-derive difference-as-threat as the enabling condition of representation, and could do so, of course, with a textual analysis.[24] Common meanings and in-significant difference would respectively become, like exemption from pressure in escapism, politically and theoretically inadmissible. Yet to do so might elide something about the *social* making of escapist pleasure from the film – an intersubjective possibility, of which the evasion, or defusion, of difference in the film works as a kind of metonym.

This possibility arises in particular from the confining situation, the packed space and the claustrophobic passionality of the modern cinema theatre – its sociability reiterated, ideally, by the profusion of adjacent bars, restaurants, souvenir shops, video parlours, video trailer-display areas, and *other* theatres, other films. The subject of a textual analysis isn't produced in this kind of space: it emerges from relative solitude (the professional, or domestic, space of video-watching) and/or from aristocratic privilege (sitting alone or in select company, in the choice spot – mid-row, X rows back – of renaissance perspective). Above all, this subject has technical mastery over the object – can stop it, start it, 'work' it.

Crowds in theatres can't: but nor is the crowd collectively mastered by the film as a continuum of points of engulfment, each caught mesmerized, buffalo-like, in unmediated imaginary play. The crowded theatre is a conflictual space of vociferous and immediate interpretation, and of energy for distractions (the crowd as evasive machine: crowd noise, and crowd *pressure* – bumping, nudging, talking, shuffling, laughing, hooting, abusing, in response to the film, to friends, to strangers or in relative indifference to any or all of these).

It's precisely in the cinema theatre that spaces are significantly sparse or crowded, strangers coded hostile or friendly, and situations erupt with stray, inconsequential, and sometimes violent 'events'. No film need resonate with a social performance context, but *Crocodile Dundee* can do so to an unusual degree. From this observation, nothing can be inferred about audience or individual pleasure at any actual screening, and no determinative power ascribed to a supposedly stable film text. What can be said, however, is that in this reading, the film enacts escapism in two related ways.

Firstly it demonstrates, repeatedly and variously, a genial overcoming of *enormity*. The aim of evasive action as a method of escape is to cut things down to size. The film performs a set of anti-apocalyptic, non-sublime, counter-claustrophobic manoeuvres – and duly celebrates its victory in the final scene, with the joy of the subway crowd at the defeat of its own overwhelming, mass potential to bring about disaster.

Secondly, it does this by enacting escape from the social *burden* of difference – overcoming the enormity of cultural 'gulf'. Dundee evades not difference, but the social *use* of difference as a weapon for humiliation, anxiety, and torment; the menace of Richard (Mark Blum) in the Italian restaurant is not to fight Dundee for Sue, but to make a big deal about difference. There's an old pragmatic, patriarchal humanism here – but also a refusal to make difference 'nuclear', claustrophobic. Again, the subway scene is a final summation: the message runs openly from the bourgeois city woman to the bushman by way of a black and a white city worker – all performing their idioms, and understanding each other perfectly. The high-pressure crowd is not, this time, disabling: it is the material support (in subway and in cinema) of a momentary reconciliation.

For escapist cinema, however, this is not a utopian, fictive moment. It is a social event: an experience of the *possibility* of escape in real time and space.

PART II

Tooth and Claw

McFARLANE: *Welcome to the Australian outback. It's lovely, isn't it?!*

HALL: *HMMMMMMPH!*

The Memory of Eva Ryker, 1980

> '*I don't know why we're here*,' she said. . . .
> '*Out here to rot some teeth*,' he said, softening it only
> mildly with a quarter smile, glad at last to be critical,
> although aware of the effort it took to be unpleasant
> against the mood.
>
> Frank Moorhouse, 'The Coca-Cola Kid', 1972

But there's an edge to this escapist event, a limit to its spread of good will. If *Crocodile Dundee* is an anti-*Rambo*, it's also an anti-*Manhattan*.

Many critics stress that in the action-highlights of the film, Dundee does real or feigned battle with fantasmal Others of an equally fantasmal 'white, male, working class' – beasts, blacks, deviants, uppity women, snobs. These are in fact symmetrically distributed in the two main locations: city-cowboy/pretentious yuppy; predatory animal/savage pimp; woman-with-a-gun/transvestite; voyeur Aborigine/black mugger. But there is also a carefully preemptive distribution of 'friendly' (or easily mesmerized) Others: the amiable *bourgeois* at Sam's dinner, the buffalo, the dogs, the prostitutes, the baritone society-lioness, the 'tribal' Aborigines, the chauffeur ('Tonto' for one outraged critic),[25] the black in the bar. Furthermore, the film combats political critics by placing itself '*post*'; it historicizes radicalism as obsolete opinion. It parodies, and again preempts, two possible rhetorical positions from which it could be, and has been, attacked: patronizing dismissal of its 'crudity' (the posture of Richard the yuppy), and indignant protest (the stance of Sue's *past* husband, the 'prize ratbag').

The reduction of the latter to, and by, a throwaway line of dialogue points to a significant omission from the list of fantasmal Others, which I shall read as a structuring absence in the film's politics of opinion. There are no urban intellectuals in Dundee's bestiary. The closest that Dundee gets to a cartoon New York egghead is the head-wrapped society matron – whose bothersome indeterminacy is quickly reduced *to* sexual difference by a brutally practical act. Otherwise, and crucially in a film so concerned rhetorically to legitimate 'majority' opinion, and itself as majoritarian, the only intellectuality (and the only institution) admitted as credible is media-power: that *force* of public 'opinion'.

I want to use elements from both the industrial and escapist readings to return to the Australian setting which foregrounds a problem of opinion (the arms race, the nuclear) and a political conflict (Aboriginal land rights). Both involve struggles for survival (the human race, traditional Aboriginal culture); and together, they define something like the film's primal scene of appropriation.

The setting is the mythic Australian outback: for the Eurocentric discourses traversing the film, a perfect Other to the ultimate urban jungle; historically an empty (that is, violently depopulated) space for the enactment of colonialist fantasy. The perfection of the outback for this purpose is its supposed remoteness from cities (learning, modernity) and, unlike other legendary wastes, its 'isolation' in the middle of a monster island – prime territory for darwinian fancies of throwbacks, remnants, mutants, the (primitive) origin and the (apocalyptic) end of life.

The outback is an ideal site for the staging of knowledge conflicts. Its value is reversible: it can be invested with romantic, pre-technical wisdom (Roeg's *Walkabout*, Herzog's *Where The Green Ants Dream*) or surreal, degenerative ignorance (Kotcheff's *Outback*, a.k.a. *Wake In Fright*, Mulcahy's *Razorback*), and be a zone of life-and-death struggle over what it means, *in extremis*, to be human (*The Road Warrior*, *Beyond Thunderdome*). The shuttle between opposites, the disintegration of categories, is the outback's power for metamorphosis: from the midst of it surges, usually, The Beast – savage black, crazed white, man-eating pig, crocodile, dingo. The often comic, post-*Jaws/Alligator* reworking of this material by positively-unoriginal practices gives the outback great density as a space of appropriation, understood as mangled identity (the mini-series *Return to Eden*, in which a crocodile bite turns a frumpy heiress into a glamorous model – and, apparently forthcoming, *Marsupials – The Howling III*). It's from this space that what one neoconservative columnist calls the 'muscular innocence'[26] of Mick Dundee – the survivor with no opinions – is born.

Sue, too, can be given a genealogy in her role as questioning American, outback Pandora ('gotta have an opinion, gotta have a voice'). She is a creature of 10BA descent: bred from a history of experiments in cultural hybridization, and a long line, predating even 10BA, of imported figures in need of a narrative justification of their place in exportable bits of landscape. Occasionally these figures are just colonial immigrants like all other whites (Edward Woodward in *Breaker Morant*, Kirk Douglas in *The Man From Snowy River*). More frequently, they are bearers of a hermeneutic function. They are asking, learning, looking for something – William Holden seeking his son in *The Earthling*, Richard Chamberlain pursuing ultimate mysteries in Weir's *The Last Wave*. Sue's curiosity in *Crocodile Dundee* (a woman and a reporter, 'the biggest stickybeak in the world') is thus strongly overdetermined.

Moreover, these searching Americans are *critical*. As emblems of, and for, American consumption of Australian film, they often turn a '*What a dump!*' gaze on Australian scenes: grimaces, pouts, suppressed shivers and insincere American smiles launch events in David Steven's *Undercover*, Dusan Makaveyev's *The Coca-Cola Kid*, and Russell Mulcahy's *Razorback* as well as *Crocodile Dundee*. Subsequent narrative learning (marked by '*What am I doing here?*' monologues) transforms, or punishes, that gaze – often coded as a hegemonic 'world *opinion*'. Silence, evasiveness, may then act as modes of Australian resistance to the American opinionation necessary to the narrative. In *The Coca-Cola Kid*, the American patriot Becker (Eric Roberts) – on a promotional quest for the 'Australian sound' – politically interrogates the band making his commercial, only to be told they have 'no opinions …'.

There are no doubt many obscure sexual and national resentments at work in the ecology of these scenarios. In *Razorback*, for example, a pushy American TV woman – an animal rights campaigner – learns a lesson in the relativity of opinion from the outback. Less fortunate than the post-radical Sue, she is raped by pet-food producers, then eaten alive by a pig.[27] Sue, divorced from the 'original rebel' ('probably marching now for the gay nazis') is on slightly safer territory. Nevertheless, in the exchange between Dundee's muscular innocence of politics and her enfeebled liberal conscience, the very *form* of critical 'questioning' is placed as a mode of American ignorance.

The discussion of Aborigines is divided into two dark nights in the outback. Each raises a problem of appropriation, framed in two different ways: bad (whites land-taking, blacks taking-back the land), and good (reciprocal borrowing between cultures).

On the first night, Sue begins by putting the ultimate global question: the arms race. Dundee evades ('none of my business') by refuting the need for general political statements ('gotta have a voice') with a specific social context: 'who's going to hear it out here?'. Foiled by outback eccentricity, Sue tries something 'closer to home': Aboriginal land rights. Dundee still doesn't state 'his' opinion. Instead, he paraphrases Aboriginal belief – that Aborigines don't own the land, they belong to it.

This is, in one sense, true. But it is a significantly partial truth. Firstly, in the enunciative shift of paraphrase, Dundee takes the place of Aboriginal opinion (also construing it as unconflictual). While implying that a land-rights politics of reappropriation is un-Aboriginal, he discursively appropriates the right to Aboriginal speech. Of course, any enunciative shift 'appropriates': appropriation in this sense is neither displaced identity, nor colonialist invasion, but a process that takes place in both: the discursive struggle for power to fix the terms of reference.[28] The terms are fixed on this occasion with a homely reference to the timeless land, a dog with two fleas squabbling over ownership. Aboriginal land claims, however, are not made for The Land in general, but for particular sites. Dundee effaces this distinction in a discourse on (European) romantic Nature: and confirms its supremacy by casually throttling a snake.

In this scene, land appropriation as *politics* is dismissed on behalf of absent Aboriginal opinion. The second scene works as a comic counterbalance to the first: a real Aborigine appears, to demonstrate the value of *cultural* appropriation. With land rights consigned to irrelevance as a foreign city-girl confusion (and a white political argument), Sue's romanticism about Primitive Culture is then correspondingly ridiculed.

Nev (David Gulpilil) isn't really savage, like the snake and the croc. He isn't even 'tribal', as Dundee puts it. Nev is a city boy, doing corroboree duty in order to please his Dad. When Sue tries to photograph him as an exotic bearer of primitive belief, he repositions himself as the subject of basic camera skills. Nev says nothing about land rights. Nev, in fact, is a model appropriator: the culturally mobile Aborigine, a survivor in transit between tribal and modern life, evading museumification, and the closure of authenticity. So, it turns out, is Dundee. Already assimilated to Aborigines by Wally's tourist pitch, and by didgeridoo strains on the soundtrack, Dundee now comes out as a tribal initiate and postmodern hero – a 'white Aborigine'.[29] His dismissal of land-rights politics, and his claim to represent Aboriginal knowledge, is validated by kinship. Both men are children of the outback, products of metamorphosis, and brother cultural poachers.

These two scenes together effect a remarkable management of opinion. An easily recognizable conservative political discourse (*'these strangers with their protest talk don't know anything about blacks anyway, and couldn't last five minutes in the bush'*) is reconciled with a radically demythologizing critique of cultural authenticity. (At some urban screenings in Australia, the relief afforded by the appearance of Nev to audience bodies that wince, while others rejoice, at the land-rights dialogue, is palpable as it flows through rows of seats.) Indeed, the land-rights discussion is *framed* by that critique: from the first scenes in Walkabout Creek (the barmaid's deflation of Dundee's legend) to the closing scenes in New York (the chauffeur's Harlem Warlords boomerang trick), the film's comic action is to evade the confinements of myth: goanna or hot dog, '*You can live on it, but it tastes like shit.*'

Again, appropriation acts rhetorically for the film not as violence and invasion, but as negotiation and defusion of conflict. There is, however, a missing link in the evolution of this consensus. Hostility to Aboriginal land rights is not simply a function of racism, populist suspicion of privileges for minority groups, or of radical critiques of *le propre* and the pitfalls of sentimental humanism – any one of which can find its own satisfactions in the urbane figure of Nev. Hostility to land rights is a function of the pressure of mining companies – in particular, those seeking to mine uranium on Aboriginal land.

Sue's posing of land rights as *alternative* issue to the arms race to frame Dundee's opinions has already, therefore, a poignant evasive effect. Nothing in the comedy that follows allows a hint to emerge that the outback – primal space of land appropriation and cultural exchange – might now also provide raw materials for global nuclear threat. Instead, a link between local and global, Aboriginal and European, Northern Territory and New York, is supplied by a discourse on racial and sexual stereotypes, the frailties of liberalism, and the primacy of 'natural' perils.

Much as, in the New York narrative, the society matron takes the place of the urban intellectual, in the outback Sue and Nev take the place of the uranium miner. But while both work together to confound the discourse of critical protest, their functions are slightly different.

One obvious difference in the comedies of race and sex is that male Aboriginal modernity (represented as cultural) is not satirized from Dundee's outback position – while white female modernity (treated as political, like land rights), is. Another is constructed by a circuit of complicity linking two moments of reciprocal violation: the black peering at the lone white woman in the bush, and the white woman sneaking up to watch an all-male Aboriginal ceremony.[30] The first invasion is resolved by Australian-male complicity between Dundee and Nev about Sue's naivety (nothing was going to happen anyway); the second is resolved in transnational-white complicity between Dundee and Sue about the Aborigines' innocence (something did happen, but the elders don't know). The effect of this is to distance the violation of Aboriginal law and diminish its seriousness, while foregrounding Sue's frailties. Aboriginal opinion doesn't really matter, while Sue's opinions are wrong.

If Nev's role is to be an amiable vehicle for an anti-land-rights apologia acceptable in its *form* (cultural syncretism) to many modes of political thinking, Sue's role is to be an object of attack. Her position is quite explicitly assaulted as 'weak'. In the long transition between the two parts of the Aboriginal scenario, Sue is four times placed as *prey*: for the snake, for the kangaroo-shooters (in a carefully edited moment of doubt about what they've caught in their spotlight), for Dundee and the croc at the river; then, at last, for Nev. Once again, reduction *to* sexual difference (Sue's vulnerability in the outback) serves a broader purpose: here, to press home the unfitness of protestant liberalism to survive a terrain of 'real' struggle. That Sue's own political sense is, to say the least, vestigial – a remnant of an archaic phase of symbolic activity (*'you name it, we marched'*) – is the perfect outback touch.

Hence, perhaps, the cornered air to much political criticism of the film. *Crocodile Dundee* is difficult to attack not only because the escapist effect of benevolence ('good nature') is so strong, but because it so successfully manipulates a media process, the commodification of *opinion*, that left-wing critics – having profited from it in the 1970s – now often refuse to admit (or else ascribe to a 'new' condition). It certainly doesn't follow, of course, that the millions who come out 'feeling good' from *Crocodile Dundee* emerge as anti-land-rights fanatics;[31] not only because of their critical activity, but because media-opinion is a matter, not of contents, but, precisely, of *mood.* However it does follow – to an extent that culturalist theories of consumer appropriation may allow us to forget – that the film takes an active part in a politics of opinion by splitting land rights from the nuclear, the cultural from the political, and consigning the tools to make connections to a realm of discredited, and *parochialized,* critical knowledge.

One interesting critical comment on this process was made by Paul Hogan himself, who, now consecrated in media as a spokesman of Australian popular culture, is a master of the art of opinion. In 1986, a

Sydney radio 'credibility' poll gave him top, and record, ratings (just ahead of Bill Cosby and Bob Geldof, far ahead of any politicians, and opposite bottom ratings for Ferdinand Marcos, and the Bhagwan Sree Rajneesh). Asked for his opinion, Hogan defined the speaking-position of power in a perfect evasive reply: '*I can't say anything without losing my credibility*'.[32]

Colonial Candide

These movies are comforting in this time of terrible pessimism and depression when we've reached a level of cynicism which leads us to appreciate your naive optimism and vigor. Since the best of your films have been set in your colonial period, they recall the frontier spirit which we have lost. We wish that we could return to the 'good old days' when America seemed as robust and unsophisticated as Australia appears in these buoyant movies.

Kathleen Carroll, interview, 1982

It is no wonder that always and everywhere the image of the colonial is the very pattern of naiveté, or that naive work is presumed to speak to us figuratively from a far-off land.

William Routt, 'On the Expression of Colonialism in Early Australian Film: Charles Chauvel and Naive Cinema', 1984

In a savage attack on the persona and opinions of Crocodile Dundee, Phillip Adams (pundit, advertiser, and Chairman of the Australian Film Commission) mused on the marketing of innocence. In the past, 'there was something dead clever about Hogan's professed naivety', but now, he thought, Hogan had fallen for the worn-out genre of 'overstated anti-podean reactions to northern hemispherical sophistication' – Dundee was *really* naive, the innocent abroad, '*colonial Candide*'.[33] Events proved that Hogan had still been dead clever.

Naivety is an attribute of the other: there is no more blatant claim to cunning than the confession 'I am naive' (which can then be read ironic-ally as a sign of naivety). As a term to position the other, it advances the speaker in knowledge and history. Thus for Kathleen Carroll of the New York *Daily News*, the naivety of Australian films repeats an earlier phase of American history; while for Annette Blonski of the Australian Film Institute, Americans' films are pleasurably naive because 'they actually believe that what they make is good' – in contrast to the cynical bad conscience of appropriating Australians.[34]

The naive is rhetorically *distanced* from a subject-here-and-now (or, as in 'I am naive', displaced from *énonciation* to *énoncé*). So it is commonly linked to nostalgia: home-longing, the invention of origins, non-differential repetition, fullness and, in William Routt's phrase, something outside of history, untouched and unchanging forever Caliban'.[35] The subject recognizing naivety, Routt says, believes that it sees innocence (and so lays claim to some innocence for itself). But in fact, 'The predatory gaze of sophistication is the condition of existence for *naiveté*'.

With these terms, *Crocodile Dundee* can easily be read as a cynical play on postmodern passion for the naive, and the nostalgic. While not precisely an instance of *la mode retro* as analysed by Fredric Jameson, it recycles cinema myths to appeal to, and create, nostalgia: for old-fashioned entertainment, for rural innocence, for naive values of harmony and immediacy, for simple conservative virtues. Yet it is also an exercise in predation; *Caliban's Revenge* rather than *Tarzan's New York Adventure* (says Hogan, '*It's like the image Americans have of us, so why not give them one?*').[36] Who, where, is exploiting whom? What is more sophisticated, more ... postmodern than an innocent double game of simulated *faux naïf*?

This reading is certainly plausible. But Routt's stress on the circumstances allowing recognition of naive style might also be applied to radical critiques of the postmodern taste for nostalgia. There seems to be general agreement between most exponents and critics of postmodernism, as style or as cultural logic, that nostalgia is therein at stake – in naivety as lost ideal, as simulacrum – for someone. In radical critiques, it's usually at stake for conservatism, engaged in historical regression. For Jameson, postmodernism favours pastiche of 'dead styles', while for Lyotard – once one of the rare proponents of a cheerful postmodernism – it is a score against gloomy opponents to claim that 'Most people have *lost* the nostalgia for the lost narrative'.[37] And for John Frow, sceptical of the whole debate, postmodernism offers only 'the possibility of a sentimental redemption of the naive' (with the twist that for Frow, the *modernist* aesthetic is 'sentimental' in Schiller's sense, and so, as for Lyotard, includes and exceeds the postmodern).[38]

I don't wish to play Caliban to these discussions, by crushing their complexity: although some feminist Caliban might hear in all those terms for the regressiveness of nostalgia – origin, indifference, fullness, and the outside-history – just a touch of gynophobia, that horror of the maternal trap we have learned, in progressive theory, to know and love. I wish instead to use my readings of *Crocodile Dundee* to question some assumptions making it plausible, firstly, to see nostalgia in predatory practice and, secondly, to see appropriation as counterattack in post-modern scenarios of struggle.

If, for example, *Crocodile Dundee* were read (naively) against Fredric Jameson's argument about postmodernity, one might see it only as a symptom of the '*insensible colonization of the present* by the nostalgia mode'[39] – and the joy it can induce as little more than a case of late capitalist euphoria. Taking it as another bit of global-yet-American culture, incidentally from a far-off land, one might not read its local industrial strategy, its political ambivalence about different kinds of 'sensible' colonization past and present, and its joyful refusal of any, and certainly of Jameson's 'hysterical', sublime. That is to say, one would be left with something like a Paramount press-kit version of its meanings and functions – in the sense that the universality of a global-yet-American cultural logic would be accepted, and affirmed, in the moment of critique.

The problem is partly a product of the form of blockbuster diagnostic: few films anywhere or in any way negotiating a relation to Hollywood's (colonizing) history can escape the impact of Jameson's generalizations. It is 'the nostalgia mode' *in cinema* that frames his concept of appropriation as a 'cannibalizing' intertextuality. It also completes the divorce between (modern) 'real history' and (postmodern) 'history of aesthetic styles', between history proper and nostalgic historicism, that makes possible Jameson's model of postmodernity. It is this divorce, rather than *la mode retro* or the film re-make, that is anti-historical: thanks to the notion of 'style', it can't allow for mediation by *cinema* (that is, institutional and social as well as aesthetic) history constructed by films and by criticism. But leaving aside the general problems with this kind of periodization, it seems to me that the notion of nostalgia that Jameson shares with other critics, who may not share his aesthetics, obscures more than it enlightens.

Firstly, it ignores the positive force that the so-called nostalgic elements in a film can acquire. *Crocodile Dundee*'s comedy of frontier *savoir-faire*, for example, works as strongly to refuse the politics of paranoia, total conflict and helpless resignation as it does to revamp reactionary racial and sexual myths. The one doesn't justify the other, but nor do they necessarily imply each other, or derive now from some common source. In fact the former can contest the latter.

Secondly, 'nostalgia' may not really be such a useful term in the era of Star Wars for the actuality of appropriation as a territorializing mode. The outback manoeuvres in *Crocodile Dundee* are situated not only in relation to colonial and nuclear politics but also to contemporary practices of tourism, safari holidays, theme parks, locality environmentalism, that can now conflict with mining, as a reason for conservation;[40] its aggressive play for New York is a response to, and an action in, a long history of American cultural domination, and of the export rationale in conservative Australian thinking. *Crocodile Dundee* is saturated in 'real history': it may use myth, and ridicule of myth, to produce a position in real history, but a significant home-longing for the world of Davy Crockett (as compensation, or as replacement past) is scarcely what's involved.

Finally, the term 'nostalgia' in radical critique may simply reintroduce the apocalyptic guarantee of historical determinism by positing a limit – some final phase, some apotheosis of capital – *at* which an absolutist culture fabricates a past, the better to pervade in perpetuity the present, while brave remnants of progressive thought struggle to redeem the real past, and a better future. But this mode of romantic pessimism affirms the former and cripples the latter by effacing, like the terror of The Bomb, the indecisiveness of actual conflicts. That a film like *Crocodile Dundee* should bother to include a little sermon on the end of radicalism and the irrelevance of land-rights claims is perhaps a greater testimony to the liveliness of both.

It seems forced to play such a film against Jameson's argument – *Crocodile Dundee*'s territory is as far from Warhol as it is from van Gogh (though not far from the Bonaventura Hotel). The awkwardness is partly due to a mismatch with the *mood* of appropriation as nostalgia that Jameson's text derives from the high art-critical tradition enabling and regulating the genre of postmodern diagnostic. In this sense, it is exemplary in its use of cinema to supplement (frame) an argument defined by reference to art and architecture – two institutions (in Peter Burger's sense) which most tenaciously retain 'originality' and 'progress' (the values of *'advanced work'*) as *problems* still validating the professional differentiation, the critical packaging, of products. In this context, appropriation and nostalgia are cover versions of those problems. Postmodernism in architecture, for example, has provided a means for the professional distinction between innovative author-architects, and routine commercial hacks, to be maintained. That the former now claim to restore history and pleasure to the people instead of churning out cliché worker housing and office blocks in no way changes the dynamic involved. The institution remains chirpily expansionist in its territorializing tasks. To speak of architectural appropriation as 'nostalgia' is, like certain postmodern buildings, really a sort of joke.

'What would it look like not to repress the concept of the copy?', asked Rosalind Krauss in 1981, during the recent art cycle of retreat and revival in the rhetoric of originality – choosing work by Sherrie Levine as her answer.[41] It's facile to answer instead that it might look like most cultural practices, mass or otherwise, since Gissing could write *New*

Grub Street – or like the everyday landscape of post-colonial countries. It is institutionally reasonable that a fiction of 'the' copy repressed should have acted as a liberating device to retrieve not only a critical function for art (rewriting its history, commenting on popular culture) but a critical function for critics.

Something different happens, however, when this art-institutional fiction is transposed to serve as key synecdoche (like Warhol's 'Diamond Dust Shoes' for Jameson, or the myth of the simulacrum for Jean Baudrillard) in a general critique of contemporary culture. Art's old privilege as survival-principle (Canetti), and authentic voice of critique and protest, is salvaged, unpropitiously, in the effort to come to terms with the commodity erosion of that privilege, and to begin to think away from the terms its privilege imposed. Criticism swings between mourning and affirmation, installed in postmodern melancholia yet looking for radical options.

Commercial cinema fits awkwardly into this scenario, except as Caliban for commentary in art. It is unwieldy: its constitutive montage of materials, and its material involvement with architecture, makes it hard to reify appropriation as *distinctive* technique in cinema. There is no repression of the copy, but also little place for retrieving optimism from reproductibility in any sense of the term. There is no professional imperative for originality and progress (although there may be admiration). Classically, cinema *auteurs* have always emerged, like architects, in action under social constraints, not in primal creativity. But unlike architects, they are not institutionally redeemed for art by the regimes of manifesto-writing and design exhibition that preside over 'movements' (like postmodernism). While film-makers may engage in both, the primary modes of film and *auteur* packaging are advertising, review-snippeting, trailers, magazine profiles – always already in appropriation as pre-condition, not post-production, of meanings.

One might say the same, of course, of all mass culture. All-pervasive, omni-active appropriation is strictly a non-event. This may be one reason why work *about* mass culture but circulating as art (including film and video) emerges so often, in the postmodern field, packaged as critical response to melancholia – while the study of that culture really contributes little to the formulation, rather than illustration, of problems. Commercial cinema, for example, cannot strictly be said to 'mix' high and popular cultures (to take one popular postmodern formulation); it subsumes the distinction not only by appropriating art materials, but by using 'high art' as an optional promotion and distribution category (for venues as well as films).

Another symptom of the evasion of mass-cultural problems is a development that seems to move away from the problematics of art-nostalgia: the tendency in much journalistic as well as academic criticism to enshrine 'to appropriate' as the model verb of all and any action – to make, to do, to write, to read, to give, to take, to produce, to consume, to rob, to receive, to exploit, to resist, to revenge (though not to revolt). In accumulating so many functions, appropriation gains radical credibility: it outrages humanist commitments to stable property values, adds a little *frisson* of impropriety and risk by romanticizing as violation the intertextual *sine qua non* of all cultural activity, and semantically guarantees a politics to practitioners by installing predation as the universal rule of cultural exchange. As reified token of rapacious relations, 'appropriation' is a lexical mini-myth of power, a promise, if not of freedom, then of survival. All energies become seizures, and we all get a piece of the action.

As a model of modifying action, appropriation does offer to radical and conservative criticism alike the chance to save a principle of *discrimination* – in purposeful, selective and calculating action. In appropriation, the elements chosen, and the choice of elements, are not released in free play or a random heterogeneous 'shuffling' in Jameson's phrase, but, on the contrary, weighted with critical, historical, particularizing significance. Appropriation is a revisionist project, in the sense that the colonial comedy of *Crocodile Dundee* is a revision of frontier mythology, not a random 'mix' of elements from it (still less an attempt to escape it).

A robust affirmation of rapacity as the law of the cultural marketplace is certainly more invigorating for criticism than what Deleuze (speaking of action cinema) calls 'melancholy Hegelian reflections on its own death'. In radical criticism's own action-image crisis of doubt in the powers of critical action now to modify rather than intensify the situation of postmodernity – the doubt that Jameson calls 'the abolition of critical distance' – appropriation has done a lot of work to theorize just such a possibility of modification (and in that capacity, it has done a lot of work in this essay). It has a certain corporate-raider chic no doubt better adapted to the mood of the times than the industrious term 'production' – which was overworked in much the same way by criticism in the 1970s.

Yet close links between rapacity and melancholia remain in its use as buzzword in otherwise politically antagonistic discourses to raise the same or similar questions – the authority of history, the power of tradition, the status of cultural canons. The jargon of appropriation is what the postmodernisms of reaction and resistance have held in common in their different responses (and helps make them so hard to distinguish). It's a jargon that preserves a certain faith in a cultural logic of affluence, a belief that 'we' are living in claustrophobia with a glut of riches that we can (depending on politics) either sanctify or seize. Postmodernized radical criticism has mostly ceased to talk about 'impoverishment' by culture, preferring the wealth released in proliferant appropriation. As Geeta Kapur points out, it is a term implying not only aggression, but abundance.

So it's not surprising that the figure of the colonial should now so insistently reappear from all sides not as deprived and dispossessed by rapacity, but as the naive spirit of plenitude, innocence, optimism – and effective critical 'distance'. Primitivism for art is (like Dundee for action-cinema, the outback for tourism) only an obvious conservative version of this figure. Resistant postmodernism has had its equivalents in popular culture on the one hand, and idealized enclaves of colonized Others (women, blacks, etc ...) on the other. That the latter may sometimes prove slow to seize their place in postmodernity suggests a problem with the premise of surfeit.

For Peter Sloterdijk, all cynicisms provide answers to 'the question of survival, of self-preservation and self-assertion'.[42] The dead cleverness of *Crocodile Dundee* is one such answer, and a fulsome one. It has a reconciliatory, cohesive force quite at odds with the analytic spirit usually claimed for *bricolage*-appropriation, and yet a zestful entrepreneurial optimism that differs (at least in its shameless *avowal* of competitive ambition) from the lugubrious celebration of a lost past predicated so often for, or by, the conservative post- (or anti-) modernism with which it nonetheless shares many racial, sexual and political hostilities.

Rather than assert another answer, it might be best to end evasively. Yet it seems to me that radicalism might better survive the boom in postmodern opinion (for which 'appropriation' has become as commodified a catchphrase as Paul Hogan's *'G'day*) by venturing into that distance that has not been abolished but expanded to infinity by postmodern criticism: the gap between the politics of production, and of regimes of consumption, or rather, since that distinction is now engulfed, between the politics of culture and the politics of politics. This distance (so actively exploited in *Crocodile Dundee*) is presided over by the figure of appropriation and its subsidiaries – such as the rhetorical gap between *mass* culture (what the industry does) and *popular* culture (what we do with what it does). How to invent – not discover or retrieve – some connections is now a major ethical and imaginative action (and image) problem for radical politics.

It isn't a matter of nostalgia for fundamentals. Today, the distance between cultural politics and political politics has become so great, so *sublime*, that radical criticism seems unable to comprehend it. In appropriating the appropriations of popular culture as prime model of political action, criticism doesn't so much abandon old terrains of 'genuine' struggle as Jameson might say, but more seriously, loses credibility: it ceases to be able to say why it thinks that cultural 'struggle' should be so necessary, or rather – it keeps on sleepily assuming *that it knows*. The politics traversing *Crocodile Dundee* are impeded by no such reticence and no such panglossian faith in a basic, immutable benevolence somehow still guiding cultural activity. In a society in which, as Michel de Certeau points out, 'there are too many things to believe and not enough credibility to go around',[43] it is a minimal political task for critics to practise, rather than preach, a little competitive curiosity.

For classical Pangloss, everything was for the best in the best of all possible worlds, and there were no effects without causes. For postmodern Pangloss, a multiplicity of causes compete with a variety of effects, so we had best make the best of everything in the only possible world.

There is really no need for nostalgic returns to a theory of cause and effect, or of originality, to suggest that nonetheless, radical criticism needs today to invent, as well as appropriate, a few good gardening tools.

Notes

Introduction: feminism, reading, postmodernism

1. Bertolt Brecht, *Collected Plays*, vol. 2, part 2, *The Threepenny Opera*, act 1, scene 2, London 1979, p. 22.
2. Anne Freadman, 'Sandpaper', *Southern Review*, vol. 16, no. 1, 1983, p. 162.
3. Freadman, p. 172.
4. Ibid., p. 172.
5. Freadman's 'use' of formalism here is rigorously differentiated from that of North American New Criticism. For her, formalism is 'the study of forms, insofar as form is the enabling condition of signification' (and so, not opposed to 'content'). 'Form', in turn, is a theoretical object derived from, not preexisting, the practices of formalism; and, far from being 'restricted to describing the linguistic forms deployed in any text', formalist *theories* of text for Freadman are 'practices of differentiation which take as their criteria conventions or rule-governed strategies for the formation of texts'. She stresses that 'formalism must in general be characterised as the practice of differentiation. Since difference is the primary enabling condition of signification, it follows that formalism is not the principle of what has been called the 'autonomous' text, since 'difference' supposes a field of pertinent comparison. But it is the case that it takes as its domain of enquiry (and as its theoretical object) not the 'individual text', but the text as individuated'. Ibid., p. 161.
6. See in particular Michèle Le Doeuff, 'Pierre Roussel's Chiasmas: From Imagining Knowledge to the Learned Imagination', *I&C*, no. 9, 1981/2, pp. 39–70.
7. Both Sontag and (more indirectly) Baudrillard derive the terms of their *thematics* of quotation from Walter Benjamin's work, *The Origin of German Tragic Drama*, London 1977. Neither, however, retains much from the historical project – or situation – of the book.
8. Roland Barthes, *Mythologies*, London 1972, p. 112.
9. See Eleanor Dark, *The Timeless Land*, Sydney 1941.
10. See Anne Freadman, 'On Being Here and Still Doing It' in P. Botsman, C. Burns and P. Hutchings, eds, *The Foreign Bodies Papers*, Sydney 1981 (discussed in chapter 1); and the collection of essays, Anna Whiteside and Michael Issacharoff, eds, *On Referring in Literature*, Indiana 1987.
11. For a more measured account of the difficulties entailed by this tendency in moments of the work of Terry Eagleton, see John Frow, *Marxism and Literary History*, Harvard 1986, pp. 41–50.
12. David Bennett, 'Wrapping Up Postmodernism', *Textual Practice*, vol. 1, no. 3, 1987, p. 259.
13. 'Feminist theory of this sort – and however "feminist" it may be, and howsoever "feminist" is construed – does not exist outside the academy and, more specifically, is in many ways not easily separable from the general "theory" that has worked its way into

271

studies in the humanities over the last ten or twenty years.' Paul Smith, 'Men in Feminism: Men and Feminist Theory', in Alice Jardine and Paul Smith, eds, *Men in Feminism*, New York and London 1987, p. 34, p. 267, n. 2.

14. Craig Owens, 'Feminists and Postmodernism', in Hal Foster, ed., *The Anti-Aesthetic: Essays on Postmodern Culture*, Washington 1983, p. 61.

15. Andreas Huyssen, *After the Great Divide: Modernism, Mass Culture, Postmodernism*, Indiana 1986, pp. 198–99.

16. Jonathan Arac, ed., *Postmodernism and Politics*, Manchester 1986, p. xi. [Emphasis mine.]

17. The others are Rosalind Coward (as coauthor with John Ellis); Sally Hassan (as coeditor with Ihab Hassan); and Laura Kipnis, for one article.

18. For discussions of the problems of an intersection between feminism and postmodernism (and responses to Craig Owens' essay), see Barbara Creed, 'From Here to Modernity – Feminism and Postmodernism', *Screen*, vol. 28, no. 2, 1987, pp. 47–67, and Elspeth Probyn, 'Bodies and Anti-bodies: Feminism and the Postmodern', *Cultural Studies*, vol. 1, no. 3, 1987, pp. 349–360.

19. *After the Great Divide*, p. 220.

20. Ibid., p. 45.

21. See papers in Colin MacCabe, ed., *High Theory/Low Culture: Analyzing Popular Television and Film*, Manchester 1986.

22. Joanna Russ, *How To Suppress Women's Writing*, London 1983, p. 66.

23. Dana Polan, 'Postmodernism As Machine', paper to the Australian Screen Studies Association, Sydney, December 1986.

24. Andrew Ross, 'Viennese Waltzes', *Enclitic*, vol. 8, nos. 1–2, 1984, p. 76.

1. A-mazing Grace: Notes on Mary Daly's Poetics

1. Mary Daly, *Gyn/Ecology*, London 1979, p. 2.

2. Since I am not a third-world woman (nor a former Catholic), I would like to thank Laleen Jayamanne for her kind permission to appropriate her statement for my own purposes. The phrase 'Mary Daly event' is Laleen's.

3. For example in Australia, the discussions in *Girl's Own*, nos. 3–4, 1980; and 5, 1981; and the review of *Gyn/Ecology* by Jill Matthews, *Gay Information*, no. 5, 1981, pp. 18–19.

4. *Intervention* began publication in Melbourne as a marxist theoretical journal in 1972. Strongly influenced by Althusser, it defined its project as one of 'analyzing Australian capitalist reality'. In practice, this meant primarily the realities defined by political economy and by class analysis. When the journal moved to Sydney in 1982, it was more interested in the critiques of marxism emerging from feminism and other issue-based movements. However when my article was written for no. 16, *Intervention* was still dominated by the discourses of the political and social sciences. It changed direction again in the following issue, Judith Allen and Paul Patton, eds, *Beyond Marxism? Interventions After Marx*, 1983.

5. Matthews, p. 19.

6. Dale Spender, *Man Made Language*, London 1980. The term 'sign' here is mine, not theirs. Both Daly and Spender use a theory of 'naming' in which it is unclear – or rather, irrelevant – whether the 'name' corresponds to or produces a concept, a thing, a (preexisting) reality, or an experience. This blending is consistent in Daly, and frequent in Spender.

7. The vocabulary of myth and religion offers a privileged set of examples for Mary Daly's methods. But the Australian *Macquarie Dictionary* generally provides a wealth of instances of linguistic anti-feminism through code control. Its obliterations of the achievements of women are all the more obvious because this dictionary, first published in 1981, is of such recent date.

Thus we find that *sexism* is merely 'the upholding or propagating of sexist *attitudes*' (my emphasis), and that a *sexist* attitude is one which 'stereotypes a *person* according to gender or sexual preference, etc.' (my emphasis again). What is eliminated here by the notion of 'person', and the psychologizing notion of 'attitude', is the sense in which *sexism* was originally used by women attempting to produce a theory of patriarchy – and thus of the structural, not merely 'attitudinal', position of *men* (rather than 'persons') in relation to *women*. Similarly, we find that *feminism* is an 'advocacy of equal rights and opportunities for women' – thus obliterating from future standard reference all the developments which distinguish the theories and practices of modern feminism from those of the suffragettes.

While it is true that the usages defined by the *Macquarie* are standard liberal currency today, the point is that the concepts developed by feminists are not even marginalized into second place, but rather omitted entirely.

8. Daly, pp. 18–19, 25, 327.

9. Cited by Daly, p. 327. Rather unhelpfully, Daly does not point out that "*un écrivain*' is 'a writer' (masculine, understood); and that it is grammatically incorrect in French to write '*une écrivain*' – 'a writer' (feminine, understood). So in writing the sentence '*Je suis un écrivain*', the WOMAN writer in French is, as Wittig says, 'silenced/ split by the babble of grammatical usage' since she must inscribe her 'I' in the masculine. Hence Wittig's use of the split 'I' – '*J/e*'. Daly discusses the censoring of this device in the English translation, p. 327.

10. Raymond Williams, 'Literature and Sociology: In Memory of Lucien Goldmann', *New Left Review*, no. 67, 1971.

11. The couple *énonciation/énoncé* has never quite settled into a standard English translation. Variants in use include 'utterance-act/utterance', 'utterance/statement', 'enunciation/statement', 'enunciation/enunciated', and 'enunciation/enounced'. The last two have the advantage of retaining the necessary oppositional structure defining each term, as well as avoiding the ambiguity of 'utterance' in English – which can mean both the action of speaking, and its product. However they have the disadvantage of carrying the connotations of 'enunciation' in its elocution-school sense of '*pronouncing* articulate sounds' – which has given rise to an obscurantist habit in theory-writing of substituting 'enunciation' for 'speech', 'writing', 'saying' or 'formulation' on every possible occasion. For these reasons, I prefer to leave these terms untranslated when I am using them in the strict sense defined by Emile Benveniste, *Problèmes de linguistique générale*, vols. I and II, Paris 1966, 1974.

12. A.J. Greimas and J. Courtès, *Sémiotique: dictionnaire raisonné de la théorie du langage*, Paris 1979, pp. 102–6.

13. Anthony Pym, *Divagations: Towards a Political Economy of Translation*, BA(Hons) thesis, Murdoch University, Perth 1980.

14. Anne Freadman, 'On Being Here and Still Doing It', in P. Botsman, C. Burns and P. Hutchings, eds, *The Foreign Bodies Papers*, Sydney 1981, pp. 151–2.

Since my argument is in many ways an extended footnote to Freadman's paper, I quote the passage in full:

Benveniste is aware that the 'sign' is not a thing in a thing called language, but a piece of a theory; that that theory is the theory of *langue*, and that the 'sign' serves the purpose in it of being a form produced by the appropriate methods of analysis, such that the set of signs and the system will be mutually entailed. For this reason, Benveniste defines the signified not as a meaning that can be examined, but as one of the ways that the sign is identified as itself and no other. The sign cannot, for this reason, account for meaning, or form the basis of an account of it. Meaning, on the other hand, is the defining characteristic of discourse; discourse is made of propositions – reference and sense; and in order to enter into the propositional structure, a sign is considered as a propositional function. Referring is the job of the mechanism of the *énonciation* – the 'stating mechanism': the pronoun 'I' defines what is 'here' and 'now', so as to establish the 'there' and 'then', thereby organizing both the spatial and the temporal relations between the speaking and the spoken about. This special function of 'I' as the nexus of linguistic space-time co-ordinates – the tense structures, the indicative pronouns (this and that), adverbs of time and place, articles – is responsible for what we call utterance-based reference, as distinct from theories of reference that depend on denotation. It is the grammar of reference that shows, at any point of a stretch of discourse, what objects are being described by what predicates: that is, how language is dealing with the world, *what* world it is dealing with. It is the other aspects of the *énonciation* which allow us to talk about the position the speaking subject occupies with respect to those descriptions.

A lot of people have claimed that Benveniste provides a theory of the subject, but I should like to contest that reading. The theory of 'I' is the premise for the theory of the *énonciation*, and the theory of the *énonciation* is a necessary postulate for this theory of reference. The point of Benveniste's work is not to define the speaking subject; it is to show what is necessary to a theory of discourse in order to show how discourse takes hold of its world.

I would emphasize that according to this analysis, it is insufficient to consider only personal pronouns in particular texts in order to analyse their enunciative strategies. Rather, the pronouns must be analysed in terms of their relationship to tense structures, indicative pronouns, adverbs and articles.

15. Both passages are cited from Jean Decottignies' edition of Mme de Tencin, *Mémoires du Comte de Comminge*, Lille 1969, pp. 170 and 47 respectively. My translations.

16. 'Mind Field No. 1', interview with Mary Daly, *Girls' Own*, no. 5, 1981, p. 10.

17. Matthews, p. 19.

18. Mary Daly, *Pure Lust: Elemental Feminist Philosophy*, London 1984.

19. See 'Newspeak Versus New World', in Gyn/Ecology, pp. 329–33; and also the function of sentences like 'Since Gyn/Ecology is the Unfield/Ourfield/Outfield of Journeyers, rather than a game in an "in" field, *the pedantic* can be expected to see it as "unscholarly"' (p. xiii, my emphasis). Apart from the familiar closure of the category 'Journeyers', the term '*the* pedantic' here defines critics in terms of their be-ing ('those who *are* pedants'), not their do-ings.

20. Michèle Le Doeuff, 'Pierre Roussel's Chiasmas: From Imaginary Knowledge to the Learned Imagination', *I&C*, no. 9, 1981/2, p. 53.

21. Freadman, p. 139.

22. Peter Wollen, 'Some Thoughts Arising from Stanley Mitchell's Article' in Society for Education in Film and Television, *Screen Reader 1: Cinema/Ideology/Politics*, London 1977, p. 390.

23. Ibid., p. 390.

24. 'Mind Field No. 1', p. 10.

25. *Gyn/Ecology*, p. xiv.

26. 'Mind Field No. 1', p. 10.

27. Michèle Le Doeuff, 'Women and Philosophy', *Radical Philosophy*, no. 17, 1977; and 'Operative Philosophy: Simone de Beauvoir and Existentialism', *I&C*, no. 6, Autumn 1979.

28. It would be possible to argue that this 'fit' also operates in the fine detail of Daly's poetry, as well as her poetics. Her puns, for example, are rarely *productive* puns – puns which clash two concepts together to make a third, or three and four to make a fourth and fifth. They are *exposé* puns, which reveal – in the manner of a dirty joke – the essential secret already embedded in each and every sign. As such, most of them would fit fairly easily into the formulae of dirty-joke discourse: 'Stagnation, that's a *stag nation*, get it?' The point is not to assimilate Daly's work to the sensibilities of men in pubs, but to suggest that both Daly's puns and dirty jokes are based on a notion of the one truth hidden in all statements.

29. Luce Irigaray, *Ce sexe qui n'en est pas un*, Paris 1977, *This Sex Which Is Not One*, Ithaca 1985, p. 33. (All page references are to the English edition.)

30. See 'Questions', in Ibid., pp. 119–69.

31. Ibid., pp. 192–7.

32. Rosi Braidotti, *Féminisme et philosophie: la philosophie contemporaine comme critique du pouvoir par rapport à la pensée féministe*, doctoral thesis, Universite de Paris-I 1981, pp. 361–2.

33. Le Doeuff, 'Pierre Roussel's Chiasmas', p. 66, fn. 39.

34. For example, Monique Plaza, '"Phallomorphic Power" and the Psychology of "Woman"', *Ideology and Consciousness*, no. 4, 1978, pp. 4–36.

35. *Féminisme et philosophie*, p. 373.

36. Luce Irigaray, 'Misère de la psychanalyse', *Critique*, no. 365, October 1977, pp. 896–7. My translation.

37. 'Mind Field No. 1', p. 10.

38. *This Sex Which Is Not One*, pp. 166–7.

2. The Pirate's Fiancée

1. Valerie Solanas, *The Scum Manifesto*, London 1983, p. 1. All subsequent quotations heading sections of this chapter are from this text.

2. Michel Foucault, 'Truth and Power', in M. Morris and P. Patton, eds, *Michel Foucault: Power/Truth/Strategy*, Sydney 1979, p. 33. Also in Colin Gordon, ed., *Power/Knowledge*, Brighton 1980, pp. 114–15.

3. Michel Foucault, 'Theatrum Philosophicum' in Donald Bouchard, ed., *Language, Counter-Memory, Practice*, Ithaca 1977, pp. 165–96.

4.

> *Some poems fall anyhow,*
> *all of a heap anywhere, dishevelled,*
> *legs apart in loneliness and*
> *desperation*
> *and you talk about standards.*
> Sylvia Kantarizis

Cited in Kate Jennings' poem, 'All of a Heap Anywhere, Megara, Megara', in *Come to Me My Melancholy Baby*, Melbourne 1975.

5. Parveen Adams and Jeff Minson, 'The "Subject" of Feminism', *m/f*, no. 2, 1978, p. 44.

6. Monique Plaza, '"Phallomorphic Power" and the Psychology of "Woman"', *Ideology and Consciousness*, no. 4, 1978, pp. 4–36.

7. Mark Cousins, 'Material Arguments and Feminism', *m/f*, no. 2, 1978, pp. 62–70.

8. See Linda Gordon, *Woman's Body, Woman's Right*, London 1977.

9. Rosalind Coward and John Ellis, *Language and Materialism: Developments in Semiology and the Theory of the Subject*, London 1977, p. 155.

10. Ibid., p. 155.

11. For example, it is a fundamental principle of the semiotics of A.J. Greimas that the methods of analysis be such that an analysis is *repeatable* across a multiplicity of texts. This principle is in turn inscribed in the concept of *isotopie*, for Greimas an enabling condition of the intelligibility of discourse (*Sémantique structurale*, Paris 1966). In contrast, while *S/Z* might just conceivably give rise to imitations, by means of the *lexie* Barthes' analysis aspires to absolute unrepeatability.

12. Coward and Ellis, p. 154.

13. See Luce Irigaray, 'Questions', in *This Sex Which Is Not One*, Ithaca 1985, pp. 119–69.

14. Robert Castel, *Le Psychanalysme: l'ordre psychanalytique et le pouvoir*, Paris 1976.

15. Pierre Clastres, *La Société contre l'état: recherches d'anthropologie politique*, Paris 1974.

16. On the politics of 'gross' concepts, see Gilles Deleuze, 'A propos des nouveaux philosophes et d'un problème plus général', pamphlet published as a supplement to *Minuit*, no. 24, May 1977.

17. Just as I would argue that the presumed essentialism of the problematic of 'the

subject' can result from paraphrase procedures referring to (and thus constructing) '*the*' subject as problem in the first place, so I would question that Foucault ever appeals to '*the body*' in the sense that Adams and Minson suggest in their summaries of his texts and their resulting critique. For a different interpretation, which points out that for Foucault the 'pre-discursive referent' is *not a natural object*, see Paul Veyne, '*Foucault révolutionne l'histoire*', in *Comment on écrit l'histoire*, revised edn, Paris 1978, pp. 347–85.

18. I would like to thank André Frankovits for his relaxed assistance with this article.

19. Christine Delphy, 'Proto-feminism and Anti-feminism', *The Main Enemy: A Materialist Analysis of Women's Oppression*, London 1977. Works by Annie Leclerc are *Parole de Femme*, Paris 1974; *Epousailles*, Paris 1976; 'La Lettre d'amour', in H. Cixous, M. Gagnon and A. Leclerc, *La Venue à l'écriture*, Paris 1977; and, with Marie Cardinal, *Autrement Dit*, Paris 1977.

20. Delphy, p. 41.

21. Plaza, pp. 4–36.

22. Michèle Le Doeuff, 'Women and Philosophy', *Radical Philosophy*, no. 17, 1977, p. 6.

23. Georges May, *Le Dilemme du roman au dixhuitième siècle*, Paris 1963.

24. Hélène Cixous, cited by Elaine Marks, 'Women and Literature in France', *Signs*, vol. 3, no. 4, 1978, p. 832.

25. Michel Foucault, 'The Life of Infamous Men', in Morris and Patton, pp. 76–91.

26. 'Truth and Power', in Morris and Patton, p. 43.

27. Michel Foucault, 'Non au sexe roi', *Le Nouvel Observateur*, no. 644, 1977.

3. Operative Reasoning: Reading Michèle Le Doeuff

1. Michèle Le Doeuff, *L'Imaginaire philosophique* (IP) Paris 1980. All translations are by Colin Gordon.

2. *GREPH (Groupe de recherches sur l'enseignement philosophique)* was formed in 1974 to examine the institutions – and the concept – of philosophy teaching in France. Jacques Derrida was a founding member. The group was active in mobilizing resistance to the 'Haby Reform', which proposed to eliminate the compulsory teaching of philosophy in schools. See Colin Gordon and Jonathan Ree, 'The Philosopher in the Classroom', *Radical Philosophy*, no. 16, 1977, pp. 2–9; and the collective volume by *GREPH*, *Qui a peur de la philosophie?*, Paris 1977.

3. See Jacques Derrida, 'White Mythologies: Metaphor in the Text of Philosophy', *Margins of Philosophy*, Chicago 1982, pp. 207–71.

4. Lucien Dallenbach, *Le Récit spéculaire: essai sur la mise en abyme*, Paris 1977.

5. Michèle Le Doeuff, 'Women and Philosophy', *Radical Philosophy*, no. 17, 1977, pp. 2–11.

6. Michèle Le Doeuff, 'Operative Philosophy: Simone de Beauvoir and Existentialism', *I&C*, no. 6, 1979, pp. 47–58.

7. Ibid., p. 48.

8. IP, p. 152. The contrast here is between Le Doeuff's modes of writing and the femininity codes employed by a range of writers in France from Annie Leclerc to Hélène Cixous. However, to see how far Le Doeuff herself has modified some of the classic enunciative strategies of French philosophical discourse, it is useful to compare her chapter 'Galilée ou l'affinité suprême entre le temps et le mouvement' (IP, pp. 47–67), with her major reference – A. Koyré's *Etudes Galiléennes*, Paris 1966.

9. IP, p. 12.

10. IP, p. 11.

11. IP, p. 183. (The chapter 'Pierre Roussel's Chiasmas' is translated in *I&C*, no. 9, 1981/2, pp. 39–70. For consistency's sake, however, all subsequent references are to the French edition).

12. IP, p. 79.

13. IP, p. 65.
14. IP, p. 79–80.
15. IP, p. 80.
16. IP, p. 10–11.
17. IP, p. 83.
18. IP, p. 177.
19. IP, p. 167.
20. IP, p. 124: 'Utilising an image already invested by an earlier philosophy is like giving a nod and a wink, for reasons that remain in each case to be ascertained, to something in that philosophy; it is a way of reactualising a philosopheme which the philosophy that repeats the image is perhaps not able to produce for itself.'
21. IP, p. 127.
22. IP, pp. 19–30. Kant's island of pure truth introduces the final chapter of the 'Transcendental Analytic' in *Critique of Pure Reason*. Le Doeuff traces the metaphor to Bacon's *Great Instauration*.
23. IP, p. 21.
24. IP, p. 29.
25. IP, p. 24.
26. IP, pp. 30–3.
27. IP, p. 150, n. 5.
28. IP, p. 152.
29. IP, p. 136.
30. IP. p. 147. (The reference here and subsequently is to the French version, '*Cheveux longs, idées courtes*', in IP).
31. IP, p. 142.
32. IP, p. 154.
33. IP, pp. 161–2.
34. This construction is less marked in the earlier essays on More and Galileo, where an optimistic conception of philosophical work comes close enough as a possibility in her text to require explicit renunciation (e.g. IP, p. 83).
35. See The Eagles' song *Hotel California*: 'You can check out any time you like, but you can never leave ...'. A comparison of philosophical forms of menace with classic horror-house imagery would repay investigation along the lines suggested by Le Doeuff's analyses.
36. See Rosi Braidotti, *Féminisme et philosophie: la philosophie contemporaine comme critique du pouvoir par rapport à la pensée féministe*, thesis, Universite de Paris-I, 1981; and more recently, Alice Jardine, *Gynesis: Configurations of Woman and Modernity*, Ithaca 1985.
37. IP, p. 134.
38. One difficulty with these arguments is that demands for such a justification usually impose precisely the unitary notion of philosophical discourse that Le Doeuff contests.
39. Evelyn Sullerot, ed., *Le Fait féminin*, Paris 1978. 'The Feminine Fact' was a colloquium organized at the Royaumont 'Centre for the Study of Man' in 1976. It envisaged a unified theory of femininity, synthesizing the work of biologists, psychologists and social scientists.
40. An exemplary text in this respect is the section on de Beauvoir in Margaret Walters' essay, 'The Rights and Wrongs of Women', in Juliet Mitchell and Ann Oakley, eds, *The Rights and Wrongs of Women*, Harmondsworth 1976. Walters reads *The Second Sex*, de Beauvoir's novels and her autobiographies in order to produce knowledge of de Beauvoir the woman – against which de Beauvoir's texts may then be tested for their truth value in terms of a balancing of 'admissions', 'claims' and 'denials' thus extracted by the critic. The strategy produces 'Walters' as a writing/reading subject qualified to adjudicate the truth of de Beauvoir's most intimate statements.

For example, 'Reading [de Beauvoir's descriptions of dreams], I was driven back to her account of why they never married or had children. Both are decisions that I respect and even agree with; both seem to me far more difficult decisions than she claims. Memmi has argued that it was basically Sartre's decision not hers, and I think he may be right' (p. 367).

One could read in this a trace of feminist desires towards theoretical mothers; but it would probably be more pertinent to consider the role played in feminist analysis by an imaginary specific to psychologizing forms of literary criticism.

41. In fact, I think it is probably both inaccurate and unjust. Le Doeuff's paraphrase implies that for Irigaray, 'the main enemy' may be fixed as idealist logic and the metaphysical logos for all women at all times, in a way which would consistently override the need for other interventions in other discourses. This ignores the specificity of the philosophical and analytic contexts *against* which Irigaray's work is inscribed: it develops a description of her practice into a prescription which is then attributed to her, and it effaces the different tactics she herself adopts in different parts of her work (here lumped together as 'Luce Irigaray's books').

4. Indigestion: A Rhetoric of Reviewing

1. An eminent reviewer in both radio and television, John Hinde is also the author of *Other People's Pictures*, Sydney 1981.

2. The Greater Union Awards for Australian short films are decided annually by panels of local judges for the Sydney Film Festival. The twelve finalists are then screened to the Festival's international guests, who select one film to receive the Mamoulian Award.

3. David Stratton, *The Last New Wave: The Australian Film Revival*, London and Sydney 1980. Stratton was for many years Director of the Sydney Film Festival.

4. John Simon, *Movies into Films: Film Criticism 1967–70*, New York 1971, p. 171.

5. Ibid., p. 177.

6. Pauline Kael, 'Circles and Squares', *I Lost It At The Movies*, London 1966, pp. 307–8.

7. These were 'Circles and Squares', p. 300 – 'A film critic need not be a theoretician, but it is necessary that he know how to use words. This might, indeed, be a first premise for a theory.'; and Paul Rotha's introduction to Richard Winnington, *Criticism and Caricatures 1943–53*, London 1975, pp. 14–15.

8. I refer to careful editing, now a rather eccentric practice after computerization and the disappearance of hard copy. More common is the routine of cutting from the bottom up – a procedure responsible for the majority of brutally abrupt and 'dismissive' reviews ('If the film's lousy, why waste the space?'). Experienced reviewers structure their comments with this possibility in mind.

9. George Tosi, 'Geoff Burrowes and George Miller: Interview', *Cinema Papers*, June 1982, p. 209. Burrowes is a producer, whose projects include *The Man From Snowy River*.

10. Private conversation with John Flaus – film critic, historian, actor, teacher.

11. I'm not suggesting that people necessarily go to the films such critics recommend, but that both the 'plot outline' *and* the 'personality' methods of reviewing work to keep desire circulating through the cinematic institution – which includes not only films but texts about films.

12. My thanks to Peter Kemp, both for this anecdote and for his help with research for this essay.

13. This is why former obituary writers can in fact move over to become perfectly persuasive reviewers. This is also why someone who knows and cares about film does not necessarily make a persuasive *reviewer*. Whether or not one is competent in relation to film (and however such competence may be assessed), one needs first to be able to use the codes of journalism to signify 'competence' competently.

5. Apologia: *Beyond Deconstruction*/'Beyond What?'

1. John Docker, *In A Critical Condition: Reading Australian Literature*, Ringwood and Harmondsworth 1984. Docker's is one of a number of recent books attacking the politics of deconstruction *à l'americaine* by way of a comparison with the New Criticism. However, its distinctive feature is to integrate this attack with an account of how the importation of both British and American modes of 'close reading' functioned institutionally in Australia, particularly during the Cold War period, to marginalize Australian literature and literary history in general, and the writings of the so-called 'radical nationalists' in particular.

2. See John Frow, 'Limits: The Politics of Reading', *Marxism and Literary History*, Harvard 1986, pp. 207–35.

3. Felperin begins by narrating his problem as a Yale man arriving in Melbourne ('Leavisism Revisited'), while Docker ends with a tale of the trials of a Sydney man at the 'imaginary' Fletcher University ('Epilogue: A Doubter Meets the Devotees').

4. Felperin, *Beyond Deconstruction* (BD), p. 2.

5. BD, pp. 91–7.

6. Barthes, 'The Artist: *Beyond What?*', section 'Réquichot and His Body', *The Responsibility of Forms* (RF).

7. Anne Freadman says of John Docker's reading of *S/Z* as a denunciation of the realist 'fallacy': 'Barthes's word is "myth", not "fallacy". To say it's a myth is both to say that we believe, and that it's not true; that it works, and that we work it. It is not a fallacy, because we do not *fail* to represent; it is a myth, because we succeed.' 'Taking Things Literally (Sins of My Old Age)', *Southern Review*, vol. 18, no. 2, 1985, p. 183.

8. To represent Felperin's position accurately I should probably say 'interpretation' rather than 'criticism'. I am uncomfortable with that term, and so I'm producing an Australian skewing of his argument here (as he skews French material with American 'interpretive' emphases).

9. BD, p. 47.

10. BD, pp. 168, 182. See Roman Jakobson, 'Closing Statement: Linguistics and Poetics', in Thomas A. Sebeok, ed., *Style in Language*, Cambridge, Mass. 1960, pp. 350–77 (especially pp. 356–8).

11. See BD, pp. 34, 51, 147.

12. BD, p. 41.

13. BD, pp. 87–8.

14. BD, p. 215.

15. On this issue, see Anne Freadman, '*Riffaterra Cognita*: A Late Contribution to the "Formalism" Debate', *SubStance*, no. 42, 1984, pp. 31–45.

16. BD, p. 135.

17. RF, p. 229.

18. Felperin uses this term in a sense derived from Harold Bloom, *The Anxiety of Influence: A Theory of Poetry*, Oxford 1973.

19. RF, p. 230.

20. John Forbes, 'Aspects of Contemporary Australian Poetry', in *The Foreign Bodies Papers*, Sydney 1981, pp. 114–21.

21. RF, p. 262.

22. *The Rustle of Language (RL)*, p. 58.

23. RF, p. 300.

24. RL, p. 169.

25. RL, pp. 177–8.

26. The classic alternative to Kramer's reductive model of literary history, H.M. Green's mammoth two-volume *History of Australian Literature* (Sydney 1961, revised by Dorothy Green, 1984), has been until recently a casualty of precisely those institutional battles narrated by John Docker.

27. BD, p. 147.

28. BD, p. 87.

29. T.W. Adorno, 'The Essay as Form', *New German Critique*, no. 32, 1984, pp. 151–71.

7. On the 'On' of *On Photography*

1. William Gass, 'A Different Kind of Art', *The New York Times Book Review*, 18 December 1977, p. 7.
2. Colin L. Westerbeck, Jr., 'Off Photography', *Artforum*, vol. XVI, no. 8, April 1978, pp. 56–60.

8. Intrigue

1. Jean-Michel Raynaud, 'Species of Origin', in Ian Reid and Sneja Gunew, eds, *Not the Whole Story*, Sydney 1984, pp. 151–9.
2. John Forbes, '4 Heads & How To Do Them' ('The Symbolist Head'), in Robert Kenny, *Applestealers*, Melbourne, 1974, pp. 164–8.
3. In *Family History* (1932, London 1986), Vita Sackville-West attempted a spelling reform. The word 'that' sometimes appears as 'thatt' to distinguish between its various grammatical functions. That is, she wanted a difference in meaning (between conjunction and demonstrative adjective and demonstrative or relative pronoun) to be made *visible*. She agreed that it was irritating, and eventually gave up.
4. 'Grids', *The Originality of the Avant-Garde and Other Modernist Myths*, Cambridge, Mass., 1985, p. 9.
5. See Anne Freadman's analysis of Sophie Taeuber-Arp's *Aubette Triptych: Vertical-Horizontal Composition*, in 'Reading the Visual', *Framework*, nos. 30/31, 1986, pp. 136–47.
6. Richard Dunn, untitled essay in *Pleasure of the Gaze: Image and Appearance in Recent Australian Art*, curated by Bruce Adams, Perth 1985, p. 18.

9. Politics Now: Anxieties of a Petty-bourgeois Intellectual

1. This is a version of a paper delivered at a forum at the Conference on Culture, the Arts, Media and Radical Politics (CAMARP), Sydney, 14 July 1985. Other speakers were Sylvia Lawson (writer) and Denis Freney (Communist Party of Australia).
2. Katingal was a maximum security unit in Sydney's Long Bay gaol in the 1970s. It involved the use of sensory deprivation techniques, and after a protest campaign was eventually closed down. Leonie Kramer, Professor of Australian Literature at the University of Sydney and editor of the *Oxford History of Australian Literature* (1983), includes association with the Katingal scheme in her distinguished public career.
3. *Petrodollars* was a shorthand term for 'loans raised by the Australian government from Arab sources'. A scandal over the presumed economic mismanagement entailed by the raising of such loans (which were not illegal, but came to seem so in the press coverage) was an important element in the destabilization of the Whitlam Labor government in 1975.
My Little Mate was a phrase purportedly used by High Court Judge Lionel Murphy (during an illegally taped phone call) in reference to a Sydney solicitor later charged with criminal offences involving professional misconduct. When Murphy himself was charged with conspiring to pervert the course of justice, the phrase came to epitomize the mateship-nexus of criminals, politicians, big capital and the legal profession thought to be responsible for corruption in New South Wales. However, since 'mateship' is perhaps still the single most complex cultural value in Australian life, and since it it no more illegal than 'petrodollars' but for a time came similarly to seem so (as 'guilt by association'), the phrase acquired ironic, yet poignant, defensive connotations for Justice Murphy's supporters. Justice Murphy had been Attorney-General in the Whitlam government.
4. See E. Grosz, T. Threadgold, D. Kelly, A. Cholodenko and E. Colless, eds., *Futur*fall: Excursions into Post-Modernity*, Sydney 1986.

5. Cited by Charles Newman, 'The Post-Modern Aura: The Act of Fiction in an Age of Inflation', *Salmagundi*, nos. 63–4, 1984, p. 5.

6. Sylvia Lawson, *The Archibald Paradox: A Strange Case of Authorship*, Harmondsworth and Melbourne 1983; Charles Merewether, *Art and Social Commitment: An End to the City of Dreams 1931–1948*, Sydney 1984; Ross Harley, 'Neither Here Nor There? A Dossier Around *Serious Undertakings*', in P. Botsman and R. Harley, eds, *Local Consumption Series 5: Sex, Politics, Representation*, Sydney 1984; Pauline Johnson, *Marxist Aesthetics*, London 1984.

7. *New Left Review*, no. 146, 1984, pp. 53–92.

8. Ibid., p. 55.

10. Room 101 Or A Few Worst Things In The World

1. George Orwell, *Nineteen Eighty-Four*, Harmondsworth 1970. All quotations heading the sections of my article are from this text.

2. Jean Baudrillard, *Les Stratégies fatales* (*SF*), Paris 1983, p. 261. All translations from French titles are mine.

3. *SF*, pp. 11–12.

4. Jean Baudrillard, *De la séduction* (*DS*), Paris 1979, p. 84.

5. *SF*, p. 11.

6. I owe this formula to Salvatore Mele, 'Game with Vestiges: An Interview with Jean Baudrillard', *On The Beach*, no. 5, 1984, p. 20.

7. 'Le Cristal se venge: une entrevue avec Jean Baudrillard', *Parachute*, June–August 1983, p. 29.

8. *SF*, pp. 170–1.

9. *SF*, pp. 259–60.

10. *SF*, pp. 259–60.

11. Jean Baudrillard, 'Nuclear Implosion', *Impulse*, Spring–Summer 1983, p. 10.

12. Jean Baudrillard, *In the Shadow of the Silent Majorities* (*SM*), New York 1983, p. 3.

13. Michel Beaujour, 'Some Paradoxes of Description', *Yale French Studies*, no. 61, 1981, p. 47.

14. Jean Baudrillard, *Simulations*, New York 1983, p. 142.

15. Philippe Bonnefis, 'The Melancholic Describer', *Yale French Studies*, no. 61, 1981, p. 158.

16. 'Paradoxes of Description', pp. 43, 59.

17. Ibid., p. 42.

18. Jean Baudrillard, *Forget Foucault*, New York 1987, p. 46.

19. *Simulations*, p. 4.

20. *DS*, p. 223.

21. *SF*, p. 126.

22. *SF*, p. 78.

23. Jean Baudrillard, 'What Are You Doing After the Orgy?', *Artforum*, vol. XXII, no. 2, October 1983, pp. 42–6, and *DS*, p. 56.

24. *SF*, p. 83.

25. *SF*, p. 79.

26. *DS*, pp. 31–2.

27. *SF*, p. 241.

28. *SF*, p. 253.

29. 'What Are You Doing After the Orgy', p. 43.

30. *Simulations*, p. 35.

31. SM, p. 4.

32. Jean Baudrillard, *Simulacres et simulation*, Paris 1981, p. 77.

33. *Simulations*, pp. 24–6.

34. Mark Titmarsh, 'Touch me Television', *On the Beach*, nos. 3–4, 1984, p. 64. For Baudrillard, however, it is this 'instability' which defines video as *not*-an-image.

35. SM, p. 21.

36. *Simulations*, p. 12.

37. SM, p. 96. On this point, which is essential to Baudrillard's scenario of meaning's 'death', see also *DS*, pp. 123–4, and, for the notion of 'isolating' and 'proving' the real, *Simulations*, p. 41.

38. SM, p. 5.

39. See Anne Freadman, 'On Being Here And Still Doing It', in P. Botsman, C. Burns and P. Hutchings, *The Foreign Bodies Papers*, Sydney 1981, pp. 139–41.

40. *Simulacres et simulation*, p. 69.

41. *Simulations*, p. 72.

42. *DS*, p. 214.

43. *SF*, p. 91.

44. *SF*, p. 72.

45. *DS*, p. 236.

46. *DS*, p. 104.

47. *DS*, pp. 102–4.

48. *SF*, p. 109.

49. *SF*, p. 234.

50. *SF*, p. 67.

51. 'The cat came back' is the refrain of a folksong about a feline principle of eternal return.

52. *SF*, p. 103.

53. Jean Baudrillard, *Le Système des objets*, Paris 1968.

54. *SF*, pp. 215–20.

55. *SF*, p. 144.

56. *SF*, p. 234.

57. *SF*, pp. 240–1.

58. *SF*, p. 254.

59. *SF*, pp. 79–81. The analogy here is made explicitly with the 'mixity and promiscuity of races'.

60. *Simulations*, p. 23.

61. *DS*, p. 88.

62. Philippe Hamon, 'Qu'est-ce qu'une description?', *Poétique*, no. 12, 1972, p. 485.

63. 'What Are You Doing After the Orgy', p. 43.

11. Postmodernity and Lyotard's Sublime

1. Samuel H. Monk, *The Sublime: A Study of Critical Theories in Eighteenth Century England*, Ann Arbor 1960, p. iii.

2. Jean-François Lyotard, 'Presenting the Unpresentable: The Sublime', *Artforum*, vol. XX, no. 8, April 1982, p. 69.

3. See *Les Immatériaux*, 2 vols, Paris 1985, and Elie Theofilakis, ed., *Modernes, et après? 'Les Immatériaux'*, Paris 1985. Since this passage concerns the logic of suspicion in Lyotard's definition of modernity, I have not subsequently revised it to take account of the actual exhibition.

4. Jean-François Lyotard, 'Appendix: Answering the Question: What Is Postmodernism?', *The Postmodern Condition: A Report on Knowledge*, Manchester 1984, p. 79 (translation modified). This essay was first published in French in *Critique*, no. 419, April 1982, independently of *La Condition postmoderne*, Paris 1979, and is discussed as a separate item throughout my article.

5. Jean-François Lyotard, 'The Sublime and the Avant-Garde', *Artforum*, vol. XXII, no. 8, April 1984, pp. 36–43.

6. See Jean-François Lyotard, 'Introduction à une étude du politique selon Kant' in Etienne Balibar *et al.*, *Rejouer le politique*, Paris 1981, pp. 91–134.

7. 'Answering the Question', p. 82.

8. Jean-François Lyotard, *Le Différend* (*LD*), Paris 1984. On this debate, see Hayden White, 'The Politics of Historical Interpretation: Discipline and De-Sublimation', *Critical Inquiry*, vol. 9, no. 1, 1982, pp. 113–38.

9. *LD*, p. 65.

10. *LD*, p. 33.

11. *LD*, p. 11.

12. Jean-François Lyotard and Jean-Loup Thébaud, *Just Gaming*, Manchester 1985 (*Au juste*, Paris 1979).

13. Jean-François Lyotard, *Driftworks*, New York 1984. The French publication dates of these essays range from 1970 to 1973.

14. *The Postmodern Condition*, p. 15, n. 55, and p. 41.

15. *Ibid.*, p. 67.

16. For a recent discussion of Lyotard's critical strategies, see David Carroll, *Paraesthetics*, New York and London, 1987, Chapter 7.

17. *Just Gaming*, p. 5.

18. *LD*, p. 54.

19. *LD*, p. 197.

20. In relation to Lyotard's reading of Kant, see Gilles Deleuze, *Kant's Critical Philosophy: The Doctrine of the Faculties*, London 1984.

21. *Just Gaming*, p. 90.

22. Craig Owens, 'The Discourse of Others: Feminists and Postmodernism', in Hal Foster, ed., *The Anti-Aesthetic: Essays on Postmodern Culture*, Washington 1983, p. 57.

23. *LD*, p. 197.

24. First elected in 1983, the government of R.J. Hawke became in 1987 the first Federal Labor regime in Australian history to achieve a third term of office. It has combined a reforming mode of economic rationalism with the progressive revision and/or abandonment of most of Labor's traditional social programmes and political ideals. An example of Hawke's 'site-specific' approach is provided by the fortunes of a 1983 election promise of uniform land-rights legislation for Aboriginal people in all states of Australia. The bill was subsequently abandoned when the State Labor government of Western Australia warned that five Federal seats could be lost over the issue (after an expensive campaign by mining companies in that state). But it was revived as an ideal (not a promise) in 1987, when the threat of bad publicity during the 1988 Bicentennial helped Labor to renew its interest in Aboriginal politics.

25. Richard Rorty, 'Habermas and Lyotard on Postmodernity', in Richard J. Bernstein, ed., *Habermas and Modernity*, Cambridge and Oxford 1985, p. 162. Lyotard and Rorty discussed their differences in *Critique*, no. 41, May 1985, pp. 559–84.

26. *Just Gaming*, p. 70.

27. *Ibid.*, p. 25. On the general issue of 'opinion' see pp. 73–84.

28. See Christopher Norris, 'Philosophy as a Kind of Narrative: Rorty on Postmodern Liberal Culture', *Enclitic*, vol. 7, no. 2, 1983, pp. 144–58.

29. *The Postmodern Condition*, p. 19.

30. 'Philosophy as a Kind of Narrative', p. 151.

31. This song – in which a mother maligned by small-town gossip goes to a PTA meeting to confront her accusers with their own shortcomings – provides an excellent allegory of an effective *move* made in a language-game. The furtive narration and third-person reference-strategy of gossip is converted into the genre of public accusation, and an I/you exchange. This example occurred to me because a neighbour played the song over and over every day when I was writing this article. However the 'witch' in Nelly Kaplan's film *La Fiancée du pirate* provides another: the despised prostitute secretly tapes her lovers' private conversations, and 'answers' village gossip by playing them over the public address system.

32. *Just Gaming*, p. 82.

33. Jean-François Lyotard, 'Preliminary Notes on the Pragmatic of Works: Daniel Buren', *October*, n. 10, 1979, 59–68. See also 'The Works and Writings of Daniel Buren',

Artforum, vol. XIX, no. 6, February 1981, pp. 56–64.

34. Jean-François Lyotard, 'Theory as Art: A Pragmatic Point of View', in W. Steiner, ed., *Image and Code*, Ann Arbor 1981, p. 73.

35. *Just Gaming*, pp. 51–2.

36. *The Postmodern Condition*, p. 15.

37. See *LD*, p. 263.

38. *The Postmodern Condition*, pp. 9–10.

39. See Thomas Morawetz, *Wittgenstein and Knowledge: The Importance of 'On Certainty'*, University of Massachusetts 1978, p. 52.

40. Farhang Zabeeh, 'On Language Games and Forms of Life', in E.D. Klemke, ed., *Essays on Wittgenstein*, Illinois 1971, p. 363.

41. Ludwig Wittgenstein, *Philosophical Investigations*, Oxford 1968, p. 11.

42. *LD*, p. 257.

43. Thomas Weiskel, *The Romantic Sublime: Studies in the Structure and Psychology of Transcendence*, Baltimore and London 1976, p. 21.

44. 'Answering the Question', p. 79 (translation modified).

45. Bertrand Russell, *History of Western Philosophy*, London 1946, p. 679. Lyotard, of course, would not accept this essentialist and flippant summary. But Russell does describe, at least, a popular *representation* of Kant's sublime, which reflects the history of its circulation.

46. Freidrich von Schiller, *Naive and Sentimental Poetry/On the Sublime*, New York 1966, p. 209.

47. Ibid., pp. 204–7.

48. Ibid., p. 205.

49. 'Introduction à l'étude du politique selon Kant', p. 112 (my emphasis).

50. *LD*, p. 238.

51. See *LD*, p. 120: '"Every sentence is." ... *Is* should rather be: *Is it happening? (Arrive-t-il?)*, the French *il* indicating an empty place to be occupied by a referent.'

52. Edmund Burke, *A Philosophical Enquiry into the Origin of Our Ideas of the Sublime and Beautiful*, Notre Dame and London 1968, p. 41.

53. Ibid., p. 135.

54. 'The Sublime and the Avant-Garde', p. 40.

55. 'Answering the Question', p. 79 (translation modified).

56. For a different use of a similar distinction, see Paul Willemen, 'An Avant Garde for the 80s', *Framework*, no. 24, 1984, pp. 53–73.

57. 'The Sublime and the Avant-Garde', p. 43.

58. For example, see Craig Owens, 'The Allegorical Impulse: Toward a Theory of Postmodernism Part 2', *October*, no. 13, 1980, pp. 79–80, and Willemen, 'An Avant Garde for the 80s', p. 61.

59. 'The Kantian *Darstellung* is not, in spite of its name, the presentation of a sentence universe. It is the conjunction of two sentences belonging to different regimes', *LD*, p. 99.

60. *LD*, p. 29. See also pp. 9, 18–19, 198–9.

61. *LD*, p. 92.

62. *LD*, p. 200.

12. Tooth and Claw: Tales of Survival, and *Crocodile Dundee*

1. Gilles Deleuze, *L'Image-mouvement*, Paris 1983, p. 278; Hugh Tomlinson and Barbara Habberjam, trans., *Cinema 1: The Movement-Image*, Minneapolis 1986, p. 206. Translation slightly modified.

2. Cited in John Baxter, 'A Fistful of Koalas', *Cinema Papers*, no. 57, 1986.

3. I am referring to Jurgen Habermas, 'Modernity – An Incomplete Project', in Hal Foster, ed., *The Anti-Aesthetic*, Washington 1983; Jean-François Lyotard, *The Postmodern Condition*, Manchester 1984; Fredric Jameson, 'Postmodernism, or the Cultural Logic

of Late Capitalism', *New Left Review*, no. 146, 1984; Andreas Huyssen, 'Mapping the Postmodern', *After the Great Divide: Modernism, Mass Culture, Postmodernism*, Indiana 1986.

A great deal of work in film and media studies has drawn on these texts. My comment concerns only the elision of cinema in these formulations of postmodernism, not the vast associated literature.

4. Jean-François Lyotard, 'Acinema', *Wide Angle*, vol. 2, no. 3, 1978, pp. 52–9.

5. Foreword to Jean-François Lyotard, *The Postmodern Condition*, pp. xvi–ii. However, Jameson does violence to Lyotard's argument in attributing to him a commitment to 'innovation', when Lyotard specifically distinguishes between the modernist imperative to innovate from the *Ereignis*, and the procedure by paralogism, that he claims to be theorizing for the postmodern. See chapter 11, above.

6. These terms are loosely adapted from Ross Chambers, *Story and Situation: Narrative Seduction and the Power of Fiction*, Minneapolis 1984, p. 33.

7. With Laleen Jayamanne and Yvonne Rainer, 'Discussing Modernity, "Third World", and *The Man Who Envied Women*', *Art & Text*, nos. 22/23, 1987, pp. 41–51.

8. 'Urban Renaissance and the Spirit of Postmodernism', *New Left Review*, no. 151, 1985, p. 107.

9. Susan Dermody and Elizabeth Jacka, in *The Screening of Australia*, 2 vols, Sydney 1987, give an exemplary account of the interlocking of economic structures, rhetorical inventions of identity ('Australian-ness' as ideal and/or commodity), and aesthetic strategies in the development of a national cinema: and I refer to it gratefully as the basis of the terms of my discussion.

10. 1982 interview in Peter Hamilton and Sue Mathews, *American Dreams, Australian Movies*, Sydney 1986, p. 157.

11. Ibid., p. 95.

12. Stuart Cunningham, 'Hollywood Genres, Australian Movies (1983)', in Albert Moran and Tom O'Regan, eds, *An Australian Film Reader*, Sydney 1985, pp. 235–41. Comparing it to the spaghetti Western, Cunningham calls this tendency 'generic transformation'.

13. 10BA initially offered a 150 per cent write-off for film investment, with no tax payable on the first 50 per cent of profits. In August 1983 the concessions were reduced to 133 per cent and 33 per cent, and then again, in September 1985, to 120 per cent and 20 per cent. By 1985, the year of the actual filming of *Crocodile Dundee*, the level of guaranteed pre-sale income required to attract investors had reached 65 per cent. At the time of writing, the scheme was under review as no longer viable for either the industry or the government. See *Film Assistance: Future Options: A Discussion Paper by the Australian Film Commission*, Sydney 1987, pp. 1–8.

14. It may give some idea of the economic difficulties of the Australian film industry to note that in twenty-two weeks in Australia, *Crocodile Dundee* took $31 million. It then took the same amount of money in ten days in the United States (*Sydney Morning Herald*, 11 October 1986).

15. For the pleasure of American deconstructionists, we might note that instead of playing Fess Parker, Dundee plays with Sue's *fesses*.

16. I must thank Julie Rose for pointing this out to me. The bush telegraph was once a way for settlers to warn bushrangers about the movements of police. In urban society today, it usually means gossip.

17. Elias Canetti, *Crowds and Power*, Harmondsworth 1973, p. 265. *Crocodile Dundee* can be a particularly unfortunate *model* – that is, as an ideal rather than an event – for future Australian cinema because of Paul Hogan's unusual status as a recognizable American commodity (through tourism commercials); because the Paramount budget for publicizing the film in North America rivalled its local production budget; and because its success on these terms (as well as its cultural conservatism) makes the task of sustaining and justifying support for local independent film even more difficult than before.

18. T.W. Adorno and M. Horkheimer, *Dialectic of Enlightenment*, London 1979, p. 137. See Adrian Martin, 'Wishful Thinking', *Tension*, no. 8, 1985, pp. 27–30.

19. *The Age*, 2 May 1986. The second Hogan comment in this paragraph is from

Baxter, 'A Fistful of Koalas', p. 29.

20. Frances Ferguson, 'The Nuclear Sublime', *Diacritics*, vol. 14, no. 2, 1984, pp. 4–10.

21. Paul Willeman, 'Presentation', *Framework*, nos. 30/31, 1986, p. 135. Lawrence Grossberg gives a more sympathetic account of the difficulties in these theories of reading in "'I'd Rather Feel Bad Than Not Feel Anything At All'": Rock and Roll, Pleasure and Power', *Enclitic*, vol. 8, nos. 1–2, 1984, pp. 97–101.

22. *Recodings: Art, Spectacle, Cultural Politics*, Washington 1985, p. 134.

23. An example of tragic contrast to *Crocodile Dundee* might be *Cool-Hand Luke* (1967). Paul Newman's character begins as an evasive hero, but is swiftly reduced by that system's confining power to a victim banging his head against the wall. A comic contrast is *Smokey and the Bandit*: without the sheriff, Burt Reynold's evasiveness would lose its *raison d'être*. The lack of interest in either law or significant lawlessness (apart from a little poaching) in *Crocodile Dundee* is also what distinguishes the film from its American Western models.

24. A possible starting-point for such an analysis would be the construction of the scene of the hero's mesmeric gaze – in which the narrative of the exchange of looks between Dundee and the buffalo is mediated by a medium shot of Sue's gaze at the scene via a camera. An equivalence is established, animal-woman-camera-audience, defining a set of specular relations that make the male hero's action, and action *upon* those relations, possible and meaningful.

25. Frank Campbell, 'The Golden Age of Hoges', *Sydney Morning Herald*, 7 January 1987. For Campbell, the racial and sexual conservatism of the film makes it a '*soft*', not an anti-, *Rambo*, mixing a cocktail of messages for audiences 'which cannot afford to be seen taking them neat'.

26. 'The Shining Hero Inside Mick Dundee', *The Australian*, 20–21 December 1986. His innocence is compared to Sue's 'left-liberal cant'.

27. In *Razorback* the American woman is in fact played by an Australian, Judy Morris, so that the *real* American star, Gregory Harrison, can come looking for her once she's dead.

28. In this way my opening quotation to this section, from Frank Moorhouse's story 'The Coca-Cola Kid' (*The Americans, Baby*, Sydney 1972), takes two separate lines of dialogue from Australians at a party (the second of which was addressed *to*, not by an American in the story), and makes them refer here to each other, to the role of Americans in Australian films, and to difficulties in criticizing *Crocodile Dundee*.

29. The white Aborigine has been one of the privileged figures of postmodernist rhetoric in Australian art writing; see Paul Taylor, 'The Art of White Aborigines', *Flash Art*, no. 112, May 1983, pp. 48–50. It's also an old colonial metaphor ('miscegenation') of contradiction and reconciliation.

30. The reciprocal relation of Sue and Nev is underscored by the fact that Aboriginal women are nonexistent for the film. At one of their ceremonies, however, Sue might well be admitted while Dundee would not. At this level of the film's politics of opinion, it maintains the classic anthropological myth of absolute male dominance in traditional Aboriginal societies. See Diane Bell, *Daughters of the Dreaming*, Melbourne 1983.

31. Shortly after the release of the film in Australia, a mining company began illegal operations in Kakadu National Park. The fact that *Crocodile Dundee* had been shot there was used in the media to mobilize opposition to the move – by effectively divorcing the conservation issue from the touchy matter of land rights, to represent Kakadu as the 'heritage' of 'all Australians' rather than just its traditional owners. The mine was temporarily halted.

32. *The Daily Telegraph* (Sydney), 21 October 1986.

33. 'Sorry Hoges, But This Time You've Blown It', *The Australian*, 26 April 1986.

34. Kathleen Carroll, in Hamilton and Mathews, *American Dreams, Australian Movies*, p. 62; Annette Blonski, 'Independent Film ... An Historical Perspective', *Filmviews*, vol. 31, no. 129, 1986, p. 18.

35. Moran and O'Regan, *An Australian Film Reader*, p. 62.

36. See 'A Fistful of Koalas', p. 28.

37. *The Postmodern Condition*, p. 41, my emphasis.

38. John Frow, *Marxism and Literary History*, Harvard 1986, p. 117.

39. 'Postmodernism', p. 67, my emphasis.

40. See Tom O'Regan, '*The Man From Snowy River* and Australian Popular Culture', in *An Australian Film Reader*, pp. 242–51.

41. Rosalind Krauss, 'The Originality of the Avant-Garde: A Postmodernist Repetition', *The Originality of the Avant-Garde and Other Modernist Myths*, Cambridge, Mass. 1985, p. 186.

42. Peter Sloterdijk, 'Cynicism – The Twilight of False Consciousness', *New German Critique*, no. 33, 1984, p. 195.

43. Michel de Certeau, *The Practice of Everyday Life*, California 1984.